NEW WORLD
DREAMS

Canadian Pacific Railway and the Golden Northwest

H
HERITAGE

NEW WORLD DREAMS

DREAMS

DAVID LAURENCE JONES

For Lise and Glyn, Chris and Sue

Heritage House Publishing Company Ltd.
heritagehouse.ca

Cataloguing information available from Library and Archives Canada
978-1-77203-455-4 (paperback)
978-1-77203-456-1 (e-book)

Edited by Warren Layberry
Cover and interior design by Setareh Ashrafologhalai
Cover image: Detail from a promotional poster promoting joint efforts between the CPR and British government to reunite families after the Second World War. Artist unknown. Author's Collection

The interior of this book was produced on FSC®-certified, acid-free paper, processed chlorine free, and printed with vegetable-based inks.

Heritage House gratefully acknowledges that the land on which we live and work is within the traditional territories of the Lkwungen (Esquimalt and Songhees), Malahat, Pacheedaht, Scia'new, T'Sou-ke, and W̱SÁNEĆ (Pauquachin, Tsartlip, Tsawout, Tseycum) Peoples.

We acknowledge the financial support of the Government of Canada through the Canada Book Fund (CBF) and the Canada Council for the Arts, and the Province of British Columbia through the British Columbia Arts Council and the Book Publishing Tax Credit.

27 26 25 24 23   1 2 3 4 5

Printed in China

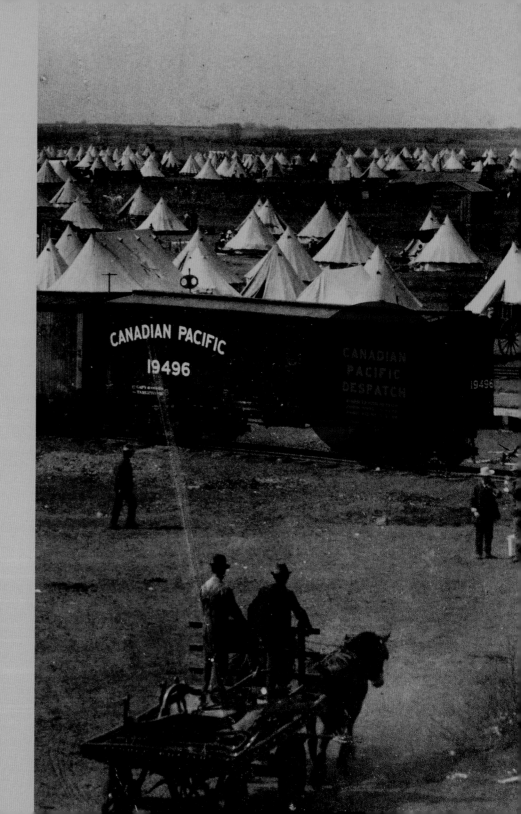

CONTENTS

PREFACE

FROM THE TIME of its founding in the 1880s to the outbreak of the Second World War, the Canadian Pacific Railway Company (CPR) invested more than one hundred million dollars to promote immigration to Canada and stimulate settlement throughout the country's sparsely populated hinterland. The financial and material contributions of the CPR outnumbered and outshone the kindred efforts of the federal government in assuring the essential role that the "Golden Northwest" would play in the country's growing prosperity and established a pattern of development in the region that is still evident today.

The iconic institution that had indeed been founded as an instrument of national unity contributed more to that end than any other private company in history. The work of the CPR's immigration agents; railway, steamship, and natural resources employees; and public relations practitioners in the cause of solidifying the nation's economic success was unprecedented anywhere in the world. Not in Australia, not in South Africa, not even in the great melting pot of the United States would a private corporation forge such remarkable bonds while contributing to the creation and development of its mother country.

But even the most publicly minded companies do not imbue their corporate agendas with a spirit of altruism. The CPR's all-encompassing need to have productive settlers along the entire length of its transcontinental railway line, settlers who would put traffic into its revenue-generating boxcars, dovetailed well with the government's desire to establish a foothold from coast to coast, free from the expansionist ambitions of its neighbour to the south. To satisfy that need, the CPR would—in the words of its first president, George Stephen—give away their own lands if they couldn't sell them.

A note on perspective

The first decision an author must make when telling a story, be it fiction or non-fiction, is one of perspective. *New World Dreams* is a book on settlement and is, by necessity, told from a settler's perspective. However, it is important to recognize that the choice of one perspective neither denies nor invalidates other perspectives. In the case of the story told here, it would be very different indeed told from an Indigenous People's perspective. The idea, for instance, that the CPR had "their own lands" to either sell or give away would be challenged in *that* story, and rightfully so. While that book might also characterize the CPR as the Great Colonizer, it would not be meant as praise.

The author invites readers to consider some of the excellent works cited in the notes to chapter one for insight into the perspective of Indigenous Peoples of Canada. These include Bob Joseph's *21 Things You May Not Know About the Indian Act: Helping Canadians Make Reconciliation with Indigenous Peoples a Reality* (Indigenous Relations Press, 2018); Lynda Gray's *First Nations 101: Tons of Stuff You Need to Know about First Nations People* (Adaawx Publishing, 2011); and *The True Spirit and Original Intent of Treaty 7*, by Treaty 7 Elders and Tribal Council with Walter Hildebrandt, Dorothy First Rider, and Sarah Carter (McGill-Queen's University Press, 1996).

1 THIS LAND IS YOUR LAND

A deal like no other

When the Canadian Pacific Railway Company (CPR) was incorporated in February 1881, the federal government granted the builders a subsidy of $25 million and 25 million acres (10 million ha) of land to construct the essential link that would bind the nation together for all time.[1] The cash would prove to be just the beginning of the large sums the CPR syndicate would need to make the world's longest railway operating under one management both self-sustaining and profitable.[2] The generous land grant, however, would position the private company to play an unprecedented role in the establishment of Canada as a viable nation, economically and politically, from the Atlantic to the Pacific.

The railway's twin bands of iron would serve as a vital link in the British Empire's "Imperial Highway" spanning the globe from the United Kingdom to its far-flung possessions in Asia. The Canadian leg of the extensive route opened to settlement the largest area of rich agricultural land the world had ever seen, inspiring the most enthusiastic supporters of the transcontinental railway to name the CPR "The Great Colonizer."

The fledgling country north of the United States had acquired an enormous land mass from the Hudson's Bay Company (HBC) just over two years after the four British provinces of Quebec, Ontario, New Brunswick, and Nova Scotia were united as the Dominion of Canada on July 1, 1867. The official transfer of what had been called Rupert's Land, which included all of the lands in the Hudson Bay watershed, was to have taken place December 1, 1869, but was delayed until political unrest in the Red River district was resolved. This was accomplished when the federal government passed the Manitoba Act of 1870 and created the new Canadian province of Manitoba. At the same time, another piece of British North America, known as the North-Western Territory, which took in a large area west of Rupert's Land, was removed from HBC control and also ceded to the Canadian government.[3]

On June 23, 1870, Queen Victoria signed an order-in-council erasing both Rupert's Land and the North-Western Territory from the map and, less than a month later, creating in their place the North-West Territories ("North-West" would change to "Northwest" in 1906).[4] The transferred lands stretched from the US border on the forty-ninth parallel to the Arctic tundra and comprised what is now the whole of Manitoba, Saskatchewan, Alberta, the Yukon, Nunavut, and the northern parts of Ontario and Quebec.[5] Before American independence, Rupert's Land had also

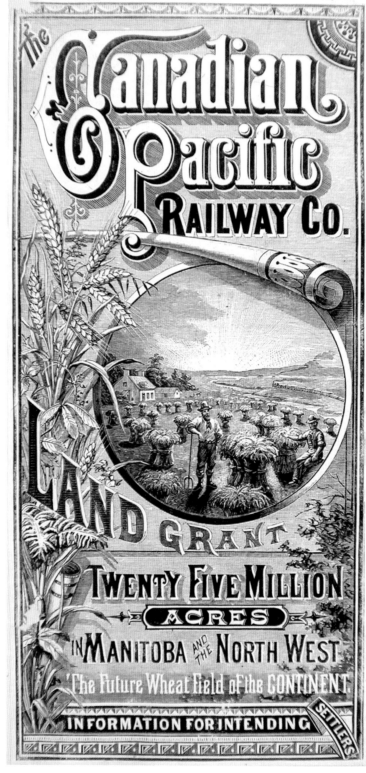

encompassed parts of what became the states of Minnesota, North and South Dakota, and Montana.

To put in motion its grand design for one country from sea to sea, the Canadian government purchased the entire holding of about 1.5 million square miles (3.9 million m²) of land for $1.5 million (more than $60 million in 2021 Canadian dollars), the largest real estate deal in the country's history.[6] By comparison, three years earlier, the United States had acquired Alaska from the Russian Empire, an area less than half the size, for about $7.2 million US.

An acknowledgment of the presence of Indigenous Peoples on land the government "owned" led to the creation of multiple treaties, beginning in 1871. That year, Sweetgrass, a leading Chief of the Plains Cree, wrote to the lieutenant governor of Manitoba and the North-West Territories,

Adams Archibald: "We heard our lands were sold and we did not like it; we don't want to sell our lands; it is our property and no one has a right to sell them."[7] Two hundred years earlier, King Charles II had granted the same lands to the Governor and Company of Adventurers of England Trading into Hudson's Bay—the HBC—as the company's "exclusive commercial domain."[8] Meanwhile, it was this dramatic handover of Rupert's Land—named for the king's cousin, who had been the first governor of the HBC—that solidified the Canadian nation into one of the largest geographical entities in the world.

The CPR was the only railway on the continent to receive a fixed amount of land as a contractual obligation, regardless of the ultimate length of its lines. Because the sale or granting of public lands in the East and in British Columbia fell under the jurisdiction of the provincial authorities, the CPR was obligated to select lands from the region where the land was controlled solely by the federal government, between Winnipeg and the Rocky Mountains. The 25 million acres (10 million ha) granted to the CPR syndicate a decade after the purchase of Rupert's Land would be chosen from within this territory, but unlike the Indigenous Peoples whose ancestral claims were all but ignored, the railway builders would have a significant say in how the land was ultimately carved up and transformed.

During the nineteenth century, the United States government had granted nearly 150 million acres (61 million ha) of land to western railroads as a means of developing the relatively uninhabited regions of the country. The Northern Pacific received 30 million acres (12 million ha), the largest grant made to a single American railroad. However, land was not awarded to railroads in the US in predetermined allotments; it was granted in specific amounts on either side of the tracks as the lines were constructed. After the CPR's initial grant, the Canadian government would follow a similar formula for all railways, awarding 6,400 acres (2,590 ha) of land per mile as track was constructed. The federal authorities stopped awarding land grants to Canadian railways altogether when the Dominion Lands Act was repealed in 1908, but the provinces continued the practice on occasion.

Fairly fit for settlement

Initially, CPR was expected to select most of its granted acreage from a belt of land 24 miles (39 km) deep, on either side of the railway's main line and branch lines, between Winnipeg in the "postage stamp province" of Manitoba and Jasper House at the western extremes of the North-West Territories.[9]

The Dominion Lands Survey System was adopted in 1871, largely to ready the expansive interior of Western Canada for settlement. Based on a model introduced and implemented in the western United States during the reconstruction years after the Civil War, the system divided the countryside into townships of 36 square miles (93 km²), each square mile known as a "section." Unlike their US counterparts, however, the Canadian surveyors were quick to include road allocations, which precluded the need for future adjustments. The grid would eventually cover more than 200 million surveyed acres (800,000 ha), almost one-tenth of Canada's entire land mass.[10]

The Hudson's Bay Company, in its sale of Rupert's Land to the Dominion government, had been awarded all of the sections numbered 8 as well as three quarters of the sections numbered 26 in every township. The remaining

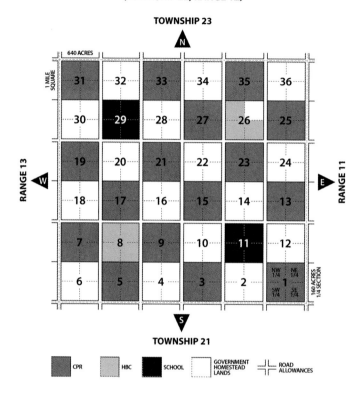

DOMINION LANDS SURVEY SYSTEM
(TOWNSHIP 22, RANGE 12)

◄ The Dominion Land Survey created a vast checkerboard of land holdings across the West. BREATHE COMMUNICATIONS, AUTHOR'S COLLECTION

quarter of each section 26 was made available by the government for homesteads. Sections 11 and 29 were reserved for schools. The CPR was given access to all of the odd-numbered sections of the remaining thirty-two, with the government retaining the even-numbered sections.

Significantly, the CPR would also be given the option to reject any sections it deemed "not fairly fit for settlement." If the amount of land within the railway belt was found to be insufficient to meet the conditions of the contract, the deficiency would be met from other areas within the

so-called fertile belt, located between the 49th and 57th degrees of north latitude, or "elsewhere at the option of the Company."[11] To satisfy the terms of the railway's 25-million-acre (10 million ha) subsidy, the government would ultimately allow the CPR to choose lands far from its own rail lines as well as a large block of contiguous sections in the semi-arid region known as "Palliser's Triangle."

In the US, where government grants provided stipulated amounts of land per mile of track laid along the entire length of the railroads in question, the agreements carried no guarantee as to the quality of the land. As a result, unlike the CPR, American transcontinental lines found themselves in possession of vast areas of undesirable land, worthy of little more than grazing cattle or sheep.

Despite the generous land concessions negotiated by the CPR's founders, the Canadian project would not be without its challenges. From its inception, not everybody had been enthusiastic about the prospects for the proposed Canadian Pacific transcontinental, the land it would run through, or the Nation of Canada itself. The English magazine *London Truth* drew a dismal picture for its readers:

The Canadian Pacific Railway will run, if it is ever finished, through a country frostbound for seven or eight months in the year, and will connect with the Western part of the dominion a Province which embraces about as forbidding a country as any on the face of the earth . . . [In Manitoba], men and cattle are frozen to death in numbers that would startle the intended settler if he knew; and those not killed are maimed for life by frostbite . . . [British Columbia] is a barren, cold mountainous country that is not worth keeping . . . Fifty railroads would not galvanize it into prosperity.[12]

But the men in the CPR syndicate who built the railway were not so easily dissuaded. Their views of the railway's potential and their judgment of what lands were "fairly fit for settlement" would be shaped largely by the extensive surveys that had been carried out by Irish-born explorer and geographer John Palliser more than two decades earlier, in 1857 and 1858, as well as by those of Sandford Fleming, engineer-in-chief for the Canadian government's initial Pacific Railway deliberations between 1872 and 1880.

The United Province of Canada, consisting of Upper Canada (now Ontario) and Lower Canada (Quebec), had also mounted a lesser-known expedition to the northwest under the direction of ex-HBC trader George Gladman around the same time as the Palliser foray.

It was the age of exploration, and the more prominent European nations were in direct competition with one another to obtain a foothold in the far-flung, uncharted corners of the world.

Gladman, son of a HBC fur trader and an Indigenous woman, was charged with exploring the agricultural possibilities of the promising new frontier, but only as far west as the Red River. With him was Simon James Dawson, a civil engineer from Trois-Rivières who would go on to map out a system of roads and waterways from Prince Arthur's Landing (now Thunder Bay) to Winnipeg that would be dubbed the "Dawson Route." Gladman also recruited Henry Youle Hind, a geologist and chemist from the University of Toronto who was more interested in the prospects farther west, where the proponents of the transcontinental railway hoped the line would go.[13]

Palliser, a self-sufficient world traveller who was fluent in five languages and reportedly a crack shot with a rifle, approached the Royal Geographical Society to support his planned trek from the Great Lakes to the Rocky Mountains. Backed by both the society and the British government, Palliser's party, which included the Scottish geologist Dr. James Hector, was granted a broad commission to "report on everything," including the possibilities for agriculture and the exploitation of mineral deposits. Notably, Palliser was also asked to assess potential transportation routes and the best areas for settlement.[14]

Based on what these two exploration parties found in the 1850s, it was commonly agreed that most of the negative aspects of the "Great American Desert" also extended past the US border into the southern regions of the Canadian West. Both Palliser and Hind, who had himself ventured farther west than Gladman's mandate called for, recorded semi-arid conditions and a lack of trees on the steppes east of the Rocky Mountains, in what is now southern Alberta and Saskatchewan. The area soon became known as "Palliser's Triangle" and was generally viewed with pessimism as far as its potential for productive farming. However, the two explorers were impressed by the more northerly wooded valleys of the North Saskatchewan River and its tributaries, where they found land more suited to settlement and cultivation. This area would constitute the "fertile belt" cited in surveyors' reports and within the CPR charter.[15]

Fleming's preliminary survey of 1871 had located a proposed route for the Pacific Railway north of Lake Superior, running west to the Selkirk settlement in the newly created province of Manitoba, and continuing on through the more northern prairie region favoured by Palliser and Gladman. Fleming and his assistant, Walter Moberly, explored several potential routes through the mountains before they had settled on the Tête Jaune, also known as Yellowhead Pass, where the grades would be far less steep, more negotiable, and less expensive for construction than those they surveyed on alternate routes farther south. From the Yellowhead Pass, the line was projected to extend to one of several suitable inlets on the West Coast. At the time, Fleming estimated the cost of the completed line would be roughly $100 million in Canadian currency.[16]

As a result of all this surveying activity, when the CPR syndicate eventually signed a contract with the federal government, the railway builders agreed to construct, complete, and equip the central and western sections of the line—as anticipated—from the Selkirk settlement to Port Moody, in British Columbia, via the Yellowhead Pass and Kamloops.[17] Despite the broad consensus to adopt the more northerly route, however, the ambitious new company was soon looking at alternatives that would bring the line much closer to Canada's border with the United States. Several factors played into the decision to consider a fundamental

change in direction, not the least of which was the syndicate's desire to have the most direct route to the Pacific. The distance from Montreal to Port Moody in a more or less straight line was nearly 600 miles (966 km) shorter than rival Northern Pacific's route between New York and Seattle. Even accounting for an additional 360 miles (578 km) of track between Montreal and New York City, the southern route would enable the CPR to offer the fastest schedule from the busiest East Coast port to Puget Sound and connections with trans-Pacific steamship lines.[18]

For more than a decade, it had been widely thought that the Pacific Railway would run through the fertile belt northwest of Winnipeg, along the route on which there were already established settlements of pioneer homesteaders and freight forwarders connected with the fur trade. As a result, land speculators were already jockeying to occupy prime locations for townsites and squat on the best agricultural lands along the intended route. By taking a more direct path due west, the CPR would pass through relatively uninhabited territories, giving the company a virtual monopoly on commercial development and a free hand in locating towns.

Influential CPR syndicate member James Jerome Hill—who was also general manager and soon to be president of the St. Paul, Minneapolis, & Manitoba Railway Company—was a man of significant influence on both sides of the Canada–US border. He knew the merits of running the Canadian transcontinental line through near virgin land, as he explained to John Macoun, a botanist who joined him in advocating for the more southerly route:

I am engaged in the forwarding business and I find that there is money in it for all those who realize its value. If we built this road across the prairie, we will carry every pound of supplies that the settlers want and we will carry every pound of produce that the settlers wish to sell, so that we will have freight both ways.[19]

In addition, the decision to reroute the CPR main line closer to the US border was strengthened by recent discoveries of large coal deposits and other minerals on the prairies and, particularly, in southern British Columbia. Without sufficient protection, these resources could easily be poached by US railroads running branch lines across the lengthy and still somewhat tenuous border between the two nations.

Left to the CPR railway builders, the transcontinental line might have run even closer to the international border than it ultimately did. Years later, CPR president Thomas Shaughnessy recalled that the railway syndicate had given serious consideration to directing the line south of Brandon, through Weyburn, and westward to Lethbridge and the Crow's Nest Pass (now Crowsnest Pass). The federal government had disallowed the plan because it feared that, in case of war with Canada's southern neighbour, the US could easily cut the line.[20] But the company never lost sight of the route's potential. Within twenty years, the CPR would build a branch line through the Crow's Nest Pass on its way to completing a second route through the mountains to the West Coast.

Ironically, botanist John Macoun, who had accompanied Fleming on the first of five government surveys, may have provided the reason for scrapping the engineer-in-chief's route through the Yellowhead Pass. Macoun declared that the land in the southern prairies was not the arid wasteland Palliser and Hind had described but rather a fertile plain on which he estimated there were more than 15 million acres (6 million ha) of arable land.[21] He was convinced that previous tepid assessments of the vast area that had been written off as unfit for agriculture had been tainted by the onset of an atypical, prolonged dry period in the climate cycle. In his mind, it could very well be a "garden to the whole country."[22]

Meeting with CPR syndicate members in Hill's St. Paul office, Macoun suggested that the westward route between Moose Jaw and Seven Persons Coulee, near what is now Medicine Hat, would be less expensive to construct than a line heading northwest that would require several large bridges across major rivers.[23] In making his case, he insisted that not only would the more direct passage through the prairies give the CPR a faster line to the West Coast, but "much of the southern district now considered fit only for pasture will yet be known as the best wheat lands."[24]

The decision to gamble on a more southern path than had been envisioned for many years was a momentous one that substantially altered the pattern of settlement in the

▶ Botanist, explorer, and naturalist John Macoun (shown here ca. 1857) was convinced that the southern prairies were not the arid wasteland Palliser and Hind had described. LIBRARY AND CULTURAL RESOURCES DIGITAL COLLECTIONS, UNIVERSITY OF CALGARY CU1103156

Canadian West. The change of course was one of the most fateful gambits in the nation's history and, as expressed by Dominion archivist W. Kaye Lamb nearly a century later, "whether the change was for better or worse is still a matter of debate."[25]

To solidify the decision of the CPR syndicate and put to rest any misgivings investors might have, the man chosen by the company to drive the transcontinental line through to completion was also put forward as its chief spokesman.

"Having now seen all of the line between Winnipeg and the Pacific, and having studied the prairie section with great care, I feel justified in expressing my opinion in the strongest terms, that no mistake was made by the Company in adopting the more direct and southerly route instead of that by way of the Yellow Head [sic] Pass," said general manager William Van Horne in a widely distributed report. "The land along the northern route is undoubtedly good, but that along the constructed line is as good as land can well be, and the worst of it would be rated as first-class in almost any other country."[26]

Despite Van Horne's glowing assessment, however, the CPR initially refused to accept a significant portion of the land set aside for the railway inside the 48-mile-wide railway belt along the transcontinental main line west of Moose Jaw. In 1883, the dry cycle had returned to Palliser's Triangle. It would last for more than a decade.

The decision to alter the route of the main line was less contentious, however, when it came to heading off potential incursions from US interests. James Jerome Hill, the driving force behind the Great Northern Railroad, had ambitions to extend his main line to the West Coast in direct competition with other transcontinentals north and south of the border. An early investor and syndicate member of the CPR, Hill resigned from the Canadian company in 1883 and sold off most of his stock when he saw that the Canadian line would ultimately run through the barren Laurentian Shield north of Lake Superior to connect Winnipeg with the established communities in the East.[27]

The disillusioned Hill had held out hope that the CPR branch running south from Winnipeg to the US border would connect with his St. Paul & Pacific Railroad—a predecessor to the Great Northern—at St. Vincent, Minnesota, and feed most if not all of its traffic from the Canadian West onto his growing US network.[28] Just such a connection would very soon occur, but the CPR would nevertheless keep most of its eastbound traffic within Canada.

By 1893, the Great Northern had completed its own line to the Pacific and, as predicted, was threatening to syphon off traffic from its Canadian competitor by running branch lines northward wherever possible. It was to have a few successes, notably in British Columbia, but probably far fewer than would have been possible had the CPR taken a more northerly route.

Looking back, William Pearce, who had a long and productive career with the federal government and later with the CPR as a strong proponent of irrigation in the Canadian West, would confirm this view. In a 1924 memorandum, he estimated that "a reference to the map will show that at least 60 percent of the wheat producing territory of Manitoba, 70 percent of Saskatchewan and about 90 percent of the present wheat producing portion of Alberta would have lain south of the line and would have been open to be served by branch lines running in from United States lines."[29]

With all of the land from Winnipeg to the Rocky Mountains secured by the federal government, and surveying well under way along the intended route of the transcontinental railway, all that remained to prepare the "Golden

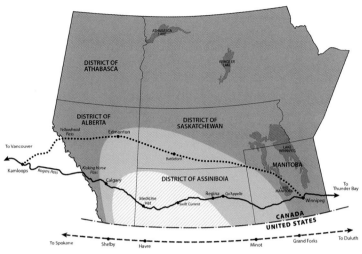

ROUTE OF THE
CANADIAN PACIFIC RAILWAY
1885

ATHABASCA LAKE

DISTRICT OF ATHABASCA

REINDEER LAKE

DISTRICT OF ALBERTA

Yellowhead Pass

To Vancouver

Edmonton

DISTRICT OF SASKATCHEWAN

LAKE WINNIPEG

Kamloops Rogers Pass Kicking Horse Pass

Calgary

Battleford

MANITOBA

DISTRICT OF ASSINIBOIA

LAKE MANITOBA

To Thunder Bay

Medicine Hat

Swift Current

Regina Qu'Appelle

LAKE MANITOBA

Winnipeg

CANADA

UNITED STATES

To Spokane Shelby Havre Minot Grand Forks To Duluth

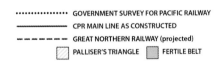

············· GOVERNMENT SURVEY FOR PACIFIC RAILWAY
————— CPR MAIN LINE AS CONSTRUCTED
– – – – – GREAT NORTHERN RAILWAY (projected)
▨ PALLISER'S TRIANGLE ▩ FERTILE BELT

The railway syndicate's decision to build the line farther south forever changed the country's pattern of settlement. BREATHE COMMUNICATIONS, AUTHOR'S COLLECTION

herein appropriated, and to be hereafter granted in aid of the railway."[31]

Clearing the plains

All of the negotiations with and decisions about the fate of Indigenous Peoples in the Canadian West would be in the hands of the federal authorities. The CPR syndicate members, board of directors, officers, and construction crews were to have no direct involvement with the outcome, but the railway company would benefit from the clearing of the plains of any impediment to the laying of track.

Speaking about potentially confrontational situations with Indigenous Peoples to the Canadian House of Commons shortly before construction of the transcontinental began in earnest, Macdonald said he intended "to wean them by slow degrees, from their nomadic habits, which have almost become an instinct, and by slow degrees absorb them or settle them on the land. Meanwhile they must be fairly protected."[32] For a time, it was a somewhat sympathetic view of what would be required, but ultimately Indigenous Peoples would be betrayed at every turn.

The end of the paternal relationship the HBC had had with the various Indigenous groups who participated in the fur trade, and the disappearance of the buffalo, led to the dissolution of the traditional Indigenous ways of life. The appearance of the railway surveyors who preceded the inevitable increasing numbers of settlers added a sense of urgency to the historic treaty agreements. In his 1880 book, *The Treaties of Canada with the Indians of Manitoba and the North-West Territories*, Alexander Morris says that "First Nations peoples saw the Numbered Treaties as a way of solidifying a peaceful and enduring kinship relationship

Northwest" for settlement and further exploitation was to extinguish the land claims of the Indigenous Peoples though a series of numbered treaties intended to affect that outcome.

By the time the CPR was incorporated in 1881, John A. Macdonald's government policy for the "pacification" of Indigenous groups that had been "an integral, if not always explicit, component of the Tory government program of development," was already being implemented.[30] The CPR contract would specify, somewhat belatedly, that "the Government shall extinguish the Indian title affecting the lands

with the Crown."[33] Later historical accounts of the treaty negotiations and their significance would confirm that, while the government representatives were determined to erase Indigenous rights to all but a few small parcels of land throughout the Northwest, Indigenous Peoples themselves viewed the same talks primarily as peace settlements.

The white negotiators spoke about newcomers to the West living in harmony with Indigenous Peoples, emphasizing that the original people of the prairies would not have to give up their rights to hunt and fish at will, and in addition the federal government would help them adapt to a more sedentary lifestyle. But what was written in the final treaties was not always what had been spoken about, and those who were being systematically dispossessed of their lands did not understand the language or the full intent of their occupiers.

The idea of partitioning land and erecting fences to delineate ownership was not known to Indigenous Peoples because to them, land could not be owned. All that

they had they shared, not just among themselves but with the settlers who were arriving in increasing numbers. The Chiefs representing the various Indigenous Peoples were persuaded to sign government treaties. However, according to their world view, land could not be signed away because it was not theirs to begin with. This was a fundamental difference in culture that the treaties failed to acknowledge, which led to future resistance to the imposition of the terms of the treaty as interpreted by the settlers.

Few of the warriors or Chiefs present at the negotiations could speak English, and the translators, though presumably well intentioned, left much to be desired. Historian Rodger Touchie, in his biography of Jerry Potts, a translator at the Treaty 7 negotiations, noted that "it is the way of traditional Euro-American history to record the words emitted by the English-language orator and presume that this was the message transmitted to the non-English speaker." Yet it is well known that the translations provided by Potts and others at the treaty negotiations "included little of what was actually said."[35]

In many cases, the critical terms that were used to ratify the treaties had no equivalency in the languages of the Indigenous Peoples. They had "no comprehension of words like 'cede' and 'surrender,'" a later spokesman for their people would emphasize. "I say this because the Indian leaders would never give up the territory that they used for their everyday survival."[36] Even Siksika Chief Crowfoot, who was considered the paramount leader among the Indigenous Peoples present at the signing of Treaty 7 and was perhaps the one best acquainted with the ways of the white man, expressed his determination to not give up their heritage. Standing before the assembly of his followers, he pleaded with the government commissioners:

Great Father! Take pity on me with regard to my country, with regard to the mountains, the hills and the valleys; with regard to the prairies, the forests and the waters; with regard to all the animals that inhabit them, and do not take them from myself and my children forever.[37]

While the signing of treaties with the Indigenous Peoples provided the federal government with the certainty that they could proceed with the building of the transcontinental railway and the settlement of the Canadian West, it provided no certainties for the Indigenous Peoples. The terms of the treaties would often go unfulfilled or would soon be arbitrarily changed or modified to suit the authorities. In many cases, lands "awarded" to First Nations in the treaties would be taken from them at a later date without permission or compensation.[38]

The treaty negotiations included rough descriptions of where the Indigenous Peoples were to be located and approximately how large would be the areas they would occupy, based on how many people in each Indigenous group were assigned to a particular reserve. Treaty 1, negotiated in 1871 with Chiefs of the Anishinaabe and Swampy Cree on behalf of about one thousand of their people, set the standard. Initially, the Chiefs had asked that two-thirds of Manitoba be set aside as their reserve, but the government had already decided what the terms would entail. In exchange for surrendering title to their lands, the First Nations would receive 160 acres (65 ha) for each family of five. In addition, the government would provide schools, keep intoxicants off the reserves, provide a one-time payment of four dollars per person, and pay an annuity of three dollars per person in cash, blankets, clothing, twine, or traps.[39]

Jerry Potts, a plainsman and buffalo hunter, served as an interpreter between the government and the First Nations but wasn't himself very fluent in any language.

Each treaty set a precedent for the next, with slightly larger payments and a few additional concessions becoming the rule, as each group of First Nations learned the lessons of the previous talks. Treaty 3 with the Woodland Ojibwe hunters and fishermen, for example, offered reserves, on the basis of five people per square mile, a far more generous concession than the government had previously considered. The Ojibwe also asked for free transportation on the soon-to-be-built CPR but had to settle instead for a better allowance of clothing and tools.[40]

When it came time to negotiate Treaty 7, which involved the Siksika (Blackfoot), Kainai (Blood), Tsuut'ina (Sarcee) as well as some Nakota (Stoney) and Piikani (Piegan), a large contingent of government officials met with hundreds of warriors and their Chiefs for a multi-day discussion of terms. The lands occupied by Treaty 7 First Nations would be the most affected by the coming of the railway. The large reserve set aside for the Siksika, Kainai, and Tsuut'ina, 4 miles (6.4 km) deep along the Bow River, and the reserve for the Nakota, in the vicinity of Morleyville—the old settlement that predated present-day Morley—would be particularly close to the CPR right-of-way.

The area that the Treaty 7 Chiefs agreed to surrender consisted of about 50,000 square miles (130,000 km²) of their ancestral hunting grounds, extending from the Cypress Hills (just west of the present-day border between Alberta and Saskatchewan), west to the Rocky Mountains, and from the US border, north to the boundary of Treaty 6 (in central Alberta and Saskatchewan). The members of the Treaty 7 First Nations would also "cede, release, surrender, and yield up to the Government of Canada for Her Majesty the Queen and her successors forever, all their rights, titles and privileges whatsoever to the lands," in exchange for

"sufficient area to allow one square mile for each family of five persons, or in that proportion for larger or smaller families," as well as the usual cash payments, clothing, tools, firearms, and a few cows.[41]

Precise surveying of the reserves was left in abeyance for several years, as the government's priority was to make sections along the route of the CPR and in other agriculturally desirable areas immediately available to homesteaders. Every surveyor that could be mustered was engaged in the task of keeping up with railway construction as it moved across the country. When the end of track was ahead of land sales, some of the surveyors locating the road bed would be temporarily loaned out to the government for the all-important task of preparing the frontier for settlers.

While the borders of the reserves remained tenuous, little attempt was made to require Indigenous Peoples to stay within fixed boundaries. Hunting parties, in particular, were given leeway to roam freely, often crossing the international border back and forth unhindered, as had been their habit previously. For the rest of the Indigenous population, the sight of steel rails and telegraph wires crossing the plains was a constant reminder of their shrinking freedom of movement, and on occasion they reacted with anger.

In the forests of the eastern railway sections, logs were piled on the right-of-way in an effort to derail locomotives. Surveyors' stakes were pulled up, and Indigenous groups squatted in rows along the line to unnerve the railway workers, who were unfamiliar with them and fearful.[42] Indigenous Peoples were beginning to greet the oncoming rails with skepticism and active resistance. Some, such as Cree Chiefs Big Bear and Piapot, continued to defy the authorities, refusing to move their people onto the reserves even as the railway advanced toward their ancestral lands.

In the summer of 1882, Piapot's warriors pulled up 40 miles (64 km) of surveyors' stakes on the line west of Moose Jaw, before setting up tents across the path of the construction crews. One railway surveyor later remarked that while the warriors "rarely tampered with survey markers or removed them, they would sometimes express their resentment by defecating upon the top of every available stake, which added nothing to the amenities of the job."[43] Piapot's defiance led to a tense showdown with two members of the Maple Creek detachment of the North-West Mounted Police (NWMP), but was resolved when the policemen asserted their authority.[44] The Chief backed down and his people were then forced to move 350 miles (563 km) from the Cypress Hills to their assigned reserve east of Regina.[45]

In many cases, their first encounter with steam locomotives was even more alarming for Indigenous Peoples than the sudden appearance of survey stakes dotting the prairies. The machine was new to them, as it had been to the white man's world some eighty years earlier, and they called it a "fire wagon."[46]

On March 24, 1882, Prime Minister John A. Macdonald announced to Parliament that all Indigenous Peoples in the territory of Assiniboia (most of which later became the southern part of Saskatchewan) would be removed, by force if necessary, from the land south of the CPR main line. Among the first to be moved was Piapot, who was persuaded to settle near Indian Head. About eight hundred of his people boarded CPR boxcars at Maple Creek for the trip east. While en route, two of the boxcars derailed and rolled down an embankment. Although there were no serious injuries, Piapot was angry, and his people continued the journey by oxen and carts. Some thought it was all part of a plot to kill them off.[47]

◄ Chief Piapot and his small group of warriors launched acts of resistance to the incursion of the railway's "fire wagons." AUTHOR'S COLLECTION

► Prime Minister John A. Macdonald was sympathetic to the plight of Indigenous Peoples but ultimately unbending in his resolve to usurp most of their lands. Ca. 1867–91. LIBRARY AND ARCHIVES CANADA C-021604

In less than a year, five thousand Cree and other Indigenous groups were expelled from the Cypress Hills. In doing so, the Canadian government accomplished the ethnic cleansing of the Indigenous Peoples from southwestern Saskatchewan.

There would be few Indigenous Peoples left in the path of the tracklayers as they spiked down steel rails across the open plains. The stragglers who clung to the only means of survival they knew took a fatalistic view of the coming of the railway. John Egan, the CPR's general superintendent for the western region, assured Van Horne of their peaceful disposition:

No doubt you have heard reports regarding trouble with the Indians at end of track. I was there all day Wednesday and Wednesday night but saw nor heard nothing to justify such rumors. There are about a dozen tepees at Maple Creek camped there on the bank of the creek. At Swift Current there are from 15 to 20 tepees. They have been there in the neighbourhood of three weeks and state that they are waiting for the buffalo to cross at that point. They say the buffalo are coming and will reach there in about a week or ten days. They appear to be very friendly and take great delight in being about the engine and cars.[48]

The original provisions in Treaty 7 envisioned three contiguous reserves along a four-mile-wide strip on the north side of the Bow River and part of the South Saskatchewan on which the Siksika, Kainai, and Tsuut'ina First Nations would settle. Before this reserve could be implemented, however, both the Kainai and the Tsuut'ina had changed their minds in favour of accepting land within their traditional territories—the Kainai in their favoured wintering grounds bounded by the St. Mary's, Oldman, and Belly rivers, and the Tsuut'ina in the foothills southwest of Calgary.[49]

As the CPR construction gangs moved past Medicine Hat toward Calgary, the railway right-of-way was headed straight for the middle of the lands set out in Treaty 7 for the Siksika, and new boundaries had not been settled. When tents were erected on the border of the disputed lands, Siksika Chief Crowfoot sent warriors to inform the railway foreman that no further work would be permitted.[50]

It was only the intercession of Albert Lacombe, an oblate missionary who maintained good relations with the Siksika, that prevented a violent incident from occurring. While preaching restraint to Crowfoot, Lacombe had sent urgent telegrams to CPR general manager William Van Horne, as well as to Edgar Dewdney, lieutenant governor of the North-West Territories, outlining the situation. The priest was asked to appease the Indigenous Peoples in any way he could until Dewdney arrived to assure them that they would be given extra land in return for the railway right-of-way. Van Horne also authorized Lacombe to make a gift to the Siksika of two hundred pounds of sugar and a like amount of tobacco, tea, and flour.[51]

The new reserve for the Siksika would be laid out with the CPR main line as the northern boundary. Because township surveys had already been completed by the Department of the Interior, the surveyors were now able to use township lines for the east, west, and south sides of the reserve.[52] Chief Crowfoot was given a railway pass to travel on the CPR for free, in perpetuity, in recognition of the role he had played in peacefully agreeing to adjust the boundaries of the reserve. Van Horne had the pass framed and fitted with a chain so that Crowfoot could wear it around his neck, which he did proudly for the remainder of his years. As a result, the Siksika Chief is widely remembered and lauded by the Canadian establishment as a peacemaker, but in

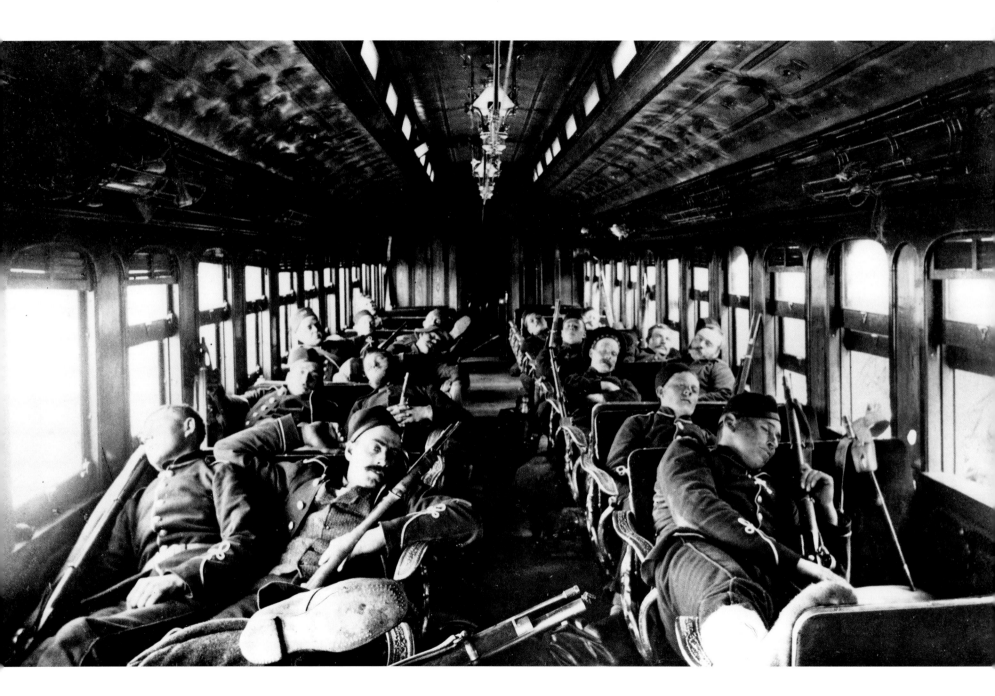

later years some of his own people remained suspicious of his motives. "He always had money," they said.[53]

The railway line passed the Siksika reserve without further incident and headed straight toward the Nakota reserve through which the railway surveyors determined the most advantageous route for the CPR lay, with predictable results.

"The line goes through their Reserve from one end to the other," Dewdney wrote to Prime Minister Macdonald. "I went over it and found that it did not destroy any of their improvements or timber. Consequently, they were entitled to no compensation; this they could hardly understand, but they were very reasonable and said that, of course, I knew whether they were entitled to anything or not; if they were they would be very glad to get it."[54] What they got from 1882 onward was precious little other than game animals scattered and killed on their reserve.[55] The domestic cattle that came later often suffered the same fate, until being fenced off from the railway right-of-way.

On a more positive note, the reserves that were located close to the CPR had the benefit of an efficient pipeline by which to obtain equipment, supplies, and consumer goods as well as a ready means for shipping to market the results of their labours, whether agricultural produce or cattle; but they were vulnerable to prairie fires caused by sparks from the locomotives. For a brief period, it looked as if the Nakota might have been able to supply the railway with timber for cross ties and telegraph poles, but William Pocklington, Indian Affairs sub-agent for Treaty 7, ruled that the initiative ran contrary to the Indian Act and quickly shut down that possibility.[56]

Reserves in more remote regions were often on lands less favourable to agriculture and did not have easy access

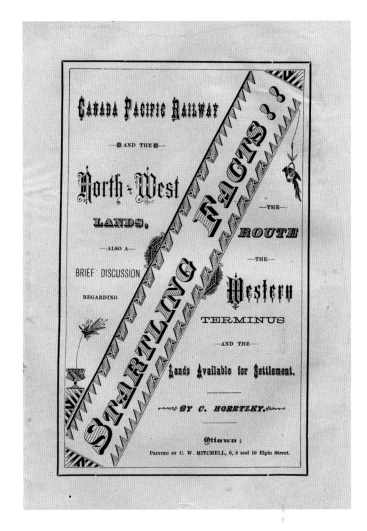

to roads, sewage facilities, and, later, electricity; but, of course, they kept local Indigenous Peoples segregated from the incoming settlers, which was viewed favourably by government officials.[57]

More than anything else, exposure to new diseases brought to the Great Plains with the arrival of Europeans would decimate Indigenous populations, by as much as 90 percent in the worst cases. As early as 1876, when

Icelandic immigrants landed on the shores of Lake Winnipeg, hundreds of Ojibwe and Cree had perished from an outbreak of smallpox brought in with the newcomers.[58]

In 1878, Indian agent M.G. Dickinson had estimated the entire Indigenous and Métis population of the North West to be about 26,500, down from the hundreds of thousands who had roamed freely in the Canadian West before the advent of the white man.[59] By the 1880s, tuberculosis was the primary killer within the indigenous population, with influenza not far behind.[60] The spread of those afflictions, as well as other contagious diseases like measles, scarlet fever, and smallpox, was facilitated by the construction of the railway and the attendant influx of settlers, particularly European immigrants, who often harboured the tubercle bacillus.[61] Crowfoot himself died from congestion of the lungs in the spring of 1890.[62]

The railway also played a decisive role in stifling opposition in the Northwest when a disparate group of discontented Métis and their supporters coalesced into armed resistance in 1885. While largely a clash between the rugged, unrestrained individualists in the West, who resisted government interference in their everyday affairs, and the more conservative and established collective in the East that wished to impose "order" in advance of large-scale settlement, a small group of Indigenous warriors joined the fray in what one historian called "their final futile gesture against the onrushing tidal wave of civilization."[63] The nearly completed railway enabled the Canadian government to rush in some eight hundred trained military men under General Frederick Middleton and quickly suppress the uprising.

Early advertising booklets and pamphlets would describe the Northwest as a vast, largely uninhabited, and mostly fertile wilderness ripe for colonial settlement. There would be little mention of Indigenous Peoples other than the occasional vague suggestion that there was "nothing to fear" for the newcomers.

When the Numbered Treaties had been signed, the Plains First Nations were still powerful, independent people who were feared by their enemies. Within a handful of years, as a result of the decimation of the buffalo, the ubiquity of infectious diseases, and the advent of the transcontinental railway, the once mighty Indigenous population was reduced to starvation, "mendicants at the feet of the bureaucrats, dependent on them for their very lives confined to their reserves, and subject to a plethora of new rules."[64]

The historian Pierre Berton, who in the 1970s mythologized the building of the CPR as the culmination of a Canadian national dream, said the rapid completion of the railway was a marvel to everybody, "that is, except the people it was replacing."

To the Indians, the railway symbolized the end of a golden era—an age in which the native peoples, liberated by the white man's horses and the white man's weapons, had galloped at will across their untrammeled domain, where the game seemed unlimited and the zest of the hunt gave life a tang and a purpose. This truly idyllic existence came to an end with the suddenness of a thunderclap just as the railway, like a glittering spear, was thrust through the ancient hunting grounds of the Blackfoot and the Cree. Within six years, the image of the Plains Indian underwent a total transformation. From a proud and fearless nomad, rich in culture and tradition, to become a pathetic, half-starved creature, confined to the semi-prisons of the new reserves and totally dependent on government relief for his existence.[65]

The bone trade

With the vast buffalo herds that once roamed the prairie grasslands decimated and the inevitable onrush of settlers that would come with the railway all but certain, the plains way of life for Indigenous Peoples was forever changed. Staying alive in the short term would mean accepting hand-outs from the federal government, and in the long term taking up a more agricultural and pastoral lifestyle.

Fifty years earlier, as many as thirty million buffalo had migrated back and forth at will across the ancestral lands of Indigenous Peoples in both Canada and the United States. The great beasts had been the main source of food for Indigenous Peoples. Their hides provided cover for tepees and robes for warmth, and their bones were fashioned into needles, knife handles, cups, spoons, and more. Tragically, by the end of the nineteenth century, there would be more of the once pervasive creatures in zoos and compounds than in the wild. Indigenous Peoples had lost the main source of their livelihood.

Ironically, the mass destruction of the buffalo would create one of the first successful industries in the Northwest since the advent of the fur trade, and the CPR would give the new entrepreneurs a ready means for shipping their product to market. With the passing of the old ways, the Métis, much like their First Nations neighbours, desperately needed a new economic lifeline, and the sun-bleached bones that littered the prairie landscape offered ready cash—if only for a brief period.

The processed remains of the buffalo had been found to be a value substance for the production of charcoal and fertilizer. For a few short years, the buffalo would once again support the prairie people. Needy Métis freight handlers

and hard-pressed homesteaders could earn up to eight dollars for a ton of the bones delivered trackside to the railway, where the skulls and other skeletal remains would be stacked into boxcars for shipment to manufacturing plants in Chicago, Detroit, and St. Louis. The native peoples tended to stay at arm's length from the industry because of their religious beliefs and the sacred status that they bestowed upon the buffalo.[66]

The business had originated in the United States during the late 1860s when white settlers began to slaughter the buffalo in ever-greater numbers, and the coming of the railroads made it profitable to ship the bones for processing in the East. Freight cars bound for the frontier with settlers' goods could be reloaded with buffalo bones for the return haul. Soon, piles of bones began to appear along every siding on the routes of the Union Pacific, Kansas Pacific, and Santa Fe railroads.[67]

When the supply began to dry up in the US, the demand for the product spiked in the Northwest, where the skeletal remains of the buffalo were still ubiquitous. Throughout the grasslands of the Qu'Appelle and South Saskatchewan valleys, the ground was virtually carpeted with a sea of bones. One Swift Current merchant, F. Fraser Tims, was said to have shipped two hundred thousand pounds of buffalo bones to Minneapolis in CPR boxcars, during the fall of 1884 alone.[68]

One early shipment from Regina of forty-seven tons was enough to fill four boxcars. A lone dealer could load up to fifteen carloads of bones in a single day. Volumes waiting on sidings grew so large they often exceeded the railway's capacity to move them. Great accumulations lingered in piles beside the track, sometimes frozen together in a solid mass.

As the business thrived and became more efficient, the bone hunters had to forage farther and farther afield from the CPR main line. When the grass grew tall, it was more difficult to find the bones, so the scavengers would burn the vegetation to expose more of their product to view. If this strategy was practiced on lands near the railway tracks, the blame could be placed on sparks from passing locomotives, and the railway rather than the bone pickers would suffer any resulting public wrath.

By 1889, most of the prairie between Indian Head and Medicine Hat had been scoured of bones. As branch lines

were opened, Saskatoon became the epicenter of the trade. At one point in 1890, the skeletons of more than 25,000 animals were waiting at the CPR's Saskatoon depot to be transported to processors in the United States. By the time the industry was winding down in the mid-1890s, James Lesley, one of the local purchasing agents, was said to have shipped 750 carloads of buffalo bones from the district, while his immediate competitors accounted for another 2,500 carloads. It was estimated that the ground remains of as many as 1.5 million of the once-plentiful beasts had ended up in charcoal filters and bags of fertilizer.[69]

◄ For several years, the bone trade constituted a lucrative business for dealers back east, largely in the United States. OMER LAVALLEE COLLECTION

► People earned a finder's fee for stacking buffalo bones in boxcar-sized piles alongside the railway tracks. AUTHOR'S COLLECTION

2 HOMESTEADERS, SPECULATORS, AND URBAN PLANNERS

Settling, not selling

William Van Horne arrived in Winnipeg on December 31, 1881, to take up his position as general manager of the CPR. The headquarters of the CPR was in Montreal, but the head office for railway construction and land sales was located in what would soon be known as the "Gateway to the West."

Van Horne was born in Chelsea, Illinois, in 1843. He spent his formative years in the United States, beginning in a telegrapher's office for the Illinois Central and quickly rising through the ranks to high-level management positions with several US railroads. He was destined to become one of Canada's most famous and celebrated railway builders. The CPR's formidable new construction boss had been lured north of the border with the promise of one of the industry's top salaries. Physically strong and capable of decisive action, he managed to complete the task of building the CPR main line in just five years.

Within months of its incorporation, the CPR had organized a land department in Winnipeg with John Henry McTavish as land commissioner. The first sale of CPR land was officially registered in the company's account books on September 21, 1881.[1] Before he was recruited by the new railway company, McTavish had been in charge of the HBC

trading post in Upper Fort Garry, at the confluence of the Red and Assiniboine rivers. He was also a former representative of the North-West Territorial Executive Council and close friend of Donald Smith (later Lord Strathcona), an influential member of the CPR syndicate and past governor of the HBC.

Incorporated as the City of Winnipeg in 1873, the thriving community around the old fort would grow to be one of the most important hubs in the CPR network. By the time Van Horne arrived on the scene, the railway's Winnipeg land office was already doing a booming business, having handled more than 1,500 applications for the purchase of 750,000 pristine acres (300 ha) of prime agricultural land in the first few months since it opened its doors.[2]

The Canadian government and the CPR were the two largest landowners in Manitoba and the North-West Territories, and sales from their holdings were inextricably linked by virtue of the checkerboard system that gave each of the two stakeholders alternate sections of surveyed lands within the railway belt and elsewhere. Since the passage of the 1872 Dominion Land Act, the federal authorities had been offering their lands for "homesteads" at giveaway prices.

"FREE HOMES FOR ALL," trumpeted the advertising flyers in bold capital letters. Homesteads consisting of a

▲ William Van Horne arrived in Winnipeg to push the railway line through the Northwest with dispatch. AUTHOR'S COLLECTION

► Colourful pamphlets encouraged settlers to range west of Winnipeg into the beckoning Northwest. AUTHOR'S COLLECTION

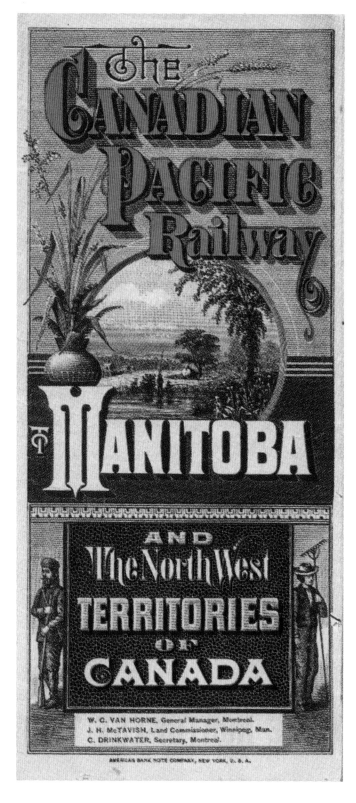

The CANADIAN PACIFIC Railway

MANITOBA

AND The North West TERRITORIES OF CANADA

W. C. VAN HORNE, General Manager, Montreal.
J. H. McTAVISH, Land Commissioner, Winnipeg, Man.
C. DRINKWATER, Secretary, Montreal.

AMERICAN BANK NOTE COMPANY, NEW YORK, U. S. A.

Opposite, left The City of Winnipeg, strategically located at the forks of the Red and Assiniboine rivers, was the "Gateway to the West." LIBRARY AND CULTURAL RESOURCES DIGITAL COLLECTIONS, UNIVERSITY OF CALGARY CU1156078

Opposite, right A government map aimed at potential settlers showed which lands had already been sold and which were occupied by Indigenous Peoples. JAMES E. LANIGAN COLLECTION

DOMINION OF CANADA

A MAP OF THE

Province of Manitoba

Showing the

DOMINION LANDS SURVEYED

ALSO

Lands Disposed of AND Half Breed Lands.

TOGETHER WITH GENERAL DIRECTIONS.
THE LAND REGULATIONS OF THE
DOMINION GOVERNMENT.
OTTAWA, CANADA, 1882:

PUBLISHED BY THE
DEPARTMENT OF AGRICULTURE
OF THE CANADIAN GOVERNMENT.

THE BURLAND LITHO. CO., PRINTERS, MONTREAL.

quarter section, or 160 acres (65 ha), were available at little cost to "any person, male or female who was the sole head of a family, or any male who had attained the age of eighteen years."[3] For the settlers' part, they were expected to take possession of their land within six months, were not to be absent for more than six months at a time, and were to reside on and cultivate the land for at least three years before they took full ownership. An administrative fee of $10 for a quarter-section homestead was the only charge.

The terms established by the Canadian government were remarkably similar to those outlined by the US authorities in their 1862 Homestead Act, but even more generous in their provisions. While an American settler could also obtain a 160-acre (65 ha) homestead for a token fee of $10, south of the border, they had to be at least twenty-one years of age to take advantage of the offer and reside five years on the land before being granted full possession.

Those receiving Canadian homestead "entries," as successful applications were known, were "entitled at the same time—*but not at a later date*—to a pre-emption entry for an adjoining unoccupied 160-acre [65 ha] tract." This meant for an additional fee of $10, homesteaders could reserve the right to acquire an additional government quarter section or purchase one of the railway sections priced at $2.50 per acre ($6.18/ha) that bordered their quarter section. They had up to three years to exercise this option. Other regulations allowed settlers to purchase nearby timber lots at $5 per acre ($12.36/ha) or to obtain additional homesteads if all conditions had been met after three years residence on their first acquisition.

The *Manitoba Free Press* carried daily ads for lands offered for sale by both the government and the railway. Flyers printed by the thousands and distributed liberally wherever potential settlers congregated emphasized the sale of the free government homestead lands but were often printed by the CPR. On the reverse side of advertisements, the railway added instructions on how to become an immediate landowner by purchasing a quarter section for $2.50 per acre ($6.18/ha). If paid for in full, the CPR would issue a "deed of conveyance" on the spot. Alternately, the purchaser of railway land could pay one-sixth of its cost in cash, and the balance in five annual instalments, with interest at 6 percent per annum payable in advance.[4] Buyers were also eligible for a rebate of half the purchase price for every acre brought under cultivation within five years.[5] CPR president George Stephen explained the rationale for the generous terms when he stated in May 1881, "It is *settling*, not *selling* that we must aim at . . . [and] if our lands won't sell we will give them away to settlers."[6]

At first glance, free government homesteads were the more attractive option, but some settlers learned there could be disadvantages as well. The requirements to live on a government homestead for half the year and the obligation to clear for cultivation a minimum of 10 acres (4 ha) a year for three years could be a burden if a settler did not have immediate funds to purchase horses, plows, seeds, and other necessary farm supplies. On the other hand, if you had the money to buy from the railway, you got the land free and clear, and you could use your land as collateral to get a loan from the nearest bank for other supplies you might need. "After all, the railroad was in the business of selling all this land," said one pioneer landowner. "There wasn't much nonsense about them. A deal was a deal. With the government there always seemed to be some fussing around."[7]

In any event, McTavish and his railway bosses realized they would have to put a lot of settlers on free government

responsibilities with other obligations in the Department of Agriculture, consigning the whole unwieldy arrangement to the overview of a single Conservative government minister, initially John Henry Pope. Adding to the bureaucratic tangle, land sales fell within the purview of the equally overburdened Department of the Interior.

In the years before the construction of the CPR, the flow of immigration to the Canadian Northwest had been a mere trickle. Lord Selkirk's settlement, founded as early as 1811 on HBC land in the vicinity of what would become Upper Fort Garry,[8] constituted one of the few groups of settlers with European origins other than HBC employees at company "factories"[9] and other posts.

The Selkirk settlers established their own fort, Fort Douglas, about 2 miles (3.2 km) north of Upper Fort Garry. The settlement founders from Scotland intermarried with French Canadian fur traders and the Indigenous population, creating a unique "Métis" culture that was quite independent politically and economically from the Canadian authorities back East. The impression of two solitudes was reinforced in the way members of the eastern establishment characterized what they saw as the less civilized denizens of the Red River Valley. After passing through the area in the late 1850s, Captain John Palliser, the renowned explorer and surveyor, gave his dismissive and condescending view: "The indolence of the people is truly wonderful … They hunt during three months of the year, and beg, borrow and starve during the remaining nine."[10]

Many of these settlers clustered around the confluence of the Red and Assiniboine rivers were caught up in the North-West Resistance of 1870 and 1885. They were mistrustful of Ottawa and increasingly under pressure from the growing number of colonizers slowly beginning to make

homesteads before they could sell much of their own land grant holdings. For the foreseeable future, the burden of promoting immigration and colonization would fall to the CPR.

Much like the railway syndicate that was struggling to pay the enormous construction costs of building the transcontinental, the Ottawa government was hard pressed for funds. For the time being, instead of making immigration and settlement a national priority, it bundled those

their way toward the new promised land from the eastern provinces, the United States, and Europe. A major bone of contention had been the incompatibility of the traditional system of land holdings within the Selkirk settlement and the new system adopted by the federal authorities. Since the founding of the settlement, individual plots had been surveyed in long strips that gave each owner access to one or the other of the two local rivers. To preserve the peace, the government back in Ottawa initially did not try to superimpose quarter-section homesteads over areas already occupied before the Dominion Lands Act came into effect.

Another significant group of settlers, which had first arrived in Manitoba in 1874 and was already firmly entrenched before the arrival of the CPR, consisted of Mennonites primarily from southern Russia, whose pacifist views had brought them into conflict back home with the government of Tsar Alexander II. In coming to Canada, they had been provided with several inducements such as exemption from military service, the right to organize their own religious schools, and ownership of eight free townships in the Red River Valley on which to farm. By 1879 about six thousand Mennonites had settled on the Manitoba prairie.

In 1881, when the CPR was incorporated, the population of Manitoba and the North-West Territories was about 120,000 souls, or more than double what it had been just a decade earlier.[11] Nearly half were living in Winnipeg and its vicinity, with the remainder made up largely of Indigenous and Métis trappers and fur traders spread out across the prairies in disparate groups. Another fifty thousand or so people were mostly in fairly small and isolated settlements along the BC coast as well as in gold mining centres in the BC interior, such as Barkerville and Fort Steele, awaiting the arrival of the transcontinental railway that had been promised in 1871 by the federal Conservative government to link them with the more populous centres in the East.[12]

Shortly after the opening of the immigration season in spring 1881, the federal agent in Winnipeg received word from his superiors in Ottawa that "information has reached [the minister responsible for immigration] from several quarters, including paragraphs in newspapers," that immigrants arriving in Winnipeg were not being met by government officials. Apparently one party arriving on a Saturday night had been forced to sleep on the floor of the CPR station until Monday morning. "The women and children especially suffered severe and cruel hardships in

the absence of fires, or any other provision for their comfort," the agent was informed, with the added caveat that the minister "finds it quite intolerable."[13]

At the same time that McTavish and Van Horne were settling in at the railway's new construction headquarters, Winnipeg was in the midst of an unprecedented real estate boom. To the west, the towns of Portage la Prairie and Brandon were also experiencing outstanding interest in the sale of town lots, a commodity which the CPR had in abundance. The quick cash these sales could generate would be sorely needed to finish construction of the railway's main line. Not far from the CPR's Winnipeg depot, a million cross ties and six thousand telegraph poles sat in the rail yard waiting to be installed, and nearly five hundred teams of horses had been hired to move construction materials to the end of track.[14] Cash was tight, and the sale of town lots would make a crucial contribution to helping the CPR ward off bankruptcy.

FRIDAY, MARCH 3

BOOM! BRANDON. BOOM!

Of all the Brandon Surveys this Admittedly Bears Away the Palm

Section Twenty-two

The Cream of Brandon put upon the market at last. Sale by Joseph Wolf, Auctioneer. Connected by bridge now being erected with the north side of the river.

AT THE GOLDEN SALE ROOM

$200,000 Already Sold by Private Sale!

MAGNIFICENT SPECULATION!

TERMS VERY LIBERAL.

Plans on view. No reserve. Title A 1.

JOSEPH WOLF

In Winnipeg, lots on Main Street owned by the government, the railway, and others sold for as much as $2,000 per foot of frontage in choice locations, more expensive at the time than prime real estate in Chicago. Not until the 1970s, nearly a century later, would prices again rise to this level.[15] The coming of the railway had set up unrealistic expectations and created a real estate bubble that, at some point, would have to burst. "If there ever was a fool's paradise, it sure was located in Winnipeg, Manitoba," said Western journalist and raconteur George Henry Ham. "Man made fortunes, mostly on paper, and life was one continuous joy ride."[16] Winnipeg was spoken of and written about in superlative terms, as the Hub of the West, the Queen of the Prairie, and the Chicago of the North-West.

New arrivals poured into Winnipeg from the East. "The 10 p.m. train of the CPR was crowded last evening with victims of Manitoba fever," reported one daily newspaper, "and it is expected that the evening trains for some time will have full fares for Manitoba."[17] The *Winnipeg Times* called its hometown the New Eldorado, and circumstances bore that out.[18] Several immigrant parties had to be lodged temporarily, once again, in the CPR depot during an early March blizzard in 1882, as all of the sleeping accommodations in the city were full.[19]

The first government immigration hall, built in 1881, had quickly been overwhelmed with the steady influx of potential settlers, and new, expanded facilities were opened in 1882 and 1887, always taking into account proximity to the railway depot where the wide-eyed arrivals would disembark onto the station platform.[20]

As to the character of the immigrants in those early years, the federal land agent at Winnipeg reported tens of thousands of new arrivals, consisting of a "superior class

of agriculturist, possessed of sufficient means to provide themselves with the outfit necessary to start upon home-steads," as well as those identified as shopkeepers, artisans, and labourers going to the new towns springing up along the railway.[21]

By January 1882, the real estate boom had spilled over to Brandon, the CPR's first divisional point west of Winni-peg, where the prices had nearly tripled. Town lots on the main street were selling for as much as $140 per foot of frontage. Portage la Prairie, between Winnipeg and Bran-don, was even pricier, at $230 per foot along the town's centre street.[22]

While CPR construction gangs were laying down track at a rapid rate, another group of men were hard on their heels building stations and ancillary structures, where frontier communities would soon spring up. A few of the more strategic locations on the banks of major rivers were already supporting a small population, but the arrival of the railway planted the first seeds of settlement at most of the spots chosen by the railway surveyors. In its drive across the prairies of the Golden Northwest, the CPR would eventually create eight hundred new communities.

In those early years, railway maintenance crews could work efficiently for about 4 or 5 miles (up to 8 km) in both directions from their home base, so towns and villages along the CPR route were created every 8–10 miles (13–16 km) along the track. Sidings were also needed at intervals of 10–20 miles (16–32 km) to allow faster passenger traffic to pass freight trains or to facilitate the meeting of trains travelling in opposite directions. In most cases, this meant the establishment of some kind of station building at these spots, no matter how rudimentary, to house the company's operator and often his family, although maybe 20 percent of stations along the main line did not warrant a full-time employee.

The entire transcontinental line would be divided into sections (later referred to as subdivisions), which were about 125 miles (200 km) long, a section being the effective distance for steam locomotive operations, before the need to change crews.[23] Water for the engine boilers was required more frequently, so tanks were situated about every 25–35 miles (40–55 km), while coal was provided around the midway point on most subdivisions. Passenger trains could cover the distance between divisional points in about eight hours, including stops, freight trains in ten.

As a result of those standard operating requirements, many communities along the CPR main line initially took on the same basic appearance. Towns might have any combination of grain elevators, loading platforms, and commodity sheds along one side of the tracks, and a main street with hotels, stores, and other commercial buildings on the other. Residential streets would be set back one or two streets from the railway, along with schools, libraries, and local offices, land for fairgrounds, and stockyards being situated toward the extremities. Railway divisional points, where crew changes and minor maintenance would be carried out, would also include engine houses and often dining halls for both railway workers and passengers, with as many as two dozen bedrooms upstairs. Water tanks were located at divisional points and at intermediate stations.

Ranging from truly utilitarian to uniquely picturesque, the CPR's formula remained basically the same: small or even portable depots for small towns, larger buildings for locations where natural resources or other commercial advantages might be exploited, and "Class A" structures for major city terminals or other sites deemed to have the potential for greatness.[24]

For many pioneer towns in their formative years, the railway station would soon become the central hub of activity. Railway agents often took on a variety of additional roles in the community, such as cab driver, insurance broker, travel agent, club organizer, or even mayor. Station waiting rooms were inviting spaces, where the local Masonic Lodge, boys' and girls' agricultural clubs, or church organizations could hold meetings around the inviting warmth of the pot-bellied stove until their own quarters were up and running.

Before Van Horne arrived in Winnipeg, the CPR had already begun construction work west of Winnipeg. Brandon's rise as a railway divisional point began in 1881, under the supervision of Major-General Thomas Lafayette Rosser, the CPR chief surveyor who oversaw the initial push of

Prairie depots sprouting up across the prairies soon became the epicentres of community life. AUTHOR'S COLLECTION

▲ Railway divisional points typically included dining halls for
workers and passengers, with
rooms upstairs for overnight
stays as required. This view is
thought to be at Broadview,
Northwest Territories.

► Dining halls, like this one
at Moose Jaw, were mostly
patronized by railway passengers with deep pockets.

As soon as track was laid west of this commodious station in Winnipeg, railway passenger service was opened, heading west in stages as construction progressed. AUTHOR'S COLLECTION

the main line across the Manitoba prairies. Rosser was a colourful figure, a dashing Virginian gentleman and a West Point graduate who had chummed around with fellow cadet George Armstrong Custer. The former army officer's term with the CPR was cut short when Van Horne discovered his inappropriate involvement with land speculation. Along with Rosser, the railway's general superintendent, Alpheus Beede Stickney, was fired for the same reason. Stickney had previously held a similar position with the St. Paul, Minneapolis & Manitoba Railway, and had been recommended to the Canadian railway by that company's pioneering railroad magnate, James Jerome Hill. In light of what Van Horne considered to be Rosser's and Stickney's severe conflict of interest, the CPR general manager set a rigorous standard for how the railway would deal in the future with other in-house speculators who sought to profit from unauthorized side deals.

Back in 1880, when the Pacific Railway was still a project of the Canadian government, it was expected that the next divisional point west of Portage la Prairie would be at a place where the railway could cross the Assiniboine River with relative ease. In the spring of 1881, Rosser arrived in Portage la Prairie to turn the first ceremonial sod for the new CPR company and headed toward the would-be community of Grand Valley, a likely location for the anticipated bridge, where astute speculators had already squatted.[25]

The pioneer settlers of Grand Valley, anticipating the arrival of the railway, created a small land boom in the area. Local residents Dugald and John McVicar came from Quebec in 1879 and had built the first sod building in the district. By the time Rosser arrived with plans to build a major depot on the McVicar homestead, the town had already erected a general store, a sawmill, and a hotel in a large canvas tent.[26]

In various contemporary accounts, Rosser is said to have offered the McVicars anywhere from $25,000 to $50,000 for the piece of property he had in mind; but apparently the owners were determined to hold out for considerably more.[27] In any event, Rosser and the CPR resolved the issue by simply moving the townsite 2 miles (3.2 km) farther west to the present site of Brandon, on the opposite bank of the Assiniboine. A precedent had been set. Whenever the CPR was faced with an extortionate price to acquire land already owned by speculators, the railway would bypass all of the obstacles and set up its townsites on land it already owned, or on a section where it could negotiate a favourable deal.

The CPR site at Brandon was divided into town lots by a team led by Dominion land surveyor, Josephus Wyatt Vaughan. In June 1881, Charles Whitehead, son of railway contractor Joseph Whitehead, purchased the first lots from the railway in a public auction. Many of the buildings erected by speculators in Grand Valley were then moved to Brandon. By mid-summer there were four banks, a flour mill, sawmill, two planing mills, two churches, and several other industrial and commercial structures in what was rapidly becoming an important centre for the CPR. There were saddleries, harness makers, blacksmiths, carriage makers, furniture manufacturers, grocery and dry goods stores, butcher shops, jewellers, and a waterworks.[28]

The railway's new division point would become the jumping-off point and supply depot for people homesteading in the immediate area and throughout the frontier further north.

To ward off the potential stain and adverse publicity of land speculation and the persistent rumours of insiders taking advantage of their position to buy town lots along the line before their availability was officially announced, Van Horne placed a notice in the Winnipeg newspaper stating that successful buyers in all CPR towns would be chosen "without regard to any private interest whatsoever."[29] Soon after, the railway boss announced that he would have 500 miles (800 km) of railway constructed by the end of the year.[30] He would face many obstacles chasing that goal. Above all, the spring weather would create severe challenges, blanketing the landscape with punishing snowstorms and leaving CPR work crews to struggle with their aftereffects.

In the spring, the first passenger train to leave Brandon for Winnipeg after severe flooding had three coaches full of men and woman quitting the Northwest, never to return.[31] One settler, J.M. Wallis, who had boarded a train for the West in Winnipeg on April 3, 1882, was caught up in a blizzard before he could even reach Brandon. He wrote to his mother:

There is not a thing to eat on the train and it is impossible to get any assistance until they dig out the road. I have a small flask of whiskey which I am sharing with my fellow passengers but it won't last more than a few hours. There are a great many women and children on board and the prospects are there will be terrible suffering and cold.[32]

A relief train took the passengers back to Winnipeg. They started out again for Brandon a few days later, reaching their destination successfully. Wallis told his mother that on his first night in town, there was no door on the house where he was staying, which made it rather cold. "However," he wrote, "compared with my train experience it was paradise." His missive did not put the CPR or Brandon in a very favourable light:

My valise has been lying here for four days and I could not get it until I hunted through a dozen baggage cars and walked off with it. Everyone helps himself to his own baggage without reference to the baggage man. The greatest confusion prevails at the station. Hundreds of immigrants cannot even get shelter. Whole cars of stock have been starved and frozen to death. The reckless destruction of baggage and freight is something appalling. The snow blockade has prevented things from being sent down from Winnipeg and one cannot get the smallest trifles.[33]

Many pioneer settlers made the mistake of not taking into account living conditions in the new lands, particularly the nature of the climate, and this led to failure and a less than robust population growth. In the early years, as many settlers were leaving the Northwest as were arriving.

Land commissioner McTavish and the CPR were resolved to sell lands only to actual settlers or those agreeing to cultivate and improve the land. In that way, they might avoid,

With proper sleeping cars in short supply, the railway initially carried most settlers west by day coach. AUTHOR'S COLLECTION

in the words of the CPR president George Stephen, "the pernicious evil of speculators buying large tracts and locking them up."[34] To discourage speculators, CPR raised the sale price of prairie land to $5 an acre ($12.36/ha), a quarter of which was to be paid at the time of sale and the balance in five years without interest. At the same time, the rebate for land placed under cultivation was raised to $3.75 an acre ($9.27/ha), so that bona fide settlers who worked the land would still only pay $1.25 an acre ($3.09/ha). Those who bought land hoping for a quick turnover, or to hold it until prices rose substantially, paid four times as much.[35]

Townsite policy

By 1882, with a bullish economy rapidly turning bear, and the initial land sale euphoria in the Northwest having been exhausted, the CPR was in dire need of any funds it could muster. In the spring, the railway had entered into an agreement with the minister of the interior, whereby both the government and the railway would contribute land to constitute the townsites of Virden, Qu'Appelle, Regina, and Moose Jaw.[36] The first of those town lots were surveyed early that year and offered for sale under the management of McTavish, with the proceeds to be divided equally between the two chief landholders. To retain better control of where townsites would be located, the department of the interior temporarily withdrew for sale the government's even-numbered sections located within a mile of the railway for homestead settlement.

Settlers were now coming west at a slower pace and would continue to do so until the turn of the century. For that reason, and to quickly secure badly needed cash for everyday operations, the CPR agreed to sell 5 million acres (2 million ha) of prime land to a British–Canadian syndicate, the Canada North-West Land Company.[37] Those lands consisted of the railway's odd-numbered sections in every township along the main line railway belt from Brandon to the eastern boundary of British Columbia. The newly incorporated land company would also take over responsibility for holding, administering, and selling the property in all of the railway's new townsites. Profits from the sale of town lots would be split between the CPR and the land company, one-quarter each, while the government would be entitled to the other half.[38] Land was transferred to the company as it was needed because, as soon as it changed hands, it was liable to taxation.[39]

The new land company was chaired by Thomas Skinner, a London-based financial journalist and HBC shareholder. Along with acquiring a significant amount of land from CPR, the firm also agreed to buy $13.5 million worth of land grant bonds from the railway.[40]

To administer the sale of town lots and the division of profits, CPR set up a four-man "Joint Townsite Trustee

Board." Representing the railway's interests were Donald Smith and Richard Angus, while the Canada North-West Land Company appointed Edmund Osler and William Scarth. All four would become major players in the development of the Canadian Northwest.

Arriving in Canada decades earlier from Scotland, Smith had risen to prominence with the HBC. As the HBC's executive officer, he had played a leading role in negotiating the transfer of his company's lands in the Northwest to the Canadian government, one of the largest real estate deals in the world. As a member of the syndicate that promoted and built the the CPR, Smith pledged his personal fortune to keep the project viable and was rewarded with the honour of driving the last spike in the transcontinental line at Craigellachie, on November 7, 1885. In later years, as Baron Strathcona and Mount Royal, he would go on to serve as Canadian High Commissioner in London and would be remembered as a businessman, politician, diplomat, and philanthropist.[41]

Angus began his ascendancy in the business world as a banker but made his biggest breakthrough when he partnered with Montreal businessmen George Stephen and Donald Smith, along with James Jerome Hill, their colleague from Minnesota, to purchase the bankrupt St. Paul & Pacific Railroad. Much of the profits they derived from the St. Paul & Pacific were from land sales. All four of those men would build their personal fortunes on the foundation of that fateful deal, and all would become founding

members of the CPR syndicate largely based on that success. The experience they gained with land matters in the US would influence the syndicate's later negotiations with the Canadian government. Angus would serve as a railway director and member of the CPR's executive committee for the next forty years.[42]

Like Smith, Osler was a businessman, politician, and philanthropist. From a young age, his Toronto firm offered expertise in stockbroking, investing, and insurance services. In 1882, he was a founder and managing director of the Ontario & Qu'Appelle Land Company. His role as an advisor to CPR president George Stephen helped him to land a position on the CPR board of directors as well as the presidency of the Ontario & Quebec Railway. Increasingly, he concentrated on western investments and, as a co-founder of Osler, Hammond, and Nanton, managed key colonization railway projects, most of which were later incorporated into the CPR network.[43]

Scarth set himself up in the 1870s as a shipowner and timber merchant. Along with a variety of involvements in insurance, railways, mining, and real estate, he was instrumental in establishing the North British Canadian Investment Company and the Scottish Ontario and Manitoba Land Company. Shortly after the formation of the Canada North-West Land Company, Scarth assumed sole administrative responsibility for the joint enterprise.[44]

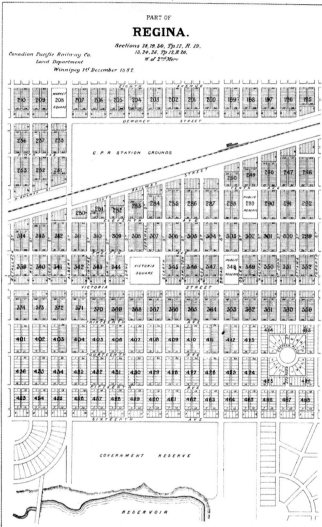

THE COMPLIMENTS OF

THE REGINA LEADER,

THE LEADING NEWSPAPER IN THE NORTH WEST TERRITORIES.
SUBSCRIPTION, $2 A YEAR.

PART OF

REGINA.

Sections 18, 19, 30, Tp 17, R. 19,
13, 24, 25, Tp 17, R 20.
W. of 2nd Mer.

Canadian Pacific Railway Co.
Land Department
Winnipeg 1st December 1882.

Under the arrangement between the CPR and the federal government, the railway could have the land it needed for its station buildings and other facilities, and the government could take whatever land it required for official and public offices and buildings.[45]

One of the most important townsite developments that same year occurred near a creek with the distinctive name Pile of Bones (now Wascana Creek), a reference to the vast quantities of skeletal remains in the vicinity from the great buffalo slaughter in recent years. Under a blistering August sun in 1882, track construction had raced toward the future town at breakneck speed, setting a one-day record of 4 miles (6.4 km) laid down just west of Pilot Butte.[46]

The federal census in 1881 had revealed that the large area of the Territories that now constitutes the Province of Saskatchewan had a total population of nearly 19,000, of which about 15,000 were Indigenous Peoples and 3,000 were Métis. There were only 615 landowners on nearly 14,000 acres (5,700 ha) of cultivated land, and a lot of wide-open spaces.

Once again, to thwart speculators, the railway laid out a town about a mile from where squatters had anticipated. Built in the midst of an uninspiring region of the prairies, with few trees and a barely adequate water supply, an unimaginative, rectangular grid of lots would set the stage for the early years of the town to be named Regina. As orchestrated by the CPR, the lackluster frontier railway stop would shortly be chosen as the legislative centre of the North-West Territories, replacing the former capital of Battleford for that honour. The official transfer of the government apparatus from one location to the next would take place in March 1883. Folks in the former capital were not impressed by the political machinations, as newspaper laments made clear:

The CPR land department created an orderly grid of town lots on streets named for railway officers and their associates. AUTHOR'S COLLECTION

The choice of this capital [Regina] has but one thing to recommend it—it lies on the railway; but that advantage is also enjoyed by hundreds of other places which have in addition both wood and water. Pile of Bones [as Regina, like the creek, was formerly known] has little of the later and none of the former, standing as it does in the midst of a bleak and treeless plain. However rich the soil may be, the lack of wood and water in the vicinity must militate against its becoming a place of very great importance.[47]

For the townsite trustees of the Canada North-West Land Company, the potential downside of serving two masters, the CPR and the federal government, must have become clear when Van Horne chose a spot for the railway station that was a couple of miles east of the two original sections that had been surveyed by the land company for the townsite—on a railway section, of course. Edgar Dewdney, appointed in 1881 as lieutenant-governor of the North-West Territories, built the territorial council building and his own residence in separate areas farther west, on HBC land.[48]

Despite the obvious differences of opinion on how or exactly where the capital should be developed, however, CPR president Stephen sought to assure the Canadian prime minister that all was well as far as townsite cooperation and land sales were concerned:

We want to do all we can to make Regina a great success and anything and everything we can do to make it a success will be done, and I hope you will not allow anyone to even suggest to you, that the fact of the Gov't having a half interest in the site is going to make us any less eager for its success than if it all belonged to the Coy [sic].[49]

When a pair of immigrant brides arrived in Regina in 1882, though, they were less than impressed by their surroundings. "It was a dirty little town consisting of a one-roomed station, a few stores and several shacks," recalled one of the intended in later years. They had found no accommodations, so everybody had slept "on the floor, men, woman and children, rich and poor, side by side," and they all apparently woke up "stiff and sore."[50]

In March 1883, the federal government would open a Dominion Lands Office in Regina, and by the end of the year the moratorium on selling even-numbered sections of land within a one-mile belt along the CPR main line would be lifted. Within a year, more than four thousand homestead entries were recorded in the district around Regina, a greater number than had been sold through any other land office in the North-West Territories.[51]

To handle sales for the long haul, the CPR and the Canada North-West Land Company would set up agency offices throughout the central prairie region in the railway stations at Carberry, Brandon, Virden, Moosomin, Broadview, Wolseley, Regina, and Moose Jaw. The region had lighter but no less fertile soil than that of the Red River Valley, but little timber for building and fuel, most of which had to be brought in from Ontario or BC. The agents at the land offices distributed maps of the lands available for sale, along with plans of town plots and pamphlets describing the detailed assessments of CPR land examiners.

The CPR was instrumental in establishing seventy-eight towns along its main line between Brandon and Calgary, at the confluence of the Bow and Elbow rivers and the approach to the Rocky Mountains. Divisional points would be created at Broadview, Moose Jaw, Swift Current, Medicine Hat, and Gleichen.

Qu'Appelle became the jumping-off point for settlers and supplies moving north to off-line towns such as Prince Albert and Carlton. Moose Jaw and Swift Current, in turn, became the transfer spots for people and freight farther

Two Cree women in northern Alberta, 1882. Old east–west prairie cart trails were reoriented to head north and south of the railway main line as it progressed westward.

west, whose lands were located north and south of the railway. Where Métis cart trails had tended to run east to west, freight forwarders now began to map out new routes north and south of the railhead as it progressed across the country. Shippers from as far away as Edmonton came south to load supplies brought in by the CPR and hauled goods to connect with paddlewheelers that plied the South Saskatchewan during the spring.

The early pattern of settlement at Swift Current reflected how the Indigenous Peoples and the newcomers to the region would choose to be segregated. The white people built their houses and businesses along the tracks, across from the CPR station, while the Métis and Indigenous Peoples who had not yet moved to reserves set up their tepees and erected rough shanties along the local creek, which the

French fur traders called Rivière au Courant, or Swift Current. It was not unlike the dynamic that had played out in Winnipeg's pioneering days.

For whatever reason, the Canada North-West Land Company did not expend much energy in advertising town lots in Swift Current. For its first twenty years, the town would consist mostly of railway workers and their families. Until the turn of the century, a half-dozen business establishments, a school, two churches, and a handful of houses, strung out north of the tracks along Railway Street, were the only structures in town other than the CPR's operating facilities.

At Medicine Hat, surveyors had laid out the townsite some time before the arrival of a Canada North-West Land Company land sales agent. In the interim, there had been a gentlemen's agreement among the local businessmen to respect one another's pre-emptive claims for town lots where various individuals had already begun to ply their respective trades. When William Scarth arrived in town and announced the land company's prices for the lots, there was an immediate cry of indignation from the prospective buyers, as the prices were much steeper than anticipated. As a result, the sale of town lots was set back by several months.[52]

Along with keeping costs affordable, there were aesthetic considerations for the CPR to ponder. An early initiative to encourage immigration and settlement across the prairies was the development of vegetable and flower gardens on the grounds adjacent to many of the railway stations, where the bounty of the land could be made readily apparent to all who passed through or stopped off in those towns. The gardens developed by CPR employees at divisional points were particularly elaborate.

This public relations idea, which would serve as a powerful testimony to the fertility of the soil to be found in the Northwest, was the brainchild of David Hysop, an Irish immigrant who arrived in Canada with his parents in 1847. Taking up residence in Toronto's fashionable Parkdale district, Hysop earned his railway bona fides with the Grand Trunk, at first as a member of a surveying party and later as a conductor. By 1881, he had answered the call of the new Canadian frontier and made his way to Manitoba. He soon took a position with the CPR and began to invest in real estate. A few years later, he made the acquaintance of William Whyte, the railway's then general superintendent of the Western Division, who was impressed with Hysop's ability and good judgment.[53]

Initially, Whyte assigned Hysop to the task of investigating the claims of farmers residing close to the railway that

fires started by sparks from CPR locomotives were damaging their properties and threatening livestock. While settling what were sometimes valid claims and filing a report to that effect with the railway company, Hysop included in his summation that to guard against future incidents of this nature, fireguards should be plowed along the right-of-way wherever feasible. A seed company from Chicago had offered free grass seed to manicure the bare spots cleared of flammable wild vegetation, but Hysop was intent upon what he considered to be a far better solution, as he advised Whyte:

Good grass there [along the right-of-way] would be setting up a free lunch counter for all the cattle in the country. Just think of the train wrecks and the lawsuits about cattle killed by the trains! If you want to show how good the soil is, why not have

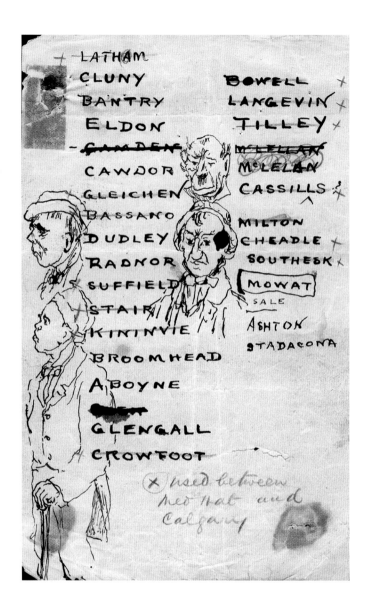

gardens at the railway stations in which flowers and vegetables can be grown? The company can supply the seeds, the station agent and the section foremen can look after the gardens, and, if water is needed, the locomotives can supply it, and it can be kept in barrels along the track. The vegetables and flowers can be used in the dining cars and shown at fairs far and wide.[54]

In Europe and the United States, it had long been the practice to landscape railway grounds where station construction had marred the immediate area around them, and often CPR employees who were gardening enthusiasts had unofficially pursued that same strategy. With Whyte giving a thumbs up to Hysop's suggestion, prospective settlers were soon being enticed with prominent displays of local flora and produce.

By the time the transcontinental was up and running, the CPR was providing stations along the line with trees and shrubs—and later perennials—from a large nursery at Wolseley, just east of Indian Head. By 1907, the railway would establish a second nursery at Springfield, Manitoba; soon after, the CPR would supply seeds and flowers from its own greenhouses at Fort William, Kenora, Winnipeg, Moose Jaw, Calgary, Revelstoke, and Vancouver.

As time went by, the station gardens were often bordered by trees and ornamental shrubs, or a plethora of colourful perennials. Abandoning all subtlety in later years, the CPR station in Broadview featured a large display of the word "produce," spelled out with leafy lettuce plants.[55]

During 1883, the federal government set a record for surveying, driven by the rapid advance of the railway across the prairies and the need to award land grants related to construction accomplishments. The 27 million acres (11 million ha) surveyed that year established the high-water mark

◄ President Van Horne drew character sketches on a list of suggested prairie station names sent to him for consideration. CRHA/EXPORAIL CANADIAN PACIFIC RAILWAY FONDS A494

► The wide open and flat expanses of the southern prairies enabled speedy construction, but offered railway passengers little in the way of scenic vistas. LIBRARY AND CULTURAL RESOURCES DIGITAL COLLECTIONS, UNIVERSITY OF CALGARY CU1151760

in the history of land subdivision for North America, a feat that is unrivalled to this day.[56]

As construction of the CPR main line approached Calgary in August 1883, land commissioner McTavish and the Canada North-West Land Company trustees were well aware that a considerable amount of squatting had occurred near the confluence of the Bow and Elbow rivers, where it was anticipated the railway might locate its station, particularly on the east side of the Elbow.

Eight years earlier, the North-West Mounted Police had established Fort Calgary on the west bank of the Elbow River. The area where the two rivers meet had long been a wintering spot for local Indigenous Peoples, as it was both aesthetically pleasing and practical for hunting and fishing. The Montana firm of I.G. Baker had also built a small store beside the fort, while the HBC had moved its trading post from the Ghost River to the east bank of the Elbow River opposite the fort. At a stopover point on the wagon trail between Fort Benton, Montana, and Fort Edmonton, a number of Métis had thrown up rough dwellings for their families on either side of the Elbow.[57]

By 1880, the buffalo were all but extinct. The nomadic Siksika, who had formerly roamed the region, had been largely confined to reserves after the signing of Treaty 7, negotiated in 1877. Only four Mounties remained stationed at Fort Calgary. But with CPR's dramatic decision in 1881 to change its transcontinental route to a more southerly one, rampant speculation descended on the lands surrounding the underused fort. Although odd-numbered sections were normally reserved for railway lands, the mounted police were well established on Section 15 and the whole section had been kept largely free of squatters so that it could be used by the force for pasture land.[58]

Fort or no fort, CPR's James M. Egan was determined to locate the townsite there. Egan replaced Alpheus Stickney after Van Horne fired the former general superintendent for speculating on land sales. Arriving at Calgary a couple of weeks ahead of the CPR construction crews, Egan fired off a letter to Van Horne to outline the merits of his favoured site:

At Calgary on Section 15, there is a very good location for a Town site. No squatters are on this Section, as the Mounted Police have kept them off here. Mr. Hamilton [of the CPR Land Office] has arranged to lay out a town, and I have no doubt that when you see the place it will please you. It is west of the Elbow, and the north line of the Section runs across the Bow River. It is a natural Town site, and far ahead of any location that we have on the line of the Road.

As you perhaps are aware, there is considerable strife between the people east of the Elbow and those West. The buildings of the Mounted Police, I.G. Baker and several others are West of the Elbow, and the Hudson's Bay Coy's stores and a number of settlers are East.

In locating the Station Grounds, I have placed them towards the west end of the section as I think by that location, the strife between the places will be ended.

We now have seventeen stations for which we are anxiously awaiting names.[59]

When the construction crews arrived in the area, a temporary, portable station was deposited right where Egan had suggested, but despite the superintendent's glowing account of the ease with which the townsite might be established on Section 15, there were a few small details to attend to. Among them was the need to deal with one settler who had managed to establish a foothold in the desired area.

Before the year was out, the board of directors of the Canada North-West Land Company passed a detailed resolution confirming that "the Townsite Trustees reported having paid $1,000 to Baptiste Anouse for consideration of his abandonment of Squatter's Claim to the SE¼,

Sec 15, Twp 24, Range 1 West 5th Meridien, which section has been chosen by the CPR as the Calgary Townsite."[60]

Four months after Egan's letter, railway construction continued westward, but little progress had been made in finalizing the precise location for the townsite. To resolve the issue once and for all, townsite trustee William Scarth dispatched CPR land commissioner John McTavish to Calgary in January 1884.

McTavish set up his office in a railway car on a siding beside the CPR station. Along with William Thomas Ramsay, an agent of the Canada North-West Land Company, McTavish soon arranged a meeting of stakeholders, many of whom already held substantial land holdings east of the Elbow River on Section 14.[61]

To sway the hostile crowd toward giving fair consideration to locating the townsite on Section 15, McTavish went well beyond what the CPR had authorized him to offer. Afterward, he sent a lengthy explanation for his actions to Scarth, who, in turn, forwarded the update to CPR's corporate secretary:

I felt that to prevent a total failure I would be obliged to make some concessions, so I fixed the price for inside lots at $300, corner lots $450, and as I knew there was very little money in the place I only called for $50 down, $50 in 6 months, balance in equal instalments in one and two years with 6% interest. I further offered a rebate of half the purchase price to those who built and were in occupation on [Section] 15 by the 1st of April [1884].[62]

Parties wishing to buy parcels of land were then invited to draw numbers from a hat to determine the order in which they would select lots from a large surveyed townsite map pinned to the wall. John Glenn, the oldest inhabitant in the

► The Calgary townsite took on a familiar pattern with the railway tracks on one side of the CPR station and a main street dotted with hotels and other businesses on the other side. AUTHOR'S COLLECTION

neighbourhood, picked ticket number one and chose seven lots in all, three of them being corner lots, two of which were immediately opposite the CPR station, north of the tracks. The rest of the buyers followed suit, and by the end of the week McTavish and Ramsay had recorded sales of 263 lots, for which they received $86,500.[63]

Once again, the CPR had outmaneuvered the land speculators and located its townsite in a spot where the railway and its chosen agents could control all of the land sales and economic development.

The CPR federal charter granted the company freedom from taxation on its land grant holdings for twenty years after they were selected unless the land was sold. The Canada North-West Land Company claimed that it was also entitled to this concession by virtue of its agreement with the railway. At the time, government surveyor William

Pearce was instrumental in clearing away red tape in the way of town development.

Forty years later, he remembered the taxation issue as a bone of contention between the elected officials in the Calgary town council and the townsite trustees: "After wrangling over the matter for some time," he recalled, "a compromise was effected by the Corporation [of Calgary] relinquishing its rights to taxation up to a certain date, in exchange for the townsite trustees conveying to the Corporation of Calgary the block of land which became Central Park."[64]

The Canada North-West Land Company would also reach agreements with the township administrations in Regina, Qu'Appelle, and Moose Jaw to share the terms of its tax exposure with the CPR and the federal government.

The towns established by the Canada North-West Land Company in partnership with the railway and the federal government would grow at a steady pace. In particular, Calgary's strategic location at the crossroads of the east–west transcontinental railway and an important north–south trade route established during the fur trade era would serve the CPR well in the coming years. Before the turn of the century, Calgary would emerge as the railway's most important divisional point between Winnipeg and Vancouver.

Looking farther afield

By 1884, the CPR was suffering from the effects of a full-blown, worldwide depression that would continue to some extent until the late 1890s. During the period from the end of 1883 until 1896, the company sold fewer acres of land than it had in 1883 alone.

In the face of faltering sales, the Canada North-West Land Company was driven to reduce the amount of its proposed land purchase from the 5 million acres (2 million ha) originally agree upon to a more manageable 2.2 million acres (890,000 ha). This reduced the land company's indebtedness to the CPR from $13.5 million to $6 million. When it was reorganized in 1893, the Canada North-West Land Company became—in fact, if not in name—a CPR subsidiary, with Van Horne as president and CPR directors holding the lion's share of the stock. The following year, the railway's own land department took over the administration and sale of the land company's real estate.[65]

As construction moved across the prairies toward the Rocky Mountains, the CPR had found it increasingly difficult to select prime agricultural land for settlers from what was available in the railway belt. The most generous estimate of acceptable agricultural land within this

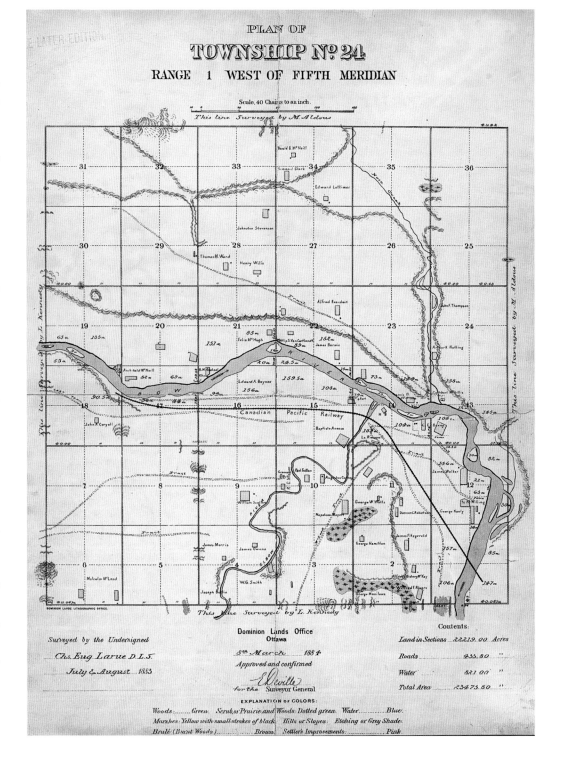

48-mile-wide (77 km) strip placed the total at 6 million acres (2.4 million ha). To compensate for this, the company was compelled to acquire four large land reserves far removed from the main line.

The first of these was located in what was known as the fertile or "garden belt" running through Western Saskatchewan and Northern Alberta, comprising some of the finest land in the Dominion. It was estimated that this region would yield nineteen million odd-numbered sections from which the CPR could choose. Even accounting for lands rejected as "unfit for settlement," it would guarantee the company more than half of its total land grant.[66]

In addition, arrangements were made to grant the CPR about 2.5 million acres (1 million ha) between the original western boundary of Manitoba and the uplands of the Missouri Coteau, known in Canada as Palliser's Triangle. A few months later, the government agreed to extend this reserve to include all the odd-numbered sections from the transcontinental line to the US border and between the Red River and the original western limit of Manitoba.[67]

The lands in southern Manitoba would be sold off relatively quickly, as their location became increasingly desirable with the company's construction of branch lines throughout the region. Meanwhile, the lands in the fertile belt to the north would sit idle until such time as the cultivation and development of free government homesteads within the area brought about a corresponding appreciation in the value of the railway's own sections.

In the 1890s, two more areas from which to select large blocks would be chosen by the company to fulfill the government's land grant obligations. Those allotments, which were also remote from the railway's main line, would come to be known as the Lake Dauphin Reserve and the Second Northern Reserve. The former included odd-numbered sections in the fertile and highly desirable Swan River district, due north of Brandon, where the CPR's competitors would eventually build railway lines. The latter was east and northeast of Edmonton "so far removed from the main line that there would be slight chance of any real colonization for many years to come."[68]

3

A HARD SELL

Home on the range

Even before the CPR refused to accept land grants along its main line west of Moose Jaw, the Canadian federal government had acknowledged that the semi-arid lands in Palliser's Triangle were more suited to grazing cattle than to planting field crops. Under an 1881 amendment to the Dominion Lands Act of 1872, an order-in-council enabled individuals or companies to lease up to 100,000 acres (40,000 ha) of pastureland for a period of 21 years, at a paltry rate of one cent per acre (2.5 cents/ha) annually.[1] The birth of large-scale ranching in Western Canada was about to begin. The arrival of the CPR, two years later, would finalize the deal.

In North America, a boom in cattle production was spurred by the demands for meat made by the Union army during the US Civil War in the 1860s.[2] The growth in the industry soon spread north toward Canada. When the North-West Mounted Police established Fort Calgary in 1874, they developed a small local market for beef products and secured lands surrounding their post for open grazing. Around the same time, Joseph MacFarland, an Irish-American frontiersman, and George Emerson, an ex-Hudson's Bay man, drove small herds into the Canadian West from Montana to meet the increasing demand. The pioneer Methodist missionary Reverend John McDougall and his father, George, also began raising a herd near their mission at Morleyville (now Morley, Alberta).[3]

The people who initially took up ranching in the Canadian West were mostly British, not American, and the industry was dominated by a wealthy and politically powerful elite from Eastern Canada, epitomized by Senator Mathew H. Cochrane of Ontario's Wellington County, who lobbied hard for the rights of ranchers and became one of the most prominent cattlemen in Alberta.[4] Along with his Cochrane Ranche, other large concerns were the Bar U, Oxley, Walrond, Winder, Quorn, and Cross ranches. In the first half of the 1880s, twenty-three cattle companies were established in the Northwest, with capital linked to powerbrokers in Montreal, Toronto, and Ottawa.[5] The British connection was strengthened by the arrival of Englishmen attracted by the heavy publicity that the British media accorded the North American cattle business. English and Scottish newspapers reported on opportunities for investment, with the result that three major investors from overseas put together British-Canadian cattle companies.[6]

The Western ranchers banded together to form stock associations to deal with issues of mutual interest, such as

the depredation of wolves and the relations of the industry with the various levels of government. Horse and sheep ranching never reached the same lofty numbers of practitioners, size of herds, or strength of lobbying power.

The large gangs of government surveyors and railway construction workers that converged in the Northwest with the advent of the CPR, and the accompanying growth of settlers, provided a local demand for large quantities of beef. More importantly for the cattle industry, when the CPR main line reached the prairie ranchlands in the early 1880s, it gave ranchers ready access to distant markets in the eastern provinces and overseas.

The Northern Pacific had reached Montana in 1883, but its rail line was far away from much of the grazing lands in the northern part of the state, so the large-scale ranchers

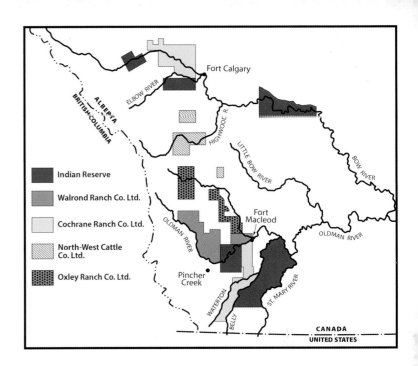

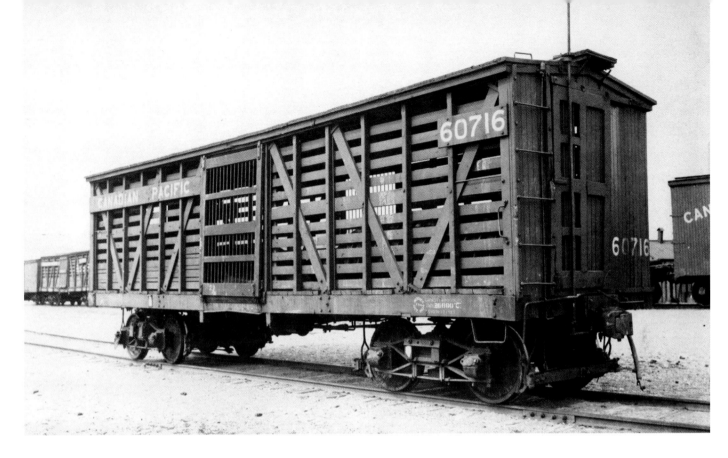

south of the border negotiated an agreement with the Canadian government and the CPR to drive their cattle to the railway's loading facility at Maple Creek, from where the livestock could easily be shipped to the busy abattoirs of Chicago.[7] The business contributed enough revenue to the CPR's bottom line in 1886 that the company's annual report made a point of informing shareholders about the significant numbers of American herds that had been brought across the international boundary to Canada. "The experience of the past winter, which was the most severe for many years, has shown the great advantages of the Canadian North-West over the adjacent territory in the United States

for cattle raising," it explained, "the percentage of losses in the neighbouring territory of Montana having been greater than on the Canadian side of the International Boundary."

Two years earlier, Canada had exported as many as 54,000 head of live cattle by rail and steamship to England, via the CPR's Montreal stockyard in Hochelaga. By the turn of the century, that annual tally had doubled, with heavy exports going to the United States as well.[8]

The earliest North American railway cars designed specifically for cattle were developed around the time of the US Civil War, in the 1860s. The cars had similar dimensions to a standard railway boxcar and featured solid, covered roofs with slatted sides for proper ventilation. In addition, they were equipped with sliding doors on either side to facilitate the loading and unloading of their bovine passengers. This basic configuration did not change dramatically for the next 120 years, by which time the practice of shipping livestock by rail had been phased out.

To the chagrin of the ranchers, who were zealous in their efforts to preserve the open range for the cattle industry, the advent of the railway not only facilitated their access to markets, it enabled an influx of homesteaders and other settlers to invade what had previously been exclusively their turf. The grazing law of 1881 stated that settlers already engaged in farming in the regions where large parcels of land were being leased for pastureland would be allowed to stay and pursue their livelihood.[9] By mid-decade, with the arrival of the CPR, the competition for land would only increase.

In 1885, Sam Livingston, one of the first pioneers to take up farming in the Calgary area, founded the Alberta Settlers Rights Association and fought for the rights of squatters and other settlers looking to farm their lands and to prove that the region was suitable for pursuits other than ranching. As a result of the association's lobbying efforts, Prime Minister John A. Macdonald cancelled some of the grazing leases held by land speculators and announced that future leases of ranchlands would not be allowed to interfere with homesteader settlement in any way.[10]

Nevertheless, the area in the Northwest under lease to the cattle industry grew rapidly during the 1880s and 1890s. But putting productive farmers on the land and creating a steady amount of traffic to fill both freight cars and company coffers was proving to be a hard sell. Some expansion of the areas available for rangeland came about from

the reversion of failed homesteads as well as from the leasing of lands that lacked the necessary fertility for large-scale agricultural development.[11]

For twenty years, the CPR did more to sustain ranching than it did to promote farming in the semi-arid region of the prairies. An early railway advertising booklet proclaimed that part of the Canadian Northwest as "peerless among the cattle countries of the world." The business was only marginally profitable for the CPR, but it did provide early settlers, many of whom had at least a few head of

FARMING AND RANCHING IN WESTERN CANADA

Manitoba, Assiniboia, Alberta, Saskatchewan.

cattle, with another means besides agriculture to generate capital and remain on the land. As the railway informed prospective investors, "Some idea can be formed of the profits accruing to cattle raisers from the fact that for the four-year-old steers comprised in the shipments [to Europe] as high as $45.00 per head was paid on the foot at Calgary, while the cost of raising, consisted almost entirely for management and herding, the animals having been fattened solely on the natural grasses."[12]

To a lesser degree, sheep ranching also benefited from having the railway to facilitate the movement of wool and mutton to market. As was the case with cattle, the first large flock of sheep was imported from Montana in 1884. By 1900, there was an estimated forty thousand of the fleecy interlopers in the Western ranching district.[13]

In addition, the northern ranchlands, with their high altitude, dry atmosphere, mild winters, and in many cases luxuriant grasses and plentiful supply of pure water, were considered to be highly conducive to the development and growth of horse breeding. There were also the beginnings of a ready equine market locally. The North-West Mounted Police required a regular source of saddle horses, and incoming settlers required a growing number of heavy draft horses. CPR pamphlets told those coming west to "bring as many first-class brood mares as you possibly can, and if you should not desire to settle here you will find a ready market for your stock at prices that will yield you a handsome profit on the investment, and indeed the same thing may be said of all domestic animals."

Whether one settled in the West or just wanted to enjoy a pleasant sojourn on the new frontier, the CPR could assure you that a carload of any "good trading animal"—horses, cows, sheep, or pigs—would defray your expenses "and pay you well for your time while enjoying a trip to the great ranching and farming country of Canada."[14]

A marketing nightmare

On Friday, October 12, 1883, a special fourteen-car train left the CPR's Winnipeg yard, bound for the West. The team of men on board was assigned the task of establishing a series of experimental farms along the railway's main line between Moose Jaw and Calgary, the very region through which railway surveyors had rejected land grants as not "fairly fit for settlement." The CPR was reluctant to take ownership of any of the lands within the controversial area known as Palliser's Triangle, but the railway had few hesitations about attempting to lure settlers and future customers to the government's free homestead lands in the region.[15]

Despite their own misgivings about the fertility of the land west of Moose Jaw, the company's propagandists were offended when prominent men and eastern newspapers belittled the territory. The media naysayers had gone so far as to assert that the large tract in question was made up of desert and alkali lands, entirely unfit for cultivation, as the following quotation from a prominent paper shows:

The Company have been permitted to divert their main line so far to the south that for hundreds of miles it runs through land which is unfit for settlement. When they asked for such an alteration of the contract in their favour, they should have been warned that they would still be compelled to take the chief part of the land subsidy along the line of railway. They knew what the lands they wished to traverse were like. Their general character has been known for a quarter of a century. They constitute the northern portion of a great American desert, which is projected like the apex of a cone into Canadian territory.[16]

The CPR wished to prove how utterly at variance with the facts assertions such as these were. The damaging effects of several consecutive years of drought in the Northwest would reveal themselves fully over the next few years, but for now the company was engaged in wishful thinking. An official memorandum prepared by officers of the CPR in December 1882 had boldly stated that "the railway between Winnipeg and the foot-hills of the Rocky Mountains, 900 miles [1,450 km] long, traverses one of the finest agricultural regions in the world, the settlement of which has been hitherto impeded by the want of railway facilities, but is now making remarkable progress."

► The CPR's experimental farms in the mid-1880s were really nothing more than test gardens that showed early promise, before collapsing during the following years of drought. BREATHE COMMUNICATIONS, AUTHOR'S COLLECTION

CPR EXPERIMENTAL FARMS 1883

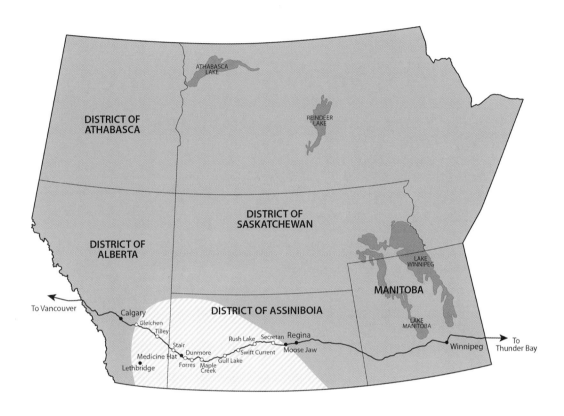

DISTRICT OF ATHABASCA

ATHABASCA LAKE

REINDEER LAKE

DISTRICT OF SASKATCHEWAN

DISTRICT OF ALBERTA

LAKE WINNIPEG

MANITOBA

LAKE MANITOBA

To Vancouver

Calgary
Gleichen
Tilley
Stair
Rush Lake
Secretan
Regina
Medicine Hat
Dunmore
Swift Current
Moose Jaw
Lethbridge
Forres
Maple Creek
Gull Lake

DISTRICT OF ASSINIBOIA

Winnipeg
To Thunder Bay

○ CPR EXPERIMENTAL FARMS 1883

▨ PALLISER'S TRIANGLE

The report went on to state almost completely erroneous facts:

In this district nearly the entire Land Grant of the Company is located. The country is a gently undulating prairie, well-watered throughout, and requiring no irrigation anywhere. The soil is uniformly deep and rich, and fully equal to that of the best agricultural lands in any part of North America.[17]

The United States had instituted a system of land-grant agricultural colleges in the 1860s, some with experimental stations. In Canada, experimental farming work was carried on in connection with the Ontario Agricultural College, founded in 1873. But it would not be until 1886 that the federal government set up a country-wide system of experimental farms.[18] The CPR's rush to demonstrate the superiority of its southern route across the prairies with positive results from its own network of experimental farms would be more window dressing than scientific enterprise.

The workers first broke ground in the vicinity of the railway's station at Secretan. Under the direction of a railway field inspector, the farming team and necessary equipment was unloaded each morning at a selected location and put to work preparing a small bed in which a variety of crops could be planted. CPR land commissioner McTavish would then have the locomotive pull his private car in search of a "suitable place for the next day's operations, returning to the first point in the evening to load up and move the entire outfit during the night to the location chosen."[19] In this manner, additional experimental gardens were established, in rapid succession, at Rush Lake, Swift Current, Gull Lake, Maple Creek, Forres, Dunmore, Stair, Tilley, and Gleichen.

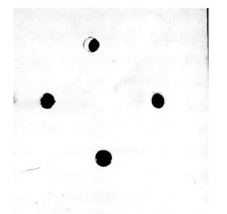

SAMPLE
OF
NO. 1 HARD WHEAT
(RED FYFE)
GROWN IN THE
Canadian North - West,
ON THE
EXPERIMENTAL FARM
AT
GLEICHEN
(785 miles west of Winnipeg),
ALONG THE LINE OF THE
CANADIAN PACIFIC
RAILWAY.

In every case, the CPR reported the soil to be "good and in most instances excellent." The following spring, on March 27, 1884, another special train was dispatched with boarding cars, men, implements and seed grain to begin planting. At each farm, a small plot was sown with a variety of vegetables and grains and harvested in the fall, with satisfactory results. At the end of the season, the railway reported that the experiment had been even more satisfactory than anticipated. The land in the section of the country under study was found to give "as large a wheat yield per acre as the heavier lands of Manitoba," resulting in "a fair crop can be obtained the first year of settlement." Cereals, root crops, and other garden produce were all shown to have been successfully raised at an elevation of 3,000 feet (914 m) above sea level.[20]

In little more than a year's time, the entire Northwest was afflicted with a severe drought that lasted, for the most part, until the late 1890s.[21] The CPR let its "experimental farms" fall by the wayside with little fanfare.

The return to the prairies of extremely dry conditions in the mid-1880s was a wakeup call for the federal government. Farmers were forced to adapt or leave, and the government realized the need for more extensive agricultural research throughout Canada and, in particular, in the Northwest. As a result, the Dominion Experimental Farms system was inaugurated in 1886. The following year, a 680-acre (275 ha) site was chosen at Indian Head, not far from the CPR station. A second prairie farm, at Brandon, would soon be added.[22]

Initially, the government specialists spent a great deal of time trying to interest and train Indigenous families in agricultural pursuits, but even the white settlers with considerable farming experience were having difficulties.

Along with the drought, homesteaders had to contend with early frosts and farming techniques with which they were unfamiliar. The pioneering research, conducted at the experimental farms, on when exactly to sow crops, as well as how to use newly developed farm machines would serve government homesteaders and CPR landowners alike.[23]

As had been the case with the observations of early railway surveyors such as Palliser, Hind, and Macoun, much depended on which years were chosen to evaluate the lands west of Moose Jaw.

"I have never failed in raising a good crop of wheat, oats, barley, and vegetables of all descriptions during each of the successive years," reported early Fish Creek resident, John Glenn, in 1884. Glenn raised tomatoes and cucumbers every year in the open air on his land just south of Calgary. "Of wheat I have averaged 37 bushels; oats 57 bushels; barley 71 bushels to the acre [91, 141, and 175 bushels/ha]; and have some this year not behind that standard. Average yield of potatoes, on 8 acres [3.2 ha] last year, was 225 bushels to the acre [556 bushels/ha]."[24]

The following year, Arthur Wellington Ross, a member of Parliament for Lisgar, Ontario, stood up in the Canadian House of Commons to complain about some of the negative views that were prevalent. "Immigration," he said, "has been stopped largely from Ontario, by complaints coming from the West, and also, I fear, by the action of some portion of the Ontario press in dwelling too persistently upon unfavourable aspects, though no doubt based upon former official reports. I found a general impression to this effect prevailing among intelligent men in the North-West, the general effect of which was prejudicial to the best interests of the settlement."[25]

He might have been referring to newspaper reports such as the one that appeared in the [Toronto] *Globe* on June 13, 1884, which described Palliser's Triangle as "400 miles [640 km] of this part of the line [that] can never earn enough to pay for locomotive tallow, unless alkali should become of great commercial value."[26]

The CPR maintained a positive narrative in its promotional materials for the lands along the entire length of its main line, but a large chunk of southwestern Saskatchewan and eastern Alberta remained a wasteland as far as cereal agriculture was concerned. One settler's daughter remembered in later years that the reputation of the area was so poor that, whenever possible, the CPR scheduled its trains to cross the country between Regina and the Alberta border at night, "lest prospective settlers glimpse its dismal character."[27]

Despite the best efforts of the CPR to advertise the merits of the Northwest, along with the federal government's initiative to speed up the surveying process and make more lands available to settlers, even the lure of free homesteads was not attracting many takers. The government had left much of the land sales to the CPR, knowing that the railway's own holdings would only be marketable when free homestead lands became scarce; and the railway needed settlers on the land as quickly as possible to generate the revenue necessary to sustain its business. But tens of millions of those free acres were remote from the CPR, and they were unlikely to be served by railway branch lines any time soon.

To speed up the process of settling lands within these vast areas, the government came up with a scheme to multiply the number of players involved in the land sales business, without having to expend too much effort itself or commit funds that were in short supply.

The same year that the CPR was incorporated, the Ottawa government adopted regulations that allowed companies to purchase lands remote from the railway for colonization purposes. To buy odd-numbered sections at $2 per acre ($4.94/ha), prospective buyers would agree to place two settlers on each even-numbered section within the same area. In turn, the established homesteaders would aid with land sales through their eligibility to reserve lots attached to their own as a pre-emptive option. After five years, if a company had colonized the even sections, it would receive a rebate of $1 per acre ($2.47/ha) on a corresponding number of odd-numbered sections that it had acquired for resale.[28]

Initially, there was a rush of would-be colonizers eager to take advantage of the government's offer. A total of 260 applications were received, from various religious denominations, philanthropic organizations, and financiers, of which 106 were accepted as viable.[29]

One of these colonization companies, the Saskatchewan Land & Homestead Company, would play a leading role in the early settlement of central Alberta. Founded in 1882 by Toronto interests with strong ties to the Methodist Church, the newly formed company applied for grants of 200,000 acres (81,000 ha) in three large blocks in the Northwest: two in what would later be the Province of Saskatchewan, and a third consisting of 115,000 acres (46,500 ha) in the vicinity of Red Deer River Crossing on the Calgary–Edmonton Trail.[30]

As early as the summer of 1882, John T. Moore, who was the managing director of the Saskatchewan Land & Homestead Company, led an exploration party to inspect the lands they hoped to acquire, taking the CPR to end of steel at Moose Jaw and bumping across the prairie by buckboard

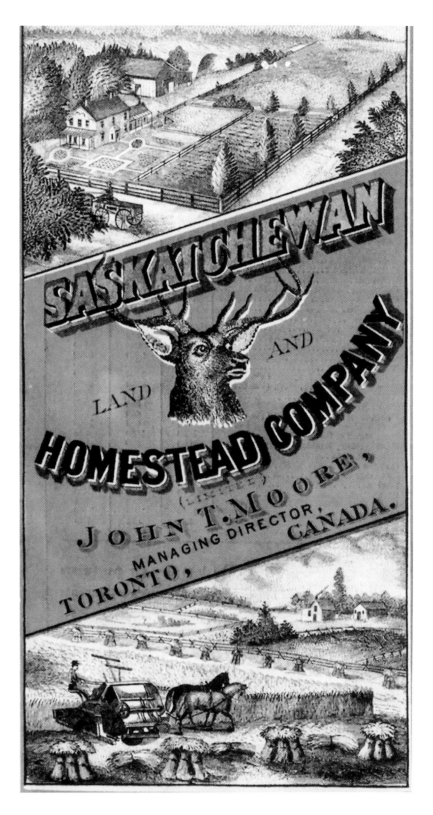

for the remainder of the trip. Moore would eventually relocate from Toronto to Red Deer and become one of its most prominent citizens, serving as the publisher and editor of the *Alberta Advocate* and president of the Alberta Central Railway, and becoming one of the founders of the Western Telephone Company and Western General Electric Company. In 1905, when Alberta became a Canadian province, he was elected to the provincial legislature for Red Deer.[31]

Another company director, Reverend Leonard Gaetz, a Methodist, was the Saskatchewan Land & Homestead Company's first land agent in central Alberta, taking up residence in 1884 at Red River Crossing. Gaetz would be an effective promotor of his company's lands and of the Northwest in general, but in the near term, the Northwest Resistance effectively stifled immigration, and the situation would not improve for the remainder of the nineteenth century.[32]

Overall enthusiasm for large colonization projects waned as the new companies discovered the difficulties of putting together the necessary financing in the face of a stagnant economy, at a time when prospective immigrants and other potential settlers could still get good agricultural land close to a railway line in the United States. As a result, the government entered into contracts with only twenty-six companies, covering 2,842,742 acres (1,150,417 ha). Nine of these companies failed to place any settlers on the land, while the others brought in a total of only 1,243 settlers.[33]

Disappointed with the results, the Macdonald government ordered the program to be halted in June 1883, although the companies that were somehow managing to make a go of it continued to operate for the time being. For a few brief years, any settler willing to look farther afield than the railway belt could contact a representative of the Saskatchewan Land & Homestead Company, the York Farmers'

Colonization Company, the Dominion Lands Colonization Company, the Touchwood and Qu'Appelle Colonization Company, the Montreal and Western Land Company, or the oddly named Primitive Methodist Colonization Company, all of which were dissolved before a decade had passed.[34] The last of these pioneering enterprises, the Temperance Colonization Society, had its contract cancelled in 1891.[35]

One year after the government's foray into the business of sub-contracting colonization, the CPR had also felt compelled to give some consideration to individuals and companies who wished to buy large amounts of company land within the 48-mile (77 km) railway belt. CPR priced the land at five dollars an acre, but the purchasers had only to pay one quarter of that in cash. If at least one-half of a buyer's land was cultivated and a crop sown and reaped within five years, the balance would be waived. The CPR sold more than 800,000 acres (324,000 ha) in this way to hastily formed colonization companies, but several of them failed to comply with the conditions respecting cultivation and settlement, so the railway cancelled their contracts. The initiative failed to bring in as many settlers as the CPR had hoped, and it would not be until the following century that interest in similar undertakings would be revived.[36]

All eyes on the exhibition car

In the early years of CPR promotion, the most effective innovation for attracting settlers from Eastern Canada and enticing emigrants from the United States was an exhibition car loaded with agricultural and geological exhibits extolling the virtues of the "Golden Northwest" for all to see. The specially outfitted advertising vehicle was originally a CPR baggage car built in 1882 by the Cobourg [Ontario] Car Works. Much of the railway's valuable silk traffic in the early years was carried in this type of car, which featured a single door on either side rather than two, thereby providing greater protection for its cargo from pilferage and weather damage. Converted in 1884 for the CPR Land Department to house exhibits, the car would tour Eastern Canada and the US for the next twelve years in collaboration with the federal Department of Agriculture.[37]

One of the early settlers who collaborated with the CPR to outfit the exhibition car was Leonard Gaetz, land agent for the Saskatchewan Land & Homestead Company in Red Deer. Gaetz provided samples of wheat, oats, barley, potatoes, turnips, two kinds of onion, and two kinds of carrot for the car's 1885 tour.[38]

"Equipped with samples of products gathered along the line between Calgary and Winnipeg, this car penetrated into all portions of the eastern provinces which had railway facilities," according to James Hedges, a former professor of American History at Brown University and a leading authority on CPR land and colonization policies. "The exterior of the car was sufficiently gaudy in appearance to attract the attention of the curious and lure them to the railway stations where it was on exhibition. Once inside the car, the prospective settler found the exhibits, conveniently and tastefully arranged, impressive evidence of the possibilities of the new land."[39]

The Gananoque [Ontario] *Reporter* described the interior of the exhibition car as "a little world in itself." On each side of the car's central passageway were small bins covered with wire grating, in which various sorts of grain were showcased. On ledges above were roots and vegetables, and over those were framed views of the Northwest,

► The railway's exhibition car, outfitted to promote the products of Manitoba and the Canadian Northwest, was painted up like a circus car to encourage potential settlers to view its contents. J. BRUCE, AUTHOR'S COLLECTION

from Winnipeg to the Rockies. "The medals, gained by the North-West grains at the [recent] Amsterdam [agricultural] exhibition, are conspicuously displayed," reported the paper. There were also specimens of ore: copper and iron from the Bow River; freestone from Calgary that was said to equal the best Ohio sandstone; and coal from Western Canadian mines, "as good as anybody wants." There were stuffed heads of mountain sheep and antelope; soil samples in glass jars; and a profusion of wild fruits, among them black and red currents, strawberries, plums, crab apples, and Saskatoon berries.

Each female visitor to the exhibition car was given a copy of "What Women Say of the Canadian North-West," a pamphlet circulated with the intention of convincing them to join their sisters in touting the benefits of taking up residence in the new West. In the first couple of years, the car hosted an average of three thousand visitors per day.[40]

Van Horne himself was a great proponent of the Land Department's chief promotional vehicle and often sent brief messages with suggestions to tweak its effectiveness, as he did in this letter to CPR land commissioner McTavish:

The "Exhibit Car" which is now in Montreal is working much good down here amongst the French Farmers with whom "seeing is believing"; and it is doing in a day what we could not do in weeks by means of pamphlets...Samples of tobacco leaf, as grown by the Mennonites would sell well with the French Canadian and I think some specimens of timber of different kinds would go far to convince the unbeliever that there is wood to be found in Manitoba and the North West.[41]

An employee of *The Times* in Chicago wrote to CPR general superintendent John Egan about the exhibition car's potential effectiveness in the United States:

It has been apparent for some time that the "Canadian Northwest," or Northwestern Provinces of British America have not been thoroughly advertised. Our landed interests have gathered in all of the "immigration" and to a certain extent have prevented much of it going to your territory. Now I verily believe that if your car with a good talker and an excellent descriptive writer, run from here to New Orleans by one route and return by another, would net you a great deal.[42]

The exhibition car never did operate that far south, but it spent several years touring the US Midwest, where little effort to induce immigration had previously been made. The CPR regarded the eastern states as the ripest for exploitation. Farmers in those states were still sending their children west in search of productive, free land, and there was a chance to divert them to Manitoba and the Canadian Northwest. In addition, many French Canadians who had relocated to New England were good candidates for repatriation to Canada under the right conditions. When feasible, the CPR would man the exhibition car with at least one French-speaking agent, or even a Catholic priest, for this audience.[43]

The car's popularity prompted the CPR to continue its tour through the fall and winter. Company colonization agent Louis Olivier Armstrong outlined some of the challenges of operating in the off-season to Thomas Shaughnessy, the railway's assistant general manager who would succeed Van Horne as CPR president:

My experience last year would lead me to advise the putting in of hot water pipes on a stove at each end of the car. Last year with a stove in the middle of the car, the stuff froze at each end. I should like to have more light let into the car. Wire screens to keep the crowd from handling and stealing. Revarnishing of car and some painting. Double

▶ The CPR manned its exhibition car with agricultural specialists, French-speaking agents, and even Catholic priests in its quest to woo prospective settlers to the Northwest. AUTHOR'S COLLECTION

windows as the ice forms on single windows and damages things when melting. Cupboards or drawers to put literature and supplies in. We damage things that kick about. We have no time to lose if we are to get over the territory laid out for us this fall and winter. Last winter was not long enough to enable us to do much more than half the country laid out.[44]

By the mid-1890s, when CPR and its Ottawa allies were in the midst of an aggressive propaganda campaign in the American Midwest, Van Horne expressed his misgivings to Thomas Mayne Daly, the minister of the interior, about overusing the exhibition car:

I am far from sure that it would be wise to send our Advertising Car into Kansas and Nebraska. Its movements in the Eastern States are not noticed, but if it were to go out into the territory of the transcontinental lines, which have been fighting us so viciously at Washington, it would create a disturbance, which would work to our prejudice in Congress. We would not haul such a car in Canada for such railways as the Northern and Union Pacific, and I am so certain that they would refuse to haul ours on any terms, that I would not like to ask them to do it. And I doubt very much if the car would ever come back to us if it should go out there. You will remember the ill will that

was manifested against our propaganda in North Dakota, and the people of North Dakota are very moderate as compared with those of Nebraska and Kansas, especially the latter. I have lived among them, and I know pretty well what they would do. A Canadian agent or lecturer would be roughly handled out there—tar and feathers would be the least he could expect. It would not be the farmers who would make the trouble, but the people of the towns, who would resent any attempt at enticing the farmers away, and it is in the towns where the worst element is to be found.[45]

In the 1890s, the exhibition car's tour was also aided and supplemented by a horse-drawn advertising van with a lecturer on board. The team and van would precede the railway car to each new location, blowing a horn outside residences along the way and distributing advertising flyers to the occupants with information about the exhibition vehicles and the scheduled lectures. In the evenings, while awaiting the arrival of the railway car, the two horses with the road van were saddled up to convey riders out into the countryside with more flyers. The result was good attendance. "The car advertises the lecture and the lecture the car," reported the travelling passenger agent who accompanied the road van.[46]

Left Residents of small-town Quebec were invited to view the free show in the railway's exhibition car and pick up some pamphlets. AUTHOR'S COLLECTION

Right The car's popularity prompted the railway to continue the tour for several years, opening to the public whenever the weather allowed. AUTHOR'S COLLECTION

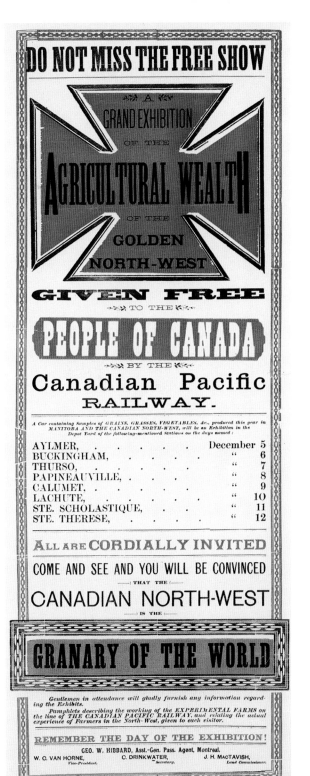

4 THE CALL OF THE NEW WORLD

Keeping it British

Soon after the CPR was founded, the ambitious new railway company organized an emigration department for Britain and continental Europe. The first modest office space consisted of two rooms rented from a banking firm on London's Bartholomew Lane. After a few months, the company moved its operations to the first floor at 101 Cannon Street. By the fall of 1881, the London staff members had already launched the beginnings of an advertising campaign with the publication and distribution of an attractive booklet entitled "The Great Prairie Provinces of Manitoba and the Northwest Territories."

At the time, the ethnic origin of Canada's settlers was overwhelmingly British, and the Anglo-Canadian majority sought to expand its economic and political dominance through an ongoing program of emigration from the Mother Country. The larger cities in the United Kingdom were overcrowded with workers who had become urbanized in the country's rapid industrialization during the last few decades, while a large portion of the agricultural community consisted of tenant farmers who did not own the land on which they toiled. Both groups were ready targets for both the Canadian propagandists, who wished to lure them overseas, and the British government, which encouraged them to go.

Within a year of the arrival of the CPR's emigration agents on London's Cannon Street, magnificent displays of prairie produce were drawing appreciative crowds to the prominent picture windows of the railway's offices. Enormous jars filled with rich soil samples gathered at various points across the railway's transcontinental system provided graphic evidence of the country's vast potential for agricultural exploitation.[1] Giant vegetables grown and harvested from those same fertile soils started many a lively conversation of ever-expanding superlatives.

"It is no uncommon thing to see potatoes which weigh from a pound and a half to two pounds each," wrote emigrant advisor Hugh Fraser. "You can see in the proper season cabbages which are from three to four feet [0.9–1.2 m] in circumference." Not to be outdone, a correspondent from the *London Times* was quoted as saying he saw a cabbage measuring five feet, one inch [1.6 m] in circumference and a cucumber grown in the open air, which measured six feet, three inches [1.9 m] in length.[2]

Apart from an article in the influential London weekly *Truth*, which dismissed the entire Canadian transcontinental project as an outright disaster, the biggest problem for the CPR was not bad press but rather the lack of any interest in the Dominion whatsoever. When the first CPR president, George Stephen, travelled to England to promote immigration to the Northwest and drum up support for CPR land bonds, he was bumped from the newspaper headlines by a famous pachyderm. The London Zoo had recently sold Jumbo the Elephant to the American circus owner P.T. Barnum, and concerned members of the local citizenry were making every effort to stall the popular animal's departure.[3] "Jumbo the big elephant recently bought by Barnum is a matter of ten times more interest than twenty Colonies," Stephen moaned to Prime Minister Macdonald.[4]

Exacerbating the problem for Canadian publicists was the ongoing efforts of emigration agents representing American interests. Railroad companies south of the border, in partnership with the leading steamship lines on the North Atlantic, had already been luring settlers from Britain to the US Midwest for the past couple of decades. As a result, much of the British public, as well as potential colonists from Western Europe, were of the opinion that the best economic and social opportunities awaited them in the United States.

In 1883, proponents of the CPR first published the *Canadian Gazette*, mainly to supply the British public with factual information about life in Canada. The goal was to encourage emigration to destinations other than the United States as well as to counter the antagonistic attitudes of the Grand Trunk Railway and other established financial interests opposed to the upstart Canadian transcontinental. Stephen was a prominent supporter and secret financial backer of the publication, and the publisher, Thomas Skinner, was one of Stephen's financial advisors and soon to be a lifelong member of the CPR's board of directors.

To add vigour to its campaign, the CPR had engaged Alexander Begg as its overseas general emigration agent.

Begg had been a respected journalist in the Canadian Northwest, publishing and editing the *Manitoba Trade Review* and the *Gazette and Trade Review* during the 1870s, before going on to edit the *Daily Nor'Wester*. The plucky Scot was appointed sergeant-at-arms to the Manitoba legislature in 1878 and served for six years as deputy treasurer and auditor in the provincial government of the Honourable John Norquay before joining the CPR.[5]

By the spring of 1884, the CPR was distributing maps and pamphlets in English, German, French, Dutch, Danish, Finnish, Norwegian, Swedish, Welsh, and Gaelic through a network of thousands of agencies in Britain and more than 200 centres in northern Europe. Begg placed advertisements for Canadian immigration on a regular basis in 167 journals in Great Britain and 147 continental publications.[6] Many of the European governments had their misgivings about allowing other countries to lure away their young men who were fit for military service. Norway and Sweden, for a time, imposed a complete prohibition on emigration literature.[7]

Like a massive, industrial emigration engine, the London office was producing large-format posters to display in railway stations, hotels, and other public places. Begg was also sending company representatives in prodigious numbers to the remote corners of England, Wales, Scotland, and Northern Europe. The islands and highlands of Scotland received special attention from agents who were thoroughly conversant with the Gaelic people and their ways.

The work of the travelling representatives was aided by special lecturers, recruited for their social and community connections and equipped with newly developed "lantern-slide projectors."[8] While professional speakers were used wherever possible, the CPR was often able to

► Alexander Begg was a respected journalist and a whirlwind of marketing ideas.
NOTMAN PHOTOGRAPHIC ARCHIVES, MCCORD STEWART MUSEUM 11-61300.1

▼ Working from his Cannon Street office in London, Begg distributed immigration propaganda across Britain and throughout the continent.
AUTHOR'S COLLECTION

For Maps, Pamphlets (sent free of charge), and full information about the Country, its climate and resources, address, personally or by letter,

ALEXANDER BEGG,
88, CANNON STREET,
LONDON,
ENGLAND.

recruit local clergymen or other notables to deliver a credible message.

From 1883 onward, the London staff collected and compiled from the overseas press any and all uplifting items related to the Western Canadian economy as well as clippings from the railway's own offices that would aid in their promotional efforts. To meet and counteract misinformation about the Golden Northwest and the CPR's efforts at colonization, they also kept a complete record of all relevant materials published in London.

By the mid-1880s, competing interests—the Grand Trunk Railway of Canada prominent among them—were putting forth all manner of slanderous statements in both Eastern Canada and Britain. Crop failures, droughts, early frosts, storms, and the vagaries of weather were front and centre in these narratives, with just enough of the truth to create a convincing negative impression of the conditions awaiting prospective settlers. Stephen denounced the Grand Trunk's "paid inkslingers," anti-CPR columnists who wrote under pseudonyms such as "Ishmael" and "Diogenes."[9] The CPR's very own sycophant, a reporter with the *Toronto Mail* who styled himself "Mohawk," would fire off equally scornful rebuttals to even the rhetorical score, while himself remaining incognito.

Upon being appointed president of the CPR in 1888, and presiding over his first annual meeting at the head of the besieged corporation, Van Horne was compelled to speak out about what he felt were nasty and uncalled for attacks on the company by the rival Grand Trunk:

I feel that I am more than justified in what I have to say by the increasing freedom of his [Sir Henry Tyler, Grand Trunk Railway Company president] remarks concerning this Company, with which his shareholders are entertained at their half-yearly meetings, and which clearly indicate that he lacks the first requisite of good neighbourhood, the faculty of minding his own business.[10]

In retaliation for negative press aimed at his British audience, Begg developed a simple but effective strategy. In pamphlets with titles such as "Plain Facts and Practical Hints from Farmers in the Canadian Northwest" and "Manitoba, The Canadian North-West: What the Actual Settlers Say," Begg employed testimonials from those already on the land in Canada, along with names, locations, and particulars about their frontier experiences. Questions about the crop yield per acre for wheat, barley, and oats drew the expected numbers, from 25–30 bushels (62–74 bushels/ha) for wheat, and as high as 75 (185 bushels/ha) for oats "on land broken last year." Enquiries about the yield for vegetables inevitably emphasized their gigantic proportions. "Have had carrots 12 inches (30 cm) round," said one farmer. "Beans and potatoes very good, better than I ever raised in England with 20 years' experience."

The main point was to show the superiority of the northern frontier over any other possible destination. "After more than five years' experience in this country, I am satisfied that no other country in the world can approach the Canadian North-West as a field for agricultural productions," said S.W. Chambers of Wattsview, Manitoba. "I consider this the greatest grain producing country in the world without any exception," enthused A.R. Speers of Griswold, Manitoba.

The answers to a survey of some four hundred women in Manitoba, Assiniboia, Saskatchewan, Alberta, and Athabasca resulted in a fifty-page pamphlet called "What Women Say of the Canadian North-West," in which prospective settlers got a personal view of the family and social aspects of life in the New World. None dwelt on the extreme debilitating loneliness that would often overwhelm the pioneer farmer's wife. In its stead, the shortage of women and the corresponding enthusiastic welcome they could expect to receive was a central theme, along with the abundant opportunities that awaited those with energy and a can-do attitude. Young, healthy women were needed, not just as farmers' wives, but also as domestic servants, boarding house and hotel cooks and chambermaids, milliners, and seamstresses.[11]

The weather was often cited as a prime inducement to choose the Northwest over the American Midwest, or for that matter a more far-flung destination such as Australia. In the 1886 edition of the railway booklet "What the Actual Settlers Say," settlers who were asked whether they had suffered any serious loss from storms during winter or summer settlers typically answered with the expected "not worth mentioning," "no loss whatsoever," and "none yet of any kind."

To maintain credibility, the railway included a few mildly negative responses such as, "I lost part of my crop this year by hail storms," which was quickly followed up with "but it is the first I lost since I came here 5 years ago." Another homesteader conceded that he had losses "from hail this summer, but crop has come along well again." While one forgiving settler reported "not any" to the question of serious losses, "except by thunder and lightning, which destroyed outbuildings, stock and implements." And a firm believer in the glass half full reported that: "I had my house roof blown off in June 1881, but no other damage."

For the most part, the "plain facts" in the propaganda booklets emphasized that the Canadian Northwest was outside the "storm belt" that caused farmers in many parts

WHAT

ACTUAL SETTLERS SAY

— OF THE —

CANADIAN NORTH-WEST

— AS AN —

AGRICULTURAL COUNTRY.

PRACTICAL INFORMATION FOR INTENDING
SETTLERS.

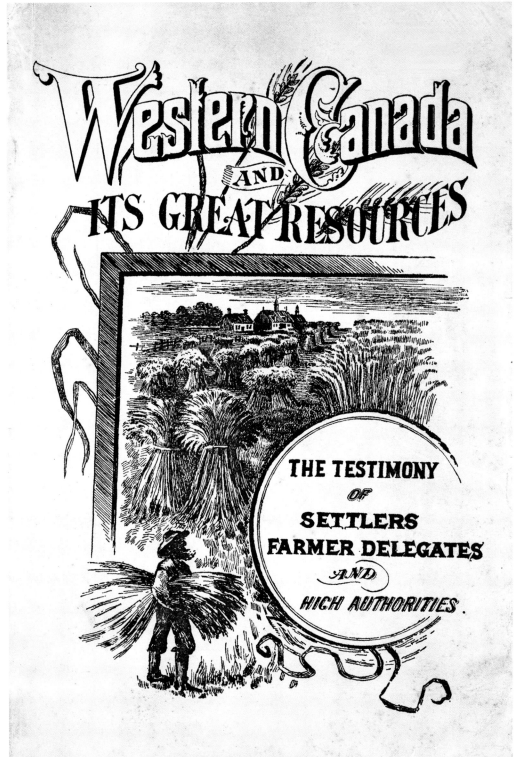

Western Canada

AND

ITS GREAT RESOURCES

THE TESTIMONY
OF
SETTLERS
FARMER DELEGATES
AND
HIGH AUTHORITIES.

of the United States to feel anxiety. The benefits of the cooler, drier temperatures prevalent in the Northwest for much of the year were touted by the proponents of "climato-therapy"—a nineteenth-century pseudo-science based on observations that cool, dry air was healthier than warm, humid air—as one of the best reasons to settle there.[12]

In the 1870s, Canada's governor general, the Marquis of Lorne, had warned potential immigrants about regions in the US "notorious for their cyclones, snakes and centi-pedes, or for ague and fever," and urged them to note "how healthy the conditions of life in the North are, and to what a great age men [there] usually live." The CPR's Begg ran with the theme, waxing philosophically: "What use to the immigrant are fair fields and meadows, beautiful crops and the acquisition of wealth if, to obtain them, he is obliged to sacrifice his own health and that of his family."[13]

While the British were being inundated with a flood of emigration propaganda in favour of the Canadian North-west, the CPR's agents did not entirely ignore the prospects on the other side of the English Channel. Immigration work on the continent was conducted by R.R.H. toe Laer, under the supervision of Begg's London office. Toe Laer visited 30 prominent immigration centres in Northern Europe over the winter of 1883–84, while appointing 196 agents throughout the continent and answering more than 4,000 inquiries about Manitoba from prospective emigrants.[14]

The British media sent emissaries to watch and report on the extent of the CPR's literature distribution through-out Europe. A full record was kept for one year, and it was found that three million pamphlets were put into the hands of potential settlers. A prominent printing firm suggested at the time that, as their machines had been kept running day and night for six months turning out Manitoba pamphlets,

"the business would justify their paying for a private tele-phone from the CPR office to their works."[15]

In 1884, Begg submitted a full report to CPR president George Stephen of the work being carried on overseas. In it he wrote about the need for good, active agents in New York City, where most of the emigrants sailed en route to either the United States or Canada. He thought "no better class of settlers can be obtained" than the Dutch, and that exhibits in Amsterdam of products sent from Canada "will do much to make the Canadian Northwest well known not only in Holland, but also on the continent [generally]."[16]

In 1903, the *Canadian Gazette* reported on the many agricultural shows at which the CPR expended consider-able resources:

In those days in Europe, Manitoba was the Canadian Pacific Rail-way, and but for the Canadian Pacific Railway Company little would have been heard of this new Eldorado in the West. The Royal Agricultural Shows, which take a year to prepare and were held in a new district every year, were attended frequently. The Prince of Wales, our Sovereign of today, usually visited the Man-itoba Stand, giving a tremendous value to the company's display. Great English firms spent thousands of pounds annually on their Royal Show exhibits, so the Canadian Pacific Railway Company's Manitoba show involved heavy expense. At York, Shrewsbury, Pres-ton and Norwich sensational Manitoba exhibits were made by the company. His Royal Highness evinced special interest in the Pres-ton exhibit, and remained a long time with his attendant nobles making a careful inspection of the exhibits, which included glass tubes filled with samples of soil taken every 20 miles [32 km] from Winnipeg to the Rockies... In the early eighties, a fenced and fully equipped Manitoba farm was laid out on ground adjoining the Antwerp Exhibition.[17]

Three quarters of a million people passed by the new CPR office on London's Trafalgar Square every day. AUTHOR'S COLLECTION

From the beginning of the CPR's emigration efforts in Britain, large-format photographs had been displayed prominently in company offices and at exhibitions and fairs. In the spring of 1886, railway president George Stephen added fine art to the public offering by sending a packing case of paintings to Begg for use in the upcoming Colonial Exhibition, including works by John Fraser and Lucius O'Brien. Begg also managed to have featured a selection of agricultural trophies awarded for products from the Northwest. Thereafter, the company's promotional representatives in Britain made sure that photographs and paintings were kept in constant circulation at railway stations and hotels, reading rooms and mechanics institutes, and at agricultural fairs around the country.

In the late 1880s and early 1890s, the work that had been accomplished by Alexander Begg and his staff was expanded and perfected under the direction of Archer Baker. A Yorkshireman who had come to Canada to seek his fortune, Baker had been secretary-treasurer and general manager of the Brockville & Ottawa Railway before taking up employment with the CPR. His return to the mother country had been marred when the Beaver Line steamship, *Lake Manitoba*, sank off the coast of French-held Miquelon Island, in June of 1885. "My linen, pictures, china, bric-a-brac, books, sewing machine, all my photographs, the illuminated address presented to me with the silver are now reposing at the bottom," he informed Van Horne three months later.[18]

In London as the company's European traffic agent, Baker opened an office at 67 King William Street.[19] In 1891, the CPR's operations were consolidated in a new headquarters on Trafalgar Square, and Baker was promoted to European traffic manager. Two years later, he was simply the CPR's

European manager and had taken on all aspects of the company's activities in the UK and on the continent, while reporting to the second vice-president, William Whyte, in Montreal.

The *Canadian Gazette* called the new offices "as handsome a pile as any railway company in this country can show,"[20] and Baker had gone to great lengths to tout the merits of its prime location to his bosses in Montreal:

Ask any four persons in the country who have come up to London, say on an excursion ticket, whether they know the C.P.R. London office, and the chances are that three of them will either know the office by that name or as the Canadian Emigration Office near London Bridge. Southern Railway Terminals, Tower Bridge, Tower of London, the Monument [Nelson's], Electric Railway, London Bridge, Billingsgate and St. Paul's Cathedral, all playing into our hands and tending to direct a stream of persons past our windows either on foot or in vehicle as it would be impossible to parallel anywhere else in the world. No government, corporation or individual interested in colonization occupies an office in a similar commanding situation, owing partially to official ideas of respectability, to the great expense which would be involved, and partially to the fact that such positions are rarely obtainable at any price.[21]

At ground level, the large picture windows, with their perfect view of the exhibits of grain and minerals and photographs of Canadian scenes, provided a constant source of fascination for the estimated three-quarters of a million people who passed by every day. The top row of windows, five floors above, showed a "moving panorama, night and day, of coloured pictures of Canadian Pacific scenery." A constant flow of inquirers demanding attention from the headquarters staff walked away every day with more than two thousand information pamphlets under their arms.[22]

As had been the case in Eastern Canada, one of the most effective tools aiding office-bound staff members with their propaganda efforts turned out to be a travelling exhibition vehicle, described in the press as "a veritable Canada on wheels." The road van was sent out to various towns around Great Britain on market days when agriculturalists and other interested parties would gather together. Flyers distributed in advance to local hotels and public houses, often with the help of accommodating ministers and clergymen, ensured a good turnout at the various venues, while talks delivered by farmers with first-hand experience of the Canadian Northwest increased the likelihood of the exhibits making a favourable impression. In 1893 alone, the CPR staff on the travelling van visited 516 places, covering 1,825 miles (2,940 km) by road, and distributing 81,675 information publications.[23]

As early as 1891, the CPR had begun to use what were called "return men" in its British advertising campaigns. That year, seventeen settlers who had been successful in establishing themselves and their families in the Northwest were sent by the company to London to tell their stories.[24] Baker's staff carried out the experiment for the next four years, before deciding that the expense outweighed the benefits. Many of the men had been glad to raise their hands for service but had mostly been looking for a free holiday in their former homelands. A good farmer did not necessarily make for the most articulate spokesperson. The practice of sending out return men would later be revived on the continent, where peasant farmers were more likely to trust information presented in their own tongue by old acquaintances with first-hand knowledge of conditions in the Canadian Northwest.

The CPR's European staff continued to pursue potential emigrants among the most promising northern agricultural communities, but they ran into a number of political headwinds. Baker outlined for Van Horne some of the problems they encountered in the Prussian-dominated German Empire: "The laws in regard to emigration vary, the particular bar against Manitoba being I understand confined to Prussia," he wrote in 1894, "but the fact that in one part of the kingdom Mr. Dyke [a Canadian government representative] was imprisoned for six weeks, toe Laer [CPR's continental European manager] had to leave hurriedly another part of the country, and that our own agent was ejected from the country at Berlin is the most practical proof one can have of the general intentions of the Government in these matters."

Baker went on to say that the German Hamburg America steamship line had recently won a concession from the government to allow the distribution of pamphlets from the Canadian government, but only to "such people as ask for them." He was also very critical of the Dominion government's lack of effort in promoting emigration from France, though he viewed the country as a "not very fertile field."

The views of CPR's European traffic agent perhaps reflected those of the company as a whole, when he concluded his remarks with a nod to the merits of private enterprise versus the public sector:

In my opinion, the best thing in the interests of Canadian immigration would be for the Government to go out of the business altogether. The same reasons that disqualify them from running a railway successfully operate so far as emigration is concerned. There is too much departmental jealousy and too much political pressure permeating all that they do and an unsuccessful result is fore-ordained.[25]

The North Atlantic crossing

When helping potential settlers come to Canada, it was always desirable for CPR colonization agents to arrange for a single through ticket with a fixed fare that would get their clients across the ocean and overland to their destination in the Northwest on either a government homestead or a railway quarter-section. To that end, Alexander Begg and his London staff maintained an active correspondence and business arrangement with steamship companies on both sides of the Atlantic that were involved in the St. Lawrence trade as well as those steaming to New York City and Boston, the most common destinations for North American immigrants.

By the 1880s, the Allan Line and the Dominion Line had become the dominant forces in the North Atlantic steamship service to Canada, and both had business connections with the well-established Grand Trunk Railway, CPR's chief rival in the eastern part of the country. As a result, the CPR soon aligned itself with The Canada Steam Shipping Company, more commonly known as the "Beaver Line" because of the emblem on its house flag.

The railway and the steamship company worked out a schedule to issue a single ticket and divide the revenues for passengers travelling from Liverpool to Halifax or Quebec, and on to the Northwest. While westward sailings were dominated by emigrant traffic, eastbound cargoes consisted largely of Canadian exports such as grain, flour, cheese, butter, apples, livestock, dressed beef, and other provisions, much of which was moved to the ports by the CPR.

Agents acting for the CPR to negotiate ocean steamship connections were also successful in coming to an agreement with the Robert Reford Company that represented

EMIGRATION TO CANADA!

SEASON 1884.

A Special Party of Emigrants will leave

LIVERPOOL for CANADA

ON OR ABOUT

THURSDAY, APRIL 24th,

PER

DOMINION LINE STEAMER.

This Party will be personally conducted by

Mr. FREDERICK WROE, Salford,

Who so successfully conducted the one in Sept., 1883, under whose care and guidance they will proceed to their destination, where employment will be found for those requiring it.

Persons wishing to join these Parties can book at the ordinary rates of fare, and no extra charge whatever will be made for services rendered to Emigrants who compose them.

IMPORTANT!!!

An Emigration Club has already been formed to enable the Working Classes to contribute by Weekly Instalments of not less than 1/- towards their Passage and Outfit in April, 1884.

For further particulars, and to secure berths, apply to

FREDERICK WROE, Stationer and Bookseller,

202, Regent Road,

SALFORD.

◄ Dominion Line steamers were among the most competitive conveyors of British emigrants to Canada. AUTHOR'S COLLECTION

Opposite, top left The Montreal Ocean Steam Company, better known as the Allan Line, had business connections with the CPR rival, Grand Trunk Railway. AUTHOR'S COLLECTION

Opposite, right The Beaver Line advertised (CPR) trains departing from Montreal for the Northwest alongside their ships arriving from overseas. AUTHOR'S COLLECTION

Opposite, bottom left The Elder Dempster Company's Beaver Line steamships aligned themselves with Canadian Pacific. AUTHOR'S COLLECTION

the Donaldson Line to Glasgow, the Great Western Line to Bristol, and both the Thomson and the Ross lines to London. It was agreed that traffic from those ports destined for points along the CPR would be subject to the same railway/steamship percentage divisions that had been arranged with the Beaver Line.

Dealing with the competition would be a different story, as CPR vice-president Van Horne outlined to his European freight manager:

The Allans live in mortal fear of the Grand Trunk and however well they may talk to us, we cannot count on fair play from them. The Dominion Line is in the same fix. The Beaver Line has, as I have already written to you, been entirely thrown over by the Grand Trunk on account of their disposition to work with us, and I am satisfied that we can only count on the Beaver Line to break up the Grand Trunk, Allan and Dominion combination, and that our best policy is to help the Beaver Line in making all the trouble possible.[26]

While conducting his work in Britain, Begg had maintained close contact with the St. Lawrence steamship companies, supplying them with free propaganda booklets about Manitoba and the Northwest and making sure their advertisements were featured on the back pages. Although the CPR was distributing in excess of one million pieces of such material annually, the emigration staff estimated they would need to double that figure if they were to adequately supply the five thousand agents with whom they dealt.[27]

Despite his best efforts, however, Begg had not been able to negotiate a satisfactory through rate to Western Canada by way of New York City. While the CPR was happy to use all-Canadian routes during the summer, it was important to establish a working arrangement with New York steamship lines for the winter months. One of the problems seems to have been the reluctance of connecting US railroads to hand off potential settlers to Canada, as Van Horne was at pains to explain to a traffic exchange agent in New York:

The Canadian Department of Agriculture undertook to arrange these matters with the New York lines last season. We put them in a position to make a $12.00 rate from New York to Winnipeg. The New York Central [Railroad] refused to cooperate or to sell tickets. The Erie [Railroad] played with the question until too late... The continental steamship lines for various reasons could not be induced to use the low rate offered, and I have no doubt that their refusal was based on the action of the rail lines running west from New York, who look with jealousy upon the diversion of the immigrant business to Canadian Territory. The steamship lines running to New York do not dare to work contrary to the wishes of the pooled rail lines.[28]

The urgent need to come to a reasonable working arrangement with New York steamship lines and connecting US railroads to provide immigrants with a through rate to Canadian destinations had been brought on by the inability of the Beaver Line to strike a deal for winter service with the Intercolonial Railway. The Intercolonial was controlled by Canada's Department of Railway and Canals, serving the Port of Halifax in connection with the provinces of Nova Scotia, New Brunswick, and Quebec, and had a longstanding relationship with the Grand Trunk. As a result of the Intercolonial Railway's antagonistic stance toward the CPR and steamship lines friendly with the company, the CPR anticipated more of its winter business would come through US ports.

Opposite, left In 1879, the Intercolonial Railway served the Port of Halifax and had a stranglehold on European immigrant traffic entering Canada directly. MAP BY OMER LAVALLEE, AUTHOR'S COLLECTION

Opposite, right The Intercolonial had acquired a connection with Montreal by 1890, but maintained its longstanding relationship with the Grand Trunk and its antagonistic stance toward the CPR. AUTHOR'S COLLECTION

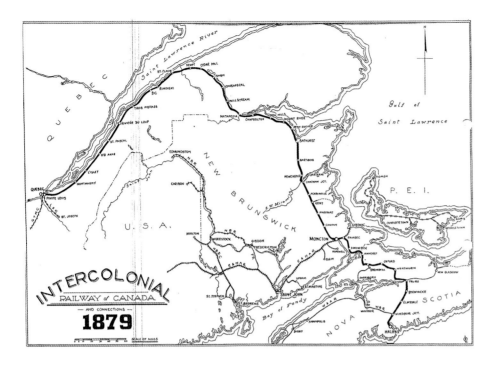

"The Intercolonial refused them [the Beaver Line] the same rates as given to the Allan and Donaldson Lines, except on certain conditions, as to maintenance of through rates," Van Horne informed his freight manager. "We also asked the Intercolonial people to take our freight from Halifax and deliver it at Montreal at the same rates charged by the through lines, which the officers of the Intercolonial said they would be unable to do."[29]

The need for constant, ongoing negotiations with the various steamship lines to maintain the CPR's Atlantic connections would be one of the key reasons the company purchased its own ships for the St. Lawrence service, not long after the turn of the century. For the time being, though, the CPR would cooperate closely with the Beaver Line

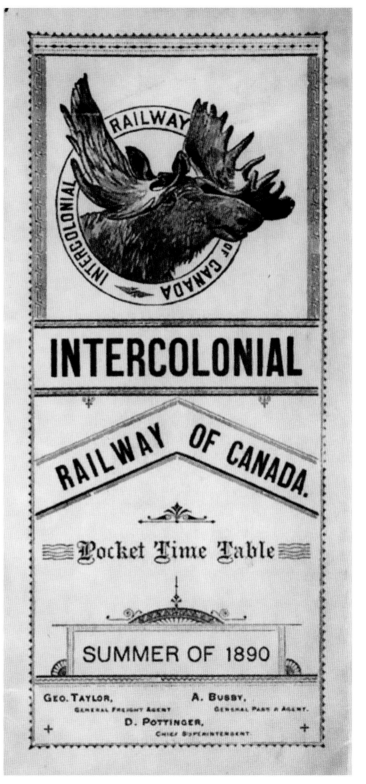

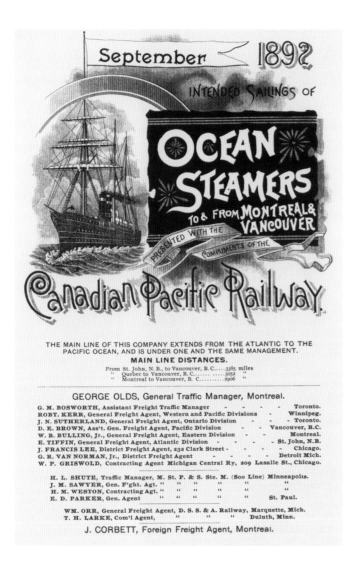

and, a few years later, with the Allan Line to bring as many settlers as possible directly to the "Golden Northwest."

Liverpool was the most popular port of departure for emigrants from Britain and the European mainland to the United States and Canada because of well-established business links created by the cotton and timber trades. A common route from Northern Europe involved a crossing of the North Sea to Hull and then train travel to Liverpool. If a passenger had secured his ocean ticket before leaving home, for as little as four pounds Sterling, an agent of the steamship company would be on hand at Liverpool to take charge of his baggage and get him and his possessions safely on board.

In the days of sail, before the 1870s, the voyage across the North Atlantic had occupied about thirty-five agony-filled days. Apart from seasickness, passengers often suffered from such diseases as cholera and typhus, and scores died before reaching the New World. By the 1880s, virtually all emigrants came to North America by steamship. The crossing time was reduced to between seven and ten days, and the strong competition for passengers improved travelling conditions to some extent. The voyage to Quebec had the advantage of being in sheltered waters for hundreds of miles once the steamships entered the Straits of Belle Isle and sailed through the gulf of the St. Lawrence River.

Most emigrants travelled in the cheapest class of accommodation, known as steerage. Sleeping, eating, and life in general were carried on below deck, although access topside was allowed during the day, weather permitting. For sleeping arrangements, hammocks were hung or rough-hewn bunk beds were built in, dormitory style. Long tables amidship served as a communal dining area.

◀ In its second decade of operations, Canadian Pacific published schedules for a full slate of ocean-going steamships and their sailings on both the Atlantic and Pacific. AUTHOR'S COLLECTION

▶ Most passengers on the Allan Line steamship *Scandinavian* travelled in spartan steerage accommodations. AUTHOR'S COLLECTION

Emigrants were required to provide their own bedding, plate, knife, fork, spoon, and water can, all of which could be purchased at Liverpool, Glasgow, and other ports.[30] Typically, breakfast would be served at seven or seven thirty, consisting of coffee with milk and sugar, fresh bread, and butter. Dinner at noon was more substantial, with soup, beef, and potatoes, and maybe a dessert such as plum pudding with sauce. Tea was at five, once again with bread and butter, and there was gruel every night at eight o'clock.

"The food was good and wholesome," said one traveller on the Allan Line steamship *Sardinian*, in 1882. "The wonder to me was that, with about one thousand steerage passengers aboard, the stewards managed to get them their meals with such order and precision . . . Where there was fault found, it was generally by someone who, from his appearance, had left a worse table at home then he found on board ship."[31]

Passengers were allowed to bring a maximum of 150 pounds of freight with them to the New World, but the 1884 edition of the *Englishman's Guide Book to the United States and Canada* tipped off readers that luggage was never actually weighed. While most immigrants used whatever they could find in the way of carpet bags, canvas duffle bags, or early versions of leather suitcases, the more affluent remittance men, or second sons, coming to the Northwest with family money in their pockets came equipped with sturdy "steamer trunks," with brass corners, hasps, and locks, that fit snuggly in the space between the floor and the berth in a saloon-class cabin.[32]

Generally, families were berthed together; single males and single females were in separate areas. Stewardesses were available "to attend to the wants of women and children during the voyage . . . also a doctor who supplies medical comforts free of charge."[33]

The length of the transatlantic voyage and the apprehensions of leaving familiar surroundings for the unknown could make for a trying passage. A missionary making the crossing on the Allan Line's *Sarmatian*, in 1885, found many of the Irish on board in tears from severing home ties.

How shall I describe that first night on board? Some whistling, some singing, some talking, and many others in a sorrowful mood. The weather during the first two or three days was beautifully fine, thus giving me an opportunity to get acquainted with a number of my fellow passengers, amongst whom were many young men of genial spirit and sterling quality. Three days out, our ship began to rock and pitch, and for some days subsequent we were "of all men most miserable." Here at this time, I noted that, notwithstanding the boasting of many during the first two days as to their seaworthiness, they now became just as fallible as the rest of us, that is, when the

◄ During the day, when the seas on the North Atlantic were not too rough, it was beneficial to sit topside, like these Allan Line passengers taking a break from the odiferous conditions below decks. AUTHOR'S COLLECTION

► A large contingent of Welsh-Patagonians sail to Canada on the Allan Line steamship *Numidian*, on June 12, 1902. LIBRARY AND ARCHIVES CANADA C-037613

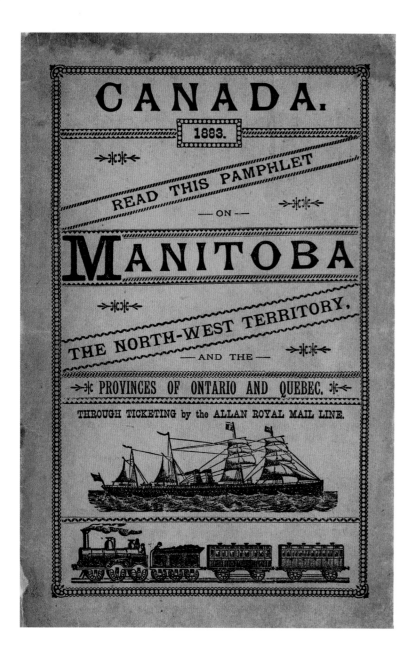

testing time came. On account of the large passenger list, we were very much crowded in our hammocks.[34]

Polish immigrant Lucan Smzt had his pockets picked aboard a ship bound for the New World, and he docked in Halifax without a penny. Undeterred, he managed to borrow two dollars from a fellow immigrant who later became his father-in-law, and with that and his prearranged railway ticket, he travelled by CPR to Edmonton. There he went to work for the railway as a section hand at a dollar a day, changed his name to Luke Smith, and after four years had saved enough for a down payment on a quarter section of prime CPR land.[35]

Upon arrival at Quebec or Halifax, passengers with through tickets were transferred, along with their baggage, at no extra cost to trains waiting alongside the vessels at the wharf. Those who hadn't planned ahead for the railway portion of their trip had to seek out one of the many available ticket sellers under the authority of an exchange ticket agent. Depots or immigration sheds for the reception of immigrants needing assistance were provided by the government at Quebec, Halifax, Sherbrooke, Montreal, Ottawa, Hamilton, London (Ontario), and Winnipeg.

Land routes to the Northwest

It took the CPR a few years to piece together a comprehensive network of rail lines in Eastern Canada, whereby it could offer immigrant transportation all the way from Atlantic ports to the Canadian Northwest. However, prospective settlers were a determined bunch, and they continued to drift westward in relatively small numbers by pioneer routes through Canada and the US.

Upon landing immigrants could read about conditions in Manitoba by consulting the pamphlets they received from the "Allan Royal Mail Line" with their through tickets. LIBRARY AND CULTURAL RESOURCES DIGITAL COLLECTIONS, UNIVERSITY OF CALGARY CU11054141

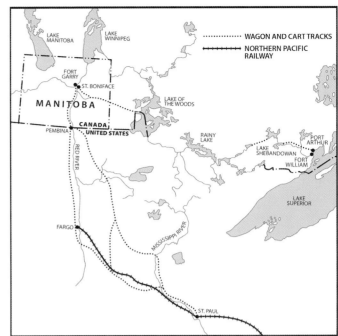

During the 1870s, farmers seeking free land had emigrated from the older Canadian provinces, primarily Ontario, settled in the Red River Valley and southern Manitoba. The introduction of the federal government's homestead land policy encouraged some to sell off their holdings in the East and move to what was then the Canadian frontier. The primary lifeline between the Red River settlement and the eastern provinces was the so-called Dawson Route, which connected Prince Arthur's Landing (later Port Arthur, and now Thunder Bay) with Fort Garry. The route was an arduous one, consisting of about 450 miles (725 km) of rough road and lengthy water travel in several stages. From Toronto, determined trekkers could connect with the Dawson Route by way of the Northern Railway to Collingwood, on Georgian Bay, and various steamboat services on the Great Lakes, one of the most important of which was the Northwest Transportation

Left A transfer station at Lake Shebandowan on the Dawson Route. CANADIAN ILLUSTRATED NEWS, DECEMBER 7, 1872, LIBRARY AND CULTURAL RESOURCES DIGITAL COLLECTIONS, UNIVERSITY OF CALGARY CU2120934

Right From Eastern Canada, one could travel to Winnipeg via Port Arthur by river craft and wagon road, in a series of stages; or use US railroad connections to reach Fargo, before negotiating the waters of the Red River or bumping along its western bank by wagon. BREATHE COMMUNICATIONS, AUTHOR'S COLLECTION

◄ James Hill and his American partners plied the Red River with their sternwheeler *Selkirk* when the water levels allowed for safe navigation. AUTHOR'S COLLECTION

▲ The first railway locomotive in the Northwest, soon to be named Countess of Dufferin, arrived in Winnipeg by barge from the United States, on October 9, 1877. AUTHOR'S COLLECTION

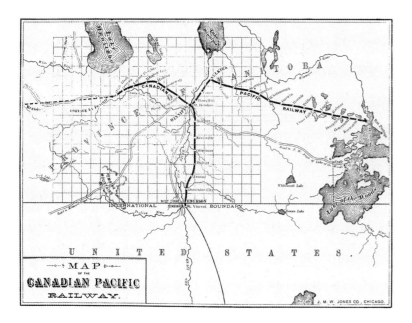

MAP OF THE CANADIAN PACIFIC RAILWAY.

Company. This navigation concern was managed by Henry Beatty, who would go on to organize the CPR's own Great Lakes steamship services in the mid-1880s.[36]

At the same time, a few adventurous Americans were crossing the border to seek new homes and expanded opportunity, aided by the rapid development of stagecoach and boat services along the Red River in both the United States and Canada. The Northern Pacific completed a railway line from the Great Lakes through St. Paul to Fargo in 1872, further enhancing the commercial prospects as well as the connectivity of the Red River Valley.

James Jerome Hill and his American partners had been among the first to exploit the cross-border river route, when they launched the steamboat *Selkirk* in 1871 at McCauleyville, Minnesota. The vessel was named after a community on the Red River, 23 miles (37 km) north of

Winnipeg. Within a year, the *Selkirk* and what was previously the HBC's *International* were both being operated by Hill's new company, the Red River Transportation Line. Steamboats could only negotiate the Red River sporadically, from April to October each year. In the spring, high waters could make the roads from the Twin Cities to the river station impassable, and in summer, low water often seriously impeded steamboat operations, so the rapid development of a parallel rail connection was inevitable.

In 1873, Alexander Mackenzie's federal government signed a contract with Joseph Whitehead, a pioneer Canadian railway developer and politician, to build a railway link between the international boundary at Emerson and St. Boniface, across the river from Winnipeg. Whitehead brought to St. Boniface the first railway equipment to be seen in the Canadian Northwest, when on October 9, 1877, the paddlewheeler *Selkirk* pushed a barge loaded with a locomotive, conductor's van, and six flatcars from Fisher's Landing in Minnesota.

The locomotive, soon to be named Countess of Dufferin, would be used to enable tracklaying on the Pembina Branch line between Winnipeg and the international boundary. Canadian Pacific acquired both the locomotive and the railway line a few years later. After the famous little engine completed many years of active service, it would become a showpiece in a Winnipeg park in front of the CPR station. Today it can be viewed in the Winnipeg Railway Museum, housed in VIA Rail's Union Station in that city.

Whitehead's contract to build the Pembina Branch was awarded in anticipation of an American railroad, the St. Paul & Pacific, soon being built to connect Emerson with St. Paul, Minnesota.[37] That enterprise would get a fateful boost when Hill approached Donald Smith of the

◄ The CPR's first system map in 1881 showed the completed line to the US border at Emerson, as well as the track that had been laid east and west by the federal government. AUTHOR'S COLLECTION

Opposite, top The company's first emigrant sleeping cars, soon renamed "colonist" cars, were acquired by the CPR at a cost of $4,200 apiece. AUTHOR'S COLLECTION

Opposite, bottom The Crossen Car Company of Cobourg, Ontario, would be a reliable supplier of early railway rolling stock, including twenty colonist cars for the CPR in 1884. COBOURG MUSEUM FOUNDATION

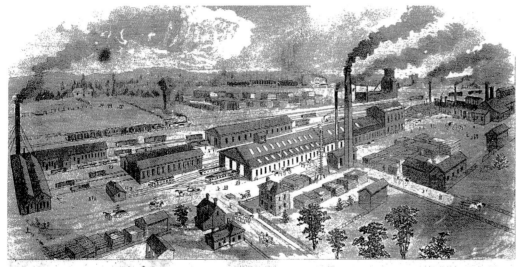

Hudson's Bay Company and George Stephen, president of the Bank of Montreal, with the deal of a lifetime. Together with Norman Kittson, known as the "commodore" of the Red River Transportation Company, the four venture capitalists would buy the St. Paul & Pacific for $280,000 Canadian (approximately $3.9 million today), which Hill estimated was about 20 percent of its real value.[38]

The rail line was completed to the Canada–US border in 1878, driven by the ambitions of its new owners. The lessons learned from operating the railway, soon reorganized as the St. Paul, Minneapolis & Manitoba, would position the canny businessmen to play a leading role in the birth of the privately held Canadian Pacific Railway Company just three years later. Their experience in dealing with the generous land grant they inherited with the purchase of the US railroad would lead them to drive a hard bargain in their later land negotiations with the Canadian government.

Unmatched rail service

US railroads had been catering to the immigrant trade since the 1830s, using whatever old pieces of equipment could be mustered for the task, often boxcars hastily fitted out with benches and not much else in the way of accommodations. By 1855, the Illinois Central had modified twenty boxcars with windows on either side of the centre doors and seats that could be removed to load freight when the cars weren't moving their low-fare passengers like cattle.[39]

In Canada, the Grand Trunk made the industry news when the *Railway World* reported, in an 1867 issue, that eight or nine hundred Germans were crammed into ten boxcars on their way west. No windows, benches, stoves, or toilets were provided. The journal called it the most "inhumane and shameful" scene imaginable.[40]

When the CPR ordered its first twenty colonist sleeping cars in 1884 from the Crossen Car Company of Cobourg, Ontario, for $4,200 a piece, they would be based on a functional design developed earlier by an official of the Central Pacific Railway. James Crossen was an early Canadian car builder, whose company eventually supplied railway equipment to nearly all of the major Canadian railways, as well as many local regional lines, in direct competition with American firms such as the Pullman Company, the Barney and Smith Car Company, and Harlan and Hollingsworth. His colonist cars—known for a short period of time on the CPR as emigrant cars—featured fourteen or sixteen open sections, each of which had face-to-face seats that folded together to create a sleeping platform, with additional berths above that pulled down from the ceiling. The seats were made with wooden slats, with no upholstery, and must have been fairly uncomfortable.

Unlike the more luxurious accommodations in a first-class sleeping car, which required passengers to pay an extra fare to secure a berth or compartment, the first-come, first-served sections in a colonist car came with no extra charge. However, passengers did have to provide their own bedding. A complete outfit of mattress, pillow, blanket, and even optional berth curtains for privacy could be obtained from a CPR agent at the point of embarkation for $2.50 (10 shillings). The colonist cars were fully functional, self-contained, rolling hostelries, equipped with toilets and washbasins, as well as stoves for both heating and cooking purposes. At each end were open-air platforms.

Sleeping berths, whether outfitted with curtains or not, posed more logistical problems for female travellers than they did for men, as a Winnipeg newsman explained:

A man can get into a berth and shuck himself very comfortably. He can stand on his knees and duck his head and take off some of his clothes, and then he can lay down on his shoulders or the back of his neck and kick off other articles of wearing apparel, because when the buttons are unbuttoned his clothes are as liable to come off in the dark as in the light. But it is different with a woman. Her clothes are pinned on with all kinds of pins, from the safety pin to the darning needle, tied on with strings, hooked on with hooks and eyes, buckled on with buckles, and put on in many ways only known to the fair sex. Give her a large enough room, three or four gas lamps and a large mirror and plenty of time, and she can buckle, etc., and what she can break at night and tie up in the morning. But place her in a small berth in the dark, with only her two eyes to watch all the holes in the curtain to see if anybody is looking, and only two small hands to find things to unfasten, and she is in a bad box.[41]

The CPR ads, of course, said their colonist cars were "really first-class sleeping cars, modeled after the style of the first-class Pullman," but not everybody was a fan of their communal facilities. One pilgrim, on what he termed the "Queen's Highway," wrote in his journal:

It is rather fun to pass down these cars and see the babies squatting round, and the people, some eating, some cooking, and some sleeping (they make up their beds for themselves, so they often go to bed at odd times), if only they would not all contribute to the atmosphere. I never saw any of them take the slightest interest in the scenery; in fact, they did not find anything to interest them except tobacco, tinned food, and bed.[42]

While the transcontinental line was still under construction, very little effort was made to follow strict operating schedules. Priority was given to moving manpower and supplies to complete the task, and much of the trackage had

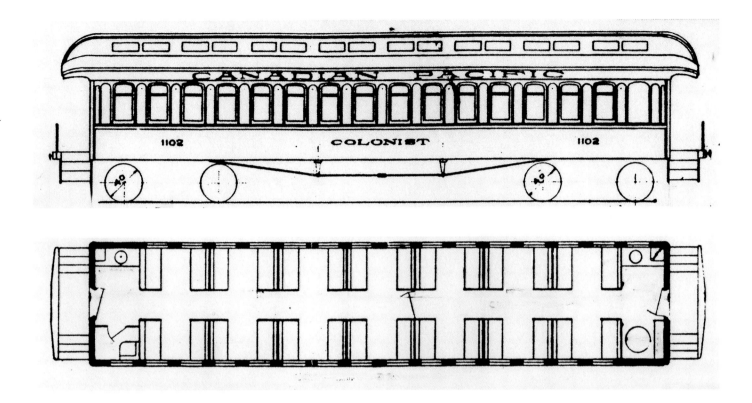

Profile and top-down plans of a CPR colonist car. Modelled after first-class Pullman coaches, the CPR colonist car presented an elegant exterior. Inside, at the far end of the smoking room (the right side of the drawing), were the car's stove and coal bin (both at bottom right). At the other end was a water closet (washroom), and there were washstands at both ends. DOUGLAS R. PHILLIPS COLLECTION

enforced speed restrictions because of the haste with which it had been laid down, sometimes without the optimum number of spikes and ties, and often without adequate ballast to fully stabilize the roadbed. As a result of those factors, coupled with the vagaries of climate in the Northwest, delays and frustrations were common.

One pioneer, William S. de Balinhard of Yorkton, recalled a snowstorm in 1882 when immigrants on their way west were stuck in one spot for three days with nothing to eat. A year later, the family of Andrew Hunt, en route from Glengarry County, Ontario, to their new homestead west of Moosomin, spent eight days getting there. The father described the trip as the train moving on "when the railway had nothing else to do." When they arrived in Moosomin, the CPR did not want to put the boxcar with the family's effects on a siding for unloading. Hunt had to go to Broadview and arrange for his belongings to be shipped back to Whitewood. From there, he got his livestock driven further east to the family homestead, and then returned to Moosomin by horse and wagon to retrieve his family members.[43]

Despite the problems that could occur, the CPR was providing immigrants with a rail service that was unmatched anywhere in North America, and sometimes unscheduled

stops came with a silver lining, offering passengers a welcome opportunity for berry picking, gathering flowers, or closely observing the abundant wildlife along the line. In Canada, the Intercolonial and the Grand Trunk railways would soon follow the CPR's lead signing contracts for colonist cars with the Crossen Car Company. In service, the mahogany-stained and varnished cars were coupled behind the mail, baggage, and express cars, and in front of the first-class coaches, dining, and sleeping cars, on all but the most prestigious trains. A little more than a year after the CPR took delivery of their first colonist cars, Van Horne was looking for ways to make the immigrant experience even more pleasant.

"We intend to provide immediately some emigrant sleeping cars in two compartments," he informed his general manager, "so that women and the more decent class of second-class passengers especially from abroad can travel without being mixed with the loggers and laborers who so commonly ride in these cars at present, and where they will not be suffocated by tobacco smoke."[44]

Despite their shortcomings, the quality of the ride in a CPR colonist car, particularly when not filled to capacity, was sufficiently comfortable that even passengers of means would often opt to sleep in one to avoid the extra charge of more up-scale quarters. However, it came as no surprise that class consciousness and xenophobia entered into the equation, as one American passenger from Nebraska wrote to his former town newspaper in 1887. While he had no issues with the "English pioneers" on board his colonist car, "there were others of other nationalities whose personal habits and general atmosphere were such that I quite agreed with the youth from Chicago who said to me, 'I would rather walk first class than ride third class.'"[45]

Until the CPR completed its route around Lake Superior, first with steamboats on the Great Lakes and a rail connection from Prince Arthur's Landing (now Thunder Bay) to Winnipeg, followed shortly by an all-rail link, most travellers on their way to the Northwest used existing railway lines in Canada and the United States to get to St. Paul. While the CPR worked to consolidate its position in Quebec and Ontario, the Grand Trunk Railway handled much of the traffic, connecting with its affiliate lines in Canada and links to US roads such as the Chicago & Grand Trunk (later Grand Trunk Western) and the Michigan Central.

As early as March 1881, the Great Western Railway, which operated in southern Ontario and into Michigan, was running immigration excursion trains twice a month from Toronto. Leaving Toronto on March 2, a trainload of 250

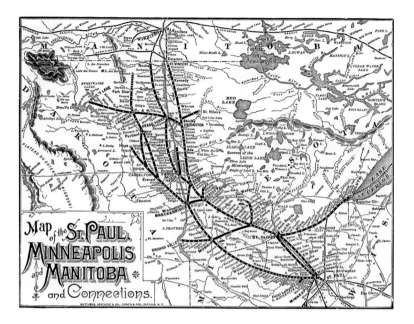

Map of the ST. PAUL, MINNEAPOLIS and MANITOBA and Connections.

people on six first-class passenger coaches called at Hamilton and London, before connecting with the Michigan Central at Detroit bound for Chicago. In the Windy City, the excursionists were transferred onto a Chicago, Milwaukee & St. Paul train for the run to St. Paul, where they boarded the St. Paul, Minneapolis & Manitoba, for the last leg northward through the US.

By May 1881, the St. Paul, Minneapolis & Manitoba was running through coaches and elegant sleeping cars on two routes between St. Paul and Winnipeg, daily except Sunday. One route ran along the west side of the Red River through Neche, North Dakota, connecting with the CPR at Gretna, Manitoba, while the other took the east bank through St. Vincent, Minneapolis.

Left The St. Paul, Minneapolis & Manitoba ran comfortable coaches and elegant sleeping cars from St. Paul through to Winnipeg, daily except Sunday. OMER LAVALLEE COLLECTION

Right Before the CPR had consolidated its own railway lines in Eastern Canada, it was already advertising routes west through the United States. AUTHOR'S COLLECTION

▶ As the fortunes of the railway improved, so too did the quality of the advertising printers' art. NOTMAN PHOTOGRAPHIC ARCHIVES, MCCORD STEWART MUSEUM M930.50.5.188

Burlington & Quincy, then the Burlington, Cedar Rapids & Northern, and finally the Minneapolis & St. Louis, before climbing aboard the St. Paul, Minneapolis and Manitoba to connect with the CPR.[47] One can only imagine that when the CPR completed its own through line, there would be less opportunity for luggage to go astray.

Eastern network

The CPR lost no time building and consolidating its lines in the East. The company's charter specified Callander (now Bonfield), just east of Lake Nipissing, as the nominal eastern terminus for the transcontinental.[48] Four months after Canadian Pacific was incorporated, the company acquired the charter of the Canada Central Railway, which would enable the CPR to extend its main line from Lake Nipissing to Ottawa. It also allowed Canadian Pacific to lease or acquire lines from the nation's capital "to any point at navigable water on the Atlantic seaboard."

At the same time, some of the CPR syndicate members and their associates were also acquiring private holdings in strategic locations. President George Stephen had been investing in the Credit Valley Railway even before Canadian Pacific was incorporated. Now he viewed that property as a potential nucleus for his company's railway network in southern Ontario.

In 1881, Edmund Osler, a Toronto financier who worked closely with the founders of the CPR and who would, three years later, become a partner in the Canada North-West Land Company, became president of a revived Ontario & Quebec Railway, originally incorporated to build from Ottawa to Toronto via Peterborough. The railway's charter

When the March 2 excursion from Toronto reached St. Vincent, a CPR special was awaiting the immigrants, whose large consignment of effects had arrived the day before in twenty-five boxcars. After passing customs into Emerson, half of the party disembarked for farms in the district, while the remainder went on to arrive in Winnipeg, about eight days after they had started out. Several delays due to severe snowstorms, coupled with layovers between connections, had made for a fairly slow passage, but all reached their destinations without any mishaps.[46]

Two months later, the Winnipeg papers were noting the arrival of "another batch of pilgrims" in their fair city. This time, the trainload of immigrants had made even more transfers after the stop in Chicago, taking first the Chicago,

TORONTO GREY AND BRUCE RAILWAY.

DIRECT AND ONLY LINE
BETWEEN

TORONTO and OWEN SOUND

LAKE ONTARIO TO GEORGIAN BAY.

3 TRAINS DAILY EACH WAY

Close connections at TORONTO with trains from

EAST AND WEST

QUEBEC, MONTREAL, DETROIT, NEW YORK, BUFFALO and HAMILTON,

And at OWEN SOUND with Steamers of the OWEN SOUND
STEAMSHIP LINE for

Georgian Bay, Lake Superior and the Great Northwest.

QUICK TIME!   LOWEST RATES!
NEW PASSENGER EQUIPMENT!

D. McNICOLL,   **EDMUND WRAGGE,**
Gen'l Freight and Pass. Agent.   General Manager.
OFFICES—TORONTO, ONT.

had lain dormant for nearly ten years. The O&Q became a not-so-secret weapon of the CPR when George Stephen and CPR vice-president Duncan McIntyre joined its board within months of its revival.

Not long afterward, Stephen's associate, George Laidlaw, president of the Credit Valley, leased the Toronto, Grey & Bruce Railway, which included a line from Toronto to Owen Sound. By 1883, the CPR would absorb both the Credit Valley and the TG&B, giving the transcontinental a port on Georgian Bay from which to launch a fleet of steamships for the Great Lakes trade. Within a year, the CPR had extended its southern Ontario lines to St. Thomas, with connections to Detroit and Chicago.[49]

In 1882, the CPR was able to acquire the western portion of the money-losing Quebec, Montreal, Ottawa & Occidental Railway to gain access to Montreal, despite the strong objections of the Grand Trunk Railway and its eastern establishment allies. Five years later, the CPR would extend its Ontario & Quebec line from Smith's Falls to Montreal, creating a shorter line from Toronto than its route through Ottawa. In 1888, the line would again be extended to a new Montreal terminal at Windsor Street. Augmented with several major additions, the imposing, greystone Windsor Station would grow to become one of the city's most iconic structures and serve as Canadian Pacific's headquarters for the next 110 years.

Looking to the east and south, Stephen also set his eye on two key railways that would expand the CPR's reach. He was interested in the charter for the Atlantic & North-West Railway because of its authority to build a bridge across the St. Lawrence at Lachine, just west of Montreal. He also realized the potential value of the South Eastern Railway, a small operator in southern Quebec with the ability to provide a through line to Portland and Boston.[50] Both would soon be in the CPR's possession.

In 1883, the CPR moved to bring all of these railway lines under the control of the parent company. In April, it petitioned Parliament for authority to lease the Credit Valley, the Ontario & Quebec, and the Atlantic & North-West, which was granted in May. In July, the O&Q leased the TG&B, and added the Credit Valley in November. The next month, CPR purchased the Atlantic and North-West. As a *fait accompli*, early in 1884, Canadian Pacific then leased the O&Q and all of its subsidiary lines in perpetuity, solidifying the three-year-old railway's now-formidable eastern network.[51]

By the end of April 1884, the CPR was advertising its new "Palace" sleeping car service between Chicago and Toronto, in conjunction with the Michigan Central. Immigrant traffic and freight had already been moving

over the two railways between Montreal and Chicago for about a month. While that development made it easier for Canadian Pacific to move settlers and their effects to the Northwest via the United States, a more portentous event was unfolding on the all-Canadian route.

Great Lakes steamships

Two years in the making, at the Aitken & Mansell and Charles Connell & Company shipyards on the River Clyde in Scotland, the CPR's new iron steamships, the *Algoma*, *Alberta*, and *Athabasca* steamed into the harbour at Owen Sound in the spring of 1884, ready to bridge the gap between the eastern provinces and the head of navigation at Prince Arthur's Landing, while the railway line was being completed around the north side of Lake Superior. The railway had already been operating a small, ragtag fleet of working boats on the Great Lakes, largely to move construction materials, but these new vessels were said by the CPR publicists to be "the finest steamships on inland waters."[52]

The locals had long enjoyed steamship service to their town. The Owen Sound Steamship Company ran a tri-weekly service to Manitoulin Island and ports on Lake Superior. In recent years, they had laid claim to being "the short and favorite route for tourists and emigrants, between the East and the West." Their main competition was the North-West Transportation Company, which operated several vessels in connection with the Toronto, Grey & Bruce and the Grand Trunk Railway in Ontario, and the Northern Pacific at Duluth, in Minnesota. Henry Beatty, general manager of the family's steamship business, acted as the CPR's agent during the construction of its Great

Lakes steamers, and became the line's first manager when it went into service between Owen Sound and "the Lakehead," which is to say the head of Lake Superior (i.e., its western end) and thus the Great Lakes.

The new vessels would be a cut above anything previously calling at the sheltered Georgian Bay harbour, as the editorial staff of the *Owen Sound Advertiser* pointed out:

No such vessels have ever been seen on the Great Lakes, but their excellence lies not in the gorgeousness of their furniture or the gingerbread work of decoration, but in their superiority over other lake craft in model construction and equipment and in their thorough adaptability for the business in which they will engage.[53]

As the steamships would only run from Owen Sound every other day, immigrants often had a layover of twenty-four hours, so it was important to erect an immigrant shed there. In March, Van Horne had advised the secretary of the Canadian Department of Agriculture that the CPR had a large force of carpenters at Owen Sound working on the necessary railway and steamship facilities. He indicated that if the government were ready to provide funds for the shed to be built, the CPR would undertake to construct the building.[54] When the government declined to do anything about the matter, Van Horne and his general superintendent, William Whyte, arranged to provide the shelter themselves.[55] The federal government did, however, build a large and commodious reception house for immigrants at Port Arthur.

In the days leading up to the inaugural run of the *Algoma*, which was to be the first of the three vessels to reach Owen Sound, Van Horne was anxious to ensure that a large number of immigrants then on their way across the Atlantic

◀ Arriving in Port Arthur by one of the CPR's new steamships, the *Alberta*, *Athabasca* and *Algoma*, was always a more pleasant event during the summer months. AUTHOR'S COLLECTION

Top Settlers could join the first-class passengers in the elegant dining halls aboard CPR's Great Lakes steamships, if their means allowed. For many, paying the less expensive fares meant they also had to rent their own mattresses and bedding and eat in a more spartan area below deck. AUTHOR'S COLLECTION

Bottom The CPR lobbied the government to change the name of the railway's steamship terminal, originally known as Prince Arthur's Landing, at the Lakehead to Port Arthur. OMER LAVALLEE COLLECTION

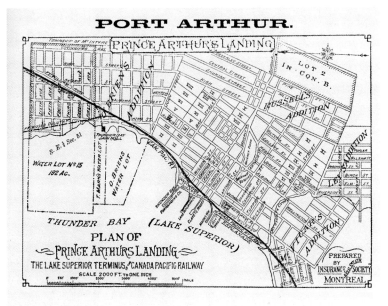

would be made comfortable should they arrive at the Great Lakes port ahead of the steamship that was to convey them westward. "It is exceedingly important that no bad reports go back from these first parties," he emphasized to Whyte.[56]

The CPR's Great Lakes steamships were of sufficient length that on the way to their home port, it had been necessary to cut them in half—between special bulkheads installed for that purpose—to pass through the locks in the Beauharnois and Cornwall canals. After reassembly in Port Colborne, the *Algoma* arrived in Owen Sound on May 10, 1884, and loaded her cargo and passenger complement the next day. More than twelve hundred passengers clambered aboard for the maiden voyage from Owen Sound to the Lakehead, about a thousand of whom were immigrants headed for the Northwest.

The new steamships were fitted out with 180 berths for first-class passengers and 200 bunks in well-lit steerage quarters, but in a pinch—such as occurred on the *Algoma*'s first outbound trip—up to one thousand immigrants could be accommodated in steerage with the addition of more bunks and a profusion of hammocks. Unlike their more pampered first-class shipmates, however, those in the

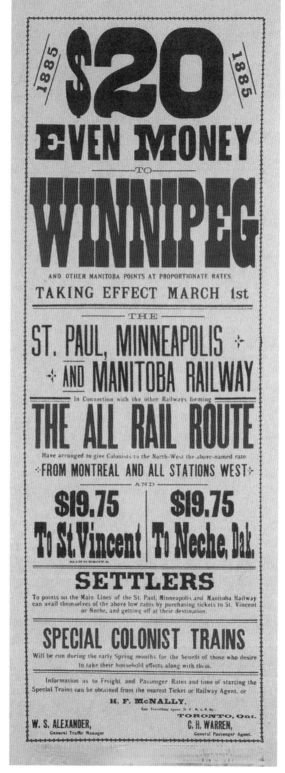

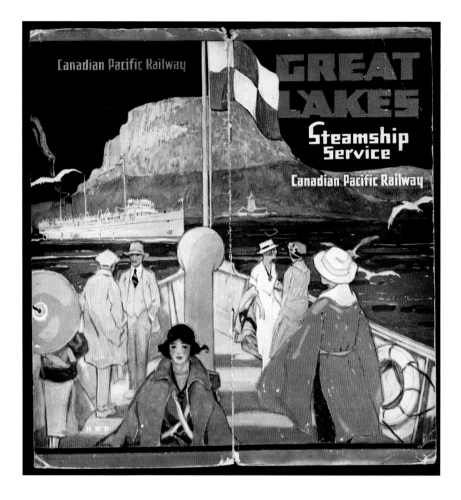

more spartan communal quarters had to rent their own mattresses and bedding.[57]

That summer, Van Horne sailed on the *Alberta* to assess the overall quality of the new service. Generally, he found things much to his liking, but he did suggest that breakfast be served from seven to ten in the morning, rather than waking passengers at the ungodly hour of six for the scheduled morning repast. Meals were complementary for first-class ticket holders and twenty-five cents each for steerage passengers, a charge that company fliers suggested was well below cost.[58]

While the railway line was still under construction along the rugged north shore of Lake Superior, the steamship service on the Great lakes would be of particular value to the CPR's immigration business. The track work would not be completed, and the line put in first-class shape, until the fall of 1885. Regular freight service between Montreal and Winnipeg was inaugurated in the last week of October. On Monday, November 2, the first scheduled through passenger trains began operations. Immigrants and their baggage could now traverse the entire route within Canada from Montreal to Winnipeg by rail. The Great Lakes service would hereafter mostly cater to the first-class and tourist market.

On virtually the last day of the shipping season, tragedy struck the steamship line. November 7, 1885, the same day the Last Spike on the transcontinental railway was being driven at Craigellachie, BC, the *Algoma* foundered on the ragged shores of Isle Royale, not far from the safety of Port Arthur (originally Prince Arthur's Landing, renamed by the CPR in 1883). On board were five hundred tons of construction supplies and general merchandise as well as fourteen unfortunate passengers, all but two of whom died in the wreckage. Snow and freezing rain had reduced visibility to virtually nil, and the ship's captain had made a fatal navigational error, allowing the winds and waves to dash the *Algoma* to pieces against the rocks. No immigrants had been on board.[59]

5 TRUE BELIEVERS HEAD WEST

Imperialists and empire builders

With both the government and the railway favouring British immigrants, it's no surprise that the first large-scale publicity tour of the Northwest was organized for the British Association for the Advancement of Science, a distinguished professional organization that met in Montreal for its annual convention in August 1884. The association held a yearly meeting in a different city each year, at which scientists presented new ideas and discoveries to their peers and publicized their work. The Montreal meeting was the first to be held outside of the United Kingdom, so it garnered a lot of interest from the press and the public. About 800 members had taken advantage of the offer of reduced ocean fares and free railway trips on the CPR, subsidized with a $25,000 contribution from the Canadian government to offset costs.[1]

The group came to Canada aboard three transatlantic steamships: The Allan Line's *Parisian* and *Polynesian* and the Dominion Line's *Oregon*. At the end of the formal sessions in Montreal, 117 members of the association took the CPR up on its offer to tour the railway's Western Division, from Winnipeg to Kicking Horse Pass in the Rocky Mountains, travelling in considerable style in the confines of seven luxurious sleeping cars.[2] They travelled to Manitoba through southern Ontario, Chicago, and St. Paul.

The CPR wished to showcase the West's potential for settlement to this august group, in the full knowledge that many words would be written in overseas journals about every detail of the association's trip. The railway's general superintendent, John Egan, and immigration agent, Alexander Begg, hosted the publicity tour. The party was reported to have returned from the West with many scientific specimens gathered in the field. It made its way to end of track and back with only one untoward incident. At the western extreme of the excursion, the well-respected geologist Alfred Selwyn had put himself at undue risk while walking across a temporary wooden scaffold over a ravine. Struck by an avalanche while negotiating the shaky structure, and carried a considerable distance by the impact, the plucky scientist had emerged from a pile of battered timbers virtually unscathed.[3]

The highlight of the tour for both the excursionists and certainly for the railway's advertising men was a reception at the Qu'Appelle Valley Farming Company, better known as the Bell Farm. The owner, Major William Robert Bell, and his wife greeted the group at their farmhouse.

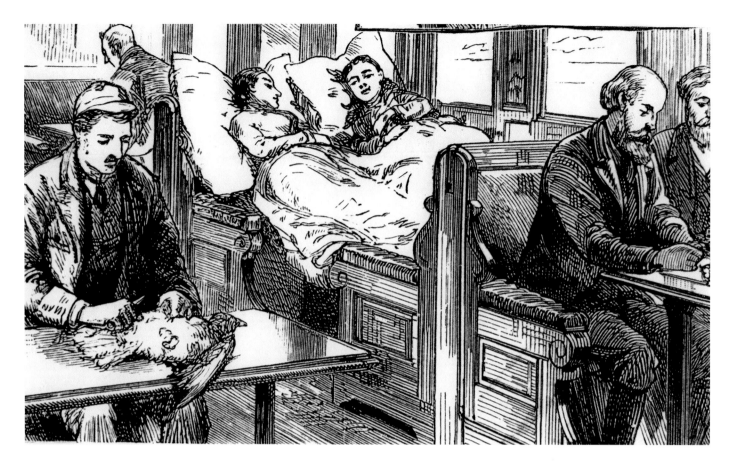

Three years earlier, Major Bell, a militia officer, sportsman, farmer, and businessman from Brockville, Ontario, had gotten it into his head to launch a large-scale agricultural operation in the Northwest. In the summer of 1881, he walked westward from Brandon, Manitoba, along the proposed route of the CPR, until he reached a site that met with his approval in the vicinity of present-day Indian Head. The following winter, he purchased more than 23,000 acres (9,300 ha) from the federal government and 29,000 acres (11,700 ha) from the CPR in the same area.[4] Financed chiefly by his British and Canadian capitalist backers, Bell now held more than 80 square miles (210 km²) of some of the best potential wheat-growing lands in North America and the largest farm of contiguous lands in the world.

On May 12, 1882, the ambitious major formally incorporated the Qu'Appelle Valley Farming Company with Edward Dewdney, the newly appointed lieutenant governor of the North-West Territories, as a board member. Bell

wanted the farm to serve as a vehicle for advertising the potential of the region. The federal government and the CPR were more than happy to help out. The farm company embarked on an ambitious construction program, erecting some seventy buildings by the spring of 1883, several of stone. Among them were a granary and storehouse, a large stable for horses, a shed for cattle, an icehouse, and a dog kennel. That same year, there were said to be "twenty-six self-binder reaping machines, fifty sulky ploughs, two steam threshing machines" and eighty-seven men employed to operate them.[5] The nearby townsite of Indian Head was developed on lands owned by both the Bell Farm and the CPR.

The task of breaking the land got under way immediately: 2,500 acres (1,010 ha) by the end of the first summer, 7,000 acres (2,800 ha) the next year. Five thousand acres (2,025 ha) were under cultivation for wheat and 2,000 acres (810 ha) for oats by the time the group of British

Sir John Lister-Kaye cut a
dashing figure, as he transformed from British entrepreneur to Canadian Northwest
land baron, farmer, and livestock owner.

scientists arrived for their tour. The farm's furrows were reputed to be so long that the teams plowing them would turn just once a day, at lunch, to return to where they had started. Unfortunately for Bell, the first few harvests suffered from drought and early frosts, although in 1884, the farm did manage to sell more than 50,000 bushels of wheat to the Ogilvie Milling Company at a dollar a bushel. The outbreak of the Northwest Resistance was a further blow; men and horses from the farm were recruited to transport military supplies. By 1886, the farm was running heavy losses. To stave off a complete collapse, portions of just over 200 acres (81 ha) a piece were sold to about 100 "thrifty and intelligent" bona fide settlers, though few had prior agricultural knowledge of the Northwest.[6]

By 1886, the company was refinanced as the Bell Farm Company Limited. The new company divested itself of its holdings in the townsite of Indian Head. It also sold 674 acres (272 ha) to the federal government for a new experimental farm. In 1889, the farm was broken up further and sold to small owners. Bell retained about 13,000 acres (5,260 ha) and tried to carry on his original concept on a smaller scale, but creditors seized his holdings in 1896.[7]

Major Bell had taken on a bigger project than he could sustain. But he was able to prove the undeniable fertility of the land around Indian Head and, for a short time, had grown some of the best wheat in the world, as he had dreamed of doing. The ultimate fate of his endeavour showed how precarious the life of a farmer in the Northwest could be, given the vagaries of climate, politics, market conditions, and just plain bad luck.

During those tentative early years of passenger train operations on the transcontinental railway, Bell had provided the CPR with a fascinating attraction along a ten-mile (16 km) stretch of tracks that showed immigrants anything was possible. The Bell Farm was the Northwest's first tourist attraction. For a few short years, its farming operations were so huge that even trains on a strict schedule would routinely stop to let passengers watch the work in progress.

The Bell Farm also served as an inspiration for another would-be empire builder who arrived in the Northwest in 1884, fresh from successfully promoting a land settlement project in California.[8] Sir John Lister-Kaye was an English entrepreneur who liked what he saw at Major Bell's vast farm east of Regina. That summer, with financial support from Lord Queensberry and others, he purchased nearly seven thousand acres (2,800 ha) from the CPR and the Dominion government at Balgonie, not far from the Bell Farm. He began immediately to import high-quality livestock, planted wheat, oats, and barley on two sections and, despite the outbreak of the Riel Resistance in 1885 and its accompanying demand for men and supplies, managed to bring in a decent yield and made a tidy profit on his investment.[9]

It was at this point that Lister-Kaye made his biggest gamble. Despite the drought that had struck the south-central portion of the Northwest in 1886, he turned his eye toward the Swift Current district to look for more land, making a reconnaissance tour along the route of the CPR all the way to Calgary in a private car bearing the name of his wife, Natica. He was apparently favourably impressed with what he saw, for he soon purchased ten 10,000-acre (4,050 ha) blocks of land from the CPR and the federal government. He agreed to make six annual payments and to cultivate a significant portion of his holdings in short order. In return, the railway and the government reduced the price of the land to less than $1.50 per acre ($3.71/ha), if the conditions agreed upon were met. The CPR also granted Lister-Kaye freight rate concessions to help him get established.[10]

Seven of the properties were located at intervals west of Swift Current at locations named Crane Lake, Kincarth, Dunmore, Stair, Bantry, Namaka, and Langdon. The others were within the Swift Current district: one on the plains of Rush Lake, another just south of Swift Current, and a third at Gull Lake, near one of CPR's pioneer experimental farms. At all of the locations, the wealthy Yorkshire baronet hoped to establish ranch-farms modelled on typical English estates. With an ambitious flourish, Lister-Kaye began to promote the group of farms as the Alberta and Assiniboia Land, Stock and Coal Company, but the semi-arid conditions on many of his properties at the best of times, and the onset of a few consecutive drought years throughout the Northwest, nearly sank his prospects.

Early in 1888, he set sail for England to convince his investors of his project's worthiness. Accompanying Lister-Kaye was D.J. "Joe" Wylie, a four-year resident of Maple Creek, a charming Englishman who had also become somewhat of an authority on the prospects of the Canadian Northwest. Together the two men were able to drum up renewed enthusiasm for the company, and it was soon reorganized as the Canadian Agricultural, Coal and Colonization Company (CACC Co.).

The new company bought out Lister-Kaye's holdings—making him a fortune—and hired the former owner as manager. Sparing no expense, the empire builder ordered two million board feet (4,720 m³) of lumber to erect farming and ranching facilities on the CACC Co.'s properties. He also purchased an entire herd of 5,800 American range cattle from the Powder River Ranch Company, an English-owned firm in Wyoming with headquarters in London. Since the cattle already bore the brand "76," the CACC

COLONIZATION

THE
CANADIAN AGRICULTURAL, COAL & COLONIZATION

COMPANY, LIMITED,

Are prepared to place

FARMERS

on completely equipped and stocked

FARMS OF 160 ACRES EACH,

on their property at BALGONIE, in the
CANADIAN NORTH-WEST.

Towards the purchase of the

Land, Stock, Buildings and Equipment,

amounting to a value of about £600, more or less according to the Farmer's wishes, the Farmer will be required to find a Cash

CAPITAL OF £100,

the balance, about £500, will be treated as a Loan, repayable by instalments.

For further particulars apply to

Sir JOHN LISTER KAYE,

3, ST. GEORGE'S PLACE,
HYDE PARK CORNER, LONDON.

OR TO

SUB-AGENT.

THOMAS & SONS, PRINTERS, 83, COLEMAN STREET, LONDON, E.C

[1887 or 1888]

◄ Lister-Kaye's ambitious company purchased one hundred thousand acres of land from the CPR and the government and sold quarter sections to settlers to set up ranch-farms modeled on typical English estates. LIBRARY AND CULTURAL RESOURCES DIGITAL COLLECTIONS, UNIVERSITY OF CALGARY CU1100450

► Lister-Kaye's corral at Maple Creek often contained several hundred sheep. LIBRARY AND CULTURAL RESOURCES DIGITAL COLLECTIONS, UNIVERSITY OF CALGARY CU181039

Co.'s whole enterprise in the Northwest came to be known as the 76 Ranch. Adding to the company's livestock, Lister-Kaye sent his agents to the northwestern United States to buy thousands of Merino ewes, renowned for their wool. He then had large numbers of pedigreed rams, Yorkshire boars, and pigs shipped from England, and he bought hundreds of good mares from Ontario for field work and breeding purposes.[11]

To market the ranches' produce, he opened slaughterhouses and butcher shops in Dunmore and Medicine Hat and built a large meat packing plant in Calgary to sell the company's own beef, mutton, and pork.

The 76 Ranch recruited its substantial workforce largely through newspaper advertisements in England, offering free passage to Canada, a one-year contract that included room and board, plus ten dollars a month in wages and a chance for recruits to buy "free" 160-acre (65 ha) homesteads adjacent to one of the company's properties when their contracts expired.[12] The successful recruits arrived aboard CPR colonist cars.

Ultimately, however, Lister-Kaye's overspending and reckless decisions led to his dismissal, and he was replaced as manager of the CACC Co. More troubles followed. An 1890 prairie fire started by sparks from a CPR locomotive killed or badly burned more than one thousand of the company's sheep that were grazing near Gull Lake. The same year, a devastating hailstorm of sufficient magnitude to shatter the windows in CPR passenger coaches destroyed the crops in the Swift Current region. Plagued by financial woes, the CACC Co. was forced to sell all of its holdings to a new London-based company, the Canadian Land and Ranch Company Ltd. For a few years, the new company made a healthy profit by selling off livestock, dismissing many employees, and reducing overhead, but it was dealt a mortal blow during the winter of 1906–7 when two-thirds of its cattle died on the open range. Two years later, the Canadian Land and Ranch Company gave up altogether and sold its properties to the firm of Gordon, Ironsides, and Fares of Winnipeg.[13]

Though the company's overwhelming influence in the area came to an end, its legacy lived on in the men and women who came to the Northwest to work for the CACC Co. and its successor. Many of them stayed on the prairie to begin small farms, ranches, and other businesses of their own.

Other Brits obtained a foothold in the Northwest through the immigration and colonization work of the Canada North-West Land Company. The company's executive administrator and spokesperson, William Scarth, had come across a likely sponsor with deep pockets in the course of propaganda work carried on in Scotland.[14] Lady Emily Cathcart owned large estates in the Hebrides with more crofters living on the land than it could economically bear.

Crofting was a traditional social system in the highlands and on the islands of Scotland, characterized by common working communities that engaged in small-scale agriculture, raising livestock, and pursuing a number of other activities to earn their livelihood. Whether to further enrich herself by removing tenants dependent on her largesse for their survival or out of sincere concern for their future well-being, Cathcart proposed to sponsor some of these crofter families from her estates in Benbecula and South Uist to emigrate to the Canadian Northwest. Her substantial number of Canadian Pacific Railway Company shares no doubt helped her to get a considerable amount of logistical aid from the railway and its overseas officers.

The first contingent of crofters left Glasgow in April 1883 under the guidance of Donald McDiarmid, an agent and inspector who worked for Lady Cathcart at Cluny Castle, her home in Aberdeen, far from the Hebrides. After a two-week crossing of the Atlantic, during which time they endured near constant iceberg warnings, they arrived in Quebec. Seven hours later, the group of forty-eight settlers was on its way west aboard CPR colonist cars.

"We were in the train for five days and nights without an hour's rest until we arrived at Winnipeg on the 9th May, after having come 2,000 miles [3,200 km] by rail, and, believe me, we were quite tired of it," wrote Alexander McPherson, two months later. "We stayed only a day in Winnipeg, and then we started west to another town, 132 miles [212 km] distant, called Brandon."[15]

The party of settlers had twelve days in that town to get their bearings and purchase supplies, while McDiarmid and CPR surveyor Lachlan MacTavish staked out sixteen homesteads near the towns of Wapella and Moosomin, on the railway main line about a 100 miles (160 km) west of

Brandon.[16] Lady Cathcart and the Canada North-West Land Company split the cost of advancing each family one hundred pounds for the necessary equipment to make the improvements on their homesteads that would secure the title to the land.[17] Once they were settled, the crofter families were expected to pay back the loans at 5 percent interest.

"Ourselves are well pleased for our journey here," wrote Salina MacDonald to a friend, three months after arriving in Wapella. "We are doing improvement on the land; we have 16 acres [6.5 ha] ploughed ready for next year. We have 480 acres [194 ha] of the best land in the world. Our crop is looking splendid. We got up the winter home and stable for our cattle, but we expect to make a better house next summer."[18]

Buoyed by the success of the first group, Cathcart sponsored a second party of crofters in 1884 who landed in Quebec and travelled in the spartan confines of a colonist car to Owen Sound, where one of the CPR's new Great Lakes steamships awaited them. After boarding a train at Port Arthur, the large group, which included many children, arrived at Moosomin. From there it was a short haul by oxen and cart to their new homes.[19]

In 1883–84, nearly three hundred crofters settled the St. Andrew's and New Benbecula colonies near Moosomin and Wapella. These early Scottish settlers experienced considerable hardship during their initial years, particularly in winter when one of the few sources of ready cash was working for the railway. Some abandoned their homesteads; those who stayed, prospered in the end. And their success encouraged others to follow. The following year, about a hundred additional families came from the estates of Lady Cathcart, the Duke of Argyll, and the Earl of Dunmore to the area south of Moosomin, Wapella, and Red Jacket. In 1889, a crofter settlement was also founded in Saltcoats, more than 50 miles (80 km) to the north.[20]

Other Scottish settlers were also attracted to the Northwest, homesteading in the Qu'Appelle Valley around Abernethy, and at Indian Head, close to the Bell Farm. Some from Ontario relocated farther from the railway, north of Regina in Lumsden, Craven, Condie, Tregarva, and Brora. Scots also spread eastward across the prairies to Glenbrae, Markinch, Cupar, Dysart, Dalrymple, and the McDonald Hills.[21]

The crofters in the Wapella area had neighbours who came over from the Old Country with aristocratic sponsorship around the same time they had. In 1884, Baroness Angela Burdett-Coutts and Lord Francis Walter de Winton, two more monied imperialists with CPR connections, brought twenty families out of London's working-class districts to what they called the East London Artisans' Colony. The baroness hired an experienced farmer to instruct the city dwellers, and in time they adapted to mixed farming.

Perhaps the most unusual settlement founded in the 1880s was Cannington Manor, 40 miles (64 km) south of the railway town of Moosomin. Established in 1882 by a British officer, Captain Edward Mitchell Pierce, the colony was named for a village in Somerset, England. Here Pierce attracted British remittance men to learn farming techniques at an agricultural college for a fee of a hundred pounds a year, while creating a community that emulated upper-class English society. Many of the students took up residence in a twenty-six-room mansion built for that purpose by three of the "pups," as Pierce's pupils were known.[22]

In its prime, Cannington Manor featured thoroughbred racing on its own private racetrack, complete with imported steeplechase jockeys, polo matches, and a hunt

club replete with authentic foxhounds. The students, most of whom were second sons and other upper-class boys, played cricket, soccer, tennis, and billiards and staged amateur theatrical plays. They didn't fraternize much with longer-term Canadian settlers in the colony. While neighbouring homesteads were barely eking out a living, the Cannington residents were operating a school, dairy, blacksmith, flourmill, and carpenter shop. The stock farm included a pork packing plant and two cheese factories, while the Moose Mountain company trading store and the Mitre Hotel supported the economy of the burgeoning community.[23]

In the early years, all of the construction materials and other supplies were brought in by wagon from the railway line at Moosomin, while the colonists waited for a branch line to be built through their community. In 1902, when the CPR built a new line about 6 miles (10 km) south, rather than in the vicinity of Cannington Manor, the elite school's days were numbered. Drought and low grain prices created a depressed economy in the area for many years. The remaining businesses associated with the college estate slowly drifted to other communities on railway lines, and Cannington Manor gradually disappeared. The site where its former glory years once unfolded is now a provincial historic park.

Two former students of Pierce, the Beckton boys, remained in the area, built themselves a large stone house, and bred thoroughbred racehorses, maintaining a bit of the old British aristocracy in the Wild West.

Not too far away at Whitewood, on the CPR line between Wapella and Broadview, some displaced French counts "attempted to maintain the accoutrements of fine society" by growing sugar beets and chicory, while raising sheep and producing their own Gruyère cheese. And a little

farther west at Indian Head, Lord Thomas Brassey set up the Canadian Co-operative Colonization Company on a large piece of land that he purchased from the Bell Farm, where he invited families new to the Northwest to learn farming techniques and benefit from his support.[24]

Branch lines and colonization railways

When the Canadian Pacific Railway Company was incorporated to take over the task of building a national transcontinental railway, the private company inherited 710 miles (1,440 km) of railway track that had been built by the federal government as public works, some of it in British Columbia and some in the Northwest. The line in Manitoba from Selkirk, near Winnipeg, to Emerson, on the Canada-US border, was the first part of government-owned CPR to be operated. The section of track from Winnipeg to Prince Arthur's Landing, on the Lakehead, was opened in 1882. The CPR changed the rather unwieldy name of the town to Port Arthur the following spring. Through service east of Port Arthur would not be opened until 1885. The government also built the main line westward from Winnipeg for about 100 miles (160 km), which was transferred under a separate provision that required the new operators to pay back the cost of its construction.

A key term in the CPR charter was a provision known as the "monopoly clause," which protected the company from immediate competition from US lines that might draw away revenue-generating traffic from the Canadian West. The agreement, in large measure, was meant to compensate the railway for building an all-Canadian connection between the eastern provinces and Manitoba, around the north shore of Lake Superior, a line that would not be profitable for many years to come, if ever. The monopoly clause enraged many in Manitoba who thought it would hinder growth in the Northwest, and it only stayed in effect for about seven years before being rescinded; in the meantime, the CPR was free to set whatever freight rates it wanted across the West. The notorious Clause 15 specified:

For twenty years from the date hereof, no line of railway shall be authorized by the Dominion Parliament to be constructed South of the Canadian Pacific Railway, from any point at or near the Canadian Pacific Railway, except such line as shall run South West or to the Westward of South West; nor to within fifteen miles [24 km] of Latitude 49. And in the establishment of any new Province in the North-West territories, provision shall be made for continuing such prohibition after such establishment until the expiration of the same period.[25]

The exception referred to government-built lines over which CPR was given complete control. The provincial authorities retained the authority to charter railways to be built entirely within their own borders, but the federal government intended to disallow any connections of those lines with CPR's American competitors.

Settlers east of the Red River were primarily French Canadians, Métis, and groups of Russian Mennonites who had come to Manitoba in the 1870s. They were scattered over swampy, wooded areas that were not favoured by newly arriving immigrants for agricultural purposes. The CPR began to lay branch lines on the west side of the river.

The Manitoba South-Western Colonization Railway had been chartered in 1879 to build southwest from Winnipeg

for about 30 miles (48 km) and then head west toward the Souris coal deposits. In the summer of 1881, the Northern Pacific had managed to get financial control of the charter, with the hope of turning the line southward to connect with its own lines in North Dakota. To thwart this backdoor challenge to the monopoly, it had negotiated south of its main line, the CPR rapidly built what it called the Pembina Mountain Branch. This line ran south from Winnipeg down the west side of the Red River to within 13 miles (21 km) of the US border. It then turned westward and ran roughly parallel to the boundary line, effectively blocking any ambitions the Manitoba South-Western might have of connecting with US roads.[26]

The CPR added a 13-mile (21 km) link between Rosenfeld on the Pembina Mountain Branch and Gretna that would later connect west of the Red River with the St. Paul, Minneapolis & Manitoba, which was, of course, controlled by the same interests as the CPR. By 1885, the CPR would extend its westbound branch line to Deloraine.

And to remove any future threats from the Manitoba South-Western, the CPR acquired its charter under a long-term lease of one million dollars. It came with the usual government grant of 6,400 acres (2,590 ha) of land for every mile (1.6 km) of track the railway built, eventually bringing its new owners nearly 1.4 million acres (566,600 ha) of prime agricultural land for colonization and settlement. With the country in a depression, however, the CPR would sell less than 18,000 of those acres (7,300 ha) per year during the next decade.[27]

Even before the arrival of the CPR in Manitoba, a visionary Ontario pioneer named Thomas Greenway had acquired 1,600 acres (650 ha) of land southeast of Winnipeg, not far from the US border. Here he established his Home Stock Farm, which was described to a visitor from back east as "a shining example of what can be done with mixed farming on the prairies." For several years, beginning in 1879, Greenway cultivated wheat, raised purebred cattle, and encouraged horticulture among the first trickle

of newcomers to the land. His property, in effect, was an experimental farm, far in advance of those that would be set up by the federal government and the CPR. But his long-term goal of creating a planned community was thwarted when the railway branch line constructed through the region in 1885 bypassed his property by a couple of miles.[28]

The chief sources of immigrants in the early 1880s were Eastern Canada and the United States, with small groups from the United Kingdom and Germany. Nearly all entered Canada at Emerson, and soon Gretna as well. Some French Canadians who had taken up residence in Vermont, Massachusetts, and Michigan came back across the border to St. Boniface and St. Alphonse, just south of the Manitoba South-Western Colonization Railway. Despite this promising but short-lived trend, however, the number of immigrants coming to southern Manitoba in the mid-1880s declined in most areas except Brandon.[29] New

CANADIAN PACIFIC RAILWAY
COMPANY.

Land Explorers
EXCURSION
TO
MANITOBA
AND
NORTH WEST.

THOSE WHO SHOULD GO ARE :

1. Those who want to farm and have no land.
2. Those who have sons to settle.
3. Those who cannot make both ends meet farming here.
4. All those who have $550 or more to settle with.
5. All those who are suffering from Asthma or Bronchial Affections.
6. All those who want to enjoy the nicest kind of a pleasure trip.

THESE EXCURSIONS BEGIN ON
JUNE 26
AND WILL LAST ALL THE SEASON.

Single Fare Tickets from Montreal to any Point at Lowest Prices.

RETURN FARES WILL BE AS FOLLOWS :

Brandon, $34.00.   Oak Lake, $35.30.
Whitewood, $38.70,   Broadview, $39.30.
Regina, $40.00.
Calgary, $64.10.   Canmore, $67.60.

And Other Points at Proportionate Rates.

A SPECIAL GUIDE

Knowing thoroughly all districts of the North West, the Land and its Regulations, will accompany the Excursion. It is the best chance yet offered. No Customs annoyance, no useless expense or trouble. Free Colonist Sleeping Cars. To do the journey at the smallest cost the Explorer should carry his own provisions and a pair of blankets. For all information, and for tickets, apply or write to

COLONIZATION BUREAU,
NEAR C. P. R. STATION, MONTREAL.

We have a better Free Grant Country than any in the United States. If you do not believe, come and see. To see is to believe. We fear no inspection.

EXCURSIONS
DES
EXPLORATEURS DE TERRES
AU
MANITOBA
ET
NORD OUEST
PAR LE PACIFIQUE.

CEUX QUI DEVRAIENT Y ALLER :

1. Tous ceux qui veulent se mettre à cultiver et qui n'ont pas de terre.
2. Tous ceux qui ont des enfants à établir.
3. Tous ceux qui dépensent plus qu'ils ne gagnent, mangent leurs biens malgré tous leurs soins.
4. Tous ceux qui ont $550 ou plus avec lesquelles ils veulent s'établir.
5. Tous ceux qui souffrent de l'asthme ou d'affections des bronches.
6. Tous ceux qui veulent faire le plus beau voyage de plaisir possible.

NOTRE PAYS A L'OUEST EST MEILLEUR

Que l'ouest des Etats Unis et les avantages y sont supérieurs. Si vous ne le croyez pas, venez voir pour vous convaincre.   Venez, voyez, examinez.

LES EXCURSIONS COMMENCERONT
LE 26 JUIN
ET DURERONT TOUT L'ETE.

Les Billets d'Aller de Montreal Seront au Plus Bas Prix.   Ceux de Retour pour

Brandon, $34.00.   Lac des Chenes (Oak Lake),
$35.30.   Whitewood, $38.70.   Broadview, $39.30.   Regina, $40.00.
Calgary, $64.10.   Canmore, $67.60.
ET POUR AUTRES PLACES, PRIX EN PROPORTION.

UN
GUIDE SPECIAL

Connaissant a fond tous les endroits, les terres et les conditions pour s'en emparer, accompagnera le train.   C'est la meilleure chance qui ait jamais été offerte. Il n'y aura pas de droits, de dépenses ni troubles inutiles.   Des Chars Dortoirs seront fournis gratis.   On devrait emporter provisions de bouches et chacun une paire de couvertes.   Pour toutes informations, s'adresser au

Bureau de Colonisation,
PRES DE LA GARE DU PACIFIC, MONTREAL.

settlers coming to the Northwest from Britain and other parts of Europe from 1885 to 1896 did little more than replace the number of English-speaking immigrants who had left Canada for the United States.

CPR tried desperately to reverse the southward flow and boost the number of settlers on the land. Beginning in 1887, the railway offered "Land Explorers Excursions" to Manitoba and the Northwest, largely to entice as many people as possible to relocate from Eastern Canada. "Those who should go," the public postings maintained, "are those who want to farm and have no land, those who have sons to settle, those who cannot make ends meet farming in the East, those who have $550 or more to settle with, all those suffering from asthma or bronchial affections, [and lastly] all those who want to enjoy the nicest kind of pleasure trip."

The relatively cheap excursions offered prospective homesteaders a chance to witness first-hand the potential of the Canadian Prairies while encouraging permanent settlement along the company's railway lines. From Montreal, a return fare to Brandon was as low as $34, to Calgary $63.10.

In 1883, militant settlers had formed the Manitoba and North-West Farmers' Co-operative and Protective Union to lobby the government for fair treatment from the CPR, reductions in the rates for shipping grain, and an end to the railway's monopoly in the West. The group tabled a petition of rights at a convention in Winnipeg that December. Among their grievances, reported in the local papers, were "oppressive duty upon agricultural implements, the monopoly of the carrying trade now enjoyed by the CPR Co. and the improper and vexatious methods employed in the administration of the public lands in Manitoba."[30] Delegates at the convention also advocated for a railway line to Hudson Bay to provide another outlet to market their crops.

The pressure from farmers came to a head in 1887 when the CPR failed to handle a bumper crop of grain satisfactorily, allowing both product and discontent to pile up and fester in Manitoba. The monopoly clause, in particular, was becoming a political nightmare for the railway's standing in the West.

The following year, CPR president George Stephen agreed to the early demise of the offending privilege in return for the federal government's guarantee of interest payments on a substantial new issue of Canadian Pacific securities that would solidify the company's financial and competitive position vis-à-vis its America rivals. This gave the company a sterling credit rating and allowed it to gold plate its facilities and purchase sufficient ancillary equipment to hold its own against other North American transcontinentals. The problematic Clause 15 was removed as an issue.

Just two months earlier, in January 1888, the Manitoba government had changed from John Norquay's Conservatives to Thomas Greenway's Liberals. Norquay's government had recently authorized the construction of yet another rail line from Winnipeg to the US border, to be known as the Red River Valley Railway. Greenway's government, upon winning office, quickly decided to share ownership of the railway with the Northern Pacific, creating a subsidiary of the American company called the Northern Pacific and Manitoba Railway (NP&MR). The CPR was not amused.

About 15 miles (24 km) south of Winnipeg, the NP&MR had to cross the CPR-controlled Manitoba South-Western, which led to the confrontation known to Canadian history as the Battle of Fort Whyte. When the Northern Pacific installed a railway "diamond" to cross over its rival's tracks, Van Horne instructed the CPR's western superintendent, William Whyte, to rip it out. The ensuing standoff between workers mustered by the two railways lasted about two weeks—with the province swearing in special constables and calling out the militia—before the CPR gave in to the inevitable and allowed the new line to cross the Manitoba South-Western.

In the end, the threat to the CPR was a minor one. The NP&MR built a station, freight sheds, repair shops and an engine roundhouse on vacant HBC land north of the confluence of the Red and Assiniboine rivers. The railway was a relatively small operation and generally operated at a loss. A 145-mile (233 km) branch line extending from Morris, on

the Red River, to Brandon was completed in 1889, but the company's financial situation remained shaky. Though the provincial government had set out to lower freight rates on the new line, the reductions offered by the new player were small and, within a few years, differed very little from those offered by the CPR.

Another of the early so-called colonization railways, to which the federal government granted charters in the hope of opening up more of the Prairies to settlement than the CPR could immediately handle, was originally called the Portage, Westbourne & North Western. The railway was chartered to build a line between Portage la Prairie and Yorkton, about 280 miles (450 km) northwest of Winnipeg. Construction began in 1881 and reached Gladstone the following year.

The Portage, Westbourne & North Western was renamed the Manitoba & North Western (M&NW) when the Montreal shipping magnate Hugh Allan purchased a controlling interest in the company. Allan had hopes for extending his railway south to the US border and all the way west to Edmonton, but it was not to be.

Branch lines were built, in 1886 and 1887, from Minnedosa south to Rapid City and from Binscarth north to Russell. Construction work on the M&NW offered an opportunity for settlers in the area to supplement their farm income by engaging in even more hard labour. The M&NW's main line finally made it to its original destination at Yorkton in 1889.

The M&NW received a land grant of 1.4 million acres (566,000 ha), but drought, early frosts, and a depressed world economy conspired to sink the railway's prospects. It also had to deal with expensive operating costs as a result of the steep grades involved in crossing the Little Saskatchewan Valley at Minnedosa and the Assiniboine Valley at Millwood. By 1894, the M&NW was bankrupt. The CPR had a strong hand in the negotiations to take over the railway, particularly as the larger company was supplying the colonization railway with most of its locomotives, rolling stock, and even snowplows. By the turn of the century, the CPR had been successful in purchasing most of the remaining shares of the M&NW.[31]

The M&NW was built through an excellent agricultural region, and the lands granted to the railway before its bankruptcy were of great benefit to the CPR. In 1885, the philanthropist Count Paul Oscar d'Esterhazy had settled fifty Hungarian families on land about 20 miles (32 km) northeast of Minnedosa, not far from the line of the M&NW.

CPR agents operating in the United States had encountered Esterhazy during his involvement to save his compatriots from what he thought to be "a hopeless life in the mining towns" in the anthracite coal regions of Pennsylvania.[32] At the invitation of the railway, he was soon searching the Canadian frontier to establish what he hoped would become "New Hungary." Before the year was out, the count was in the employ of both the CPR and the Canadian government as an immigration agent and had established the Hungarian Immigration and Colonization Aid Society, with headquarters in Pittsburgh.

The first group of thirty-eight families came to Toronto from Hazelton, Pennsylvania, in July 1885, to be followed a month later by an additional twelve families. From there the CPR provided free transportation to Winnipeg and arranged for a land agent to settle the Hungarians on homesteads near Minnedosa, at a place they called Hun's

Count Esterhazy's ambition was to establish "New Hungary" in the Canadian Northwest.

Valley. There they founded the colony of Kaposvar, named after a Hungarian city. The heterogeneous flock of settlers, consisting of Magyars, Slovaks, Ruthenians, Czechs, and South Slavs, was aided by officials of the M&NW, who provided liberal credit to the settlers for purchasing farming implements, cattle, and other necessary supplies.[33] The M&NW also agreed to exchange three of the odd-numbered sections it had been granted in the valley of Stony Creek for lands elsewhere so the Hungarians could settle more closely together, a practice that Canadian Pacific would follow on many occasions for similar reasons.

Later that year, another group of ninety-five families established a second colony of Hungarians on the CPR main line, near Whitewood in the Qu'Appelle Valley, which they called Esterhaz (later Esterhazy). Many in that party worked during the winter on railway construction crews or were employed cutting cordwood for fuel. Stephen, the CPR president, took a special interest in the settlement and advanced $25,000 to the group for farm implements and stock animals. A third Hungarian colony was settled outside the town of Neepawa, aided by the Canadian government and the M&NW. Through hard work, farming in the warm weather and cutting cordwood for sale during the winter months, the settlers were able to pay back the loans extended to them within six years.[34]

The success of the Hungarian settlements prompted the CPR, the Allan Line steamship company, and the federal government to jointly sponsor a representative by the name of Theodore Zboray to travel to Hungary in search of additional colonists. Though Zboray's mission was cut short by his arrest for conducting illegal emigration propaganda, the potential of the Canadian Northwest gradually became known to the various nationalities living within the Austro-Hungarian Empire. A decade later, large waves of Poles, Russians, Austrians, Bukovinians, Galicians, and Ruthenians would begin to arrive from Eastern Europe. Count Esterhazy continued to serve as an immigration agent for the CPR until 1904, and the Hungarian communities that he helped to establish spread to other parts of Saskatchewan as well as to Manitoba and Alberta. Later colonies in the region around Esterhazy would include Swedes, Czechs, Germans, and Welsh.

Joining the pioneer settlers of the 1880s, not far from the count's Hungarians, a group of Scandinavians established a colony near present-day Stockholm, Saskatchewan. They too received substantial financial support from CPR president George Stephen. At the same time, yet another colony, New Scandinavia, was begun 20 miles (32 km) north of Minnedosa. Like the Hungarians, the Swedes, Norwegians, and Finns raised cattle and also grew grain to hedge their bets against adverse economic conditions or bad luck with the weather.

Small-scale German and Ruthenian settlements were established north of Balgonie. Along with favourable transportation arrangements, they received loans from the CPR for farming implements, which they quickly paid off within a couple of years.

Immigrants of predominantly German origin arrived in the region northeast of Esterhazy, around the same time the M&NW was furiously laying track across the prairie with the aid of local cash-strapped homesteaders willing to wield a railway spike maul. Their original settlement was called the Hohenlohe Colony, after Prince Hohenlohe von Langenburg, a German nobleman who travelled through the Northwest three years earlier and subsequently recommended to his wandering countrymen that they emigrate to Canada rather than the United States.[35] The railway station and the town that grew up there were both named Langenburg.

Not far to the west, an Icelandic colony named Thingvalla was begun by a small group of homesteaders. A few received loans from the CPR, but most were able to get by raising sheep and cattle.[36]

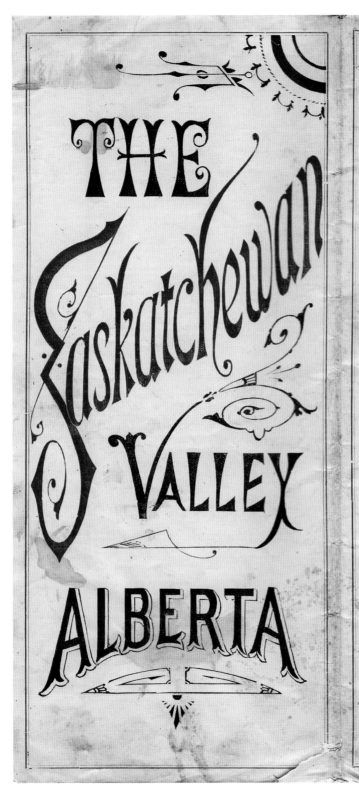

Vast tracts of inexpensive land in the Qu'Appelle and Saskatchewan valleys opened the expansive interior of the Northwest to European settlement. JAMES E. LANIGAN COLLECTION

THE Saskatchewan VALLEY ALBERTA

THE UNDISPOSED OF

C.P.R. LANDS

Shown on this Map of the Saskatchewan Valley are

FOR SALE

at the uniform price of

AN **$3** ACRE

Winnipeg, 4th April, 1892.

L. A. HAMILTON,
Land Commissioner.

Two so-called colonization railways, in particular, would receive massive land subsidies from the federal government: The Qu'Appelle, Long Lake & Saskatchewan Railroad and Steamboat Company and the Calgary & Edmonton Railway. The CPR would control the former during its formative years, before eventually handing it over to its rival, Canadian Northern Railway. It would also quickly absorb the entirety of the latter, which would become Canadian Pacific's most important north-south branch line. The financial firm of Osler, Hammond & Nanton—a concern that had intimate involvements with several of Canadian Pacific's chief officers—would help raise funds for the construction of both the Qu'Appelle, Long Lake & Saskatchewan and the Calgary & Edmonton. The influential financiers would also ensure the quality of lands granted to the two colonization railways by the government and administer the sale of quarter-sections along their lines to prospective settlers.

The Qu'Appelle, Long Lake & Saskatchewan was incorporated in 1883 with a charter to build a line from Regina in the direction of Prince Albert, via Craik, Saskatoon, and Rosthern. Initially, the company suffered from financial problems and only managed to build 25 miles (40 km) of track in its first three years. However, a construction company formed by James Ross, who had managed the building of the CPR through much of the Rockies and Selkirks, along with financier Herbert Holt and railway entrepreneurs William Mackenzie and Donald Mann, completed the line thorough to Prince Albert by 1889. The promotors secured an agreement for CPR to furnish the railway's locomotives and rolling stock. The CPR leased the line the same year.

The Qu'Appelle, Long Lake & Saskatchewan earned a subsidy of more than 1.5 million acres (607,000 ha) but

held out for lands it considered favourable in both location and quality.

The same team of Ross, Holt, Mackenzie, and Mann formed the Calgary & Edmonton Railway Company (C&E) in 1890, with authority to build north from Calgary to a point at or near Edmonton, and south to the international boundary with the United States.

The C&E had two antecedents, neither of which fulfilled their ambitions to build similar lines. The Alberta & Athabasca Railway Company was incorporated by a group of Minneapolis financiers in 1885 to build from the CPR line east of Calgary, across the North Saskatchewan River near Edmonton, and on to Athabasca Landing. When the owners failed to secure the necessary capital, they forfeited land grants that would have given them fifty-five townships along their railway line and twenty additional sections.[37] In 1889, the charter of the Alberta & Athabasca was amended and transferred to accommodate a new company incorporated by James Ross and Andrew Onderdonk, the railway contractor who built the original CPR main line in BC from the West Coast to Craigellachie. As the Alberta & Great Northwestern, the Montreal-based company planned to build its initial rail line from Red Deer to the Peace River District, with ambitious plans to expand. The federal government was ready to award the new company a land grant of 10,000 acres per mile (2,515 ha/km), up to 3 million acres (1.2 million ha), but again the financing fell through.[38]

During this time, a group of Toronto promoters sought a charter for their Chinook Belt & Peace River Railway Company, which they hoped to build from the St. Mary's River in southern Alberta, to Macleod, Calgary, Edmonton, and Peace River, but the Canadian parliamentary

▶ The Honourable Edgar Dewdney, member of parliament for Assiniboia East and former lieutenant-governor of the North-West Territories, turned the first sod for the construction of the Calgary & Edmonton Railway at Calgary, with an appreciative crowd in attendance. LIBRARY AND CULTURAL RESOURCES DIGITAL COLLECTIONS, UNIVERSITY OF CALGARY NA-237-8

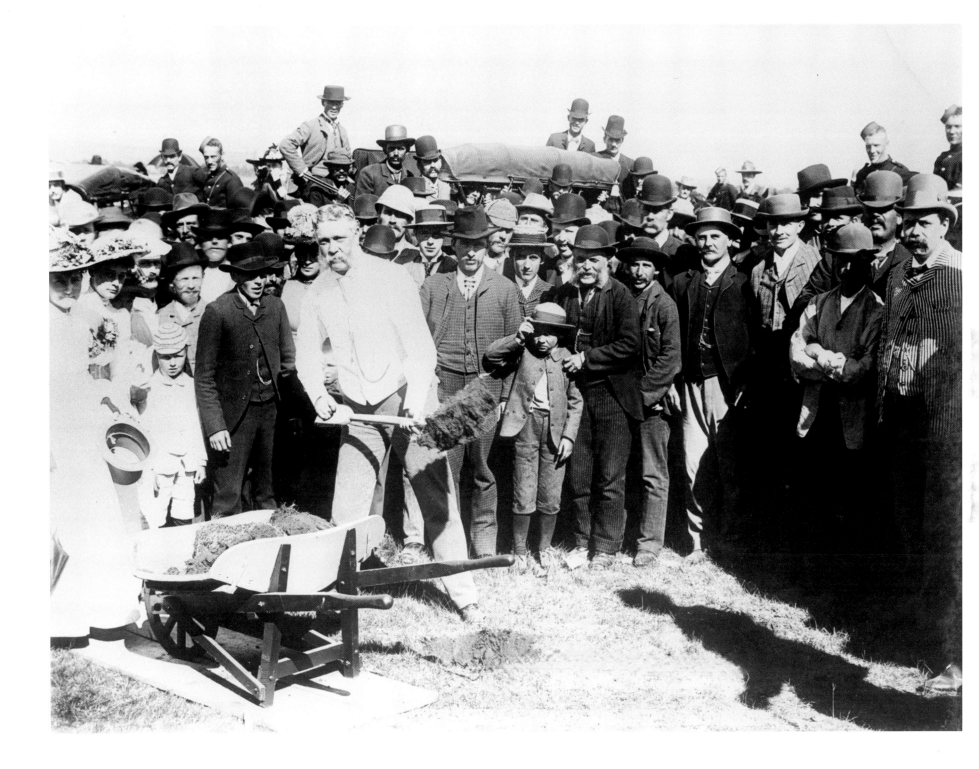

The first train pulled into the CPR terminal in South Edmonton in 1891. It would be several years before the railway would cross the North Saskatchewan River into the downtown area. CITY OF EDMONTON ARCHIVES EA-10-2760

Railway Committee rejected the company's bid in view of the existing charter covering the same territory, held first by the Alberta & Athabasca and then by the Alberta & Great Northwestern.[39]

In February of 1890, the charter of the Alberta & Great Northwestern was officially transferred to the C&E. The new company was nominally independent, but a clause in its charter gave the directors an option to lease or sell the line to the CPR once it was completed. Those in the know did not have to look far beyond the names of the principal builders, along with the close ties the C&E's financiers and land agents—Osler, Hammond, and Nanton—already enjoyed with Canadian Pacific, to see in which direction those options might play out.

"The building of the C&E railway will make our town the most important railway centre now existent, or ever will be, in Canada west of Winnipeg," a Calgary newspaperman enthused.[40] The C&E would be built in "one of the most favoured localities in the Great North-West for immigration, and for the investment of capital in cattle-raising and other industries," Prime Minister John A. Macdonald added to the public record.[41]

The C&E was granted the usual 6,400 acres for every mile (1,609 ha/km) of track it constructed and received $1.6 million in cash to carry federal government personnel, supplies, and mail for twenty years. Within thirteen months, on July 27, 1891, the last spike on the C&E was driven at Strathcona, or South Edmonton, across the North

Saskatchewan River from the town centre. No time was wasted in announcing that the line was on long-term lease to the CPR.

Just after the C&E was finished, a group of five or six hundred homesteaders from Parry Sound, Ontario, came out to establish a colony northeast of Edmonton in the Fort Saskatchewan District. The man largely responsible for inspiring the group to make a mass pilgrimage was Thomas Pearce, an agent of the Canada Landed Credit Company, a subsidiary of the Canadian Pacific Railway Land Company.

Pearce wrote to CPR president William Van Horne to ask for a rate reduction to bring the settlers west but was refused on the grounds of railway fares already being very low for colonists. Undeterred by the rejection, Pearce then prevailed upon David McNicoll, the railway's general passenger agent, who sent out one of his men to speak with the group and assess the situation. The result was two open tickets for Pearce and a companion to examine prospective areas in the West. After riding the C&E to Strathcona, the two representatives accompanied a CPR land agent on a tour of some prime locations. In the end, they chose land northeast of Edmonton.[42]

Among the settlers new to the Edmonton area were Austrian and German families, just to the west, near Stony Plain. Other German, Austrian, and Russian groups settled close to the Parry Sound Colony in the Fort Saskatchewan District. At the same time, the first significant wave of French Canadians transplanted from Quebec arrived in St. Albert northwest of Edmonton. Others would come to Morinville, Beaumont, Saint Pierre, Vegreville, and Stony Plain. Still more German colonists chose to settle in the Rabbit Hills and Wetaskiwin districts to the south. People from the states of Idaho and Washington also favoured the country around Wetaskiwin, arriving there in large numbers during the 1890s.

The once sparsely populated land experienced a rapid period of colonization, now that a ready means to transport people, their supplies, and their produce was available. Where few settlements had existed between Calgary and Edmonton, new communities mushroomed along the tracks. Little more than a year after the opening of the line, Olds, halfway between Calgary and Red Deer, had an immigrant shed, a general store, and a hotel. A group of Swedes from Nebraska took up homesteading there. Not too far to the north, Innisfail had a growing population of more than five hundred, a half dozen stores, two hotels, and Presbyterian and Anglican churches.

In the spring of 1891, the business community in the nascent settlement of Red Deer moved from Red Deer Crossing to a new location near the CPR station on land given to the CPR by Reverend Leonard Gaetz in exchange for the railway creating the new townsite on his property. Gaetz also retained a half interest in the land. One of the first to purchase a lot just outside the townsite—for $3 an acre ($7.41/ha)—was Elias Code, who had come from Beckwith, Ontario, with his wife, six sons, and a daughter.[43] After an inaugural exhibition of the Red Deer Agricultural Society in the town's Wilkins Block the following year, the annual affair was moved to the CPR roundhouse.

By now one of Red Deer's most prominent citizens and a local land agent for the Saskatchewan Land & Homestead Company, Gaetz was a regular contributor of produce to the railway's exhibition car that toured through Eastern Canada and the United States. His fine samples of grain, native and cultivated grasses, and flax were favourably commented on by journalists from the *Nor'-West Farmer*,

THE
Calgary & Edmonton
Railway Company
HAVE NEARLY

2,000,000
ACRES
CAREFULLY SELECTED
FINE AGRICULTURAL LAND
Lying in a Belt about 40 Miles wide along the Eastern Slope of the Rocky Mountains in

ALBERTA
Canadian Northwest,
FOR SALE
AT $2.50 PER ACRE UPWARDS.

No Cultivation
OR
Residence Conditions

The even numbered Sections in this Belt are open for Homestead to Actual Settlers, and as they will all be taken up within the next two years the Company's liberal terms

One Tenth Cash
And the balance, if so desired, in

Nine Annual Payments
With Interest at 6% insure to present purchasers

A Paying Investment.

OSLER, HAMMOND & NANTON
GENERAL AGENTS,
381 Main Street, WINNIPEG.

Left Settlers in Wetaskiwin transload their goods from horse-drawn sleds to CPR boxcars. LIBRARY AND CULTURAL RESOURCES DIGITAL COLLECTIONS, UNIVERSITY OF CALGARY CU1104546

Right The general agents for the C&E were closely affiliated with the directors of Canadian Pacific. AUTHOR'S COLLECTION

the Toronto *Globe,* and the *Toronto Empire.* CPR's European traffic manager, Archer Baker, was suitably impressed by Gaetz while touring railway lands along the C&E, as he reported to the *Canadian Gazette:*

At Red Deer, halfway between Calgary and Edmonton, we met Mr. Gaetz, who had farmed there for ten years. He was rightfully proud of those ten years of labour, as he showed us with evident satisfaction the original hut in which he began prairie life, the improved farm house into which he moved as he got on, and lastly, the prairie mansion, as one must term it, in which he now lives at ease. He was most enthusiastic and showed us samples of grain and roots from his farm, and his yields would be hard to beat, I fancy.[44]

In 1894, two female Scottish journalists, Franziska Marie Imandt and Elizabeth Maxwell, were sent by the *Dundee Courier* to scope out the new territories opened for settlement. They boarded a coach on the newly built C&E, where they encountered "the immigration agent, who travels in the car constantly, and is known by his uniform and badge, his duty being to help all immigrants with advice and practical guidance."[45]

At every station, they stepped down from their train to exchange information on the platform with those they encountered. "It is easy to spot the Englishmen here in the North-West towns and on the ranches," they wrote. "They too often pride themselves on being unkempt, unshorn, decked in coats of many rags, and on having hats of a nature abominably bad." They noted tents erected "at all points where immigrants were likely to rest before proceeding to settle on their allotments" and railway stations along the line "fitted with brawny settlers and decorated with specimens of grain in small glass boxes."[46]

Some of those brawny settlers might have been Moravian immigrants who arrived in Canada weeks before from the province of Volhynia, in western Russia. Members of a religious body known as the Evangelic Brotherhood, the newcomers had been persecuted by the Russian authorities and forbidden to hold property. The CPR had been more than happy to help them find their way to the Canadian Northwest to purchase railway land.

Arrangements were made through local steamship agents for the Russians to board a ship in Libau, on the Baltic Sea, and Canadian Pacific representatives accompanied the nearly one hundred families all the way to an available township in Alberta, northeast of Edmonton. The settlement was named Bruderheim. Until 1914, Libau (modern-day Liepāja, Latvia) was one of the main ports of the Russian Empire and in later years was a busy centre for Eastern European emigration to North America. The Alberta township had been scouted out earlier by Reverend Andreas Lilge, representing the group of about six hundred individuals.[47]

More methodical than the government

An article in the *Manitoba Free Press* toward the end of 1889 described the CPR's extensive efforts in promoting the formation of immigrant colonies throughout the Northwest. Among those mentioned were New Stockholm, the Swedish settlement north of the Qu'Appelle River, near Whitewood Station, and the Roumanian (i.e., Romanian) group at Balgonie. German settlements at Rosenthal and Josephsburg, south of Dunmore, were said to have borrowed $3,000 from Canadian Pacific to get started but had prospered and grown from an original thirty-two settlers to more than four hundred. Other colonies worthy of mention were a Russian Jewish settlement at Wapella, another Swedish group at Fleming, the New Finland community north at Whitewood, a German colony north of Grenfell, and an Icelandic group at Medicine River, north of Calgary.

"Foreign immigrants regard it as an additional inducement to be able to settle among their fellow-countrymen, as they dislike settling among people who do not understand their language or customs," the newspaper reported, "so the Company adopted the plan of forming colonies of the different nationalities, and now the Germans, Swedes, Icelanders, etc., may immediately upon their arrival, go among their own people to take up land."[48]

It was noted that all the settlements had been assisted by Canadian Pacific, though some of them were not founded by the company:

The efforts of the C.P.R. in the matter of settling Manitoba and the North-West has been as great, and probably more methodical, than the government's. It has sent its agents into all parts of Western Europe, through the Eastern Provinces and also through the northern and western states of the neighboring Republic, and its immigration department has been the direct means of settling thousands of people on these northwestern plains. The Company has expended thousands of dollars in advertising the country and exhibiting its products, and is still carrying on the good work.[49]

Through and from the United States

To complete its system, CPR sought a winter port on the Atlantic coast to lessen its dependence on Halifax and the government-controlled Intercolonial Railway. The company's officers were not against purchasing lines to make a connection with Portland, Maine, but the Canadian government and, in particular, Maritimers were absolutely opposed to that option. The Grand Trunk had long used Portland, Maine, as its winter port, and public opinion strongly suggested that the substantial financial and land grants given to the CPR by the Canadian people called for a greater sense of national loyalty on Canadian Pacific's part than following the lead of its older rival.

As an alternative, the CPR cobbled together a number of smaller railways in southern Quebec and northern Maine, with a view to connecting with the New Brunswick Railway and terminating at the Port of Saint John. Dubbed the "Short Line," because of its direct alignment between Montreal and the Maritimes, the work started in 1886 when crews with CP's subsidiary, Atlantic & Northwestern, began to build toward Lennoxville, in Quebec's Eastern Townships.

The CPR acquired the International Railway from Lennoxville to Megantic (now Lac-Mégantic), Quebec, and then formed a separate subsidiary, the International of Maine, to build through that state to the town of Mattawamkeag. CPR then secured trackage rights over the Maine Central to Vanceboro, Maine; from there, its trains could be handled by locomotives and crews of the New Brunswick Railway to Saint John, New Brunswick.[50] In addition, it was necessary for Canadian Pacific to build several short stretches of new track in Quebec and Maine to link up various pieces of this complex line. By June 4, 1889, the CPR was operating a passenger service on the Short Line.

The CPR would take over the New Brunswick Railway in 1890. Eighty-five years would elapse before it was able to purchase the 56 miles (90 km) of track between Mattawamkeag and Vanceboro to achieve full ownership of the route.

The CPR now had a winter port in Saint John, New Brunswick, but it still coveted a connection with nearby Halifax, which provided a much more convenient Atlantic connection with Britain and continental Europe, as it eliminated the need to sail around the southern portion of the Nova Scotia peninsula. For several years, the CPR had been trying to either purchase the Intercolonial Railway or at the very least to get permanent running rights for its trains over that railway's lines. With the building of the line to Saint John, CPR president George Stephen apparently thought he had a deal with the federal government to finalize such a connection for the short stretch between Saint John and Halifax. His whiny missive to Prime Minister Macdonald, shortly after the Short Line was completed, makes that clear:

How deeply I repent the confidence and credulity through which I was cajoled by Tupper [Charles Tupper, prominent Nova Scotian politician] and Pope [Joseph Pope, secretary to the P.M.] to undertake the building of the short line. Anything you can possibly do now to facilitate the C.P.R. reaching Halifax, under the most favourable conditions, can only mitigate the injury to the C.P.R. Company for which I am, to a great extent, personally responsible, by its ever having anything to do with the short line.[51]

The prime minister's response ignored any assurances the CPR might or might not have previously been given by his administration, and framed Stephen's complaints as sour grapes over poor CPR traffic figures at Saint John versus the Intercolonial's at Halifax or, more pointedly, the Grand Trunk's at Portland:

I was rather "irate" on first perusal of your note of the 11th. The charge of unjust treatment of the C.P.R. at my hands, and from you, seemed to me inexplicable—but an angry discussion won't help matters. I shall do my duty to the country according to the best of my judgment, and suffer even the threatened hostility of the company, if need be.

With respect to the short line, I regret that your expectations of traffic have been disappointed. That is no fault of the Government, and will, I hope and believe, be but temporary. The Government must treat the two systems of G.T.R. and C.P.R. with perfect impartiality and equal fairness. Parliament would, I am sure, not permit any other course.[52]

Canadian Pacific never did get permanent running rights over the Intercolonial, though there were periods when that railway handled CPR trains over its lines using its own locomotives and crews, and seasons when Canadian Pacific steamships docked at the Port of Halifax or made calls there after leaving Saint John to cross the Atlantic. Over the years, Canadian Pacific improved the landing and immigrant facilities at Saint John and made do with the slight inconvenience of its location.

Just as important in its implications for Canadian immigration was the emergence of a US railroad that would become Canadian Pacific's most significant subsidiary and provide a couple of well-travelled routes to the Northwest for Americans and repatriated Canadians. The origins of the Minneapolis, St. Paul & Sault Ste. Marie Railroad go back to 1883, when a group of Minneapolis flour millers began to acquire a number of railroad charters to further their business interests. Primarily, they sought to secure a route to transport wheat between Minnesota and the Twin Cities of Minneapolis and St. Paul as well as to ship processed flour to markets in the east through a connection with CPR and Sault Ste. Marie, thereby bypassing the congested railway lines in and around Chicago. The CPR syndicate members and others with connections to the Canadian transcontinental helped finance these efforts, and in 1888, a single company emerged with Canadian Pacific as the principal stockholder.

From its first years of promoting immigration to Western Canada, the CPR looked upon the American Midwest as one of the areas of the world with the most potential for attracting new settlers. Not the least of those were colonists from Britain and northern Europe, who had streamed across the Atlantic over the previous few decades, as well as many former inhabitants of Canada's eastern provinces, who had been lured by the promise of vacant—and easily accessible—agricultural lands in the United Sates.

"The people of the States seldom see more than one Eldorado at a time," Van Horne wrote to Prime Minister Macdonald in 1891. "In late years they have had in turn Minnesota, Nebraska, Kansas, Texas, Dakota and Oklahoma. They have had on the whole bad luck in the last four of these and now have not anyplace to go."[53]

Along with the general impression among new arrivals to North America that the climate in the US was less severe than in Canada, newspaper articles on both sides of the border reported, often erroneously, that the rates for shipping produce to market were much less expensive south of the border. Following a series of items in the Toronto *Globe* criticizing the high cost of shipping wheat from Winnipeg to Liverpool, and a complaint by a Canadian senator that as a result of the economic inequities settlers were moving south in droves, Van Horne responded:

With reference to the item of November 21st to the effect that Minnesota and Dakota are rapidly filling up and largely with Canadians, I will say that I am pretty well acquainted with what is going on in those States, and the increase in settlement in that direction does not begin to compare with that of the Canadian North West. It is an unfortunate fact, however, that a great many people from Ontario and the other eastern provinces of Canada have settled in Minnesota and Dakota but they were influenced to do so mainly by such newspaper articles as you quote from the "Globe": A number of these, however, have picked up and moved over to Manitoba.[54]

At the time, it was a combination of wishful thinking and patriotic posturing from the former American who had embraced his new Canadian homeland with a passion, but in the not-too-distant future, when the best lands in the United States were becoming scarce, the north-to-south trend of settler movement *would* begin to reverse itself.

For their part, the American railroads pursued an aggressive immigration campaign in Eastern Canada, often using the public facilities of their northern counterparts and rivals to do so—as was pointed out to the Canadian minister of the interior by a concerned citizen:

A gentleman who does a great deal of travelling in Ontario and Quebec informs me that it is a strange sight to see the US as a country to settle in, advertised in nearly every Railway office of the C.P.R. and Grand Trunk—great big glaring posters praising up the western States, their lands, minerals, climate, etc., and gushing cheap rates are stuck up all over.[55]

◀ The passenger who held this colonist sleeping car ticket was travelling from Toronto to Boston. JAMES E. LANIGAN COLLECTION

Opposite, left Canadian Pacific ran luxurious new railway cars on its "Chicago Flyer" to that city's World's Fair in 1893. CPR railway equipment on display at the fair won top awards for the company. AUTHOR'S COLLECTION

Opposite, right Joining Canadian Pacific and the federal government at the World's Fair to promote free 160-acre farms was a giant 22,000-pound cheese, shipped in from the Northwest. B.W. KILBURN, LIBRARY AND CULTURAL RESOURCES DIGITAL COLLECTIONS, UNIVERSITY OF CALGARY CU1103423

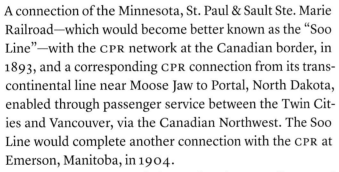

A connection of the Minnesota, St. Paul & Sault Ste. Marie Railroad—which would become better known as the "Soo Line"—with the CPR network at the Canadian border, in 1893, and a corresponding CPR connection from its transcontinental line near Moose Jaw to Portal, North Dakota, enabled through passenger service between the Twin Cities and Vancouver, via the Canadian Northwest. The Soo Line would complete another connection with the CPR at Emerson, Manitoba, in 1904.

The CPR was soon offering US immigrants a flat rate of five dollars to all points in the Canadian West. The company's land agents also arranged free transportation for any delegates of American farming communities who wanted to take a look at what its northern neighbour had to offer, including the many free homestead lands still available in what the publicists would soon be calling the "Last Best West."

One of the best opportunities for showcasing the merits of the Northwest was the 1893 World's Fair in Chicago. The exhibition's Transportation Building, featuring the "Railways of the World," prompted the CPR to upstage all of its American competitors. Its display included a locomotive, tender, and several coaches, and dining and sleeping cars, brought to life from the drawing board of the company's renowned architect, Edward Colonna, every part constructed in the railway's erecting shops in Montreal. The upstart Canadian railway won an award for "excellence of design and construction of a handsome transcontinental passenger train, having special features of merit in its colonists' sleeping cars."

In the Agricultural Palace, a building that was said to be crowded with farmers and their wives, sons, and daughters from early morning until dark, samples of produce from many points along the CPR line were featured prominently. There was wool from Indian Head, a buffalo robe, and an artistic Mexican saddle from Hutchings & Riley in Calgary, grains and fine flour from various mills, and a full collection of stuffed Northwest game and wild animals.[56]

Agents of both the federal government and the CPR met trains routinely upon their arrival in Canada to take charge of immigrants and provide assistance and advice. "The newcomer need not fear that when he reaches Winnipeg he will fall into the hands of thieves, imposters or unfriendly people," CPR literature insisted. "If he follows the directions of this pamphlet, he will put himself in the hands of real friends who will look after him."[57]

The *Calgary Herald*, noting that immigration from the US for 1892 and 1893 had been "very considerable," found that many of the Americans were thoroughly satisfied with the benefits they found in Canada. "The roads and bridges are made for us by the northwest government, the railways are built by the aid of the Dominion government, causing no special tax to fall on the locality," said one newcomer, who apparently found the tax regime back home onerous. "If such a state of things as this existed in any part of the United Sates the people there would think they were in clover."[58]

The settler experience

The checkerboard pattern of settlement set out by the Dominion Lands Survey System made the marketing and selection of lands fairly easy, but it also posed some vexing problems that stalked the everyday lives of pioneer homesteaders. In the early years of migration to Manitoba and the Northwest, not surprisingly, there was a rush for the free government lands. Initially, one 160-acre (65 ha) government quarter section would be taken up by a settler, surrounded by three other unclaimed homesteads. Even when all four free homesteads in an even-numbered section had been occupied, on all sides would be vacant CPR lands, alternating in that way through township after township.

"It made the development of a district higgledy-piggledy," said one early settler, "like you had a checkerboard as a land development and you settled only on the black squares. Oh, you could graze on the C.P.R. land, and the Hudson Bay land, but it made for a rather disjointed way of building up a community."[59]

Decades later, Van Horne observed that the largest buildings in both Western Canada and the western American states had often been insane asylums. "I believe that isolation has had more to do than anything else with filling them," he wrote to Rudyard Kipling, who at the time was seeking advice while working on a settlement project in South Africa. "It does not matter so much to the man that his nearest neighbor is a mile or more away, for he is out all day with his work, but it matters much to the woman who eats out her soul in her loneliness."[60]

Both the railway and the government realized the benefits of being flexible with the standard checkerboard survey of the lands. In many cases, the CPR relinquished its odd-numbered sections for units of equal area and value elsewhere, so that colonists could establish communities that were more compact and communal than would have been possible if only the government homestead lands—on the even sections—had been available to them.

Many settlers came to the Northwest with at least small contingents of others of the same nationality and place of origin, often sharing resources such as farm implements and manpower to get established in a foreign environment. Shared experience and a fierce determination to improve their lot despite their differences could often bring disparate groups together for the common cause of survival. Joining together in various associations, casually and formally, the pioneer settlers' trials and tribulations forged the beginnings of both Western community and Western alienation.

Winters were particularly bad for the lone homesteading pioneer in his rough-hewn cabin or sod hut, with little to do apart from the maintenance of any livestock he might have or small repairs to his shelters. With no other settlers on the same government section, chances are your nearest neighbours were at a fair distance. Bachelors and others living by themselves had nothing for company but the occasional antelope that flitted across the plain during the day or the coyotes that howled mournfully through the night. One traumatized pioneer recalled,

The loneliness Is beyond belief or description ... I experienced solitude such as I never dreamed could exist. At first the illusion that I was haunted seized me only at night, and I sat up at night after night nervous, completely unstrung and so fearsome that every noise was terribly magnified. But that was Heaven to what came afterward when I used to hear my name shouted from the sky at clear noonday while I walked out of doors, and it was not only my name but frightful warnings came to my ears and I took to talking and laughing and shouting to give myself company.[61]

In some districts, settlers arriving in the Northwest to break ground were said to have brought with them so many dogs for company that the animals outnumbered the men. Even an unwanted cat could fetch a settler two to five dollars from some poor soul, so desperate were the pioneers for any companionship whatsoever. That's if you could find one. In the early years of settlement, cats were extremely scarce. Those who had them were keeping them, and in most towns, you couldn't find one to buy at any price.[62]

An early pioneer remembered an instance when a birdcage was knocked out of the hands of a woman during a scramble for a train at Brandon, while another recalled her first real view of the prairies occurred during an 85-mile (137 km) buggy ride north from the CPR station at Broadview with a canary in a cage on her lap. At times, settlers would arrive at their new home with a full menagerie. The Hislop family came to Moosomin in April 1883 with two horses, four cows, three sheep, a little white sow, a dog, a cat, eleven hens, and a rooster.[63]

Some even blamed the rush to build the transcontinental railway, far out in front of the nation's ability to populate the new lands that were opened for exploitation, for the ensuing sparse settlement, and worse, as one newspaperman lamented during the resistance of Indigenous Peoples in 1885 in the Northwest:

The events of the past few days in the North-West prove unhappily too well how great was the folly of hastening the construction of the railroad, and thus causing the people to form scattered settlements along its whole length. If today the settlements extended only a few hundred miles from Winnipeg, there would probably be no rebellion; or if there were, it would not be so formidable.[64]

Successful homesteaders on government lands, or those with deep pockets, often enhanced their holdings by purchasing adjacent lands from the railway, gradually increasing the density of settlement. Prices often varied depending on the condition of the soil, proximity to services and other factors,

but while the railway was under construction, CPR land was usually available for $2.50 Canadian per acre ($1 per ha) or 10 shillings. Within a few years, a uniform price of $3 per acre ($1.21 per ha) was established for the lands the railway had accepted within the first 400 miles (644 km) west of the Red River and $2.50 per acre ($1 per ha) in the mountains and beyond.

The Department of the Interior was also notorious for being inordinately slow in processing homestead documents, sometimes taking two or three years between the time a settler fulfilled his obligations and the awarding of official title. In the interim, it was next to impossible for the settler to sell or lease the land or to borrow money using the land as collateral.[65]

The railway company's practice of being very fastidious about choosing only land that was "fairly fit for settlement," as its charter had allowed, remained controversial with the chattering classes, but found favour with those who had to eke out a living from their holdings. "This is a most unfortunate occurrence for the country," said one federal politician, when the CPR accepted a mere 5 million acres (2 million ha) of its 25-million-acre (10 million ha) land grant along the main line in the Northwest, "and all the damage that will ensue from it is the direct consequence of the gross blunder made by the Dominion Government two years ago when the southern diversion was sanctioned."[66]

As a result of the CPR's attention to accepting only sections with the most agricultural potential, however, the land department had very few unhappy settlers among its purchasers, unlike this homesteader on government lands, who apparently was less than satisfied with some of the offerings:

What throws a lot of people off is the word "prairie." Miles and miles and days and days of flat fertile land, like a pool table. Horsefeathers. There are ranges of hills on the prairies. You can go through miles of what would be called desert in California and Arizona. It's still there too. Sandy soil. Rocky soil. Light soil. Hills and valleys, deep trenches, gulleys, coulees. The badlands. Hundreds of square miles of badlands. Land too light for farming, land which is semi-arid just as the Arctic is, just as the lands in Africa you're reading about today are. Unfit for human population.[67]

In an attempt to counter the strong pull the United States exerted over potential emigrants, publications distributed in Britain by both the Canadian government and the CPR emphasized Canada over the US as a more desirable destination. "Law and order prevail everywhere," a guide for intended settlers informed its readers about life in the Dominion, "and he [the British settler] will enjoy a sense of security, both of life and property, which he may fail to realize in some parts of the United States, where respect for the law is only nominal, men's passions unrestrained, and acts of violence of frequent occurrence."[68]

Artisans, industrial workers, and other city dwellers were not courted, as they were considered to be too soft for the harsh life of a pioneer frontiersman. Rural folks and those involved in agricultural pursuits, however, were looked upon as more self-reliant and much more likely to make a go of it. Those were found more in the far western areas and northern regions of the United Kingdom: Wales, Ireland, and Scotland. They were the target audience for the travelling immigration agents representing the Canadian government and the CPR.

The *Lethbridge News,* in 1893, outlined for its readers why Canada was an attractive destination for a UK citizen with the right background: "To the tenant farmer of Great Britain," it instructed, "the West offers free homesteads, good markets, civil and religious liberty under the protection of the same old flag which has sheltered them in the past ... No class or creed distinctions exist, and merit alone is the stepping stone to promotion and positions of trust and responsibility."[69]

Land agents and propagandists from the United States had been scouring these same lucrative regions for several decades and the pickings of good settler stock were becoming scarce. In response many in Canada spoke up for increased efforts to attract immigrants from Germany, Scandinavia, and Russia.

"Tens of thousands of Russians are now immigrating annually to the United States," wrote Frimann B. Anderson, an early advocate for increased Canadian immigration. "The Germans in that county are estimated at thirteen millions, and the Scandinavians are numbered at about two millions. In Canada, the German population is not one quarter of a million, and the Scandinavians not ten thousand."[70]

Other countries besides Canada and the United States were also vying for British and northern emigrants with agricultural experience, among them Argentina, Australia, New Zealand, India, and South Africa. But there were still serious prejudices among Canadians, not least of which were held by new arrivals from Britain.

"Suitable land is not the only thing a man wants when he is making up his mind to settle in a new country," cautioned Ernest Elkington, a xenophobic colonist from the

Old Country. "Many a man has unwittingly planted himself on a section of land and found that none but Finns, Dukhobors and Galicians surround him for miles."[71]

In particular, there was a general—though usually unspoken—boycott of Eastern Europeans: Ukrainians, Poles, Romanians, Slovenians, Ruthenians, and Galicians. When agents representing the CPR assisted the emigration of a large group of Russian Jews to the Northwest, the company was criticized in Western newspapers for diluting the country's racial purity with "a people whose filthy habits and usurious character have made them detested in the country from which they come ... the very dregs of the most ignorant and barbarous country in Europe."[72]

Whatever their origins, most farm people felt the cost of manufactured goods, especially agricultural tools, was too high in the West. Freight rates were deemed excessive, while the railway's monopoly was regarded as a yoke around the neck of the workingman that left him at a competitive disadvantage vis-à-vis his counterparts in the eastern provinces. And perhaps most annoyingly of all, the relatively small and scattered populations throughout Manitoba and the Northwest ensured that their collective political influence, particularly at the federal level, was marginal at best.

Living in proximity to the railway helped with some of these issues, however. Where most farm implements and stock animals had come from the US before the completion of the CPR, it was now more common and generally less expensive to purchase the same items in Ontario. Food such as wild game, garden produce, grains, and fruits could be obtained locally. Sugar, syrup, salt, baking soda, tea, and coffee arrived at the railway station on the daily express trains, as did other essentials such as cloths, boots, drugs, and often fuel. Money could be made from selling eggs, milk, and vegetables to the townspeople, but serious wages could best be earned by hiring on with a large farming operation, road building, or—yes—signing with the CPR to pound in spikes or string telegraph wires.

While the most important requirement for a viable farmstead was to be close to a rail line, other critical factors were the availability of water and a fuel source. If your property was not located on a river or lake, you could perhaps get water from a slough, subject to boiling it before ingesting it, of course. Or you might dig a well to ensure a permanent and clean source of drinking water. A ready supply of wood meant you could both build a house and have a steady supply of fuel for cooking and heating. Out on the open plain, you might have to build your first home from prairie sods, until such a time as you could import lumber on the railway from Ontario or BC.

Pioneer settlers generally lived on an insufficient diet, depending on their ability to hunt and quickly establish a vegetable garden. If you were lucky enough to live close to a railway divisional point and had some income to take care of your basic requirements, you could probably supplement your dietary needs from a general store in town, or splurge on the occasional meal from the CPR dining hall. These railway centres were also the most likely places to find a doctor, either a Mounted Police medical officer or a general practitioner hired by the CPR to tend to the various ailments and accidents to which railway workers were prone.

For the most part, settlers stayed in reasonable health by sharing what they had or by living on what they could kill or grow. Lack of proper sanitation, however, could lead to health problems or even death. Outbreaks of typhoid would occasionally occur, as happened in the fall of 1888 when fifteen cases were recorded in Swift. Current.[73] The next year, diphtheria claimed the lives of two small children

► The first car in Medicine Hat was owned by a CPR medical officer, Dr. C.E. Smith, seen here with his wife and two children in 1905. LIBRARY AND CULTURAL RESOURCES DIGITAL COLLECTIONS, UNIVERSITY OF CALGARY CU185907

HOMESTEAD REQUIREMENTS	COST
One yoke of oxen	$120.00
Five cows	$175.00
One wagon	$70.00
Ox harness	$10.00
Cook stove and pipes complete	$28.00
One plow double share	$27.00
Small tools	$30.00
Four-roomed house	$250.00
Stable	$45.00
Extra lumber	$10.00
Preparing 20 acres of land	$80.00
Seed	$25.00
Provisions	$100.00
Poultry	$5.00
Pigs	$10.00
Homestead fee	$10.00
Locating and incidental charges	$25.00
Mower	$60.00
Harrows	$15.00
Binder twine	$5.00
One third share in binder	$45.00
TOTAL	$1,145.00

of Mr. and Mrs. J.T. Barker, managers of the dining hall in that town.[74]

In 1894, CPR land commissioner Lauchlan Alexander Hamilton sent Van Horne a detailed list of what a farmer needed to get properly established on a homestead and what the corresponding costs were to obtain those items:

This, he said, would make a total of $1,145, leaving a margin of $355 to provide against misfortune and interest on loans, and requiring the prospective settler to invest an overall sum of $1,500.

"I have enumerated oxen and not horses, because it is very difficult for farmers unless they have plenty of means to start with horses," Hamilton wrote. "The horses would require to be fed grain through the winter and are very likely to be taken sick, and the oxen can eventually when the farmer is in a position to buy horses be sold off for beef."[75]

When the "free" government lands became scarcer along the transcontinental main line as the nineteenth century came to a close, the railway's own lands would become increasingly valuable. While many had issues with the CPR because they were captive to the railway's rates and services, some also held the company in grudging respect, as one old-timer reflected:

Remember not everybody was homesteading, filing a 10-buck bet that he could beat the government on a homestead. Thousands bought good C.P.R. land at very, very reasonable prices and very happy many of them were with the terms and the treatment from the mighty monster of the West, that's what it has been called; very happy they were with their deal. They thought … my own grandfather did for that matter, he thought he was really putting one over on the company … I realize that these railroad big shots were a bunch of pirates. Should have been sailing the Spanish Main. But remember this, they got the job done.[76]

The empire's granary

The CPR promoted mixed farming for settlers trying to establish a permanent footing in the Northwest, as that pursuit did not require all of one's eggs to be put into a single basket, as it were. For many pioneer farmers, however, a good crop of wheat would be the best bet for generating a steady and reliable income. In a few short years, their bumper crops of this "staff of life" would be prized around the world and put the gold in the Golden Northwest.

In May 1883, jurisdiction of the railway line from Port Arthur to Winnipeg was finally transferred from the Dominion government to Canadian Pacific. The company had waited impatiently for the track to be brought up to an acceptable standard for safe and efficient train operations, and little had been done in the way of building things like sidings, station and freight sheds, yards, and engine facilities. In the end, the government had accepted the railway's offer to complete the task in return for an appropriate, agreed-upon payment of $940,000. A little more than a month later, CPR had the line up and running for scheduled passenger service. More importantly, the railway could now move grain to market entirely within Canada.[77]

Before the arrival of the CPR, the principal mode of transport in and out of the Northwest was by steamboat on the Red River between Winnipeg and Fisher's Landing in Minnesota, and from there eastward by the US railway network. The first harvest of export grain, 857 bushels of Red Fife wheat, had been shipped from Manitoba to markets in Ontario in the fall of 1876. The following year, Winnipeg farmers had upped their exports to 20,000 bushels of the hardy wheat, and they were getting as much as 80 cents per bushel in Toronto for their efforts.[78]

Red Fife was developed as early as 1842 by Ontario farmer David Fife, and its properties were extremely well suited to the soil conditions and prevailing temperatures to be found in the Canadian West. Its most important feature was that it could ripen fully within 120 days, within the short frost-free window afforded by the climate on the northern prairies.

SAMPLE
No. 1 HARD WHEAT
(RED FYFE),
FROM THE
CANADIAN NORTH-WEST,
ALONG THE LINE OF THE
CANADIAN PACIFIC RAILWAY,
On Land extending from 400 to 800 miles
West of Winnipeg, Manitoba.

Even before the railway's main line was completed, CPR allowed anybody willing to build grain warehouses or large storage sheds on railway land to transport building supplies for that purpose at half the usual freight rate. In the fall of 1883, railway workers loaded prairie grain by cart and wheelbarrow from a temporary warehouse in Port Arthur onto the steam barge *Erin*, owned by the Conlon Brothers of Thorold, Ontario. The *Erin*'s historic cargo was bound for Buffalo, on its way to markets overseas.[79]

Van Horne, the CPR's general manager at the time, was already engaged in a one-man campaign to ensure that wherever possible new grain "elevators," like those that had been developed and were now quite common in the United States, would quickly replace warehouses in most locations. Unlike mere storage sheds, grain elevators held the distinct advantage of allowing buyers to keep wheat in transit separated by grade and relatively free of contaminants. Grain mixtures or grains damaged or uneven in quality were valued at little more than would normally be paid for the lowest grade.

To hasten the upgrade to elevators, Van Horne offered free rent to any person who wanted to build one of the new facilities on railway grounds. If municipalities in the Northwest wanted to erect and operate elevators for the public good, CPR would "transport over its own line free of charge all materials used in the original construction of the buildings."[80]

CPR towns across the system were assessed for their business potential and designated for buildings with a minimum bin capacity of ten, fifteen, or twenty thousand bushels. "The small size for such stations as Niverville, High Bluff, Marquette, etc., the medium for such as Carberry, Virden, etc., and the large size for Brandon, Portage la Prairie, etc.," Van Horne instructed his building crews. In a letter to the editor of the *Manitoba Free Press*, the railway boss laid out his arguments for elevators versus warehouses:

The elevators are provided with separate bins for the different kinds and grades of grain and with cleaning apparatus, and are able to handle grain more cheaply and to get much more value out of it than can be done by means of a warehouse, and I feel sure that every farmer, who has had experience with both systems, will agree with me that, notwithstanding the occasional abuse of their opportunities by the elevator men, the elevators benefit the producer as well as the carrier and should be encouraged and protected, and it is only by prohibiting the flat warehouses that we can secure elevators.[81]

The CPR contracts required the elevator operators to receive, store, and load grain at reasonable rates without discriminating against any grower. The rate in 1883 was two cents per bushel, as low as anywhere in the Western US.[82]

While the CPR was contracting steam barges to move grain from the Lakehead, the railway's bridge and building gangs were erecting an enormous grain elevator at Port Arthur. Dubbed "The King," its bins could hold 350,000 bushels of grain. When operating at capacity, it could unload nine railway boxcars simultaneously.

In 1884, Canadian Pacific's three new Clyde-built lake steamships—the *Algoma*, *Athabasca*, and *Alberta*—arrived in Port Arthur and were put into service moving passengers and freight between Owen Sound and the Lakehead. They would greatly improve the railway's ability to move large volumes of grain. The first wheat from the Northwest to be shipped overseas by the all-Canadian route was handled by Canadian Pacific that year. Brought across the prairies in freight cars and by lake boat to Owen Sound, the grain was again moved by train to Montreal, where it was loaded aboard an ocean steamship bound for Glasgow, Scotland.

By the end of the 1884 shipping season, the CPR had completed the large new Elevator A, with a capacity of 1.2 million bushels of grain, on the banks of the Kaministiquia River in Fort William (combined with Port Arthur, now Thunder Bay). A considerable amount of dredging was required to allow the schooner *Slidge* to load the first seventeen thousand bushels the following spring, followed shortly by the *Algoma* taking on a full load. That season alone, the CPR would move more than 1.5 million bushels of grain to market, and the numbers would continue to grow.

To manage its burgeoning presence in the grain storage and transportation business, CPR hired Matthew Sellers, formerly of the Northern Elevator Company of Toronto, as its superintendent of elevators. Among his many duties, Sellers acted as grain inspector, shippers' agent, and vessel

agent, becoming one of the busiest and most respected officials in the business.[83]

In 1887, grain growers experienced the best harvest that Manitoba and the Northwest had ever known. Fields that were estimated to yield 25 bushels per acre (10 per ha) were producing forty and more. In Brandon, Red Fife wheat was earning farmers as much as 48 to 51 cents a bushel. The CPR was hard pressed to move more than 12 million bushels of marketable wheat to the Lakehead and earned the scorn of growers by running short of railway rolling stock to move the vast build-up at some locations.[84]

To keep up with the rapid growth in the industry, the CPR built four more large elevators on the Kaministiquia, beginning with Elevator B in 1889, which had a capacity of 482,000 bushels, and Elevator C with a capacity of 1,195,000 bushels the following year. The first three Fort William elevators gave the railway a combined storage capacity of a little more than 2,700,000 bushels. By 1897, Elevator D, the CPR's first all-steel grain storage facility, and Elevator E, which was an annex to the company's Elevator B, added an additional 1.5 million bushels and 1.9 million bushels respectively to the storage capacity at the Lakehead.[85]

In 1880, there were already twenty flour mills in Manitoba and the North-West Territories in various locations from Emerson to Battleford. A decade later, with railway facilities available to handle the movement of both grain and processed flour, that number exceeded forty. A.W. Ogilvie & Company, a major eastern milling firm, became a key player, building a flour mill in Winnipeg in 1881 and erecting its first Canadian grain elevator at Gretna, Manitoba.

In 1885, the Ogilvie company exported a small quantity of flour to Scotland—a trial shipment of grain from the

◀ By the turn of the twentieth century, the railway had built five new grain elevators along the Kaministiquia River in Fort William (with Port Arthur, now Thunder Bay), with combined storage capacity of several million bushels. AUTHOR'S COLLECTION

▶ At the east end of the CPR's transportation conveyor belt for grain were the company's elevators at the Port of Montreal. NOTMAN PHOTOGRAPHIC ARCHIVES, MCCORD STEWART MUSEUM 79155140

Northwest—and as a result of its positive reception, the company received a request from the British Army and Royal Navy to supply half a million dollars' worth of their product. Unfortunately, it was a much larger order than they were able to fill at the time.[86]

That same year, Alexander Begg, CPR's general emigration agent in Europe, confirmed the enormous interest that Northwest wheat was generating on the English market, as conveyed to him by the proprietor of industry journal, *The Miller*. He informed Van Horne of the developments:

It appears that this gentleman sent out some time ago samples of Manitoba wheat to a number of the millers in this country, and he shows me many replies the general tenor of which were the highest recommendation possible of the wheat and an expression of regret that it was not obtainable in his market, some replies even going so far as to suggest that it might be a good thing for several millers to combine and send out an agent to purchase on their behalf...

Mr. Dunham is quite certain that if what he calls Manitoba No. 1 hard wheat can be introduced to the millers of this country there will be a large demand for it at good prices and he suggested very strongly my having some agent to work up the matter on this side.[87]

Of course, this appeal was beyond Begg's station to arrange, but the CPR agent assured Dunham that he would lay those opinions before Van Horne, who "takes a lively interest in the success of settlers along our line" and would pursue the matter strongly.

In 1888, a group of investors opened a major flour mill in Keewatin (now part of Kenora), Ontario, to take advantage of western grain production and the CPR's ability to move it to market efficiently. Among the original shareholders of the Lake of the Woods Milling Company were the railway's senior officers, George Stephen and William Van Horne. With a peak daily production of turning 62,000 bushels of wheat into 10,000 barrels of flour, at the time it was possibly the largest flour mill in the British Commonwealth. The flour was marketed under the name Five Roses, which would soon become a world-famous brand.

By 1890, there were 90 grain elevators and 103 warehouses operating at 63 points on CPR lines in Manitoba and the Northwest. At the turn of the century, that number had blossomed to 410 elevators and 116 warehouses at 192 delivery points. Much of that development was the result of Canadian Pacific's standard elevator policy and generous terms for the development of local facilities.[88]

Top The English and European markets took enormous interest in grain grown in the Canadian Northwest. AUTHOR'S COLLECTION

Bottom Senior CPR officers George Stephen and William Van Horne were key investors in the Lake of the Woods Milling Company, a major flour mill in Keewatin (now part of Kenora), Ontario. AUTHOR'S COLLECTION

▸ In very short order, hundreds of grain elevators were operating at points all up and down CPR railway lines in the Northwest. Some towns, like Indian Head, shown here, sported several of these prairie sentinels. NOTMAN PHOTOGRAPHIC ARCHIVES, MCCORD STEWART MUSEUM 025-430

6

THE TWENTIETH CENTURY BELONGS TO CANADA

The Sifton era

In the 1891 federal election, Wilfrid Laurier's Liberals had campaigned on a policy of reciprocity, or unrestricted free trade with the United States. William Van Horne, the CPR's president, who was born an American but was now a fervent Canadian nationalist, believed that would hurt both the country and the CPR.

"I am well enough acquainted with the trade and industries of Canada to know that unrestricted reciprocity would bring prostration and ruin," he stated bluntly in a letter to Conservative senator George Drummond that was published in the *Montreal Gazette*. The CPR, he claimed, "has built up or been instrumental in building up hundreds of new industries in the country, and it is the chief support of many of them."[1] Van Horne felt the Liberal trade policy would ruin Canada's manufacturing, make New York the distribution point for the Dominion at the expense of Toronto and Montreal, and "make Eastern Canada the dumping ground for the grain and flour of the Western States, to the injury of our Northwest."[2]

The CPR was a strong proponent of the federal Conservative party that had worked hand in hand with the company to build the transcontinental line and more than once had come to the rescue with additional loans to see the "national dream" through to completion. But despite their close relationship with John A. Macdonald's government, the CPR's founding fathers had, for the most part, tried to avoid the appearance of meddling in politics. Whether the company's outspoken advocacy for the Conservation position in the 1891 election was an important factor or not, Macdonald's death later that year would strip the railway of its greatest parliamentary asset.

By the time the next general election was called five years later, Van Horne was able to resign himself to the changing political landscape. "I am doing my best to keep on the fence," he told Laurier, with whom he was on friendly terms, "although it turns out to be a barbed wire one."[3] The victory of Laurier's Liberals in the national poll would mark the end of the CPR's political honeymoon years. A new chapter was dawning for the settlement of the Northwest.

The new federal government would benefit from a promising upturn in the economy that was driven by a number of diverse factors. The devastating droughts of the early and mid-1890s were over, and the price that farmers could get for their grain relative to the cost of transporting it to market had leveled off at a much more advantageous

ratio than had been the case since they put their first crops into the ground. Red Fife wheat, which was broadly planted across the prairie, matured within the West's short growing season, thereby eliminating the frost damage that had brought so much discouragement and economic loss to the pioneer growers before the 1860s. The dry years had also led to the introduction of dry farming techniques suitable to areas prone to light rainfall.

For fifteen years, the CPR had struggled to put settlers on properties along its main line and branch lines. The company had long resigned itself to make it a priority to put homesteaders on free government lands, to boost the value of its own holdings, and to put life-giving traffic onto its railway. Where possible, individual settlers had been favoured over speculators and those who would acquire

and hold on to large tracts of land for future gain. Though the price for an acre of railway land had risen from $2.50 to $5 ($6.18/ha to $12.36/ha), a down payment of $1.25 was the full price if the land was under cultivation within five years. In effect, this meant that a speculator would pay four times as much for land as a bona fide settler. The value CPR placed on productive farmers along its lines was demonstrated by the lengths to which the company would go to keep them on their properties during hard times, including postponed payments and cancelled interest on their land contracts.

Drought, economic depression, and strong competition for immigrants from the US had conspired to keep land sales modest, as did the slow pace of government surveying. Revenues from the railway's land grants had not lived up to the expectations of the company's officers, and homestead entries had, in general, been unsatisfactory to both the CPR and the federal government. James Hedges, in his comprehensive study of Canadian Pacific's land and colonization policies, expressed both the frustration and the determination of the company that had single-handedly taken on the settlement of the Canadian West:

Large sums of money had been expended in the cause of immigration but, in the main, the period which closed in 1896 was void of results at all commensurate with the efforts and means employed. It was a discouraging business, this settling of a frontier country… The railway, however, must stand or fall, prosper or decline with the settlement and development of its country, and there could be no turning back.[4]

Hot on the heels of the election victory of the federal Liberals in 1896, a significant player from Manitoba politics arrived on the national scene. A main plank in the platform of the Laurier government was to accelerate the development of the Northwest with an aggressive program of railway expansion and competition to the CPR's near monopoly, coupled with an energetic and broad focus on peopling Canada's vast prairies. Leading the charge would be Laurier's minister of the interior, and the man who would be responsible for immigration and the settlement of the Northwest: Clifford Sifton.

Sifton was born in Arva, Canada West (now Ontario), in 1861. His father, John, was a railway contractor who received contracts to build two sections of the Canadian Pacific Railway when it was still a project of the federal government.

Clifford first came to prominence when he was elected to the Manitoba Legislature from Brandon North in the

government of Thomas Greenway, the Manitoba Liberal party that opposed CPR's monopoly in the West and the accompanying high freight rates that they blamed on the railway's too-cozy relationship with Prime Minister Macdonald's Conservative government. As Manitoba's attorney general and lands commissioner, Sifton championed the cause of increased railway competition. Significant among his moves was the introduction of a new system of financing railway construction, in which the Manitoba government guaranteed the principal and interest on railway bonds, making new investment far less risky. He worked closely with railway contractors Donald Mann and William Mackenzie to facilitate the building of the Lake Manitoba Railway and Canal Company, in direct competition with the CPR, which ultimately would be the beginning of the Canadian Northern Railway system.[5]

Ironically, when Sifton came to Ottawa with Laurier's Liberals, he embraced the main tenets of John A. Macdonald's National Policy, including protective tariffs, railway expansion, and settlement of a productive agricultural population in the Northwest.

Van Horne had recommended Sifton to Prime Minister Laurier. The CPR president respected Sifton's organizational abilities and thought that a strong personality was needed to clean out the cobwebs in the ministry of the interior. It was apparently a view shared by Sifton, judging by the minister's own description of his new fiefdom: "A department of delay, a department of circumlocution, a department in which people could not get business done, a department which tired men to death who undertook to get any business transacted with it."[6]

In 1897, Sifton was instrumental in negotiating an agreement with Van Horne that enabled the railway to build

a second line through the mountains of British Columbia to later reach the West Coast. The CPR branch line known as the Crow's Nest Pass Railway gave Canadian Pacific a cash subsidy of $3.3 million and access to the lucrative mining districts in the BC interior in return for reduced rates for shipping grain and flour east and manufactured goods west, both of which benefitted settlers.

The provision in the Crow's Nest Pass Agreement to maintain the new rates in perpetuity would soon become a millstone around the railway's neck, giving shippers freight rates that for decades to come were well below what the railway required to recover its costs. Initially, the reductions were not a hardship on the railway, yielding a modest profit in the first decade of the line's operation, but the statute stated specifically "that no higher rates than such rates or tolls shall be hereafter charged by the Company between the points aforesaid," regardless of inflated costs and price levels. In time, that crippled the railway's ability to make a profit on the movement of a wide variety of products, notably grain.[7] As a result, the CPR was often hard pressed to invest in new locomotives and freight cars for that traffic.

Sifton's main concern was to settle the Northwest with the type of settler that he thought would quickly become productive and integrate readily with the existing population, such as it was, primarily Americans, British, Germans, Scandinavians and—more controversially—selected Eastern Europeans. Above all, he wanted farmers. Anybody considered to be a non-agricultural immigrant, including Jews, Blacks, East Asians, southern Europeans, and British urbanites, was basically unwelcome.

"Northerness" was the key: Scots, Scandinavians, Germans. Northern English were ranked higher than southern English; Mediterranean people, especially southern Italians, were on the "non-preferred" list.[8] In May 1898, when the CPR hired a carload of Italians from New York to work on construction of the Crow's Nest Pass line, Sifton denied them entry to the country and had them sent back.[9]

His fervour for discrimination and conformity led him to advocate for a single system of schooling in the West, which alienated Laurier's French Canadian and Catholic constituency. And his lack of concern for Canada's Indigenous Peoples was evident when he approved the passage of Treaty 8, by which the Crown simply took from Indigenous Peoples an additional 330,000 square miles (850,000 km²) of land in the North-West Territories and BC, opening it to settlement.

In 1897, Sifton established a commission of immigration to coordinate the various activities of the government's immigration board, the Dominion Lands Office of the Department of the Interior and the land office of the Canadian Pacific Railway. The first commissioner, William Forsythe McCreary, was a lawyer, former Winnipeg mayor, and political supporter of Sifton. Four years later, he was succeeded by John Obed Smith, who remained in the position until 1908, when he went to London as Canada's commissioner for immigration.[10]

One of the commission's greatest assets, although he was never an official staff member, was Almon James Cotton, a Manitoba farmer whose enthusiasm for the potential of the Northwest led to his active involvement in several aspects of immigration policy. After Cotton was named Manitoba's "Wheat King" in 1899 for producing 18,632 bushels of wheat on 650 acres (263 ha), his story was featured in a number of Canadian newspapers and as a result, he received many unsolicited letters from potential immigrants seeking his advice. That same year, Cotton's

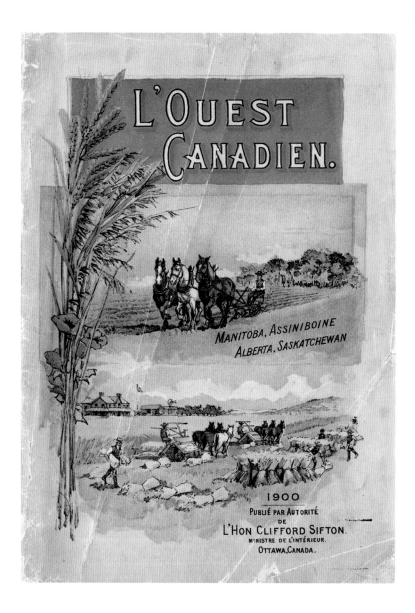

wife contributed to a CPR pamphlet of testimonials entitled "What Women Say of the Canadian North West." In the early years of the century, Cotton was said to have corresponded with nearly 2,000 prospective settlers, and continued to do so as late as 1922.[11]

During the years 1896 to 1905, Sifton and the CPR would engage in what one reviewer a half century later would call "the largest, noisiest and most successful medicine show in history. It covered two continents and was conducted in a dozen languages. Its message was simple and direct: whatever ails you, come to Western Canada!"[12] "Remember," wrote the iconoclastic Western journalist Bob Edwards, "the Trinity of Canada is the C.P.R., Clifford Sifton and the Almighty."[13]

One of the government's first priorities was to open immigration halls, sheds, and staging camps where bunkbeds, cookstoves, and land survey maps were available. Immigration agents and interpreters were often on site to dispense information and advice free of charge, and CPR representatives were close at hand, since invariably the facilities were located in close proximity to the railway's depots.

The immigration hall in Calgary was typical of those in larger centres, with a spacious room downstairs furnished with tables and chairs and a stove where food could be prepared. Upstairs was divided into cubicles with straw mattresses on wooden bedsteads. "After the cramped quarters on the train, this was almost luxurious," one English settler wrote of her experience. "The [CPR] station agent and his wife, who lived in a small house nearby, were very nice people and showed great kindness." Apparently the "foreigners" staying in the immigration facility were a different matter:

◄ The railway and government "medicine show" had the same central message for Eastern Canadians, whether French or English, as it did for those coming from the United States and Europe: Whatever ails you, come to Western Canada. LIBRARY AND ARCHIVES CANADA 971-2-C2120

► The government immigration hall in Calgary, just one block south of the CPR depot, was typical of those in larger centres, with cooking and eating facilities on the main floor and sleeping cubicles, complete with wooden bedsteads and straw mattresses, upstairs. LIBRARY AND ARCHIVES CANADA PA-046612

Mrs. Wynn [the agent's wife] invited us all for supper that first night; the others in the hall were foreigners and not very compatible. Mrs. Wynn informed mother of some other quite different type of foreigners that inhabited that place and mother took prompt action! She purchased, upon advice, quantities of sabadilla powder and other horrible smelling stuff, and so saturated all our clothes and possessions with it that we dripped and smelled of it for weeks. It was unpleasant but preferable to American bedbugs, as they were called at that time. And mother won out.[14]

The CPR agent hired the young woman's father and brother to help with laying out and planting the station garden, and after a few days at the immigration hall, the family found more private accommodations a few blocks away on Stephen Avenue.

Men in sheepskin coats

Sifton was well aware that settlers from Britain would be the most acceptable immigrants to Canadians as far as their cultural compatibility was concerned, but the number of people ready and willing to be transplanted across the ocean was dwindling fast. After several decades of intense campaigning from US and CPR immigration agents, the potential recruits from the agricultural community had been nearly tapped out, other than from the far northern reaches.

In later years, Sifton complained that people who knew little about his immigration policies assumed that the government valued quantity over quality. "As a matter of fact that statement is the direct opposite of the fact," he wrote for *Maclean's Magazine*. "In those days settlers were sought from three sources; one was the United States. The American settlers did not need sifting; they were of the finest quality and the most desirable settlers. In Britain we confined our efforts very largely to the North of England and Scotland, and for the purpose of sifting settlers we doubled the bonuses to the agents in the North of England, and cut them down as much as possible in the South."[15]

On the continent, most of the trolling for emigrants was done by steamship company agents. In northern Europe, this was coordinated mostly through agents in the port of

Hamburg, through which men from outlying agencies were sent. "We made an arrangement with the booking agencies in Hamburg, under which they winnowed out this flood of people, picked out the agriculturalists and peasants and sent them to Canada, sending nobody else," Sifton recalled.[16]

Typically, shipping agents were paid a dollar or two for every legitimate would-be emigrant, but their recruiting tactics were often unscrupulous. As described by the Canadian historian, Pierre Berton, "They slipped into villages, disguised as pedlars and itinerant journeymen, signed up anybody they could, promised the moon, and cheated their victims."[17] In 1899, William Thomas Rochester Preston, the Canadian inspector of immigration in London, turned over the role of immigration recruitment to the North Atlantic Trading Company (NATC), which received from the government $5 for each head of a family and $2 for each additional family member.[18]

Preston had apparently come to an understanding, in collusion with James Smart, deputy minister of the interior, and Lord Strathcona, Canadian high commissioner in London, to arrange an exclusive agreement with this organization of booking agents, which undertook to carry out emigration work throughout Europe and select the best prospects for Canada. The principals of the NATC stipulated at the outset that their names were to remain unregistered, as protection against prosecution from the foreign governments of the countries in which they were seeking young, healthy agriculturalists, a contingent that was also wanted in those states for military duty.[19]

In a missive to Sifton after the negotiations had been concluded, Strathcona said: "I need hardly point out that the new arrangement must be regarded as very confidential and that it must not be made public in any way."[20]

◄ In 1899, Lord Strathcona, a former CPR director and now Canadian high commissioner in London, arranged an exclusive agreement with a secretive organization of booking agents to carry out immigration work in Europe. LIBRARY AND ARCHIVES CANADA E010973341

Opposite, left With the well of prospective immigrants from Great Britain running dry, the efforts of the railway agents focused on northern Europe and farther east, as evidenced by these Russians that made the transatlantic voyage to Canada in the early years of the Laurier government. LIBRARY AND ARCHIVES CANADA C-038706

Opposite, right Much of the hunt for northern Europeans was coordinated by steamship company agents in the port of Hamburg, where this group of Germans was recruited for Canada. LIBRARY AND ARCHIVES CANADA E010958702

For the next seven years, the NATC had a monopoly on all Canadian immigration work throughout Europe. While Sifton and the Laurier government maintained that the NATC brought thousands of people to Canada and gave good value for its services, after Sifton left office in 1905, critics of the company claimed that it was a fraud and had taken large sums of public money illegitimately.[21]

Berton described the NATC as "mysterious," at best: "To this day, nobody knows exactly what the company was, who its principals were, who formed its board of directors, or, indeed, how many immigrants it actually persuaded to come to Canada."[22] To fulfill its primary role, presumably the NATC organization must have included leading representatives or agents of the continental steamship companies.

In defence of his London official and his department, Sifton claimed that the NATC had been useful as a screening agency in regard to the quality of immigrants. In his view, the NATC had "selected the immigrants and gave us the pick of all those who were booking from continental ports, letting the riff-raff go to the United States and South America."[23] More than seventy years after the fact, Berton begged to differ. "Any investigative reporter poring over the sworn evidence taken before two parliamentary committees must come to the conclusion that it was very largely a boondoggle created by Preston for his own personal profit with the connivance of Sifton's deputy, James Smart."[24]

Well before the NATC scandal erupted, however, Sifton had his hands full with the controversy he was creating over his choices of favoured immigrants. Thousands of

▲ The North Atlantic Trading Company brought thousands of people to Canada from a variety of countries in Europe, some of which did not want their young and healthy countrymen to leave when they were wanted for military duty.

► Western Canada held infinite promise for farming, ranching, and owning your own home, all in a safe environment protected by the government.

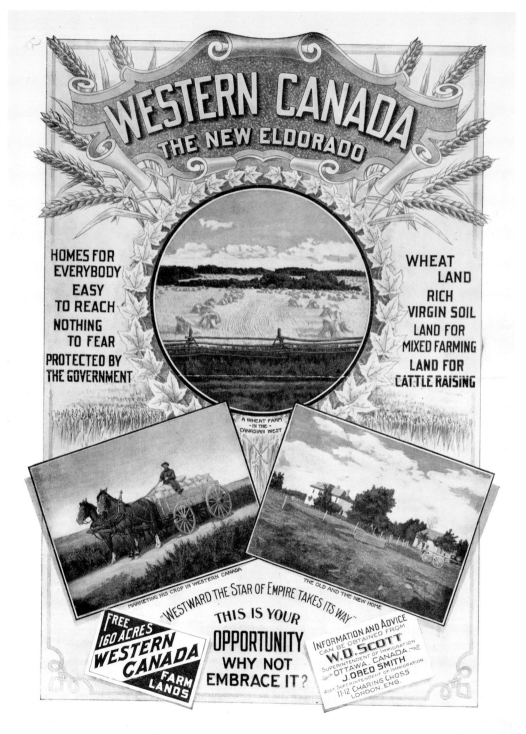

Galicians such as this family at the Quebec City immigration sheds, circa 1909, were among the first Slavic people to arrive in the Northwest. Many more would follow before the First World War. LIBRARY AND ARCHIVES CANADA C-004745

Scandinavians had already left for the United States, and in Germany, increasingly, military service was a mandatory rite of passage before one could receive the necessary authorization to leave the fatherland for another country. As a result, Sifton and his immigration office looked toward Austria-Hungary, the European country that had the largest proportion of farmers.

Sifton was particularly interested in the various Slavic peoples from the provinces of Galicia, Bukovina, Poland, and Bohemia, all of whom were referred to collectively in the Canadian press as Ukrainians or Galicians. The

Canadian minister's association with the people of this region is forever intertwined with his well-known quote from a 1922 address to the Toronto Board of Trade, and repeated in an article for *Maclean's* magazine the same year, reflecting on his motivations as Canada's former "immigration csar":

When I speak of quality I have in mind, I think, something that is quite different from what is in the mind of the average writer or speaker upon the question of Immigration. I think a stalwart peasant in a sheep-skin coat, born of the soil, whose forefathers have been

farmers for ten generations, with a stout wife and a half-dozen children, is good quality.[25]

A small trickle of Ukrainians had begun the Canadian odyssey in September 1891 aboard the Dominion Line steamship *Oregon* when two Galician peasants, Ivan Pilipiwski and Wasyl Elaniak, arrived in Montreal. They took the CPR to Winnipeg and settled south of the Manitoba capital, in Gretna.[26] On July 22, 1896, the first group of twenty-seven Ukrainian-speaking families under Sifton's tutelage arrived in Quebec City, on the SS *Sicilia* of the Hamburg America Line. They also came by CPR to Winnipeg and stayed there for a week in the immigration hall. Six men in their group travelled with government and CPR agents to view land, selecting a site for their colony about 70 miles (113 km) southeast of Winnipeg, which they called Stuartburn. Another ten families joined the group a few weeks later.[27]

Roger Harrington, a government bureaucrat in the office of Clifford Sifton, sent to tour the West soon afterward, reported from Winnipeg on how the immigrants were doing:

The station was positively teeming with the bedraggled masses disembarking from the one o'clock train. It had gathered its passengers from Toronto, Montreal and Quebec City. One colonist car after another disgorged its human cargo. Harvest time was just getting underway so in addition to the immigrants, hundreds of working men from the east were arriving for a temporary stay, expecting to make their year's wages in the coming weeks.[28]

Boarding a southbound train for Dominion City, now part of Emerson, Manitoba, Harrington shared a coach with some of the newly arrived Galicians. He described them in his report to Sifton:

The men wore thick moustaches and carried bundled sheepskin coats. The women covered their heads with flowered or black scarves and wore shirts of a coarse material. All were laden down with baskets and cloth bundles. The children were scrawny urchins, many of them blonde and sandy-haired moppets, all of them with dirt under their nails and dirty black rings around the collars of their white shirts.[29]

An editorial in the *Alberta Tribune*, printed in Calgary, objected to negative comments about the new arrivals in the Ontario press:

With a persistency worthy of a better cause, a section of the Conservative press is pounding away at the Department of the Interior on account of the number of Galicians [Ukrainians] who are coming into the country. These papers declare, with more regard to the picturesqueness than to the accuracy of their statements, that these people were the scum of the earth, if not a little worse; that they are being driven from their own country by the authorities; that the government is giving them $5.00 a head to come to Canada; that they are bringing moral, mental and physical disease with them; that they are shiftless, worthless and improvident; that they are not self-supporting and will always be a charge upon the country; that abroad other settlers in the section where they are located are complaining of their lawlessness and laziness and that it is only a question of time before murder and arson, robbery and rapine, with every other form of lawlessness, ancient and modern, will be rampant in every place where the Galicians are located.[30]

Most of the Ukrainians came to the Northwest with little or no money for farm tools, animals, and basic necessities.

The first large groups also came late in the year and were unable to grow any crops that season. Many got through the winter working for the CPR or cutting cordwood to sell in the villages. By the following spring, however, they were already starting to show signs of progress. To counter some of the virulent and racist attacks by the more xenophobic elements in the press, the local Winnipeg newspaper carried a story in which CPR president Van Horne expressed his admiration for the honesty and stick-to-it-iveness of the Galicians who had made it a point to reimburse the Canadian Pacific for the free transportation which it had supplied to early contingents from the point of embarkation to their destination in the West.[31]

In the next decade, the CPR would set up its own agencies in Austria-Hungary and carry immigrants from Eastern Europe to the New World in the steamships of its newly acquired transatlantic fleet.

Ukrainians who settled successfully in the West played an important role in helping the immigration agents identify others among their countrymen who might follow in their footsteps. They also wrote to their friends and neighbours back home, describing the richness of the land, and even provided financial assistance to help them make the move. As a result, Ukrainians ultimately became one of the largest and most prosperous ethic groups in the Canadian mosaic, second only to the Anglo-Saxons.

By the time Sifton's immigration network was operational on the European continent, a more effective promotional campaign, combined with word of mouth from the pioneering groups that had already made the momentous westward migration, was building momentum. The men in sheepskin coats had grown to include the thousands of Poles, Jews, Slovaks, Hungarians, and Czechs fleeing poverty and persecution on ships departing from the ports of Hamburg and Odessa.

Spirit wrestlers

Another marginalized people that Sifton helped emigrate to the Northwest was the Doukhobors, or "spirit wrestlers," who escaped persecution in Russia. In January 1899, the first group of twenty-one hundred Doukhobors steamed into Halifax on board the Beaver Line steamship *Lake Huron*. The massive amount of aid and logistical wrangling required to get the refugees settled into their adopted home would require months of close coordination with the CPR. It would also subject Sifton and his department to farther charges from more conservative quarters of unduly pampering questionable candidates for immigration.

After the standard medical and immigration screenings to which all new arrivals were subjected, the *Lake Huron* proceeded to the Canadian Pacific docks at Saint John, where five passenger trains awaited the largest single body of emigrants ever to have crossed the Atlantic in one ship. Each of the eleven-car trains included a commissary car loaded with 1,700 two-pound (910 g) loaves of bread, 1,700 pounds (770 kg) of baked beans, 850 pounds (385 kg) of hard tack, 80 gallons (300 l) of milk, 55 pounds (25 kg) of salt, 6 bushels of onions, and 50 pounds (23 kg) of coffee. Twice as many provisions would be waiting on the station platform in Ottawa.[32]

Housing such a large contingent of immigrants in the Northwest while more permanent accommodations were being erected was problematic. After a lot of scrambling around, immigration commissioner McCreary was able to throw up a large frame shed near Yorkton, which could take three or four hundred people in a pinch, on land the Doukhobors had selected for one of their colonies. The rest were crammed into government immigration halls and sheds that Sifton's department had erected in Winnipeg, Brandon, Dauphin, Birtle, and Qu'Appelle.

The government had managed to house more than two thousand Doukhobors in temporary quarters, and another couple of thousand were on their way aboard the Beaver Line's *Lake Superior*. McCreary and Sifton were given some extra time to prepare for the arrival of that large group when it was held for twenty-eight days in quarantine due to an outbreak of smallpox on the ship.[33] While work gangs were cutting timber and erecting houses in what were now the locations of three planned colonies, the CPR turned over to the department of the interior an old roundhouse at Selkirk that it had inherited from the government in 1881 but had soon abandoned when the railway moved its shops to Winnipeg. McCreary had thirty Doukhobors build and plaster partitions to make the cavernous structure livable and semi-private for large numbers of transient families.

The Doukhobors settled on homesteads in two locations north of the CPR's M&NW subsidiary, one 30 miles (48 km) north of Yorkton and another 40 miles (64 km) still farther north. The railway exchanged its odd-numbered sections for land of equal value elsewhere so that the colonists could settle on contiguous properties. These two settlements became known as the South Colony and the North Colony. The third was located on the Qu'Appelle, Long Lake & Saskatchewan between Saskatoon and Prince Albert. It was called the Rosthern Colony.

Within a couple of years, fifty-seven villages had been established in the three communities. Many of the men worked on the railway to earn enough to buy farm animals, tools, and other necessities, while the women broke the ground for planting crops. By the summer of 1901, the

▲ Without exception, these Doukhobor men in the Yorkton area of Saskatchewan, in 1902, posed for the photographer in their distinctive hats.

► While the men cut timber and erected houses for their families, in the absence of work horses or oxen, these Doukhobor women pulled the plough to cultivate the virgin lands they had recently acquired in the Yorkton area of Saskatchewan.

Doukhobor colonies had amassed a number of implements from the Massey-Harris Company, partly on credit, including 40 binders, 70 mowers, and 120 "ploughing machines." They were well on their way to self-sufficiency.[34]

The flower of England

In Sifton's reckoning, they were "better than imperialistic Americans; better than Eastern and southern Europeans who were, after all, foreign and probably Catholic, and most certainly, better than Blacks, Jews, and Asians whose very origins made them unsuitable for farming."[35] They were the British, and as long as they didn't come from the urbanized shopkeeper and industrial classes, he figured they were the best potential immigrants on earth.

On March 31, 1903, 1,960 British men, women, and children crammed themselves on board the Beaver Line steamship *Lake Manitoba* in Liverpool, bound for their new home on a large parcel of land in the Canadian Northwest. Their sponsor was Isaac Montgomery Barr, an Anglican clergyman and promotor of British colonial settlement schemes. This impressive contingent assembled by the ambitious Barr constituted what a local newspaper termed "the flower of England"—Boer War veterans, clergymen's sons, butchers and bakers, warehousemen, coal miners, jewellers, office clerks, furnacemen, dressmakers, even some of the much-desired farmers. Despite the paper's colourful, nationalistic appellation for the group, it included about one hundred Scots and about the same number from Ireland.[36]

Barr was a great admirer of Cecil Rhodes and his mission to spread British influence around the world. In 1902,

he had seen that the English economy was in dismal shape, exacerbated by the thousands of unemployed soldiers returning from the war in South Africa. That same year, he sailed to Canada to arrange for his dream of planting a colony of pure British culture in the Canadian West. After successful meetings with Canadian government, the Elder Dempster Company, and CPR officials at which all were anxious to provide Barr with various incentives to move forward with his plan—including free rail and steamship transportation for his own explorations—Barr returned home to finalize the details. He assured his Canadian supporters that the settlers would be experienced farmers; maybe four hundred or so actually were.[37]

The *Lake Manitoba* was one of several Elder Dempster ships that had ferried British and Canadian soldiers to and from the Boer War. When it was launched a couple of years earlier, the ship had been outfitted to hold about one hundred first-class passengers and five hundred more in steerage. It had been stripped down and drastically modified for transporting large contingents of troops, but for the voyage of the Barr colonists, the high numbers of immigrants were shoe-horned in beyond decency, perhaps three times as many as a normal complement.

The vast majority of the passengers travelled in steerage, with men and women in large, separate, dormitory-style cabins built into the holds below deck, where they slept in tiered bunks. "Even in calm weather the stuffy atmosphere would be redolent with stale tobacco smoke as well as assorted human odours," recalled one chronicler of the transatlantic crossing, "while in rough weather the stench of vomit would be nothing short of nauseating."[38]

"No sea voyage in those days was a pleasant experience," wrote Pierre Berton in his book *The Promised Land*, "but this vessel was so badly overcrowded that whole groups of families were squeezed together below decks, with little privacy. There were far more passengers than the lifeboats could accommodate, and there was not nearly enough fresh water. The colonists were forced to get along on partially distilled salt water, so brackish it ruined the tea. The food in steerage was dreadful... The potatoes were rotten, the meat tough, the cutlery dirty. There was no bread and butter, only ship's biscuit."[39]

Despite the abysmally overcrowded conditions on board, the inedible food, and the tainted water, the *Lake Manitoba* reached the CPR docks at Saint John harbour ten days after leaving Liverpool. There they waited for days while Canadian customs inspectors worked their way through the mountain of accompanying trunks and odd miscellany, which included bathtubs, bicycles, gramophones, pianos, piles of furniture, cases of books, and sewing machines. A small menagerie of parrots and canaries in cages and more than one hundred howling dogs added to the noise and confusion.[40]

The *Lake Manitoba*'s huge contingent of immigrants would soon be followed by more of Barr's "lambs" on board the Elder Dempster's *Lake Simcoe*. "For a while all was chaos," colonist Alice Rendell wrote to a friend about her send-off. "Bewildered looking groups sitting on their baggage waiting like sheep to be allotted their pens. However, after a somewhat severe test of our patience we found ourselves safely housed in a very comfortable four-berth cabin."[41]

Although Rendell's passage was somewhat more comfortable than most of her fellow travellers, it too had its harrowing aspects. "Monday proved a terrible rough day, the waves breaking right over the ship," she wrote. "There

was a birth on board and a foreigner in the steerage cut his throat and is not expected to live. In addition to all this they have discovered no less than 20 stowaways."[42]

Barr's advertising prospectus had promised his charges that upon docking in their adopted country they would travel to the West in relative style. "The journey inland will be over the CPR in colonist and tourist cars which afford comfortable sleeping and absolute privacy," it assured the voyagers. "There is a porter in every car to look after the comfort of the passengers."[43]

Sure enough, four trains of colonist cars awaited the first contingent of Barr colonists, but the intrepid immigrants were taken aback to discover they would be rolling across the country on slatted wooden seats. The berths did not come with mattresses or even blankets. And there were no porters in sight. Fortunately, the ever-enterprising Barr had arranged to sell the passengers everything they could want. "You'll need blankets on the train," he announced. "You can buy them for two dollars each." He had stocked up before the trip on old army surplus blankets from the Boer War.[44]

"Well, I have heard a great deal about the travelling on the C.P.R., and being a shareholder too, felt a special interest in it," Alice Rendell related. "I have always understood its cars and accommodation to be unequalled for comfort and luxury, but if you substitute for the latter two terms discomfort and misery you will be nearer the mark."[45] She compared the colonist cars unfavourably with the worst class of carriages back home. "No sleeping accommodation, and as to the lavatory arrangements they were simply a disgrace to civilization... The accommodation provided for us by the C.P.R. was of the most miserable description, both as regards to comfort and cleanliness, such as no English Railway would tolerate for cattle."[46]

► The Barr emigrants who sailed to Canada aboard Elder Dempster steamships *Lake Manitoba* and *Lake Simcoe* arrive by CPR colonist cars in the frontier town of Saskatoon, where a fleet of pre-purchased wagons awaited them. STEELE AND COMPANY, LIBRARY AND CULTURAL RESOURCES DIGITAL COLLECTIONS, UNIVERSITY OF CALGARY CU176584

Barr's prospectus had also assured the colonists that "each car is provided with a range on which passengers may cook without charge, and cooked or uncooked food may be bought very cheaply at all stations on the route." Typically, the reality was a challenge even for travellers far more self-sufficient and adaptable than the Barr colonists. For the pampered British immigrants—with forty or more people in each car—waiting for a turn to cook led to bitter confrontations, and at most CPR stations, divisional points being the exception, there was precious little food, if any, to be had.[47]

Consequently, the well-armed colonists, who had prepared to leave the Old Country for life on the frontier by packing their steamer trunks with a variety of shotguns, rifles, and pistols, blasted away en route at all manner of birds, small game, and anything else that looked edible. The trains usually moved at a slow enough speed for shooters to jump down from their coaches and reboard several cars back with their kill.

The inscrutable Reverend Barr took the precaution of following several days behind his flock in the civilized confines of a first-class CPR sleeping car on the railway's regular transcontinental passenger train, the Imperial Limited. The dining car was well stocked with several choices of entrée, none of which he had to kill himself.

When their trains reached Winnipeg, a number of the single, male colonists left the group to take jobs arranged by the commissioner of immigration, J. Obed Smith, either with the railway or with farmers in the district. The local paper was much more impressed with the Brits than it had been with the earlier arrival of Sifton's men in sheepskin coats. It described them as "strong, manly, clean and well-dressed," and went on to state unequivocally that "it was

doubtful if any class of immigrants has ever created a more favourable impression in the city."[48]

The government made sure sufficient supplies were put on board each train for the last leg of the railway trip, enough to last for two additional days once they reached their destination. Two days later, the four trains steamed across a long wooden trestle over the South Saskatchewan and into the town of Saskatoon, but still 200 miles (320 km) from their intended homestead lands.

The Saskatoon newspaper was impressed with the way the colonists in the first train took matters into their own hands: "The train consisted of fourteen coaches and one boxcar, and had five hundred and ten people aboard," it reported. "After a short delay they commenced to leave the cars, and without waiting to use the regular exit, they shoved their baggage through the windows and in a great many cases the owners came the same way."[49] The paper didn't say whether or not that reflected well on the CPR.

The *Saskatoon Phoenix* was not alone in its praise of the newcomers. The *Winnipeg Tribune* found the Barr colonists to be a "fine looking lot,"[50] the *Globe* called them "a splendid class,"[51] and the *Ottawa Citizen* was just happy to report that everyone seemed to speak English.[52] The *Toronto News* focused on the women:

Rosy-cheeked English farmers' help, sinewy and graceful, and with a glitter of gaiety and intelligence about their eyes, they filed through into the platform yard, to carry with them into the unknown West the destiny of a nation. The hands that rock the West's cradle will be strong enough to rule the world of Canada in a few years.[53]

They would need more than just a glitter of gaiety to get through the trying days ahead. By the end of the month, when the last of the Barr colonists rolled westward, even the enthusiasm of the newspaper correspondents was waning. One reporter from the *Toronto Star* took particular exception to some of the immigrants' headgear. "What kind of people is this that comes into the wilderness with a top hat?" he asked. "There is the trouble, some are too luxurious." He went on to all but dismiss them as the "bathtub and piano carrying crowd."[54]

At the time, Saskatoon was truly a frontier town, with a handful of stores, a bank, a bakery, and not much else. The travellers' prospectus had painted a more fulsome picture: "Here we shall find horses, cows, farm implements, provisions, furniture, tents and all things needed to complete our outfit," it had suggested. "Arrangements will be made in advance as regards price." And sure enough, Barr had arranged with the local merchants for him to receive a 10 percent commission on everything bought by the colonists.[55]

The train carrying the tents for the colonists—more of Barr's Boer War surplus—was a day or two behind the arrival of the campers themselves. Fortunately, Sifton's deputy, James Smart, had anticipated just such a glitch and had pitched as many government-issued tents as he could put his hands on. Barr had also prearranged a restaurant tent, where he planned to charge the colonists a dollar per meal. Once again, though, Smart had gotten out in front of the avaricious clergyman. He had arranged to have CPR boarding cars spotted on site to serve meals at a more reasonable forty-five cents apiece.[56]

The remainder of the luggage—the lion's share of what the immigrants had insisted on bringing with them— showed up in Saskatoon a few days later, jammed into eighteen CPR baggage cars, with nobody to sort it out. For whatever reason, the whole lot arrived without any accompanying baggagemen and was unceremoniously dumped in piles alongside the tracks.[57] Some of the group's possessions were damaged and some never arrived.

One thing Barr did right was to erect a hospital tent in Saskatoon and, presumably, man it with medical staff. In any case, a few cases of pneumonia appeared in the camp, and two colonists succumbed to scarlet fever shortly after most of the settlers had already departed for the land that had been purchased for them near present-day Lloydminster. One of the settlers' memoirs claimed that a family of German immigrants had infected a CPR colonist car with the latter disease and that the car had not afterwards been properly disinfected before being assigned to the Barr colonists.[58]

Not surprisingly, Barr received a commission on the five hundred or so covered wagons that had been readied for the immigrants, who loaded them well above their intended capacity for the overland journey. Short of foodstuffs, the colonists lived off the land, shooting ducks, prairie chickens, and rabbit. Some of the wagons broke down from the weight of the goods on board, which the settlers had hung from them in profusion. The overloaded conveyances stalled out in the mud and tipped over on river crossings, allowing more than one treasured possession to float away downstream. Horses collapsed from overwork. Some of the trekkers took two months to arrive at the site of their proposed colony.[59]

Despite the initial absence of stores, schools, hospitals, or post office, on arrival there were government land agents in the area to help the colonists locate their surveyed lands. At the suggestion of Smart, CPR had reserved the odd-numbered sections in the district, all of which were

Surplus tents from the Boer War, acquired by Reverend Barr, housed the Anglican clergyman's flock in Saskatoon while they prepared for the next leg of their trip, a 200-mile trek by wagon to Battleford, the capital of the North-West Territories, where they held significant land holdings.

quickly bought up by the colonists to supplement the free homesteads they had acquired from the government.

About three hundred of the colonists had already found work in Manitoba. Some chose to take up residence in Regina, Moose Jaw, Dundurn, and Saskatoon. Others settled near Jackfish Lake and along the proposed route of the Canadian Northern Railway, soon to be a major rival of the CPR. About one thousand of the original Barr colonists remained on the site they had chosen near the pioneer town of Lloydminster, named for a second clergyman who travelled with the group and had been an early promotor of the scheme.[60]

Barr eventually reimbursed some of the angry settlers who felt they had been cheated by all the extra charges imposed on them, but he didn't stick around to settle down in his own prairie paradise. In fact, the whole Northwest adventure marked the end of his Canadian endeavours. Barr married his secretary, became an American, and ultimately died in Australia, still dreaming about settling British emigrants in the far frontiers of the Empire.[61]

The enthusiasm of Canadians for British immigrants tapered off when it became obvious that many of the new arrivals were not farmers at all, and farmers were what the country really needed. From the time the Liberals took over the apparatus of the federal government in 1896, with their renewed emphasis on populating the agricultural Northwest, to the outbreak of the First World War in 1914, statistics showed that only 18 percent of immigrants from Great Britain took up homesteading, while as many as 29 percent of those from the European continent did so. The others tended to head to or drift toward the cities, where they competed with established Canadians for employment opportunities in urban settings.[62]

Increasingly, Englishmen were seen to be overly entitled, arrogant, and disinclined to partake of hard labour. Newspaper advertisements and posted job notices began to include the caveat, "No Englishmen Need Apply." There was a general belief that Canada was getting the wrong kind of Britisher, and a vague suspicion grew that there was a plot to clear the cities of the unemployed, the lazy, the unsuccessful, various ne'er-do-wells, and probably criminals as well.

A 1909 study of immigration patterns by James Shaver Woodsworth, *Strangers within our Gates*, reinforced the notion that Great Britain was dumping the country's undesirables on her colony across the pond. The author quoted an English magistrate reprimanding a young offender in his court: "You have broken your mother's heart, you have brought down your father's grey hairs in sorrow to the grave. You are a disgrace to your country. Why don't you go to Canada?"[63]

As early as 1897, William Van Horne received a letter from a gentleman who had recently travelled to a meeting of the British Medical Association in Vancouver on the CPR's Pacific Express, expressing his praise for the railway's overall service, with one small exception:

I can suggest little or nothing that may be of use to you concerning possible improvements unless it be to devise some plan of murdering the English grumbler. We encountered two horrible specimens of the genus—one enjoying the hospitalities of the road, too—and by quarreling with waiters and porters and airing their ridiculous pretensions they served not a little to mar our pleasure. Can't you manage somehow to keep the animal off your cars?[64]

The displaced and the repatriated

During the Sifton era, from 1896 to 1906, British immigrants outnumbered Eastern Europeans by as many as three or four to one.[65] But the biggest influx was to come from the United States, consisting largely of recent immigrants to North America who had no particular national attachment but were looking for the best economic advantage on whatever side of the international boundary that might lie. It has been estimated that during the first two decades of the twentieth century upwards of one million Americans looked to their northern neighbour and liked what they saw.

Both the Canadian federal government and the CPR built extensive networks of immigration agents to attract settlers to the Northwest. Sifton's Department of the Interior established nine state agencies soon after the Liberals came to power and systematically added new locations until there were twenty-one by the First World War. Each of the recruitment centres was run by one or more salaried agent who sought out and hired sub-agents to work on a commission basis.[66]

An old Sifton crony from the *Brandon Sun*, William J. White, was put in charge of the government's propaganda campaign, and he soon added an additional twenty-seven travelling agents to recruit immigrants freely throughout the US. By 1901, White had more than 276 sub-agents on the hunt. They received $3 for every man, $2 for every woman, and a dollar for every child they lured to Canada.[67]

Canadian Pacific also hired full-time employees to man its offices in major centres of the United States, including land and immigration agents stationed along its Soo Line. Often the railway representatives worked hand in hand

with their government counterparts, although some conflicts did occur. One advantage CPR agents held was access to free transportation, not only from their own company but across the US. It was standard practice in North America for railway companies to extend this courtesy to one another's employees, and some of the railway agents had as many as a dozen passes for various roads in their pockets. The immigration branch of the Canadian department of the interior approached Van Horne to intercede with US railroads on the government's behalf in acquiring free annual passes for its employees, but the CPR president didn't even forward the request.[68]

However, White *was* able to negotiate agreements with several US railroads to use their ticket offices and passenger stations as distribution points for Canadian immigration literature. Some of the American companies even allowed their employees to double as Canadian agents. The American roads had discovered that an increased northern migration did not necessarily mean a loss of economic production or revenue. It was more of an indication of the normal, ongoing turnover in land ownership, or the departure of landless US settlers' sons. In 1902, officials at the Union Pacific informed an immigration agent in Nebraska that it would be happy to encourage American ranchers along its rail lines to move to Alberta so that their lands might be freed up for settlers and the more lucrative produce they would put into the railroad's freight cars.[69]

CPR agents had no qualms about promoting free government homesteads in Canada, as it put settlers on the land and generated traffic for the railway, but as a matter of policy, government agents and sub-agents were not authorized to sell CPR lands. In practice, however, it was impossible to prevent every sub-agent from earning a little extra in royalty payments under the table.

Opportunities for widespread advertising and, ulti-mately, the success of the overall immigration campaign depended on the goodwill of the so-called fourth estate. To ensure that US newspapers were well attuned to the potential of the Canadian Northwest, Sifton's Department of the Interior appointed a general press secretary to liaise and establish friendly relations with the editorial fraternity south of the border. Taking advantage of the rural news-papermen's predilection for organizing themselves into associations and taking annual holiday excursions together, the minister of the interior and Van Horne extended a joint invitation in the summer of 1898 to the Minnesota Editorial Association to take a trip through the West.[70]

As a result of the overall success of the venture in generating media coverage and a positive commentary about the benefits awaiting settlers in the Northwest, additional excursions followed in quick succession, beginning later

that summer with a trip taken by the Wisconsin editors, who formally expressed their gratitude to the CPR for the courtesies extended to them. The following year, Sifton and Van Horne arranged for more than six hundred editors with the US National Editorial Association, representing about one thousand newspapers, to hop aboard the railway's palatial coaches and sleeping cars in exchange for spilling lauda-tory ink all over the pages of their hometown publications.

Free junkets really did the trick, especially when they included extended stays at the hot springs in Banff or at majestic Lake Louise, as related by historian Pierre Berton:

Trainloads of compliant editors, lubricated by good whiskey and warmed by the best CPR cuisine, raced across the country at government expense, stopping at wheat fields and handsome farms (carefully selected) or for banquets at the major cities… When the editorial junkets began to strain the public purse, White traded free trips in return for free advertising. The press swallowed the bait. The Michigan Press Association was so eager that it offered to give two or three dollars' worth of ads for every dollar Canada expended—and all in advance of each junket.[71]

The Department of the Interior also revived an old practice that had been employed successfully by the resourceful Alexander Begg, CPR's first overseas immigration agent, who pioneered virtually all of the strategies later used to even greater effect by the expanded government and railway agencies. Enterprising farmers in various localities across the prairies were asked to fill out questionnaires to be used in advertising pamphlets, typically outlining how little they had started with when they arrived in the Northwest and how well they had done in the interim. At the other end of the promotional chain, farm delegates from the US were brought to Canada at the expense of government and railway officials with a view to providing positive testimonials for the farming audience back home about the desirability of making a move north.

Typical headlines above the testimonials in the CPR pamphlets read: "Would Not Return to Indiana"; "Dakota Farmer Succeeded Without Capital"; "Prefers the Weyburn District to the States"; and "Easily Earns Holiday Trips to Ohio."

Thousands of delegates representing farming communities across the US took advantage of free transportation from the CPR. And once the delegates had sold their friends and neighbours on the benefits of moving to Canada, the railway made it easy for the immigration agents to offer potential settlers an inexpensive means of getting

there. All Dominion agents who had bona fide settlers ready to transplant their families across the border were empowered to issue them with "Canadian Land Seekers' Certificates," which entitled the holders to travel from any point in the US to their destinations in the Northwest at the rate of one cent per mile. There were so many requests for certificates that the CPR suspected that some of the government agents were granting them to people who were using them to make pleasure trips to the Canadian West, rather than to take up residence in a new country.

For those who were not fully convinced of the benefits awaiting them in the Northwest or who wanted to see the country for themselves before committing to such a momentous move, CPR organized "Home-Seekers Excursions" for large groups of potential settlers, who were under no obligation to buy land. Railway representatives assigned to accompany the excursionists on their exploratory train trips would offer whatever assurances were necessary to sway them over. One Dominion agent, stationed at Detroit, reported that he had organized special railway excursions to Western Canada in 1897 every month during the summer and harvest seasons, "when the country is seen to the best advantage." He added that the majority of his clients returned from the trips ready to move their families the following spring.[72]

Sifton and Laurier were intent upon increasing Canada's population by as much as tenfold, mostly with immigrants from Britain, northern continental Europe, and the United States. With that lofty goal in mind, Sifton's staff in London came up with a brilliant concept for showing off Canada's Imperial sentiments, while showcasing the potential of the overseas country as a desirable emigration destination. They would build an elaborate arch across Whitehall, the road between Trafalgar Square and Westminster Abbey, in

► Special "Home-seekers Fares" offered prospective settlers from Eastern Canada up to two months stopover privileges, subject to a negotiated extension, for those serious about acquiring land in Western Canada. AUTHOR'S COLLECTION

the central part of the city, along which the main government offices were located. The route of the parade during the coronation festivities for King Edward VII in the summer of 1902 would pass underneath, and thousands of visitors flocking to London for the celebrations would view this magnificent creation and the messages which it bore.[73]

Canada's high commissioner, Lord Strathcona, had decreed that the arch should span the entire street and be illuminated for maximum effect, night and day. The structure as erected was 60 feet (18.3 m) wide and 56 feet (17.1 m) high, with a central archway 25 feet (7.6 m) wide and high enough for a double-decked trolley to pass through. Twenty tons (18,000 kg) of wheat, grasses, and other grains were said to be fastened to the frame. Maple leaves, apples, and cobs of corn were features of the decorative, agricultural-themed structure through which the royal coach would convey Edward and Queen Alexandra.[74] The brilliantly illuminated arch incorporated more than four thousand lights and carried the words CANADA / BRITAIN'S GRANARY / GOD BLESS OUR KING AND QUEEN on the side facing Buckingham Palace, and CANADA / FREE HOMES FOR MILLIONS / GOD BLESS THE ROYAL FAMILY ON THE OTHER SIDE.[75]

The Canadian government was rivalling the CPR in its extravagant campaigning. "Let me tell you, my fellow countrymen, that all the signs point this way, that the 20th century shall be the century of Canada and Canadian development," said Laurier, speaking at Toronto's Massey Hall in 1904. "For the next 100 years, Canada shall be the star towards which all men who love progress and freedom shall come ... We are a nation of six million people already; we expect soon to be 25, yes, 40 millions. There are men in this audience who, before they die, if they live to an old age, will see this country with at least 60 millions of people."[76]

▲ To commemorate the coronation of King Edward VII in the summer of 1902, Sifton's staff in London arranged to build an elaborate arch across Whitehall, under which the celebratory parade would pass. The brilliantly illuminated creation would serve as Canada's salute to the new reigning British monarch, while advertising the merits of emigrating across the pond. UNDERWOOD AND UNDERWOOD, LIBRARY AND CULTURAL RESOURCES DIGITAL COLLECTIONS, UNIVERSITY OF CALGARY CU175279

The government and the railway would bring farmer representatives and newspaper editors to the Northwest by the trainload, while printing and distributing millions of booklets and pamphlets extolling the availability and fertility of free land.

Competition arrives in force

Along with the undeniable prosperity that the twentieth century ushered in, there was much clamouring for more rail service among settlers not located on a CPR line, echoed by those who felt that the pioneer transcontinental's primacy in the Northwest could use a healthy dose of competition. The federal Conservatives had championed the CPR, but this time it would be the Liberals who would act—in the words of a CPR public relations man, John Murray Gibbon— as "fairy godmother."[77]

One major issue was that the Western grain crop was increasing faster than the CPR's ability to handle it. The acute shortage of railway cars in 1901 brought the matter to a head. A group of aggrieved farmers formed the Territorial Grain Growers' Association and took the railway to court for its failure to move grain shipments to market equitably. Farmers from Sintaluta, a small community about 50 miles (80 km) east of Regina, won a test case against the railway in the Supreme Court the following year, giving individual growers as much control over ordering grain cars for loading as the elevator companies.[78]

One of the companies that would grow to rival the CPR on a national level was the Canadian Northern Railway. Ironically, its two main principals, William Mackenzie and Donald Mann, got their start in the business as contractors

for various CPR railway lines, beginning in the early 1880s. After the CPR main line was completed in 1885, Mann obtained a further contract to build snowsheds for the CPR in the Rocky Mountains. Later, both men pooled their resources to complete four sections of CPR's Short Line through Maine to the Maritimes. And Mackenzie and Mann partnered with their contractor friends Herbert Holt and James Ross to build large stretches of the Qu'Appelle, Long Lake & Saskatchewan Railway and the C&E, both lines that were not directly connected with the CPR initially but were later leased by the company.[79]

The roots of the Canadian Northern Railway would be planted when the Lake Manitoba Railway & Canal Company was incorporated to build a line from Portage la Prairie to Prince Albert, and the charter was awarded by the Manitoba government to the two well-connected

contractors, Mackenzie and Mann. In the words of Dr. Theodore D. Regehr, former associate professor at the University of Saskatchewan and author of a lengthy history of the Canadian Northern:

The northern prairies were at last getting the transportation services essential for their settlement and development… In 1896 Mackenzie's friend Sam Hughes led an expedition which reported enthusiastically that no less than 90 percent of the lands adjacent to the new railway were suitable for agriculture and would be settled once the new railway provided the necessary transportation facilities.[80]

Almost immediately, Sifton's first groups of Galician immigrants settled along the route of the Lake Manitoba Railway & Canal Company and took jobs constructing the railway line.

The two ambitious railway builders moved into the big leagues in July 1889, when they amalgamated the Lake Manitoba Railway & Canal Company with the Winnipeg

Opposite, left The first Canadian Northern train to pull into the Ottawa depot arrived on December 5, 1909. LIBRARY AND ARCHIVES CANADA PA-165400

Opposite, right The first routes offered by the Canadian Northern Railway to settlers heading to the Northwest were in connection with American railroads. AUTHOR'S COLLECTION

▶ Though in possession of much less land than the CPR, the Canadian Northern still found it advantageous to publish attractive folders touting the extraordinary fertility of the soil in Western Canada. JAMES E. LANIGAN COLLECTION

Great Northern Railway & Steamship Company—or the Hudson Bay Railway, which they also controlled—to form the Canadian Northern Railway. The new federal charter gave Mackenzie and Mann the rights to build extensive new mileage, but specifically forbade their railway to ever be sold or amalgamated with the CPR.[81]

Mackenzie and Mann continued to put together an impressive railway network piece by piece. Among their significant achievements were assembling a series of charters that gave them the power to build a new rail line from Winnipeg to Port Arthur and, in 1901, acquiring the Northern Pacific's entire network in Manitoba.[82] The Canadian Northern was now able to handle shipments of grain from the Northwest to European markets.

An independent firm, the Saskatchewan Valley & Manitoba Land Company, began promoting Canadian Northern lands in 1903. Mackenzie and Mann, being more

concerned with railway operations than land promotion, were more than happy to turn over to them as much land as possible adjacent to their railway, which they had been awarded in grants. The land promotors launched aggressive advertising campaigns in the American Midwest, selling Canadian Northern lands at an average price of $5 per acre (or just over $12 per hectare).[83]

In some cases, the odd-numbered sections along Canadian Northern lines had already been granted to the CPR or bought by land companies and individual settlers, or they were considered unfit for agricultural settlement. Canadian Northern land agents were careful about their choice of lands and benefited from the CPR's precedent of holding out for only prime agricultural land. As a result, the company, on occasion, was forced to accept lands far from their railway lines.

In the East, the once dominant Grand Trunk Railway had been losing ground to the CPR; it began to fight back in 1896 with the hiring of a new general manager from the US Wabash Railroad, Charles Melville Hays. Hays realized that his road would have to build a transcontinental line if it was to remain competitive with the CPR. By 1902, the Grand Trunk had formulated a plan to extend its eastern network into the prairies and on to the West Coast, through a new subsidiary, the Grand Trunk Pacific (GTP).

At the time, Canadian Pacific president Thomas Shaughnessy pointed out that it would not make sense to have two railway lines running through the unproductive wilderness north of Lake Superior. The CPR boss suggested instead that the Grand Trunk reach an agreement with his road for running rights between North Bay and the Lakehead, and acquire the prairie lines of the Canadian Northern Railway, which that concern had added to considerably in the previous decade.[84] The Grand Trunk had discussed the

possibility of combining with the Canadian Northern to form a transcontinental line, but despite federal government encouragement, no agreement was reached.

There was no holding back Laurier and Sifton, however. The federal government left the Canadian Northern alone for the time being and moved to cooperate with GTP to create a potential third contender in the transcontinental railway sweepstakes.

For the government, the impetus to pave the way for two big competitors to the CPR was the need to speed up the rate at which the lands in the Northwest were being sold and, more pointedly, populated. With an upturn in the economic outlook worldwide, and immigration on the rise from both Europe and, in particular, the United States, the federal politicians were in an expansive mood.

Laurier rose in the House of Commons to express his enthusiasm in racial terms:

We cannot wait, because the prairies of the North-West, which for countless ages have been roamed over by the wild herds of the bison, or by the scarcely less wild tribes of red man, are now invaded from all sides by the white man... 100,000 came last year and will come in greater numbers to sow harvest and reap.[85]

Thomas Osbourne Davis, a member of parliament from the provisional District of Saskatchewan, opined that "the decision to build the CPR in the south kept back the country for 23 years." If it had taken the more northerly route being eyed by the rival transcontinental railways, he claimed, the population of the Northwest would have been two or three million, rather than the 300,000 or so it was then.[86]

On July 29, 1903, an agreement was reached between the government and the Grand Trunk to cooperate in constructing the National Transcontinental Railroad (NTR).

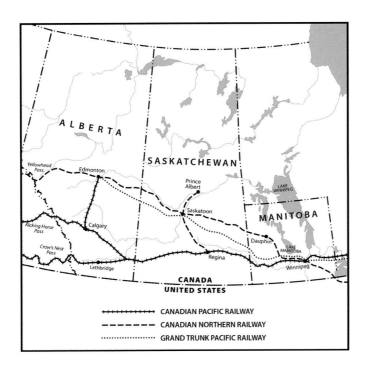

CANADIAN PACIFIC RAILWAY
CANADIAN NORTHERN RAILWAY
GRAND TRUNK PACIFIC RAILWAY

The Grand Trunk would construct and operate the NTR Western Division from Winnipeg to the Pacific coast in northern British Columbia. The government would construct the NTR Eastern Division east of Winnipeg, and upon completion, would lease it to the GTP for fifty years at an annual rental fee of 3 percent of its construction cost.

The Grand Trunk Railway's eastern terminus and preferred Atlantic port was at Portland, Maine, and there was public opposition to having the new government-assisted transcontinental line serve American interests. To benefit ports at Quebec City and the Maritime provinces, Laurier's

government insisted that the NTR Eastern Division bypass Toronto and Montreal to the north, and extend to Quebec City and Moncton, en route to Halifax by the Intercolonial Railway.

The cost of the line from Winnipeg to Moncton came in at $159,881,197, nearly one hundred million more than estimated, and the Grand Trunk, which itself was in debt for more than $200 million, refused to lease the NTR Eastern Division when completed.[87] The original plan for a unified National Transcontinental Railway having been negated, the NTR name came to represent only the Eastern Division, which was soon combined with the Intercolonial Railway and some small lines as Canadian Government Railways.

The Canadian Northern Railway continued to build up its infrastructure and challenge the CPR's dominance wherever possible, while massive cost overruns on the National Transcontinental Railway had caused the Grand Trunk to back out of a potential joint venture with the federal government and go it alone. But the Grand Trunk Pacific had been poorly conceived from the beginning. Its main line in the West was not being built as a functional colonization line. Running between the Canadian Northern and the CPR for much of its route across the prairies, the GTP was basically a trunk line with virtually no branch lines or feeders to sustain its viability. By 1912, the death of then-Grand Trunk president Charles Melville Hays, on the ill-fated ocean liner *Titanic*, was a portent of the company's own imminent demise.

7 GROWING THE BUSINESS

A new land strategy

The first decade of the twentieth century would see Canadian Pacific engage in several bold initiatives that would transform its business, expand the reach of its influence, and consolidate its standing as the primary instrument of Canadian immigration and the settlement of the North-West Territories.

The first move, in 1894, had been to take over the administration of the lands of the Canada North-West Land Company. By 1896, the upturn in economic conditions, coupled with the excellent location of the company's lands in close proximity to CPR lines, boosted sales by more than 400 percent over the previous year. About two-thirds of the sales were to people moving from the eastern provinces. The numbers would soon start to shift toward Britain, the European continent, and the United States in particular. The early response to the improved conditions was from Canadians coming west and farmers already established on the prairies who increased their holdings by purchasing CPR lands adjacent to their original homesteads.[1]

By the turn of the century, new land for farming was becoming scarce in the United States, while the Northwest was swarming with agents from south of the border anxious to get in on a market that was still booming. A couple of years of good harvests and excellent prices worldwide for cereals and produce added to the rush. With investors willing to pay a fair price for land and colonization companies once again serving a growing market, Canadian Pacific now entertained the notion of selling large tracts of land to speculators. In May 1901, sixty representatives of American land companies from Dakota, Iowa, and Minnesota were reported to be in Winnipeg. In a single day, CPR sold them more than 20,000 acres (8,100 ha).[2]

The new policy made sense for the railway on a number of levels. The US colonization companies were building elaborate networks to market and sell land that would be difficult and expensive for the CPR to try to match. Unlike a decade or two before, they were now aggressively selling their newly acquired lands to the productive settlers sought by the railway, while still walking away with a tidy profit. CPR was also beginning negotiations with the federal authorities to take the last of its government land grants within one large block of contiguous townships in the semiarid region east of Calgary. Once the railway owned all of the even-numbered and odd-numbered sections, the company could consider investing in one or more extensive irrigation projects to boost the agricultural potential of the entire

With land becoming scarce south of the border, James Peter Hansen, originally from Denmark, came to Cochrane, Alberta, to work as a gang foreman for the CPR. His family lived in a converted boxcar until they could afford a property in Standard, Alberta. LIBRARY AND CULTURAL RESOURCES DIGITAL COLLECTIONS, UNIVERSITY OF CALGARY CU191484

area exponentially. To do that, CPR needed the revenues from the sale of the large tracts of land it still held in Manitoba and southeastern Assiniboia, and it needed to move its land sales administration from Winnipeg to Calgary.

The first of the US interests to purchase an extensive chunk of CPR land was Beiseker, Davidson, and Martin, a firm owned by three land speculators from North Dakota whose success in their home state attracted the attention of the railway land commissioner, Frederick T. Griffon, who had recently taken over the position from L.A. Hamilton in 1900. At Griffon's urging, Canadian Pacific's executive committee approved the sale of 170,297 acres (68,917 ha) of railway land in eastern Assiniboia. The price was $2.75 per acre ($6.81/ha), leaving the US group plenty of room to make a profit on quick turnovers. Thomas Lincoln Beiseker and his partners formed the Canadian American Land Company, with headquarters in Minneapolis. Within five months, in cooperation with government and railway land agents, the new company had retailed all of the sections in the area to settlers from the United States.[3]

The most influential group to purchase CPR lands in Assiniboia was the Northwest Colonization Company. This

ambitious firm bought 337,090 acres (136,416 ha) from Canadian Pacific and the Manitoba Southwestern for $2.50 per acre ($6.19/ha) and agreed in their contract to re-sell the lands to settlers at not less than $4 per acre ($9.90/ha). Subsequent purchases from the Northwest Colonization Company in the same region brought their total holdings to 750,000 acres (303,500 ha). In their advertising, they characterized the region as "The Garden Spot of Canada," and by the spring of 1905, they had retailed the entire area to settlers from the US.[4]

The new generation of colonization companies employed extremely aggressive tactics and high-pressure salesmanship to make quick sales. "These companies," wrote the CPR land commissioner to the vice-president of the Canada North-West Land Company, "work on different lines altogether from any of the real estate agents here with whom we have hitherto done business. They go after their purchaser, pay railway fares, accompany them to the land,

personally conduct them over it and stay with them, eat, sleep and drink with them if necessary until a sale is made or they fail in the attempt."[5]

In 1900, a group of American land speculators had formed the Saskatchewan Valley & Manitoba Land Company and offered to buy, from the government, all of the lands that had previously been rejected by the builders of the Qu'Appelle, Long Lake & Saskatchewan. The men in this firm included such American luminaries as its president, Colonel Andrew Duncan Davidson, and Frederick Eugene Kenaston, the head of the Minneapolis Threshing Machine Company, both of whom had been previously involved with the sale of a million acres (400,000 ha) of Northern Pacific lands.[6] Another member of the land company was Walter D. Douglas of Cedar Rapids, Iowa, president of the Quaker Oats Company.

The Saskatchewan Valley & Manitoba Land Company purchased 839,000 acres (340,000 ha) from the

Qu'Appelle, Long Lake & Saskatchewan for $1.53 per acre ($3.70/ha) as well as 250,000 of even-numbered government sections within the limits of the railway's land grant for a dollar per acre ($2.48/ha), giving them a large block to market to settlers. The company was able to negotiate the low rate on condition that it would also put settlers on the homesteads in the region still under government control. It was able to get from $8 to $12 per acre ($19.80 to $29.70/ha) for the lands it had bought.[7]

The Manitoba provincial government also sold land to speculative land companies, including 202,776 acres (82,060 ha) to the Eastern and Western Land Corporation, a Toronto firm, and another 200,000 acres (80,937 ha) to the Manitoba Land and Investment Company.

Alongside these aggressive colonization companies that sold their land quickly to other speculators or secured actual settlers to purchase the land in small tracts, there were more conservative players who chose to hold onto their properties for a longer period to reap the benefit of the enhanced prices that resulted from the sale of lands adjacent to their own. One such company was Osler, Hammond & Nanton, the bankers and promotors who had been intimately involved with the building of the Qu'Appelle, Long Lake & Saskatchewan and the C&E railways. This firm handled all of the land sales along these lines for the CPR as well as the disposition of properties owned by the Winnipeg Western Land Corporation and the Ontario & Qu'Appelle Land Company. A close relationship with the CPR enabled its representatives to offer potential settlers special rates and stop-over privileges while looking to buy land.[8]

In January 1904, a group of officials representing private Canadian land interests and western business met at the Merchant's Hotel in St. Paul Minnesota to organize the Western Canadian Immigration Association. The initiative was launched by H.A. Haslam, a prominent St. Paul land promoter, who had three years earlier contracted with Canadian Pacific to buy more than 82,000 acres (33,200 ha) for resale in the United States. Other American agents with the Saskatchewan Valley & Manitoba Land Company and the Northwest Colonization Company were also keen to lobby for funds from government and public resources to promote their private land sales.

The focus of the CPR's land department was drifting farther and farther west from its origins in Winnipeg. As most of the railway lands in Manitoba and Saskatchewan were sold to individual settlers and land companies, the company's attention turned to a solid tract of about 3 million acres (1.2 million ha) extending along its main line east of Calgary that had been taken over by Canadian Pacific to satisfy its outstanding land grant claims with the federal government.

Sifton had taken a hard stand with the Department of the Interior to get railway companies to finalize their selection of lands awarded to them under various federal charters. The CPR had previously taken only lands it deemed to be "fairly fit for settlement," some along its own lines and other large tracts more remote from the railway belt. After some tough negotiations in 1903, Canadian Pacific agreed to accept a massive area of land—including all of the even-numbered and odd-numbered sections—in the semi-arid region of Palliser's Triangle. The lands would soon be subjected to one of the most extensive irrigation projects in the world.

▶ The Galt family's Alberta Railway & Coal Company opened a narrow-gauge railway between Lethbridge and Dunmore to supply high-quality coal to CPR locomotives. STEELE AND COMPANY, LIBRARY AND CULTURAL RESOURCES DIGITAL COLLECTIONS, UNIVERSITY OF CALGARY CU184721

The flow of irrigation begins

The history of irrigation in Canada is inextricably linked with the coal and railway industries. In the early years of prairie settlement, before the arrival of the railway, there were a few pioneer attempts to increase the productivity of farm lands within the semi-arid region of Palliser's Triangle, notably settler John Quirk's damming of Sheep Creek in 1878 at his ranch near Okotoks, to water a few hundred acres of hay meadow. A year later, John Glenn dug a couple of small canals to irrigate grain and vegetables on his Fish Creek farm south of Calgary. It would be nearly two more decades before irrigation was carried out on an industrial scale in the lucrative coal region around Lethbridge.

In 1882, as the CPR was approaching Medicine Hat, Alexander Galt, the Canadian high commissioner in London, formed the North Western Coal & Navigation (NWC&N) Company with several friends and associates to exploit the huge veins of coal that had been discovered a decade earlier at Coal Banks (later Lethbridge). William Lethbridge, a senior employee with the news agency W.H. Smith & Son, was appointed president. The region's largest and most important urban centre would soon be named after him. Galt's plan was to run river steamers and barges on the Belly and South Saskatchewan rivers to transport coal from Coal Banks to Medicine Hat and sell most of it to the CPR.

River navigation could be problematic, with low levels of water frequently grounding boats in dry years. The NWC&N decided to build a narrow-gauge railway from the CPR main line at Dunmore, just southeast of Medicine Hat, to Coal Banks. It would, in effect, be a branch line of the CPR.

The CPR had enough financial problems without having to invest a substantial amount of funds in its own collieries, so it clearly wanted Galt to succeed. Railway president George Stephen informed Prime Minister Macdonald of a visit from the NWC&N's promotor: "Galt was in today full of his coal. If only half he hopes from their deposits are realized, the fuel question may be dismissed as no account … We'll be glad to see his line open and carrying coal to the railway."[9]

To assume some of the financial and physical aspects of building the railway line, Galt incorporated the Alberta Railway & Coal Company (AR&CC) to handle the increasingly complex, interrelated activities that he and his son Elliot would undertake. It would be the first of several new firms the family would create in a growing web of corporate involvements in collieries, railway lines, irrigation canals and land settlement schemes.

In short order, the NWC&N and the AR&CC built the narrow-gauge line, and on August 25, 1885, the first train steamed into Coal Banks. The 110 miles (177 km) of track from Dunmore and Lethbridge had been laid in just forty-nine working days. A month later, CPR's general superintendent, John Egan, attended the official opening in the renamed Town of Lethbridge, along with Governor-General, the Marquis of Landsdowne, and the usual raft of local dignitaries. Canadian Pacific's source of coal was secured. Six locomotives and more than a hundred railway cars would maintain an economic lifeline from Lethbridge to Dunmore, with intermediate stops at Woodpecker, Grassy Lake, and Winnifred. A daily passenger train whisked travellers to the connection with the CPR.[10]

The Galt interests lobbied the federal government for land subsidies, in support of their proposal to colonize the region with American cattle ranchers through which their rail line ran. In March 1885, the government passed an omnibus bill awarding land grants of 6,400 acres per mile (1,609 ha/km) of track to the colonization railways M&NW, Manitoba & South-Western Colonization Company, and Qu'Appelle, Long Lake & Saskatchewan Railway and Steamboat Company. At the same time, the NWC&N Company was granted 3,840 acres per mile (966 ha/km) for its "resource railway," along a belt 6 miles (9.7 km) wide on either side of its railway line.[11]

The following year, the federal government introduced legislation that permitted railway companies to choose their granted lands as alternate townships rather than alternate sections, provided the HBC would agree to take its sections elsewhere. This was largely at the urging of AR&CC directors, who were looking to create large contiguous areas for ranching. The radical change in Canadian land policy would soon have a dramatic impact on the company's irrigation plans as well.[12]

In 1890, the AR&CC would open a narrow-gauge railway from Lethbridge to Coutts, at the US border (and to Great Falls, Montana).

The following year, the Galt interests merged the NWC&N with the AR&CC. The marriage brought an end the pioneer parent corporation; all of its assets and liabilities were transferred to the AR&CC. In a further complex financial manoeuvre, the Galt interests created the Lethbridge Land Company to buy $800,000 of mortgages on 45,000 acres (18,200 ha) of land outside Lethbridge and 1,500 town lots that the NWC&N Company had sold.[13]

The Galt interests were now sitting on about 1.1 million acres (445,000 ha) of land that they had earned from building the two rail lines, from Lethbridge to Dunmore and from Lethbridge to Coutts. Through the holdings of the AR&CC, Elliot Galt—who by now had taken over all of the family business from his father, Alexander—sold 10,000 acres (4,050 ha) to the charismatic Mormon leader Charles Ora Card.[14] Card had extensive experience with irrigation from his years of farming in Utah and had begun modest experimentations with the available water resources in southern Alberta. The two men discussed the possibility of Galt's coal and railway companies partnering with the Mormons from the local town of Cardston, with a view to expanding the pioneering irrigation work of Card's flock throughout Southern Alberta.

"Railway after railway may be built through a section of the country until it is covered with a network of iron

These irrigation movers and shakers in Lethbridge were W.D. Barclay, manager of the Bank of Montreal; Charles Magrath, Alberta Railway & Coal Company land commissioner; George G. Anderson, consultant; Elliot T. Galt, AR&CC president; and Jeremiah Head, consultant. LIBRARY AND CULTURAL RESOURCES DIGITAL COLLECTIONS, UNIVERSITY OF CALGARY CU1177867

rails," the *Lethbridge News* editorialized, "but the country will never be a paying speculation until there is agriculture production."[15] And in southern Alberta that meant an investment in irrigation.

The West had been plagued with droughts from 1885, but both the government and the CPR downplayed any suggestion of lasting dry conditions because they did not want to discourage land sales and immigration. By the 1890s, however, the government came to the realization that

if they didn't want settlers to leave a large portion of the Northwest en masse, a comprehensive water policy would be essential.

The chief architect of the federal government's irrigation policy was William Pearce, the inspector of land agencies with the Dominion Lands Board. Pearce began his career as a land surveyor with the Department of the Interior, where his reputation for competence led to his appointment with the Lands Board in 1882. The board was responsible for establishing regulations, formulating government policy, recommending legislation and—not inconsequentially—overseeing all of the activities around land, timber, mineral, and water resources throughout the Northwest.[16] In that capacity, the board supervised all of the Dominion Lands offices in prairie communities to ensure uniform compliance with the law by local agents.

In 1884, as construction of the CPR advanced into the Rocky Mountains, Pearce was appointed superintendent of mines, reporting directly to the deputy minister of the interior and exercising authority over a belt of land 24 miles (39 km) wide on either side of the CPR's main line from the Red River Valley to British Columbia. His considerable influence earned him the unofficial title "Czar of the West" from those who feared his disfavour. He soon came to see water management as a key area of concern.

Pearce's views on irrigation were developed during his lengthy travels in the American West, where he studied water law, water management, and dry farming techniques. He realized that without irrigation, most of southern Alberta was better suited to ranching than cereal agriculture and, as a result, began to set aside strategic locations along rivers, creeks, and lakefronts as reserves for the cattle industry. However, even before the election of the federal Liberals in 1896, government policy in the West began to shift toward the individual homesteader and away from those who would lease large tracts of land for the purpose of grazing.[17]

Pearce's contention was that progressive management of land depended upon comprehensive government management of the region's entire water supply. In July 1894, his work came to fruition when a lengthy policy document drafted by the visionary advocate of large-scale irrigation won parliamentary approval for the Northwest Irrigation

◄ The considerable influence of William Pearce earned him the unofficial title of "Czar of the West." LIBRARY AND CULTURAL RESOURCES DIGITAL COLLECTIONS, UNIVERSITY OF CALGARY CU193834

► Ukrainians employed by the CPR in the Crowsnest Pass. AUTHOR'S COLLECTION

Act. The legislation transferred ownership of water through the Northwest to the federal government, enshrining water as a public resource and enabling federal bureaucrats to management water in the public interest.

Two years later, when Sifton became the most powerful government minister in the Northwest, Charles Alexander Magrath—himself influential as land commissioner for the Galt companies—wrote, "It is but fair to say that the impetus given to irrigation development in southern Alberta came from Clifford Sifton."[18]

George G. Anderson to review the entire project, from water supply and character of the land to the planned engineering details and the prospects for settlement. Anderson was a partner in Campbell and Anderson, an American engineering firm well respected for its technical knowledge and integrity.[19] Pearce wrote a favourable report to the CPR's Van Horne about the company's success in avoiding any "wild card enterprises or swindles."[20]

Anderson's report concluded that, with the addition of sufficient moisture through irrigation, the soil in the Lethbridge region was "well suited to the cultivation of the various crops of the temperate zone, especially to all cereals and grasses." As far as the prospects for settlement was concerned, the report identified a problem common to all projects of the sort, which was "the difficulty of securing pioneer settlers who have some means, considerable knowledge of the special features of agriculture under irrigation, and a large community to follow them upon success following the original efforts."[21]

Work on the irrigation project began in the late summer of 1898. With no steam shovels nor dredges, several hundred Mormon workers with teams of horses moved an estimated 1,121,000 cubic yards (857,000 m³) of dirt.[22]

Surveys for a new CPR route from Lethbridge through Crowsnest Pass had begun in April 1897, and grading commenced later that summer. The new railway would ultimately provide access to not only the rich coal resources in the Crowsnest Valley but gold, silver, and copper mines in the Kootenays, sustaining new towns and providing a ready market for agricultural products grown on irrigated lands in Alberta. To provide a link with its own main line, CPR had purchased Galt's railway line from Dunmore to Lethbridge in September 1897, for just under a million dollars.

Sifton and another major player, John Stoughton Dennis, the deputy commissioner in the Department of Public Works of the North-West Territories, had enabled the AR&CC to consolidate its considerable land holdings into a large block, greatly enhancing the feasibility of irrigation in the entire region. But the government itself would not make the huge investment in infrastructure that would be necessary for large-scale irrigation; that task would fall to the Galt interests—the CPR and another new endeavour they had incorporated in 1893, the Alberta Irrigation Company.

The AR&CC and the Alberta Irrigation Company planned to build a major canal northeastward from a point on the St. Mary's River near the US border, passing close to where the towns of Magrath and Stirling would evolve. A smaller canal would also be dug to Lethbridge. In 1897, the Alberta Irrigation Company hired Colorado irrigation engineer

In 1898, in support of the Galt companies' plans to settle irrigated lands, Canadian Pacific began to give the Alberta Irrigation Company rebate payments of 15 percent of its gross revenues on the Dunsmore-to-Lethbridge railway line, to a maximum of $100,000 spread over ten years.[23] CPR was about to adopt a similar land, irrigation, and settlement strategy of its own east of Calgary, on the Bow River, and the Galt lands would be valuable terrain for gaining technical know-how and devising marketing strategies.

While completing the financial arrangements for building its massive network of canals and infrastructure, the Galt concerns felt the need to add yet another corporate entity into their ever-expanding empire: the Canadian North-West Irrigation Company. The new holding company purchased 73,374 acres (29,693 ha) of land from the AR&CC, and another 26,626 acres (10,775 ha) from the Lethbridge Land Company, presumably creating some financial advantage.[24]

By the summer of 1900, water was flowing freely through the 115 miles (185 km) of new irrigation canals that included the 32-mile (51 km) Lethbridge Branch and the 22-mile (35 km) Stirling Branch. A year later, the Galt concerns were ready to begin selling their vast land holdings and sign long-term water agreements with prospective settlers. The Canadian North-West Irrigation Company published a stylish brochure as it embarked upon an extensive advertising campaign in Eastern Canada, the United States, and Europe, in which the company labelled southern Alberta the "Colorado of Canada."

In 1904, reversing the trend of two decades, the various directors in Galt's labyrinthian, intertwined conglomerate, merged all of their holdings into one company. The AR&CC, the Alberta Irrigation Company, the Lethbridge Land Company, the Canadian North-West Irrigation Company, and the St. Mary's River Railway Company—formed to build a few small lines to connect Galt properties in Lethbridge, Stirling, and Cardston—became the formidable new Alberta Railway & Irrigation Company.

The largest project of its kind

With the introduction of the Northwest Irrigation Act in 1894, speculation had gone into overdrive that the CPR would accept its remaining land grants of some 3 million acres (1.2 million ha) in a solid block of even-numbered and odd-numbered sections to allow the company to irrigate the lands east of Calgary, in the region where it had previously refused to take up holdings. At an irrigation convention in Calgary, Pearce's optimistic views were echoed by Dennis, now inspector of surveys for the Dominion government, who predicted that in ten-years' time the whole

western supply of grapes, apricots, and other fruit would be grown in the district, not unlike what was happening in the once arid belt of the United States.[25]

Unfortunately, the railway and the government were unable to come to an agreement on the exact terms under which the CPR would be given such a block of land, and, with the change of federal government from the Conservatives to the Liberals in 1896, the entire discussion fell into abeyance for several years. However, with the more enthusiastic advertising campaign that both the government and the railway launched south of the border to sell agricultural lands in the early years of the twentieth century, informal negotiations resumed. By July of 1903, Sifton and Shaughnessy—who was now president of the CPR, while Van Horne served as chairman—came to an understanding on the essential conditions of a settlement.

The CPR's decision to develop a huge block of irrigated land east of Calgary had been swayed by a detailed survey plan prepared by Dennis. Effective January 1, 1903, Dennis resigned his position with the federal government and became the overall manager for the CPR irrigation project, which would grow in stages to be the largest of its kind in North America. The new superintendent of irrigation would also serve as the railway's land commissioner for British Columbia. For the next two decades, Dennis would be one of the company's most industrious and influential promotors of immigration and settlement in the Northwest, and he would soon hire Pearce as his able assistant.

The irrigation project comprised a block of about 3 million acres (1.2 million ha) along the CPR main line, taking in nearly all of the land between the Red Deer and Bow rivers, and stretching east of Calgary for about 150 miles (241 km). Initially, for administrative purposes, the block was divided into Eastern, Central, and Western sections,

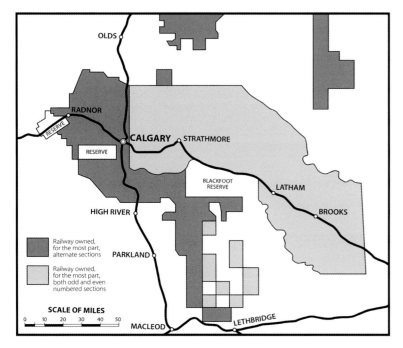

each containing about 1 million acres (400,000 ha). After the government agreed to turn over its lands, the company owned most of the sections within the block, except those controlled by the HBC and a few that had been granted to homesteaders prior to 1903.

In order to have an uninterrupted block for irrigation, the railway had to negotiate with the HBC to acquire just over 102,000 acres (41,000 ha) of land that the company owned in the area.[26] It was the biggest deal CPR had ever made with the former fur-trading giant that was rapidly becoming more concerned with its land and merchandise sales activities. Van Horne had long considered the HBC to be "one of the most hidebound concerns in existence," run by "a collection of persnickety and narrow-minded men who don't know enough about business to manage a peanut stand."[27]

At any rate, the land department of the HBC had found its semi-arid lands east of Calgary nearly impossible to sell, so was happy to turn them over to the railway. The CPR, on the other hand, was determined to give the entire area good reviews. An early CPR irrigation booklet described the general conditions to be found within the region:

The soil throughout the whole block is first-class, with heavy black loam on a clay subsoil in the Western portion and a lighter sandy loam with good subsoil in the more easterly parts. The whole block produces a most luxuriant growth of nutritious grasses, and the natural grazing is such as to provide pasture for horses, cattle and sheep throughout the whole year.[28]

Dennis and his CPR team would develop a variety of new settlement strategies and conduct some imaginative and successful advertising campaigns, which would bring increased immigration to the region right up until the First World War.

Launching the Atlantic fleet

As much as the CPR's innovative land and irrigation policies in the early years of the twentieth century changed the nature of the settlement game in the Northwest, the momentous decision to take a headfirst plunge into the turbulent waters of the transatlantic steamship trade would position the company as the dominant force in selling and delivering European emigration to Canada.

Even before the CPR's transcontinental rail line was completed to the Pacific Coast, the company's officers realized they would have to acquire ships to connect the railway with markets in the Far East. Without such a link, both the passenger and the freight business would be starved of revenue-generating traffic, particularly in the early years when large stretches of the cross-Canada route passed through wilderness, and the country could not build up much in the way of local business for the railway.

At the eastern end of the railway, it was a different story. In the waning years of the nineteenth century, several established steamship companies competed on the transatlantic routes to Europe from both Canadian and American ports. While the CPR got its financial house in order, building revenue and paying down debt, it was happy to partner with existing shipping lines, bringing immigrants inbound to Canada and the Northwest, and forwarding freight goods, grain, and livestock outbound to Britain and continental Europe. The tourist business would remain quite small and inconsequential until the 1920s.

For the CPR, two issues dominated the railway's discussions about those partnerships: the long-standing agreements between the dominant steamship companies and its chief rival, the Grand Trunk Railway, and the relative speed of ships serving Canadian ports versus those sailing to US destinations. Sometimes the two issues intersected, as is apparent by Van Horne's letter to Macdonald, alerting the prime minister that the Allan and Dominion Lines were "somewhat inclined to look upon us as disturbers of the public peace because of our advocacy of a fast Atlantic service." The CPR did not want to drive friendly steamship lines into an unholy alliance with the GTR, and the CPR "have respectfully assured them [the Dominion and Elder Dempster lines] that we would cooperate with them in preference to anybody else."[29]

Building new ships a few knots faster than the ones they already operated on the North Atlantic was a very expensive proposition for companies serving the less lucrative Canadian market, often with small profit margins. In addition, the ocean routes to Canada were generally several hundred miles shorter than the routes to Boston or New York, so a slower speed during the crossing was not always of much financial consequence. A reasonably swift passage across the Atlantic, of course, was a requirement for securing government mail contracts, and those contracts were often the difference between success and failure for competing lines.

By 1902, the CPR was flush with cash, and Shaughnessy made the bold decision that the time had come for the company to invest in the last Canadian Pacific link between the Old World and the Far East: a transatlantic steamship service of its own. Initially the company announced that it would build four liners capable of twenty knots in weekly

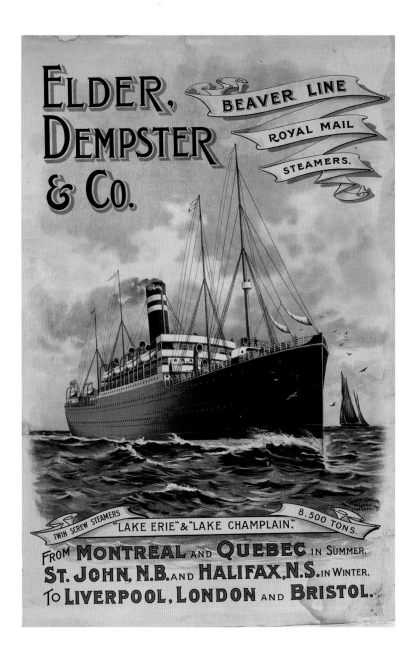

ELDER, DEMPSTER & Co.

BEAVER LINE
ROYAL MAIL
STEAMERS.

TWIN SCREW STEAMERS "LAKE ERIE" & "LAKE CHAMPLAIN." 8,500 TONS.

FROM MONTREAL AND QUEBEC IN SUMMER, ST. JOHN, N.B. AND HALIFAX, N.S. IN WINTER, TO LIVERPOOL, LONDON AND BRISTOL.

sailings as well as a small fleet of cargo ships with a speed of about half that. Shaughnessy informed shareholders of the situation:

The rapid growth of your export tonnage and the necessity for being in a position to meet the rates of any competitors, make it imperative that your Company be so situated on the Atlantic that it can quote through rates of freight and give through bills of lading without being compelled to negotiate for space and rates with independent lines.[30]

In addition, it would also allow any of the CPR's representatives at major centres in Europe to quote single fares for emigrants from ports served by the company to any of its railway stations in the Northwest.

As a rule, railway agents were authorized to negotiate bargain rates for settlers coming to Canada, particularly if they were also buying railway land. "This is one of the little jokes of the CPR," wrote a settled immigrant to his mother in England. "You can buy a ticket in London to come out here for about half the price they charge you here for one for London." To add to his beefs against the railway, he also took a rather cynical shot at the company's promotional materials: "I believe that the pass through the mountains is very fine, but you have to take a 90 percent discount off the descriptions in a CPR pamphlet. Of course, I live about five miles [8 km] from the foot of them, and one sees them every day, so one gets rather tired of them as samples of scenery. They are as barren and desolate as a pile of rocks can be."[31]

To keep competition in the Canadian trade at a minimum, Shaughnessy and the CPR negotiated a deal with the Elder Dempster Company to purchase fifteen vessels from the shipping company's Canadian arm, the Beaver

Line. The Elder Dempster Company was better known for its steamship service that began in the 1860s between the United Kingdom and the west coast of Africa, and later to the West Indies. The Beaver Line had also been formed in the 1860s as the Canada Steamship Company, with sailing ships in service from Liverpool to Quebec City and Montreal as well as to Portland, Maine, and Baltimore. Elder Dempster had controlled the Beaver Line for about five years before accepting Canadian Pacific's offer to buy all of those ships for around $7 million. "I think we have an excellent bargain," Shaughnessy expressed at the time, "and I shall be much disappointed if our Atlantic service fails to be a link of very great value indeed to our system."[32]

The purchase was a major coup for Shaughnessy. None of the acquired ships were more than a few years old. Eleven of the fifteen ships were freighters with a carrying capacity of up to 10,000 tons (907,000 kg), and the other four were similar ships that had been converted to passenger liner service. Those latter vessels—*Lake Champlain, Lake Erie, Lake Michigan,* and *Lake Manitoba*—were ideal for immigrant traffic, with accommodation for 680 to 750 passengers, mostly in second-class or steerage. All of the acquired ships could attain a speed of 12 to 13 knots, which had been sufficient to enable Elder Dempster to secure the Canadian mail contract in 1899.[33]

Van Horne, who was now chairman of the CPR board of directors, weighed in with his rationale for the purchase:

As I have said before, Canada has for some years been raising the sides of the hopper without enlarging the spout. We are simply trying to do our share of enlarging this spout . . . We are apt to get left in chartering vessels when we need them most, so we propose we have our own. This is in no way an effort to compete for traffic from New

York. Canadian Pacific has plenty of business for a line of its own, our object is to have our own ships.[34]

In one bold move, the CPR had an Atlantic steamship service of its own, and it had eliminated a potential competitor. An editorial in the *Montreal Gazette* said, "This action of the CPR should have a good effect on the trade of the St. Lawrence and of Montreal. The road's interest will be to bring by its trains all the business it can get for its steamers and vice versa."[35] The competition also recognized the significance of the acquisition. John Torrance of the Dominion Line, in expressing the views of CPR rivals, said, "This gives the Canadian Pacific the inside track over all other steamship companies and railways. This new arrangement will make Montreal a railway port, instead of a general port as at present."[36]

The influential *Financier and Bullionist* devoted several column inches to the "C.P.R. Shipping Deal." CPR's ships would compete with J.P. Morgan's International Mercantile Marine, a holding company that owned the Dominion Line, among others. If Morgan's company, the key player in a larger cartel, didn't control all of the transatlantic steamship traffic between the United States and Europe, it wasn't for lack of trying. The paper reported that Canadian freight rates would no doubt be governed by the rates from New York and Boston. "Hitherto a large portion of the Canadian Pacific Railway traffic has come to this country [England] via New York by steamers in the Atlantic trust," it reminded readers. "In future this will be shipped direct by the new service."[37]

Archer Baker, the CPR's European manager, arranged to send members of his staff to the various Elder Dempster offices in Britain that were involved with the Atlantic service and began to organize an administration to report directly to his office in London. He also asked the company's vice-president of finance in Montreal, Isaac Gouverneur Ogden, to "send over a competent steamship accountant to stay here [London] two months or longer to steer things into line and organize accounting to suit."[38]

That first year, thirty-three sailings were made from Liverpool by the *Lake Erie* and *Lake Manitoba*, carrying 860 first-class and 1,634 second-class passengers, and a whopping 23,400 emigrants in third class. A few hundred emigrants also embarked from Bristol in 1903. The next year, the service from Bristol was switched to London and Antwerp. From Antwerp alone, CPR steamships—including *Lake Michigan, Monterey, Montfort, Montreal,*

Montrose, Mount Royal, and *Mount Temple*—would carry close to 188,000 emigrants during the years up until 1913.[39]

At the dawn of the twentieth century, Liverpool was well established as the gateway to North America, not only for British and Irish emigrants, but for Scandinavians as well. The shipping journal, *Lloyd's List,* described the activity in the busy port during the inaugural year of CPR steamship service:

Evidence of the great "treck" [sic] to Canada has been very patent in the streets of Liverpool during the last few weeks. Crowds of emigrants of all nationalities have been thronging the streets, and outside offices of the several steamship companies engaged in the Atlantic trade there have been large numbers of people waiting whilst their tickets were procured.[40]

Third-class passengers on CPR steamships were provided, free of charge, what was called a "voyage outfit," consisting of bed, pillow, blanket, plate, drinking cup, knife, fork, and spoon. Emigrants were expected to keep their utensils in good order and leave them in the hands of the ships' stewards on arrival at their ports of landing.

Much like their predecessors in the nineteenth century, most of the former Elder Dempster ships suffered from having taken four-legged passengers to and from the recent South Africa War along with their human complement. "I was among 33 people in one small space," one emigrant on the way from Liverpool to Quebec soon after the war recalled. "All the men, the bachelors, were put in the hold where the horses and mules had been, below the waterline. It was in the bow and when the ship did this, up and down, we all got seasick … The men from the pantry, they didn't dare come in. We'd have killed them. They stood at the door with a great big tin pan of meat cut up in chunks and they threw it to us."[41]

At the time, the quality of food offered to steerage passengers by most steamship lines was basically dreadful, consisting largely of root vegetables well past their due date and rancid meats, often pork. One traveller on the Allan Line's *Bavaria*, in 1904, claimed he had been served pig's feet three times a day on a voyage to Canada. "I had visions of millions of pigs being sacrificed so that their feet could be given to the many emigrants leaving Europe," he said.[42]

From contemporary accounts, the CPR's early steamship offerings were at least marginally better. A typical bill of fare listed breakfast at 8 AM, dinner at 12:30 PM, tea at 5:30 PM, and supper at 8:30 PM. In a 1904 advertising leaflet, the onboard meals on offer for third-class passengers were:

Breakfast: Oatmeal porridge and milk, salt herrings, corned beef, hash, bread & butter, preserves, coffee.

Dinner: Green pea soup, boiled salt fish and egg sauce, roast beef, boiled potatoes, cabbage, tapioca pudding

Tea: Smoked herrings, corned beef, pickles, bread & butter, preserves, buns, tea

Supper: Gruel, biscuits and cheese[43]

When the ships arrived in Montreal, their sleeping berths were often dismantled to be replaced by portable stalls to accommodate horses in transit to various locations in Europe, or upwards of 1,200 cattle on their way to London's Deptford Cattle Market.[44]

One westbound steamship passenger in 1903 discovered evidence of this dual role by chance during an Atlantic crossing:

We were in what was called the forward hold. It was below the waterline. As we walked down it looked pretty nice, all painted white inside, but when we got closer we saw that it was only whitewash. Later on when we got going the whitewash got knocked off the walls as the waves hit. The whitewash would fall off the walls in chunks and there was manure under it. It had been used to transport horses.[45]

The Beaver Line steamships initiated the CPR with a baptism of fire in both the passenger and freight businesses on the North Atlantic. Nevertheless, faster ships would still be required to hold their own with the many shipping lines serving the United States, and, above all, to meet the competition from the Allan Line's two new turbine steamships, the *Victorian* and *Virginian*, operating from the UK to Canada. Accordingly, in November 1904, the CPR placed an order with the Fairfield shipping yard, on the banks of the River Clyde in Glasgow, for two eighteen-knot liners, the *Empress of Britain* and the *Empress of Ireland*.

The new ships were an immediate hit with travellers, no less so with emigrants than with those travelling in first class. In the first three years of their sailings, beginning in 1906, the numbers handled in third class were 13,871, 23,815, and 34,036, respectively.[46] Dormitory-style steerage had been eliminated in favour of cabins, lounges, and dining saloons. Chinaware had replaced metal dishes. The *Montreal Gazette* described the new experience:

The third-class accommodation of old has been revolutionized in the present vessel . . . and the old order of discomfort which formerly reigned in the steerage department has been swept away. There is even a roped off [fenced] sand playground for the little children.[47]

The two new CPR Atlantic Empresses were the fastest ships sailing to Canada, and the first steamers to offer amenities comparable to all but the very best vessels on the New York run. Where the crossing had once meant a month of being tossed about and tormented on a sailing ship, the sure and steady steamships could sail from Liverpool to Quebec City in relative tranquility, and in little more than six days.

They soon became popular staples with transatlantic passengers, as did some of the ships' well-known commanders. Captain William Stewart, the first man to take charge of the *Empress of Britain,* was said to be a fine example of the old-school North Atlantic skipper, an experienced and highly skilled mariner. He had been in command of the Beaver liner *Lake Champlain* when it was first acquired by the CPR. Captain Frank Carey was the first commander of the *Empress of Ireland*, beloved by his fellow officers and a favourite with passengers, partly because of his "delightfully soft Irish brogue." And then there was Captain Aubrey "Bully" Evans, nicknamed not for his overbearing disposition but as a result of his years of service piloting some of those cattle ships that were now doing double duty ferrying emigrants to the New World on their westward crossings.[48]

Those crossings of the North Atlantic, even on the CPR's newest steamships, could be rough for those not accustomed to the rigours of life at sea. One historical chronicler painted a vivid picture of a female immigrant on a 1907 voyage with her family aboard the *Empress of Britain*:

In the midst of the meal, the smell of the food overwhelmed her, causing her to make a mad dash for the open deck where she leaned over the railing and retched. The horizon kept rising and falling and the wind sang in the lifeboat lashings. She took out her handkerchief and did her best to clean herself up, then looked around at the vast,

watery emptiness. Was there a lonelier place on the earth than in the middle of a heaving ocean, she wondered? It was as if the whole world had disappeared and their little ark was all that was left on the planet. Then she began to cry, pounding her fist on the railing. What had they gotten themselves into? It had better be worth it, she thought bitterly.[49]

In 1906, the Allan Line had negotiated a new mail contract, which called for two additional turbine steamships to complement the *Virginian* and *Victorian* if it was to meet the specified terms of the service. When that necessary outlay of cash threatened its balance sheet with a flood of red ink, however, the shipping company's strained financial condition left an opening for Canadian Pacific to wrest a half share in the lucrative mail contract, using its two

◄ Immigrant passengers aboard the *Empress of Britain* amuse themselves with deck games. AUTHOR'S COLLECTION

▲ The third-class steerage accommodation of old was replaced with cabins, lounges, and dining saloons. Here, little children enjoy a fenced-off, sand-filled playground area.
HAROLD COPPING ILLUSTRATION,
AUTHOR'S COLLECTION

new steamships in rotation with the Allan Line's two fast liners. The partnership proved to be the first step in a negotiated merger of the two companies' shipping interests. In 1909, a formal agreement transferred all of the shares in the older firm, owned by the Allan family to the CPR. The following year, Canadian Pacific acquired the rest of the outstanding Allan Line stock and took complete control of the company.[50]

The negotiations had been conducted with a fair amount of secrecy. No official announcement of the agreement was made, and the Allan Line ships continued to sail under their former house flag. Incredible as it seems, the full details of the takeover remained clouded for several years to come. The *Saint John Daily Telegraph* report was typical of the confusion that reigned, even among industry insiders:

The sale of the Allan Line has been completed, purchase price said to be in the neighbourhood of $12 million [it had actually been $8,305,000]. It is thought that the fleet will go to the Grand Trunk, although there is a possibility that the CPR may be the purchasers.[51]

Former Dominion archivist W. Kaye Lamb believed that it was Shaughnessy's "high valuation on the popularity and good will of the Allan Line" that compelled the CPR to maintain the illusion of two separate entities. "Shipping men noted a few outward signs of amalgamation," he wrote, "notably the establishment of joint catering and maintenance staffs at Liverpool."[52]

It wouldn't be until 1913, at a meeting of CPR shareholders, that Shaughnessy would finally report: "Your Atlantic fleet has, in recent years, been supplemented by the acquisition of eighteen steamships with a gross tonnage of 146,361."[53] Even then the Allan Line was not mentioned by

name. An official announcement of the Allan Line takeover would not be forthcoming until early 1915, when Canadian Pacific applied to the Railway Committee of the Canadian House of Commons for permission to operate its railway and steamship services separately.

With the combined fleets of the Beaver and Allan lines, CPR had a substantial stake in the Atlantic steamship trade, competing head-to-head with established companies like the Red Star Line, Cunard Line, and the White Star Line. Ships arriving by the sheltered St. Lawrence route would take on a river pilot and a government immigration officer at Point-au-Père (Father Point) near the Quebec town of Rimouski. Mail bags were also loaded and unloaded there.

Down river, just above Quebec, was the historic quarantine station on Grosse Isle, first opened in 1832 during a European cholera epidemic but used most extensively a decade later to cope with the thousands of immigrants who suffered and died from typhus during the Irish Potato

▲ Baggage was tagged for its destination before being stored in the hold of the *Empress of Ireland.* AUTHOR'S COLLECTION

▶ A group of emigrants from Hamburg, Germany, pose on the deck of the *Empress of Ireland.* LIBRARY AND CULTURAL RESOURCES DIGITAL COLLECTIONS, UNIVERSITY OF CALGARY CU188613

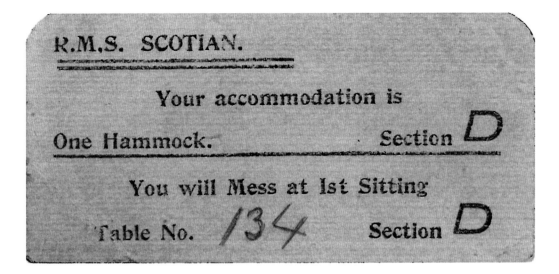

R.M.S. SCOTIAN.

Your accommodation is

One Hammock.   Section *D*

You will Mess at 1st Sitting

Table No. *134*   Section *D*

Famine. Other quarantine stations were located on Lawlor's Island off Halifax Harbour and Partridge Island near the CPR's all-season terminal at Saint John, New Brunswick.

Ships' officers and steamship company directors lived in fear of the potential losses that would occur if their vessels were stranded with outbreaks of cholera, plague, smallpox, typhus, or yellow fever. Less fatal, but equally disruptive to steamship schedules, was the onboard presence of chicken pox, diphtheria, measles, and scarlet fever. Lepers were not allowed to enter Canada and, when discovered on board an incoming vessel, would be detained at the expense of the ship owner until such a time as they could be taken aboard an outbound ship owned by the offending company.

By the opening decades of the twentieth century, it was common practice to dedicate a full day to vaccinating everyone on board as a ship approached its destination. Passengers were often required, at the port of departure, to show evidence of having been vaccinated against the major prevailing diseases. When outbreaks of disease did occur, steam and boiling water could be used to disinfect items of clothing. Other articles and surfaces were treated with a variety of substances, including mercuric chloride, carbolic acid, formaldehyde, and sulphur dioxide.

Vessels requiring quarantine inspection flew yellow flags at the fore by day and red flags by night. Any passenger leaving a ship before it was inspected and cleared by a quarantine officer was liable for a fine and six-month imprisonment.

At its summer terminals in Quebec City and Montreal, the company had access to its own piers and dockside tracks where immigrants could be readily transferred to the colonist cars that would take them to their new homes in the Northwest. The CPR also had extensive terminal facilities

at Saint John, New Brunswick, that were open year-round, and both inbound and outbound calls were often made at Halifax.

Free temporary accommodation was available in government immigration halls at port cities. Women and children had separate quarters, where matrons and assistants were on hand to attend to their needs. Groups of fifty or more immigrants arriving by ship were often accompanied on shore by a Canadian immigration officer to "protect them against imposition."[54]

After tedious civil and medical examinations, immigrants were subjected to sorting by destination, the CPR's passenger department having a large staff of agents and ticket sellers at ports of landing for that purpose. An "exchange ticket agent" was in charge of making any necessary adjustments to prior arrangements that weren't quite right or for making the proper connections with other railways and transportation companies. Passengers headed for the Soo district were issued blue tickets, those for Toronto, Detroit, and the eastern states a red one, and those for the Canadian Northwest yellow or white tickets, which were used interchangeably. Once passengers were ticketed, their baggage was checked and tagged according to the district of the country to which they were bound, thus enabling trainmen to transfer them onto the appropriate trains at junction points.[55]

The CPR's Windsor Street Station in Montreal was the busiest centre for forwarding immigrants to Winnipeg and the Northwest. With the arrival of ships, a large detachment of employees awaited the onslaught, including at least one official interpreter who could speak multiple languages fluently.

Below the station train shed were the immigrant quarters. One immense room was allocated for Asians in transit,

Left Most of the CPR's competitors had served the Canadian trade for many years, but usually had ports of call more important to their bottom lines in the United States. LIBRARY AND CULTURAL RESOURCES DIGITAL COLLECTIONS, UNIVERSITY OF CALGARY CU12926305

Right The Cunard Line was awarded the first British transatlantic mail contract and operated under the name British and North American Royal Mail Steam-Packet Company. LIBRARY AND CULTURAL RESOURCES DIGITAL COLLECTIONS, UNIVERSITY OF CALGARY CU12926306

while another capable of accommodating eight hundred people at a time was devoted to Europeans. The quarters were kept scrupulously clean, if mildly tainted by the odour of disinfectants resulting from daily maintenance and periodic fumigations.

Contributing to their reputation for displaying an attitude of entitlement, British immigrants objected to consorting with those from other countries, particularly if it meant being kept below street level, and were therefore most in evidence to the general public. Newspapers as far away as Calgary took them to task:

They insist upon being permitted to remain in the station proper, and the railway officials after vainly endeavoring to induce them to see the desirability of all immigrants remaining together, have given over the effort as a bad job ... Being able to speak the language of the country, they are in a position to argue with the officials, and that is one reason for the failure of the employees of the railway to induce them to accept the quarters provided for the generality of immigrants. The foreign immigrants, on the contrary, are amenable to reason, and are, for the most part, eminently docile.[56]

Colonist cars could be added to regular trains for small groups, but for larger contingents arriving by the shipload, immigrant specials were scheduled to leave for the West at times that would not interfere with local service and scheduled through trains. Some found the train trip to be an enormous relief after the rigours of a rough ocean crossing, others not so much. "My nights were a prolonged series of nightmares," recalled one pilgrim who wrote under the pseudonym "Tenderfoot." The conductor roused him three times during the night to check his ticket even though he was dog tired. "Is this a conspiracy on the part of

the CPR," he asked, "to have it out of colonists for the low rate at which tickets are supplied them?"[57]

"We in the colonist cars are a solemn, white-faced crowd, speaking several tongues," recalled a new immigrant, freshly from steerage on the *Empress of Britain*, "the seats a jumble of women, canvas-covered bundles, and fretful children. It is indeed a pathetic picture—this throng of newly arrived immigrants, many so uncouthly and inappropriately clad, and bearing marks of the poverty from which they have emerged."[58]

Before the turn of the century, many emigrants had come to Canada by steamship on their way to the United States. The tide had now turned, so that those who stayed—many of them heading for the Northwest—significantly outnumbered those who left the country. In the summer of 1904, the Winnipeg papers wrote about the immigrants fresh off CPR steamships from Bolivia arriving in town along with the usual numbers of British, Germans, Galicians, Scandinavians, and Russians. Others were returned from the United States:

The immigration office has just received a letter from a German residing in La Paz, in the South American republic of Bolivia. The writer says a large exodus from that country, with the faces of those migrating toward western Canada, may shortly be expected... Tomorrow the morning train will bring 100 British, 86 Germans, 17 Russians and 38 Galicians, while No. 97 will bring 70 British. These are from the steamers Montreal *and* Lake Manitoba. *This morning a party of 30 British and 20 Russians left for the West and on the same train were about 100 of Father Blais' party of French-Canadians, who are coming west to take up land. The majority of this party are from points in the eastern states, and are coming back to live under the British government.*[59]

Sailing to the New World to embark upon a life so far away from everything familiar must surely have been a bitter-sweet time of reflection. One of CPR's emigrant passengers leaving Glasgow on the former Allan Line steamship *Ionian* wrote to her relatives about the experience:

It is indeed a very sad sight seeing a boat leaving, and certainly to my idea no place for mothers and fathers, although a great many were there. It is just enough to say goodbye at the railway station, but it is nothing compared to the boat when it begins to move slowly away from the dock; such a funny feeling comes over one, it is really farewell then.[60]

8 THE BOOM YEARS

New beginnings

In 1901, Canadian Pacific strengthened its resolve to settle the Northwest with its appointment of William Whyte to the position of manager of CPR lines from Port Arthur to the Pacific Coast. He was also made assistant to the president and policy advisor on "all matters connected with colonization, proposed extensions of the company's railway system, the development of industry along the company's lines, the establishment of new business connections and the administration of the company's lands, townsites and other properties."[1]

A native of Charlestown, Fife, Scotland, Whyte began his railway career in 1861 with the North British Railway. By 1865, he was in Canada working for the Grand Trunk Railway, first as a freight clerk at Cobourg, Ontario, and later holding positions of increasing responsibility in Toronto. In 1884, Whyte was general superintendent of the Toronto, Grey & Bruce Railway when it amalgamated with the CPR. He served as superintendent of Canadian Pacific's Eastern and Ontario divisions before becoming general superintendent of the railway's Western Division.[2]

Augustus Nanton, one of the principal investors and developers of Western Canada, had high praise for the CPR's new Western boss: "I came in contact with many C.P.R. men," Nanton wrote to a colleague, "and was greatly struck with their loyalty to Whyte... With five out of six men against the C.P.R. as they are up here [in the Northwest], it is no small advantage to the Company to have a man at the head of affairs who is personally liked as Whyte is, not only by his men but liked and respected by the public."[3] A born railroader, Whyte was referred to in the *Winnipeg Free Press* as "the most distinguished private citizen of Western Canada."[4]

The upturn in the Canadian economy and the influx of new settlers to the Northwest had applied pressure not only to the CPR's land office but also to the operations departments, as is evident from President Shaughnessy's letter to an investor in Berlin in early 1902:

The development of our traffic, particularly in North-Western Canada, is beyond our expectations... our land sales indicate that settlers and land-seekers have their eyes on North-Western Canada, and that they are moving there in larger numbers than at any time heretofore... We have been deplorably short of cars during the past six months, and, satisfactory as our earnings were, we could have increased them were it possible to obtain additional rolling stock from any source.[5]

The strong tide of immigration at the beginning of the twentieth century had added an urgency to the government's insistence that CPR choose its outstanding land grants. But many of the odd-numbered sections along the railway main line had already been rejected by Canadian Pacific as too arid and unfit for agricultural settlement. As a result, an agreement was negotiated whereby the railway would accept a solid block of around 3 million acres (1.2 million hectares) of dry land between Calgary and Medicine Hat. By incorporating all of the government's even-numbered sections, most of which had not yet been taken up by homesteaders, with those allocated for railway grants, the company would be in a position to develop the entire region for extensive irrigation and dry farming.

The arrangement put to bed the issue of large areas of land being held in abeyance by the government to fulfill land grant claims, while making far more lands immediately available to immigrants for settlement. It also left Canadian Pacific to colonize the entire region alone and unaided. There would be no free government homesteads to draw settlers to the lands within the irrigation block, and no public agencies to engage in marketing them.

John Stoughton Dennis would be the CPR's superintendent of irrigation. Dennis was the son of John Dennis Sr., who served as Canada's first surveyor-general and deputy minister of the interior. He was born in Toronto in 1856, and first saw the Canadian West at the age of sixteen, when he assisted with the official government exploration and charting of lakes Winnipeg, Manitoba, and Winnipegosis and their connecting rivers. By 1879, Dennis had joined the HBC as surveyor and engineer, and helped to lay out town lots in Winnipeg, Prince Albert, Edmonton, and Kenora. He was also in command of the Dominion Land Surveys

Intelligence Corps, known as Dennis' Scouts, during the Riel Resistance of 1885.[6]

The CPR recruited J.S. Dennis in 1903 from the North-West Territories Department of Public Works, where he was chief commissioner, to manage its irrigation interests. His move from government offices in Regina to the railway's offices in Calgary, was the company's first step in migrating the administration of its lands and natural resources westward.

Under the leadership of CPR's new superintendent of irrigation, the large block of land was divided into Eastern, Central, and Western irrigation sections—later districts—for administrative purposes, to allow for incremental development. Initially, the CPR estimated that about half of the total area, or 1.5 million acres (600,000 ha), would require irrigation, while the remaining lands could be made productive through the application of judicious dry-farming techniques. The first region to be developed would be the Western Section.

Within a year of joining Canadian Pacific, Dennis would recruit another stalwart of Western Canadian irrigation, his former colleague in the Dominion surveyor-general's office, William Pearce, a pioneer surveyor, civil engineer, statistician, and public servant. Pearce was also schooled in Toronto but gained his expertise in land-use policy while working in the Northwest. He studied irrigation and dry-farming techniques in the United States and built a reputation for meticulous documentation. He was also instrumental, in collaboration with CPR's William Van Horne, for advocating for the creation of Canada's first national preserve, Rocky Mountains Park. As chief assistant to the railway's superintendent of irrigation, Pearce would be an invaluable aide in researching and planning the settlement of CPR lands.

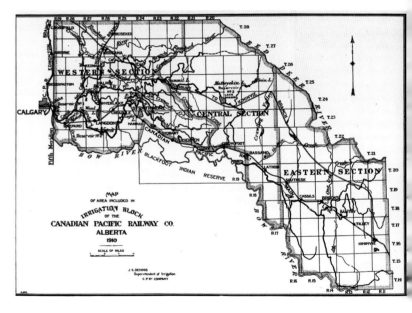

The contractor, Magnus Brown, who previously ranched in the lands around Red Deer and Edmonton, was in charge of the construction crews working on the main CPR irrigation canal. Brown would go on, in 1911, to become a Calgary alderman and earn a reputation as "the rhubarb king," on the strength of his large garden adjoining St. George's Island Park.[7]

In 1904, construction began on a weir, a low-level dam, across the Bow River in Calgary's east end. At that point, water from the river was diverted into the main canal to be carried eastward toward Reservoir #1, later named Chestermere Lake. The reservoir was filled for the first time in 1905. Downstream from the reservoir, the water was released into three secondary canals with a combined length of 254 miles (409 km) to as far away as Gleichen. The water was then "delivered to irrigators through a comprehensive system of distribution ditches totalling 1,329 miles [2,139 ha] in length."[8] Two years later, settlers were already using irrigation waters along this section of the project.[9]

Soon after arriving on the scene, Dennis would add to his responsibilities for constructing the railway's irrigation system by formulating a new strategy to settle some 98,000 acres (40,000 ha) of company land that were at too high an elevation for effective irrigation. These lands could still be used productively as grazing land or sold to wheat farmers who would employ dry-farming methods to grow their crops.

Adding to the allure, the superintendent introduced a payment plan whereby purchasers could put down one-sixth of the cost of their land, with the balance in ten equal annual installments. As a special inducement to ranchmen, he allowed a one-year extension for their second payment if they put at least one head of cattle on every 20 acres (8 ha) of land purchased. By 1905, half the acreage on offer

had been sold or leased, and the rest followed soon after.[10] More than one hundred and fifty ranches within the irrigation block were leased to the federal department of the interior for grazing purposes. Other grazing lands sold at prices ranging from $4.50 to $5 per acre ($11 to $12.35/ha).[11]

With so many Americans looking north for opportunities to acquire land, it was inevitable that US companies would be among the first to show interest in CPR's new offerings within the irrigation district. Among the companies with which the railway had already had dealings was the Canadian-American Land Company, a Dakota syndicate that had been heavily involved in colonization activities in the area around High River in Alberta and along the railway lines in the Weyburn and Milestone sections of southeastern

Assiniboia, on which CPR's Soo Line ran passenger trains up from the Twin Cities and brought home-seekers looking for land. In 1905, the leading members of this group—Thomas L. Beiseker and Charles H. Davidson, North Dakota bankers and land speculators—joined together with another US businessman, A.J. Sayre, to form the Calgary Colonization Company.

The colonization company established its headquarters in Calgary and purchased 54,000 acres (22,000 ha) from the CPR at $5 per acre ($12.35/ha), which was quickly upped to 80,000 acres (32,000 ha). Dennis was happy to arrange free transportation for agents of the company, particularly when the firm sought to acquire an additional 100,000 acres (40,000 ha) of non-irrigable CPR land at $6 per acre ($14.83/ha), under a ten-year contract arrangement.[12]

At the time, Dennis was locked in discussions with the railway's president, Thomas Shaughnessy, as well as with William Whyte, by then CPR vice-president, in charge of western lines, about policy matters. Superintendent Dennis was at odds with his bosses over whether to proceed at full speed with land companies—as he advocated—or to move slower to determine the effectiveness of the colonization companies' marketing strategies and the prices they were paying for both irrigable and non-irrigable CPR lands. Early reports supported Dennis when it was revealed that the Calgary Colonization Company had quickly sold 72 sections to individual settlers who would soon be putting their produce in CPR boxcars. To sell the land, the colonization company had spent $3 per acre ($7.41/ha) on advertising and commissions for agents and realized about $11 per acre ($27.19/ha). Since they had paid $5 per acre ($12.36/ha), this left them with a respectable net profit of $3 per acre ($7.41/ha).[13]

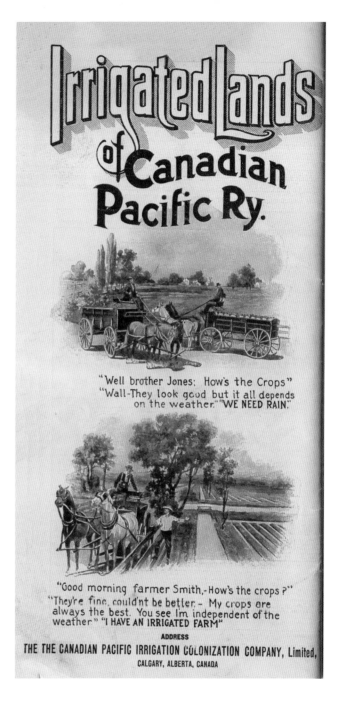

"Well brother Jones: How's the Crops"
"Wall-They look good but it all depends on the weather." "WE NEED RAIN."

"Good morning farmer Smith,-How's the crops?"
"They're fine, could'nt be better.- My crops are always the best. You see Im independent of the weather." "I HAVE AN IRRIGATED FARM"

ADDRESS
THE THE CANADIAN PACIFIC IRRIGATION COLONIZATION COMPANY, Limited,
CALGARY, ALBERTA, CANADA

Changing of the guard

The Liberals remained popular in the Canadian West as well as in the more populated eastern centres, and easily won the federal elections in 1900 and 1904. Within three months of the latter campaign, however, the government's star politician in the Northwest would resign from Cabinet. Clifford Sifton, who had done so much to promote Canadian immigration and settlement, primarily to the vast regions of underpopulated lands in the West, had packed it in following a dispute with Prime Minister Laurier over school policy in the new provinces of Saskatchewan and Alberta. Basically, Sifton opposed allowing both French and English school boards, while Laurier—with a steady eye on his Quebec constituency—insisted on maintaining separate boards.

The massive influx of immigrants that accompanied the dawning of the twentieth century and the ascent of the federal Liberal party had created a mounting need for infrastructure in the Northwest, including railways, roads, bridges, and schools of whatever linguistic persuasion. Frederick Haultain, who was the first minister—effectively the premier—of the Northwest Territorial Assembly, had long pleaded with the federal government for more and more subsidies and, preferably, provincial status for at least a portion of the Northwest. In the words of historian and former lieutenant-governor of Alberta, Grant Mac-Ewan, "The government was presenting the Territories around the world as a 'home for millions' but had no right, in Haultain's view, to invite mass settlement unless it was prepared to pay for at least a minimum of services."[15]

Sifton had consulted with Haultain and his colleagues on the matter, but he was not convinced that the population

Buoyed by their early successes, Beiseker, Davidson, and Sayre proceeded to reorganize their company as the Canadian Pacific Irrigation Colonization Company (CPICC) and were able to reach a contractual agreement with the railway company on December 21, 1905, to sell 110,000 acres (45,000 ha) of irrigable lands in the CPR's Western Irrigation Section.[14] The colonization company planned to create agencies, issue literature, bring in farmer delegates from the US, and establish a demonstration farm at Gleichen to instruct settlers and potential settlers in irrigation farming. But it would not be long before the CPR's do-it-yourself philosophy would kick in, and Dennis would recommend not only usurping the settlement strategies of the railway's namesake colonization company but taking it over entirely.

of the Northwest had reached the kind of numbers that warranted the creation of one or more new provinces. This issue may have further distanced the minister of the interior from his Cabinet colleagues. In any case, during the 1904 election campaign, Laurier had promised that, if returned to power, he would immediately begin to negotiate provincial status for the Territories.[16]

True to his word, on February 21, 1905, Laurier introduced two new bills in the House of Commons to establish self-government in the new provinces of Saskatchewan and Alberta. Because of the limitations of railway travel, and the political desirability of Laurier being on hand for both events, the inaugural ceremonies were held in Edmonton on the first of September and in Regina on the fourth.

Sifton's falling out with Laurier meant that he would not be there to preside with the prime minister over the momentous occasions; he would remain as a private member of Parliament until 1911, but he would no longer hold a Cabinet post. Taking over as minister of the interior would be Francis Robert Bowsfield Oliver, the former liberal editor of the *Edmonton Bulletin*, who would continue to implement Sifton's immigration policies, with some significant adjustments.

Oliver, a printer, merchant, newspaper editor, and publisher before turning to politics, honed his rhetorical skills with the *Globe* in Toronto and the *Winnipeg Free Press* before making his way to Edmonton and launching the *Bulletin*, soon to be the *Edmonton Bulletin*. When the CPR took a southern path through Calgary, rather than pursuing the long-planned route through Edmonton, he was embittered toward both the federal Conservatives and the CPR and became an avid supporter of the Liberals. As such, he championed the cause of squatters and homesteaders

over large land speculators and corporate interests. He was also a leading proponent of responsible government for the Northwest Territories and lobbied tirelessly to make Edmonton rather than Calgary the capital of the new province of Alberta.[17]

Shortly after taking office, Oliver shepherded a new piece of legislation into play that would focus more attention on the cultural and ethnic origins of immigrants rather than their potential for contributing to the Canadian economy. The Immigration Act of 1906 empowered the government to prohibit the landing in the country of "any specified class of immigrants," giving Oliver's department of the interior the power to discriminate freely against any ethnic group it chose. There would be far fewer of Sifton's "men in sheepskin coats" to threaten the primacy of old stock Brits and the preservation of Anglo-Saxon norms.

The Act significantly expanded the list of prohibited immigrants to specifically include Ukrainians, Poles, Russians, and other Eastern Europeans, as well as Italians and Greeks. Slavs were considered morally inferior and would surely corrupt native-born Canadians; they could never be assimilated into British culture.[18] The law also sought to exclude others on the basis of health and morality, turning back those who were blind, deaf, insane, epileptic, "feebleminded," or afflicted with "loathsome" or contagious diseases, as well as prostitutes and pimps, the destitute and impoverished, anyone likely to become a public charge, and those guilty of "crimes involving moral turpitude."[19]

The provisions of the legislation were applied to all steamship passengers arriving on Canadian shores while travelling in second-class or steerage accommodations. First-class passengers, whether or not they intended to take up residence in Canada, were not considered immigrants,

and could slip through the regulatory safety net even if they were blind or, perhaps, of a morally dicey character.[20] Despite the more stringent restrictions on the admittance of newcomers from "non-preferred countries," the demands for labour to fill the less desirable positions in industry and commerce, for which Canadians were not clamouring, necessitated the continued immigration of unskilled labour from those places of origin.

Taking exception to the more restrictive rules around immigration that Oliver had brought in with the government's new immigration act, Van Horne, the CPR chairman, could hardly contain himself:

What we want is population. Labour is required from the Arctic Ocean to Patagonia, throughout North and South America, but the governments of other lands are not such idiots as we are in the matter of restricting immigration. Let them all come in. There is work for all. Every two or three men that come into Canada and do a day's work create new work for someone else to do. They are like a new dollar. Hand it out from the Bank and it turns itself in value a dozen or more times a year.[21]

A 1903 government immigration brochure specified that Western Canadians were English, Scottish, Irish, French, and English-speaking Americans, with "a splendid lot of Germans and Scandinavians." It also claimed, perhaps with a generous dollop of wishful thinking, that "all immigrants spoke English."[22]

During the Sifton years, from 1896 to 1905, British immigrants outnumbered their Eastern European counterparts by three or four to one, and that statistic only increased with the new regulations. The problem for both Sifton and Oliver was that they could not attract the people

they wanted most: farmers and experienced agriculturalists. However, clerks, bookkeepers, machinists and factory workers, carpenters and bricklayers, students, schoolteachers, and remittance men came by the thousands.[23]

Mary Eleanor Elliot described one such displaced Englishman whom she observed on the CPR station platform upon her arrival in South Qu'Appelle in 1904:

He looked as though he belonged to his new surroundings. The Van Dyke beard currently popular in London complemented his assured walk; both confirmed his easy acceptance of an Englishman's privileged role in a still largely colonial world. The old felt hat, the best Johannesburg had been able to produce during his three-year stay in southern Africa, the Norfolk jacket, and the high leather boots merged well with the ugly red station building.[24]

She found the CPR station to be an unappealing "deep *sang de boeuf*," the colour of dried blood. That was not nearly as "appalling" as the immigration hall in Winnipeg, where she pronounced herself to be "horrified by the casual mingling of complete strangers in the much-publicized Gateway to the Golden West."[25]

In 1906, Thomas Arnold went to the Canadian Government Immigration offices in central London to find out about the prospects of moving to Canada. Things looked pretty good. He could get a 160-acre (65 ha) piece of land for free, and the young clerk at the government office offered to see if one of the railway companies could use an accounting clerk, a job for which Arnold was well qualified. When the news came through that he had secured a position with the CPR in Winnipeg, he booked passage for himself and his wife on the company's *Empress of Britain* and headed for the New World.[26]

It was a scene of total chaos when the couple arrived in the Gateway to the West. The baggage handlers at CPR's Winnipeg station were "tossing off suitcases, valises and assorted carryalls into a jumbled heap on the platform. Trunks were roughly manhandled off the baggage car and piled haphazardly as well … The result was a frustrating free-for-all."[27]

An altogether nasty start to Arnold's life in his adopted country got even worse when he discovered that nobody at the railway had heard of Thomas Arnold, and there was no job waiting for him. "I don't know who to blame," Tom said, "the Canadian Department of Immigration or the Canadian Pacific Railway." Stunned by his misfortune, he walked down Main Street to look at all the Help Wanted signs in the shop windows, only to be bowled over by what he saw: many of those signs bore the caveat, "No Englishmen Need Apply."[28]

Arnold had fallen victim to a new Western prejudice, the prevailing opinion that Englishmen were not only arrogant and self-entitled but poor and unreliable workers as well. Steamship and land agents in Britain were prone to oversell job prospects in the Canadian West at the best of times, but in their defence, they were probably unaware of the added challenges their own countrymen might find there. Fortunately for Arnold, the railways were constantly in need of labourers, and he eventually landed a job as a CPR baggage handler, giving him the chance to help new immigrants avoid a scene as chaotic as he had experienced upon his arrival in a new country.

The underlying prejudice against Englishmen among native-born Canadians seems to have been based on three premises: the United Kingdom was pawning off its inferior citizens; those who came were urban workers with little agricultural experience; and such immigrants brought with

them a poor attitude toward Canada and Canadians.[29] As a result, they may have been mocked and discriminated against, but the Britishers kept coming in ever large numbers.

The immigration campaigns carried on in the United States by the CPR and the federal government were also remarkably successful, despite the more southern country's natural advantages. "There is always a drift to the south," former minister of the interior Clifford Sifton expounded in later years. "The climate is warmer and the conditions are easier. Young men go there to better their condition in business, and for adventure and other reasons; old people go because they want a milder climate. Sick people go because they cannot stand the Canadian winter. French-Canadians go to work in the factories of New England."[30]

Nevertheless, the growing scarcity of good agricultural land in the United States, free or not, plus a number of favourable economic conditions in the North, had reversed the southward drift. Newspapers in the Northwest were enthusiastic about the "large number of desirable settlers from across the line" who were coming to make their homes in Canada:[31]

Of recent years there has been a vast immigration of settlers from the United States to the fair and fertile domains of Alberta and the Canadian West generally. This class of immigration is of the top-notch order, and every true Canadian should be proud to see it and encourage it. Thus shall our vast tracts of God's bountifulness … be peopled by an intelligent, progressive race of our own kind, who will readily be developed into permanent, patriotic, solid citizens.[32]

Indeed, Canadians and Americans had begun to intermingle indiscriminately. In towns like Portage la Prairie, Fourth of July celebrations took on the appearance of a Canadian national holiday, with revellers converging from the

▶ Settlers from Britain, the United States, and an assortment of countries in northern Europe were singing from the same songbook during Fourth of July celebrations in Portage la Prairie, with the Union Jack flying side by side with the Stars and Stripes. LIBRARY AND ARCHIVES CANADA C-081414

GERMANS   ICELANDERS   SCOTCHMEN   ENGLISHMEN   AMERICANS   FRENCHMEN   SCANDINAVIANS
                BELGIANS   RUSSIANS   AUSTRIANS   IRISHMEN

THE MAPLE LEAF FOR EVER

CANADA

"NOW THEN, ALL TOGETHER"!

surrounding countryside and arriving from other towns by train. For the 1907 event, nine cars full of members of the Winnipeg-American Association pulled into the CPR station with Canadian and British flags flying freely alongside the ubiquitous Stars and Stripes to mark the anniversary of the great republic to the south.

Mayor Brown gave a lengthy speech that was liberally applauded:

We feel greatly to the American people because the large influx of immigration which has been coming steadily our way during the last five years began from the United States. The Americans were the first to appreciate the value of our farm lands, and because of the confidence displayed by them by actual investment they assisted us materially in directing the attention of the world to our magnificent heritage. We frankly admit that the American settler is the most desirable we get.[33]

By 1906, more than twenty-seven thousand migrant workers were making their way west on CPR "harvest excursion" trains to help harvest the grain crop in Western Canada that was now approaching an annual ninety million bushels of wheat, seventy million of oats, and seventeen million of barley.[34] The call for additional able-bodied workers to put in sixteen-hour days in the fields had begun in the last decade of the nineteenth century, and the annual tide had grown by leaps and bounds in the interim.

Development of the Western District in the CPR's irrigation block continued apace. In its first years of construction, a Polish "Krakow Colony" was established along the excavated canals, as were communities of Danes, Dutch, and French-Canadians. Dennis began to set fairly stringent standards for the entire project, which were to include,

Top Thousands of workers came west to Winnipeg on CPR "harvest excursions" to help bring in the tens of millions of bushels of wheat, oats, and barley grown in the Northwest every year. LIBRARY AND CULTURAL RESOURCES DIGITAL COLLECTIONS, UNIVERSITY OF CALGARY 1125735

Bottom A harvest excursion train from Toronto stops to pose with its mostly male occupants, September 19, 1907. PROVINCIAL ARCHIVES OF ALBERTA A-10499

for example, a minimum cost of $350 for a house. Each homestead was to have a barn, several animals, and certain specified farm implements. The railway's superintendent of irrigation was beginning to formulate what CPR soon would launch as its "ready-made farm" strategy.[35]

They say it's a dry cold

It was easy, of course, for immigrants to feel right at home in Canada in mid-summer, whether they were coming to their new homes from a similar latitude on the European continent or from the northern plains of the United States, but winter in the "Golden Northwest" was another story, despite what the pamphlets had to say. "The climate of Manitoba is warm in summer and cold in winter," one CPR handout for the Northwest helpfully informed the prospective immigrant. "The atmosphere, however is very bright and dry, and the sensation of cold is not so unpleasant as that of a cold temperature in a humid atmosphere." As Western Canadians would insist from then on, "It's a dry cold."

The description of what to expect in Alberta was more explicit: "Spring is the most trying; not because it is particularly wet or severe, but because, with a mild winter, one expects to see a correspondingly early spring." Summer was deemed "superb; between the days of bright, life-producing sunshine, copious warm showers fall, bathing the rich soil like a hot-bed, and forcing vegetation forward in rapid and rank profusion." Autumn was simply "perfect ... The blue vault of heaven is unmarked with even the shadow of a cloud, the atmosphere clear and light, bright and invigorating, thrilling every pulsation of feeling,

sharpening the intellect, and infusing ruddy energy into every part of the body." And in winter, while there might be the occasional "low readings of the thermometer," one could be certain they would be "alternating with days of great warmth."[36]

Much hand-wringing occurred in the offices of the CPR public relations people in 1897 when the famous British imperialist Rudyard Kipling lauded the Laurier government's reduction of Canadian tariffs on imports from Britain with a poem that paid tribute to the overseas Dominion. Its unfortunate title was "Our Lady of the Snows." Horrors! If there was one thing that the CPR did not

want Canada becoming synonymous with in the minds of foreigners, it was snow. This was the "empire's breadbasket," after all. And what about those warm Chinook winds?

Kipling made three trips to Canada: the first in 1889 while en route to London from India; again in 1892, when he visited the Northwest with his American wife and travelled westward through the country as far as Vancouver Island; and a final visit in 1907 to see how the West had prospered since his previous trips. It was during this last tour that he famously proclaimed that Medicine Hat—a town name he admired and cited for its "uniqueness, individuality, assertiveness and power"—had "all hell for a basement," an homage to its plentiful natural gas resources. Kipling was awarded the Nobel Prize in Literature that year.

The railway had produced and distributed an enormous amount of propaganda extolling Canada as a settler's paradise, greatly influencing how the country was viewed by the rest of the world. Van Horne was particularly rankled by the efforts of the CPR's enemies to portray the Northwest as a frozen wasteland much of the year. After Kipling's widely disseminated "tribute," the order went out from President Shaughnessy's office that none of the company's campaigns and public displays were to include winter scenes. For many years, virtually no CPR advertisements or posters, with the exception of those for the Montreal Winter Carnival, were allowed to even mention snow.[37]

When Shaughnessy was asked if the CPR would donate to a fund for building an ice palace in the Manitoba capital, he telegraphed, "Not a cent for ice-palace, but five hundred dollars for a Christmas shirt-sleeve parade at Winnipeg."[38]

Canadian Pacific was joined in its protestations by Canadian rivals that also had a stake in ensuring the country had a more benign reputation. "The time has probably passed

◄ When the CPR gave Kipling exclusive use of a private railway car, he deemed it a "magic carpet" for seeing the country. *OTTAWA JOURNAL,* MAY 9, 1908

► Socked in for two days at Regina, Assiniboia, hapless passengers watch the snow-clearing efforts. LIBRARY AND CULTURAL RESOURCES DIGITAL COLLECTIONS, UNIVERSITY OF CALGARY CU178549

when the impression can exist that Western Canada has a forbidding climate," a Grand Trunk pamphlet informed its readers. "Such fabrications have been put forth freely in the past by designing persons, but the greatest factors in advertising the delightful features of the climate, which quite submerge the few slight drawbacks, are the people already settled there, prosperous and happy."[39]

When next Kipling felt the urge to drop in on the colonials, the CPR would be ready. "What would you do with a magic carpet if one were lent you?" he queried his readers in London's *Morning Post* and the *Ottawa Journal*. "I ask because, for a month, we had a private car of our very own—a trifling affair, less than seventy-foot long and thirty-ton weight. 'You may find her useful,' said the donor casually, 'to knock about the country. Hitch on to any train you choose and stop off where you choose.'"[40]

For his 1907 visit, Shaughnessy made sure that Kipling had many chances to interact with those prosperous and happy settlers, to keep his mind from dwelling on the white stuff that might have already been visible on the ground here and there during his October sojourn. In his ongoing series of dispatches to his "family" back home, the normally verbose chronicler of British possessions abroad let a Danish settler visiting his European relatives do the talking:

Three years ago I came to Canada by steerage—third class. And I have the language to learn. Look at me! I have now my own dairy business in Calgary, and—look at me!—my own half section, that is, three hundred and twenty acres [130 ha]; all my land which is mine. And now I come home first class, for Christmas here in Denmark, and I shall take out back with me, some friends of mine which are farmers, to farm on those irrigated lands near Calgary. Oh, I tell you there is nothing wrong with Canada for a man which works.[41]

Despite the best efforts of all concerned with immigration and settlement to downplay the weather, however, there were on occasion incidents that could not go unreported. Gladys M. Rowell arrived in Canada in 1903 with her family from the north of England. Though it was well into spring when their train got to Manitoba, they were met by one of the worst blizzards ever experienced there. "We saw herds of cattle bunched in tightly against the fences along the right-of-way," she later recalled, "and then, coming into Winnipeg, we passed piles of dead frozen ones where they had been dumped out of boxcars after starving to death."[42]

Settlers all across the Northwest were susceptible to the vagaries of the climate. Of the first four white people to die in Saskatoon, one was said to have drowned in the Saskatchewan River, one succumbed to exhaustion after fighting a prairie fire, and two froze to death in blizzards.[43] For the ranchers of Alberta, the winter of 1906–7 was one of the worst on record. "My brother worked for

one rancher that year, and he lost one ear and toes on his left foot from freezing," wrote one settler. "And the man he rode for, he had 800 cows and in the spring he found less than 500. That's a story."[44] Thousands of head of cattle died in the unforgiving sub-zero air, an unwanted burden for many settlers and the final nail in the coffin of many a cattleman's aspirations. Some settlers departed for milder climes, others stuck it out, but the era of enormous ranches that covered tens of thousands of acres was over.

In Manitoba, with most of the agricultural lands south of the railway having been spoken for, settlement was moving north of Winnipeg, and along with it, newcomers who were used to a more intemperate climate. By 1906, a CPR branch line had reached Gimli, and the Icelanders who favoured the area were transforming the place from its rustic foundations into a popular resort. The settlement around Gimli was christened New Iceland, and the immigrant population was allowed a measure of autonomy to set up their own schools and create their own laws. Other Icelandic communities in Manitoba included Lundar, Glenboro, Selkirk, and Morden.[45]

Just a few months earlier, an agent of the Saskatchewan Department of Agriculture stationed in Saskatoon had estimated that during the summer, 6,000 souls had arrived at that point, with 600 CPR boxcars full of settlers' effects. Many home-seekers were noted to have descended upon Swift Current, with Mennonites predominating. New arrivals from England, Ireland, continental Europe, and the United States as far as Massachusetts and Kentucky rolled into the province on the Soo Line.[46]

The department's report was not without its references to climate. It also revealed some hints of racial prejudice:

The climate of Saskatchewan, fortunately, is sufficiently vigorous to deter immigrants from the more southern and tropical countries, who are noted less for their industry than for other traits of character, from coming to the province. By a natural process of selection, we are likely to receive only those settlers who are energetic and resourceful.[47]

As much as the character of the settlers was important, new farming techniques and machinery were introducing efficiencies on an almost daily basis. Professional cerealists with the federal government's experimental farms introduced new grain hybrids that were even more hardy than Red Fife and were ready to harvest at an earlier date. A variety called Marquis became a favourite across the Northwest, winning international competitions and gaining the attention of the world. With his carefully selected two bushels of Marquis, Canadian agronomist Seeger Wheeler would win the first prize of $1,000 in gold coins for the best North American hard spring wheat at the 1911 New York Land Show—compliments of the contest's sponsor, CPR president Thomas Shaughnessy.

Women's work in the West

From the first years that Canadian Pacific set up offices in London to entice British immigrants to come to Canada, and particularly to the Northwest, the primary target audience of all the advertising campaigns and promotions had been men with farm experience or those with any agricultural expertise. Young boys with no prospects for inheriting land or those apprenticing in industry were also desirable contingents to lure to the frontier either to serve as farm

CANADA
for WOMEN

"Ten thousand Englishwomen could be ranged in a line and shot. No one would be sorry. Everyone would be glad. *There isn't any place for them.*"

Wasted Lives. "The woman who spoke these words," says AGNES LAUT, the Canadian writer, in the "Pall Mall Magazine," "was a wealthy woman of leisure, who felt in her own life, and saw in the lives of thousands of others — waste! Bodily health, education, mental ability, totalled up — Zero. Nothing done in a world where there is more to do than ever can be done. The inevitable conditions that elicited the Englishwoman's complaint are these—

First. The preponderance of women over men.

Second. Apart from domestic employment, women's labour is a drug on the market.

In short—too many women—too little work.

"What have the Colonies to offer that may adjust the matter?"

In recent years many women have been doing their best to think out a way by which the ever-increasing body of their fellow-women might pass from their native land, where their service is so cheaply held, to the land where the service of women is held to be of inestimable value, and is justly remunerated—Canada.

Such are the opening words of a remarkable pamphlet entitled

CANADA FOR WOMEN

which will be sent post free on application by any reader of *The Daily Mail* to the

Canadian Pacific Railway

62-65, Charing Cross, S.W.
67-68, King William Street, E.C. } London.

Or Local Agents Everywhere.

G. R.

OVERSEA SETTLEMENT OFFICE.

CANADA WANTS WOMEN
FOR HOUSEHOLD WORK.

SOME DOMESTIC EXPERIENCE REQUIRED.

ASSISTED PASSAGES
FOR
APPROVED APPLICANTS.

GOOD WAGES.
EMPLOYMENT GUARANTEED.

APPLY TO
ANY EMPLOYMENT EXCHANGE,
The SUPERINTENDENT OF EMIGRATION for CANADA,
1, Regent Street, London, S.W.1.
OR TO
THE CANADIAN GOVERNMENT AGENTS
at the following addresses:

TOWN	ADDRESS
ABERDEEN	116, Union Street.
BANGOR	310, High Street.
BELFAST	15-17-19, Victoria Street.
BIRMINGHAM	139, Corporation Street.
BRISTOL	52, Baldwin Street.
CARLISLE	54, Castle Street.
GLASGOW	107, Hope Street.
LIVERPOOL	48, Lord Street.
PETERBOROUGH	Market Place.
SOUTHAMPTON	8, Canute Road.
YORK	Canada Chambers, Museum Street.

Printed for H.M. Stationery Office by Waterlow & Sons Limited, London, Dunstable and Watford.

hands or become homesteaders in their own right when they came of age. But a third group of highly valued settler warranted a dedicated effort to recruit: women.

Women were not barred from owning homesteads in the Northwest, but the intricacies of the Dominion Lands Act could make ownership difficult. Technically, anybody willing to take an oath of allegiance and officially state their intention of remaining in Canada was eligible, provided they were twenty-one years of age (soon reduced to eighteen) and not "an idiot, lunatic or married woman." Women who were "the sole head of the family," which essentially meant widows or divorcees with dependents, met the necessary requirements.

Male homesteaders were, of course, encouraged to bring their wives and family members with them to their new wilderness properties to aid them in getting established, help with the chores, add a domestic touch to the home and surroundings, and stave off loneliness and madness, among other things. Single women were also sought as domestics in the cities and towns as well as among well-heeled ranchers and landowners. From its formative years, Canadian Pacific hired enterprising women from the eastern provinces and abroad to manage its early mountain chalets and later to decorate and promote its larger urban hotels.

"In London, where there'd be work for one, you'd find twenty trying for it," said one turn-of-the-century female immigrant. "Out here it's all the other way—there's twenty jobs waiting for everybody that wants to work... There's nine places out of ten where they wouldn't look at any one else if they could get somebody from England."[48]

As early as 1899, a Calgary newspaper reported that female immigrants on their way to the Northwest were being targeted by overzealous land and employment agents. The predators would board CPR trains at Port Arthur or Rat Portage (later Kenora) in search of women, who would be forced—in the words of one tabloid—to "run a regular gauntlet of persecution and annoyance." In one instance, a group of three women had been urged very strongly against coming "to such a terrible place as Calgary," which was represented as having a climate so severe in winter that it was impossible to bear. The three were led to believe that ten dollars a month was all they could expect as domestics out in the boonies, while the Winnipeg market would bring them as much as fifteen dollars.

The newspaper said it mentioned that particular case "to show the pains that are taken in Manitoba to prevent settlers of *any* class coming west." But the truth of the matter was that female workers were then, and always would be, in short supply in the Northwest. And, of course, the women in this tale were soon making twenty dollars to twenty-five dollars per month in their Calgary jobs.[49]

Perhaps the three young women avoided the bogus information offered up by following the "Advice to Settlers" set out in CPR literature of the day:

The newcomer need not fear that when he [or she] reaches Winnipeg he will fall into the hands of thieves, imposters or unfriendly people. If he follows the directions of this pamphlet, he will put himself in the hands of real friends, who will look after him. The train is met upon its arrival by agents of the Government and of the Canadian Pacific Railway Company, who take charge of immigrants and give them all the assistance and advice they need in a strange land.[50]

As immigration was flourishing in 1903, with numbers not seen since the brief influx of enthusiastic land-seekers twenty years earlier, CPR made a concerted effort to

encourage British women to come to Canada. "There is an instinct which impels men and women to deeds of heroism," one company booklet that year said in its opening paragraph. "That instinct was surely inborn in those bravehearted women pioneers who came to lay the foundation stone of this prairie home-land of Western Canada."[51] With stories such as "A Wiltshire Woman," "A Scotchwoman's Success," and "Jack Grant's Bonnie Wife," the railway outlined the challenges that were overcome by female settlers who lost their husbands, the entrepreneurial achievements of those who came to the New World on their own, and the struggles of the "deft-handed little wife" who "kept things moving."[52]

All of the testimonials in "Words from the Women of Western Canada" were from those who were living close to CPR railway lines, on land they or their deceased spouses had purchased from the railway. Widows and single women were portrayed as eminently capable of homesteading on their own or supplementing that endeavour with side businesses such as beekeeping or needlework. "Many a night the sewing machine sang the song of toil," one tale recounted. "You run the farm-work," said the wife, "and I'll rustle the cash to keep the table going."[53]

In the CPR's 1906 follow-up booklet, "Women's Work in Western Canada," as noted by a contemporary historian of women's role in British colonialism, "there was much less attention given to the untimely death of husbands."[54] The following year, the railway also issued a third pamphlet in the series. Entitled "Home Life of Women in Western Canada," it downplayed the notion of women homesteading on their own, possibly as Oliver and the Canadian government had expressed strong opposition to the issue.[55] Whether or not there were social stigmas that inhibited

"widows" and "spinsters" from going it alone, CPR land department files show 1,849 records of married women purchasing CPR land and 320 records of widows doing the same.[56]

Oliver was fundamentally opposed to granting homestead rights to single women. In 1910, he asserted his position in no uncertain terms, that it was the right of the male homesteader "to get the woman, and for the woman who wants to settle on land in the Northwest to get the man, rather than she shall have land of her own ... The single woman cannot bring the land into productiveness under ordinary circumstances, even as well as a single man."[57]

The front windows of the Charing Cross office of Canadian Pacific in London were smashed in 1913 by suffragettes, during a protest to punish businesses that did not come out in favour of voting rights for women. In retaliation, the company temporarily boarded over the windows and posted the notice WE ARE LOOKING FOR SETTLERS, NOT FOR SUFFRAGETTES. Nevertheless, the CPR continued to advertise its services in suffrage journals such as the *Suffragette and Woman's Leader*, and the *Common Cause*.[58]

Going to the movies

In the early years of the twentieth century, the federal government and the Canadian Pacific Railway both saw the potential of moving films to sell the wonders of the "Golden Northwest." In 1900, CPR had invited the Charles Urban Trading Company of England to send its cameramen, Cliff Denham, F. Guy Bradford, and Joe Rosenthal, to shoot scenes along the railway right-of-way in support of its multi-faceted immigration campaign. The railway's

European traffic manager, Archer Baker, had offered up a couple of first-class return tickets between Montreal and Vancouver, but company president Shaughnessy was quite willing to sweeten the pot.[59]

Canadian Pacific's passenger traffic manager Robert Kerr, publicity man George Henry Ham, and colonization agent Louis O. Armstrong were assigned to travel with the film crew and facilitate their shoots across the country. At the CPR's insistence, most of the filming would be done during the summer months, as the company wished to dispel any notion that Canada was a land of perpetual ice and snow.[60]

The Canadian government was more than happy to have the CPR cover most of the costs involved with this new promotional venture, and the filmmakers were keen to feature the company's locomotives and trains in their productions, as the country's dominant mode of transportation added excitement and put an abundance of motion into the motion pictures.[61] And a CPR flatcar propelled by a dedicated steam locomotive made an excellent platform from which to film the myriad attractions of the Canadian countryside, from Quebec City to Victoria.

A couple of years earlier, CPR's Van Horne had agreed to sponsor the pioneer work of James Freer, who had begun to shoot scenes of Manitoba farm life and produce "cinematograph lectures" before the turn of the century, including *Arrival of CPR Express at Winnipeg* and *Harvest Scene with Passing Trains*, which required the railway's full participation. The first tour of his finished works was considered successful enough that Sifton, then the minister of the interior, offered to sponsor a second one.[62]

In 1909, the Grand Trunk Railway Company hired Butcher's Film Service of the UK to spend four months filming along its routes in Eastern Canada as well as on the Grand Trunk Pacific in the West. The resulting films premiered in London in January 1910, introduced by speeches from Canadian and British worthies who informed the audiences that Canada could accommodate "five million workers at once" to join the "fine specimens of the Anglo-Saxon race" already settled there.[63]

The most ambitious years of film production on the CPR would begin in the summer of 1910, when the Edison Manufacturing Company of New York created thirteen pictures along the CPR and subsidiary Soo Line for its "Living Canada" series. "For a two-month period, the troop of actors and actresses, stage managers, make-up people, and a whole entourage of support staff had hotels, trains,

READING Y.M.C.A.

LECTURE HALL,

THURSDAY, FEBRUARY 9th, 1899,

At 8 p.m.

CINEMATOGRAPH

✳ LECTURE ❧

ILLUSTRATED BY . . . .

ANIMATED PICTURES

"Ten Years in Manitoba"

BY

Mr. JAMES S. FREER,

Of Brandon, Manitoba, Canada.

25,000 Instantaneous Photos upon Half-a-Mile of Edison Films, *representing the following amongst other scenes :—*

Arrival of C.P.R. Express at Winnipeg; Pacific and Atlantic Mail Trains; Premier Greenway stooking grain; Six Binders at work in 100 acre Wheat Field; Typical Stacking Scene; Harvesting Scene, with Trains passing; Cyclone Thresher at work; Coming thro' the Rye (Children play in the Hay); Winnipeg Fire Boys on the Warpath; Canadian Militia charging Fortified Wall; Canadian Contingent at the Jubilee; Harnessing the Virgin Prairie; Changing Guards at St. James's Palace (as exhibited at Windsor Castle); and other subjects.

MUSICAL ACCOMPANIMENTS.

Admission by Member's Pass or by Tickets 1/- and 6d. To be obtained of Members, or at Office.

Canadians relative to their American neighbours are showcased like a fable from a book of fairy tales.[65]

Around the same time as the Edison productions, CPR president Thomas Shaughnessy had also approved an expenditure of five thousand dollars to help finance a documentary film to encourage Canadian immigration and tourism from the United States that was shown at an Alaska-Yukon Exposition in Seattle. There are no statistics to gauge just how effective motion pictures were in luring new settlers to the Northwest, but they were one more eye-catching tool for the land and immigration agents.

By 1920, the CPR's advertising committee would take the dramatic step of forming Associated Screen News (ASN), a subsidiary company with offices in the United States and Canada, to produce and distribute newsreels to three or four thousand movie theatres across the continent. Among the company's mandates would be the promotion of Canadian immigration and resource development. ASN would grow to become the dominant force in Canadian film—far more significant than the Canadian Government Motion Picture Bureau—and, ultimately, a valuable partner in the creation of the National Film Board.[66]

The shadow of overt discrimination

If the Immigration Act of 1906 laid the country's policy of free entry to rest, the follow-up legislation only strengthened the government's discretionary powers to discriminate freely against immigrants belonging to any race deemed "unsuited to the climate or requirements of Canada." No specific, racial, ethnic, or national groups were explicitly barred from entering the country in the new Immigration Act of 1910, but the federal government was

mountain guides, railway crews, and even an ocean-going steamship weighing 9,090 metric tons at their disposal ... With titles like *An Unselfish Love*, *The Little Station Agent*, and the *Cowpuncher's Glove*, these movies were meant to be entertaining as well as instructive."[64]

An Unselfish Love was a story about an American man named John who was unable to marry his beloved Mabel because her father thought him insufficiently wealthy. Setting out to farm in southern Alberta, John draws the attentions of a local lady "by no means unattractive, but of the type and age popularly designated as an old maid." When Mabel's father fools his daughter into thinking John will marry the other woman, Mabel accepts the proposal of a new suitor. The dilemma is resolved when, to the "old maid's" credit, she finds out about the father's plot and unselfishly persuades Mabel to come to Alberta (on the CPR), where she is reunited with and marries John. The golden opportunities awaiting settlers north of the border and, not too subtly, the outstanding moral qualities of

empowered to restrict or completely exclude certain groups at will.[67] "We want to be in such a position that, should occasion arise, when public policy seems to demand it, we may have the power, on our responsibility as a Government, to exclude people whom we consider undesirable," was Oliver's matter-of-fact explanation to his fellow members of parliament.[68]

The Act also included a clause discriminating by class, prohibiting "all charity cases who had not received written authority to emigrate to Canada from the superintendent of immigration at Ottawa or the assistant superintendent of emigration for Canada in London." Valerie Knowles, a journalist and writer who published a lengthy and thorough study of Canadian immigration policy from 1540 to 2015, concluded that the clause was "inspired by the large number of impoverished British immigrants who had arrived in Canada in 1907, a year of economic downturn, with the assistance of charitable organizations, eager to rid Britain of paupers and to provide them with a new start in Canada. In 1908, 70 percent of the deportations from Canada were British immigrants, many of them undoubtedly destitute and inexperienced farmers who had landed in Canada the year before."[69] The legislated class consciousness was relatively new; the racial bias, sadly, a continuation of the semi-official, under-the-table xenophobia that was and had always been part and parcel of Canadian immigration policy.

Many Chinese workers had been brought into Canada in the early 1880s to work on the transcontinental railway. In the face of a tight local labour force, Andrew Onderdonk, a contractor for the federal government and later the CPR, had successfully lobbied the government for this measure, despite a fair amount of public opposition. Other Chinese labourers had migrated from the United States to Canada in the preceding decade to work in gold mining and construction jobs. After the rail line was completed, some of Onderdonk's construction workers stayed on in Canada. Against all odds, they started small businesses—typically restaurants and laundries, laying the foundation for Chinese communities in cities and towns throughout the country.

In an attempt to calm the outcry against additional foreign workers swamping the labour market, the Canadian government introduced the country's first piece of legislation to exclude immigrants on the basis of ethnic origin. The Chinese Immigration Act of 1885 introduced an infamous $50 "head tax" on every Chinese person seeking entry into Canada. The law created a formidable financial barrier for those seeking to bring wives and other family members to join them in the New World. The imposition of the punitive duty only temporarily reduced the number of Chinese immigrants, however, and the amount was increased to $100 per person in 1900, and $500 in 1903.

CPR president William Van Horne condemned the irrational fears in an 1896 letter to the editor of the Toronto *Globe*, while revealing his own ethnic biases:

Past experience has shown that there is no ground for your fear of a large movement of Chinese to any part of Canada. The lines of occupation open to the Chinese are very limited, comprising ordinary labour with pick and shovel, cooking or other household work, fruit and hop picking, salmon canning, and a few things of lesser importance. [Their general disinterest in North American affairs was] decidedly in their favour as against the Sicilians, Danubian Jews and other worthless European people, who are let in without a word of objection, and who have, in the United States, created festering sores on the body politic to an extent which has become most serious, especially in the large cities.[70]

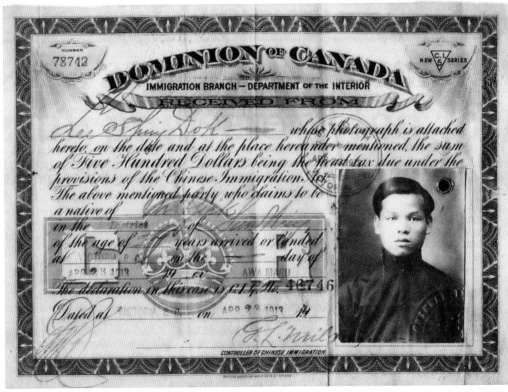

◄ Andrew Onderdonk, a contractor for the federal government and later the CPR, went against public opinion by importing Chinese labourers to build the Canadian Pacific Railway from the West Coast eastward. BOORNE AND MAY, LIBRARY AND CULTURAL RESOURCES DIGITAL COLLECTIONS, UNIVERSITY OF CALGARY CU1103679

▲ A "head tax" was imposed on Chinese immigrants coming to Canada, which began as a $50 charge, but was soon boosted to $100 and then $500. Certificates like the one above were issued by the government to show that this discriminatory practice had been carried out to the letter of the law.

AUTHOR'S COLLECTION

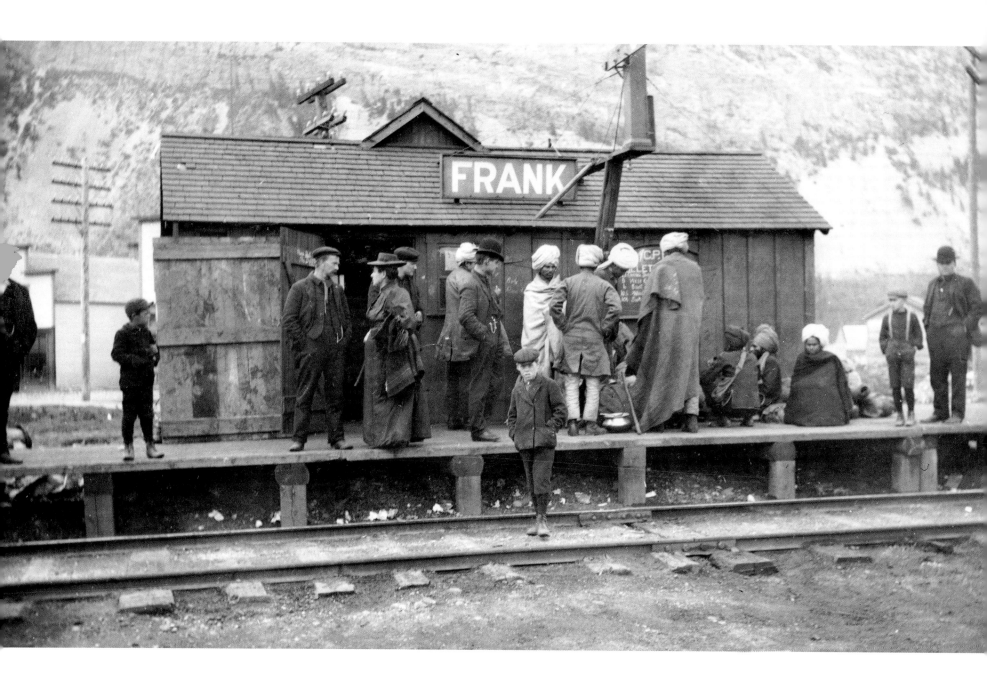

Other Asian people came in smaller numbers and didn't at first draw the same attention. Japanese immigrants began arriving in Canada in the 1880s, and Sikhs from India in 1904. These groups were affected by the Liberal government's policy that Asian immigration should not be encouraged. No promotional material was aimed at them, no agents were assigned to help them acclimatize, and no official plans were made to settle them in agricultural colonies in the Northwest.

Canadian Pacific had no such qualms about encouraging immigration from any country in Asia, as the company wished to build a larger traffic base for its steamships on the Pacific. For many years, the company's ships on the Pacific had special steerage accommodation for Asian immigrants. Steamship agents in the CPR's employ distributed circulars and notices in the Punjabi language in Kolkata, in West Bengal, and on police station walls and in the villages of Mahlipur in the Punjab. This immigration literature spelled out the route, the steamship fares, the necessary medical precautions, and the amount of money required by Canadian immigration officials to ensure entry requirements were met.[71]

In 1908, a federal order-in-council imposed a "continuous journey" rule to prohibit would-be immigrants from stopping off in any other country on their way to take up residence in Canada. As most steamships called at Hawaii on the voyage from India or Japan, the rule was intended to throw an unavoidable obstacle in the way of any Asian newcomer's ambitions.

Canadians generally held Asians to be incapable of assimilating with the country's prevailing Anglo-Saxon culture. The increased presence of these immigrants in Vancouver brought that feeling to a boil in September 1907,

when an anti-Asian riot broke out in the streets, causing extensive damage to properties owned and occupied by the "offending" racial groups, largely Japanese. The mammoth anti-Asian parade that followed knocked the remaining wheels off the welcome wagon.

That level of discrimination was not visited upon members of the various Asian communities in the pioneer towns of the Northwest, largely because of the low numbers of immigrants from those countries that came east of the mountains in the Dominion's early decades. In many pioneer towns, it was not unusual to find a Chinese café or laundry among the first businesses on Main Street, but the social status of Asians, generally, was not going to equal that of a doctor, bank clerk, or school teacher. Though they were viewed as hard-working and, for the most part, honest, and even though they deferred to their white neighbours, the government made sure to erect formidable legislative barriers should Chinese immigrants wish to bring their family members to the New World.

White racial supremacy was the order of the day in the Northwest. After the renowned Alberta rancher, John Ware, who arrived in 1882, most Black settlers arrived in Western Canada from Oklahoma in the autumn of 1909. They dispersed in small numbers throughout Alberta, Saskatchewan, and Manitoba to an undercurrent of grumblings from established settlers. In general, Canadians were big supporters of American settlers moving across the international boundary, and Department of Interior immigration statutes did not distinguish between various US citizens on the basis of race, although recent legislature had allowed for that potential.[72] But in practice, discrimination did not end at the international border.

No formal restrictions were in place on workers of African ancestry who came to Canada from the United States and the West Indies. The railways, in particular, had been keen to recruit their services as porters, and the public accepted Black men in that role. The Black immigrants from the United States appeared to want two things: to settle on land near railway tracks, for efficiency's sake, and to escape racial persecution.[73] Some settled in the Amber Valley, more than 150 miles (240 km) north of Edmonton. Others chose more accessible lands in the Parkland region, north of Maidstone, Saskatchewan, and east of Lloydminster.

Responding to protests from white settlers, Frank Oliver, the minister of the interior, sent an inspector on a fact-finding tour of Oklahoma to report on the sudden interest in the Canadian West among the Black community. The report came back that white land owners in Oklahoma wished to be rid of their Black neighbours, in a bid to raise property values. Local railroads were also said to have a major interest in promoting Black migration to Canada and regarded their replacement by white people, "as a boon to the state's development."[74]

At the same time, the Canadian government was discouraging the CPR, which had its own immigration network in the US, from cooperating with any Blacks seeking information to aid their emigration efforts. Groups of concerned citizens such as the Imperial Order of the Daughters of the Empire warned about the "uncontrollable desire in black men to seduce white women."[75] The Immigration Branch was advised about a racial incident in Estevan, Saskatchewan, that occurred when six Black men from Barbados arrived in town. The men had apparently been sent there by the CPR as harvest workers, but they were quickly arrested and jailed on a charge of vagrancy.[76]

Under pressure, the CPR came down squarely on the side of racial discrimination, agreeing to exclude Black people from organized tours of Western Canada. This decision ensured that Black people were no longer eligible for the rate reductions offered to other potential immigrants and home-seekers. The company also agreed to report back to the Canadian authorities about any government agent who encouraged Black settlement in Canada.[77]

In less than a decade and a half since the turn of the century, more than two million immigrants came to Canada, seven hundred thousand of them from the United States. Fewer than one thousand were Black.[78]

9

THE LAST
BEST WEST

The age of innovation

The year 1905 was a transformative one for Canadian Pacific, the country, and the world. In the United States, President Theodore Roosevelt's trust-busting campaign was in full swing; Japan's unexpected defeat of Russia in the Russo-Japanese war shook up international relations; and Canada was experiencing a period of unprecedented prosperity and growth that would lead to the creation of the two new western provinces of Alberta and Saskatchewan.

Two would-be transcontinental railways to rival the pioneer CPR line were pushing their lines westward, and tens of thousands of immigrants were entering the North-west from Britain, the United States, and elsewhere. The federal Liberal government had followed up on its 1896 victory with consecutive election wins in 1900 and 1904, reinforcing its support for more railway construction in the Canadian West to spur settlement and challenge the hege-mony of Canadian Pacific.

The Canadian Northern Railway reached the City of Edmonton in November 1905, and Alberta's lieutenant-governor, George H.V. Bulyea, drove a ceremonial silver spike there to mark the occasion. Frank Oliver, the min-ister of the interior, remarked that "the land which would be developed by the Canadian Northern Railway was the richest agricultural country still unsettled in the world."[1] Government homesteads were still available, as were countless acres of railway lands, owned by both the Cana-dian Northern and the CPR, along the route which the latter company had eschewed for a more southerly path, but pass-ing through a region in which the same trailblazing railway had chosen to take significant land grants. The Canadian Northern was now bringing in land-seeking settlers from its Lakehead connection at Port Arthur with steamships of the Northern Navigation Company, the Canadian Pacific Railway Steamship Line, and the Booth Line as well as by CPR trains from all points in the East.

Construction also began in the West that year on the Grand Trunk Pacific (GTP), yet another competitor headed west for Saskatoon and Edmonton, rather than on its orig-inal trajectory that would have taken the line 50 miles (80 km) north of those communities. The GTP was pri-marily a trunk line, able to handle through traffic, but with virtually no branch lines or feeder connections and little or no land for sale other than townsite lots and sections owned by the government, the Canadian Northern, and the CPR.

A couple of years earlier, when the government had begun to solidify plans for a Trans-Canada Railway to

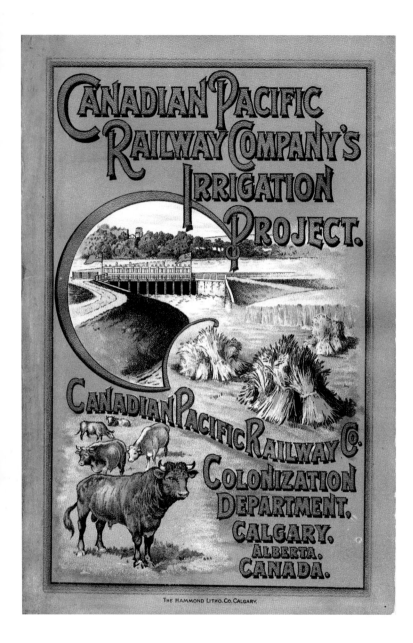

THE HAMMOND LITHO. CO. CALGARY.

compete with the CPR, Sir William Van Horne—who by then had resigned the CPR presidency, was serving as company chairman, and in 1894 had been awarded a knighthood—said in a press release, "We would hail with delight a parallel route from the Atlantic to the Pacific to help us develop the country. There is enough up there for us all."[2]

To stay one step ahead of the competition, the CPR took delivery, in 1905, of a new generation of colonist car built in Montreal by carpenters and craftsmen at the railway's Angus Shops, many of whom had no doubt themselves immigrated to Canada in recent years. The first of the all-wooden sleeping cars—that during the day could seat fifty-six people in the main section and sixteen more in the smoking area—was quickly shipped off to the manufacturing shops of the Pullman Company, in Chicago, where twenty additional cars were built to the same specifications.[3]

The attractive new cars, with all of the expected washrooms, heating and cooking facilities, and closed vestibules at either end, were built under the direction of CPR's master car builder, William Fowler, to the exterior design developed by his predecessor, William Apps. Between the years 1905 and 1912, CPR and the Pullman Company would turn out 135 of these colonist sleeping cars that would carry thousands of immigrants to their new homes in the Northwest.[4]

Now, halfway through the first decade of the twentieth century, the CPR's attention was squarely focused in Alberta on the 3 million acres (1.2 million ha) of land for sale within its irrigation block and substantial holdings in surrounding regions. American land companies had taken the lead in acquiring large holdings from the railway in the semi-arid region of Palliser's Triangle and engaging in

◄ In the first decade of the twentieth century, the CPR focused on the largest irrigation project in North America to date as a means of populating a vast semi-arid region in which the company had selected a large land grant allotment from the federal government. COURTESY OF BRUCE PEEL SPECIAL COLLECTION, UNIVERSITY OF ALBERTA

Opposite, top Second-generation CPR colonist car #1202 was restored and is on display at Calgary's Heritage Park. DAVID LAURENCE JONES PHOTO

Opposite, bottom The Luse Land Company ran its own private car from the United States into the Northwest with delegations of prominent citizens from Nebraska, Iowa, Illinois, and Indiana, many of whom would invest in CPR lands. LIBRARY AND ARCHIVES CANADA PA-021273

extensive marketing schemes. The Luse Land Company was particularly active, employing its own private railway car, the Lenza, to bring delegations of prominent citizens from the states of Nebraska, Iowa, Illinois, and Indiana, many of whom would invest in CPR lands in Alberta. On the same day a Luse Company party was leaving St. Paul in April 1906, Calgary newspapers reported that 2,000 American settlers were bound for the Canadian West on three special Soo Line trains.[5]

By the following year, the latest government statistics were showing that Canadian immigration had increased 1,000 percent over the last seven years. British immigrants were being cared for far better since the CPR's *Empress of Britain* and *Empress of Ireland* arrived on the North Atlantic to abolish "steerage" and ferry settlers in relative comfort to their new homes in the Northwest. Settler Muriel Holden, fresh off the boat with her mother, later remembered the modest home her father had prepared for them:

It was the shack dad had been 'batching' in with his friend and brother; they had graciously moved out and rented rooms. Dad had cleaned and whitewashed the place and put blue-dotted curtains at the windows. Mom was so happy to be with her man at last that she tried to hold back her disappointment, but later admitted she thought it "nowt but a cowshed." [6]

J.S. Dennis, CPR's chief engineer and superintendent of irrigation, was a visionary man, and open to any type of experimentation in land settlement that held out the promise of populating the Northwest more effectively. In 1908, he convinced the railway officers back in Montreal to take over the activities of the Canadian Pacific Irrigation Colonization Company (CPICC) from its American founders

and set it up as an in-house subsidiary, with a sub-section to be known as the Development Department. The focus would continue to be on small purchasers living in compact farming communities who would work the land, employ intensive, mixed farming methods, and ultimately put traffic in railway boxcars.

While Dennis was in charge of the company's overall development strategy, Charles Walter Peterson was chosen to manage the new subsidiary, CPICC. Peterson was born in Denmark and immigrated to Canada in 1888. After a failed attempt at homesteading, he worked as the assistant general immigration and colonization agent for the Manitoba North Western Railway, and later became the deputy

minister of agriculture for the North-West Territories. In 1906, he had been hired by the CPR as general manager of immigration and colonization; in 1908, he headed up CPICC; and from 1910 to 1912, he would serve as superintendent of irrigation.

During the early years of CPR's direct control of the CPICC, the railway deployed the tourist sleeping cars Calgary and Carsland south of the border to bring American home-seekers from the US Midwest to the Canadian Prairies in search of prime agricultural land. By 1913, excursion trains were departing Kansas City on the first and third Tuesday every month—over the Burlington Route at 11:35 AM, the Missouri Pacific at 1:55 PM, and the Chicago

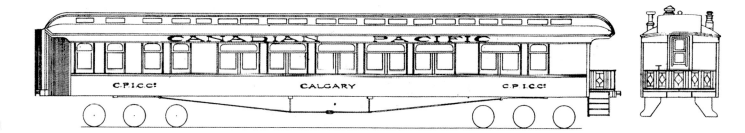

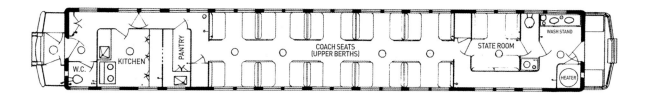

Great Western at 2 PM—with full loads of prospective settlers engaged by CPR and Canadian government land agents. Round trip tickets from Kansas City to Calgary and Edmonton were $47.50 and to Saskatoon $46, with allowance for a layover of up to 25 days.

The CPR's special home-seekers car, the Calgary, would be waiting on the Soo Line track in St. Paul's Union Station to join the excursions, accompanied by company agent W.S. Freeman. A lower berth on the Calgary from St. Paul to the car's namesake town could be had for $2.50, while an upper berth cost $2. Those on the way to Saskatoon changed trains at the CPR station in Moose Jaw.

At the same time that the CPR brought all colonization planning in-house, the CPR, the Canadian Northern, and the GTP jointly entered into a contract with the American advertising agent Herbert Vanderhoof of Chicago. The main thrust of the promotional campaign was to place articles and advertisements about the Canadian Northwest in American journals circulated in rural communities. Vanderhoof purchased a half interest in the magazine *Canada West* that was distributed liberally throughout the US and was heavily subsidized by the Canadian federal government, in effect making the three northern railways co-owners of the publication. The CPR ran full-page advertisements within the publication, and Vanderhoof used its pages to promote CPR lands whenever possible.[7]

To ramp up the company's propaganda machine, Dennis formed a Publicity Branch (later Exhibits Branch) of his growing immigration and colonization organization and hired E.T. Nolte as its creative director. The branch was in charge of advertising the CPR's lands in Western Canada as well as highlighting Canadian natural resources, mostly

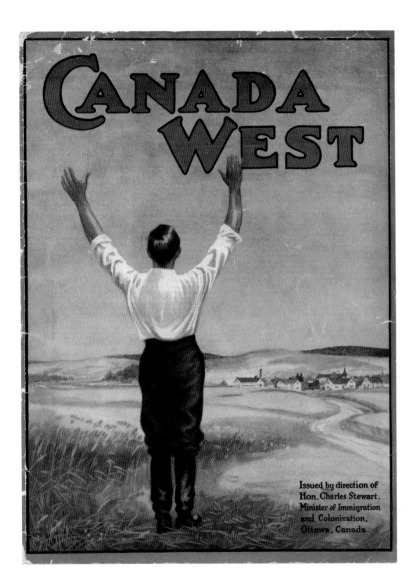

CANADA WEST

Issued by direction of
Hon. Charles Stewart,
Minister of Immigration
and Colonization,
Ottawa, Canada.

CANADIAN PACIFIC RAILWAY

SOUVENIR 1912
American Land & Irrigation Exposition
NEW YORK

GLENCARNOCK VICTOR II
GRAND CHAMPION STEER
CHICAGO INTERNATIONAL
LIVE STOCK SHOW 1913

Bred by J. D. McGREGOR
Brandon, Manitoba
CANADIAN GRAINS & GRASSES
NEVER ATE CORN

through the medium of elaborate display cases in the company's railway stations and hotels in Canada and the US.
The Publicity Branch also built a series of impressive pavilions at various international exhibitions in Europe and
continued the company's tradition of sending travelling
agents across the British countryside with a campaigning
road vehicle and a wealth of colonization literature.

The creative branch's first major project in the spring of
1910 was to erect the Canada Pavilion at a sports exhibition
in Vienna. Apart from its displays in support of sporting
activities, the pavilion featured model grain elevators and a
miniature CPR train in operation and was reported to have
"evinced a keen interest" in the Austrian emperor Franz
Josef. Two months later, Canadian Pacific inaugurated its
own pavilion at the Brussels Exhibition, where another
working model train and colonization enticements were
the main attractions.

The following year, the Publicity Branch supervised
the construction of two pavilions even more impressive
than the last: one at the Glasgow Exhibition that was
endorsed by all the leading CPR and government officials
in the UK; and another at the Festival of Empire, held on
the grounds of London's Crystal Palace, sixty years after
the Great Exposition for which the famous glass and iron
structure had originally been built.[8] A travelling information car toured the various agricultural centres in Britain on
market days, and was on hand for the major exhibitions. All
of these international events were perfect venues for advertising CPR lands in the Northwest and, in particular, the
advantages of purchasing property through the company's
soon-to-be-popular ready-made farm program.

The irrigation district was becoming the hottest real
estate market in the Northwest, for both British settlers and

▲ The Exhibits Branch assem-
bled an impressive display for
Canadian Pacific at the 1911
American Land and Irrigation
Exposition in New York. HARRY
POLLARD PHOTO, LIBRARY AND
CULTURAL RESOURCES DIGITAL
COLLECTIONS, UNIVERSITY OF
CALGARY CU1173432

those from the United States. A group of Danish settlers living on rented farms in the US relocated to the railway's irrigation block after contacting a representative of the CPICC in Council Bluffs, Iowa. A party of thirty-one repatriated French-Canadian farmers purchased twenty-eight quarter sections in the reserve, while a Dutch clergyman, Father Van Aaken of Helena, Montana, brought over two parties of colonists from Holland.[9]

The CPR retained Van Aaken to recruit Catholic immigrants in the Netherlands, with the promise of good lands in a colony settlement where they could preserve their faith. However, the settlers were not informed by either Van Aaken or the CPR about the short growing season and the primitive state of irrigation in the Northwest, so many drifted away to find employment in nearby towns, though a few managed to tough it out.[10]

Two years later, George Louis Boer, formerly a CPR water inspector at Strathmore, was appointed manager of

CPR's Land Colonization Branch in the Netherlands, where he conducted immigration recruitment lectures during the winter and spring of 1911 and 1912. Boer, like Van Aaken, understated the physical stamina and endurance that was required to succeed on 160 acres (65 ha) of unbroken land, so his eager clients suffered many hardships that might have been avoided had they been advised to do a year's apprenticeship on an established farm before buying property of their own.[11]

Individual Dutch homesteading also occurred all over Alberta, as it would in Saskatchewan and Manitoba. Apart from those settling in Strathmore, immigrants from the Netherlands took up farming north of Edmonton in a community they named Neerlandia. In Manitoba they settled in Winnipeg, Portage la Prairie, and Morden, while the CPR sold them lands outside the Saskatchewan company towns of Leoville, Swift Current, Morse, Cupar, Saskatoon, and Regina.

As an incentive to acquire railway land, the CPR's new Development Department would introduce more flexible financial arrangements for land-seekers, such as a "Crop Payment Plan," whereby settlers could pay for their land purchases with a down payment of one-tenth of the cost and the rest with a half portion of their annual crop, at 6 percent interest, over as many years as necessary. There was also a growing awareness within the company that many potential settlers, while well intentioned and hard working, were not necessarily experienced in the skills they would require to make a go of it, particularly when it came to irrigation and dry-farming techniques.

It was also apparent that the company's land agents were making "pie-in-the-sky" promises about the ease with which immigrants could slide into their newly adopted environment. The poor living conditions they would encounter, and the difficulties they would have making ends meet, drove one unsuccessful CPR immigrant to insist that he "would rather be in jail [in the Netherlands] for six months, than have to work in Canada."[12]

Dennis and his staff began to consider putting settlers on a more solid and profitable footing from the day they first arrived in their frontier homes, by perhaps fencing off and seeding part of their land in advance, and maybe providing expert advice and guidance from agricultural specialists on demonstration farms. The innovations they discussed would soon crystalize into one of the most successful colonization campaigns in history and would revolutionize the CPR's immigration and settlement strategies for what would be marketed by both government and railway as the "Last Best West."

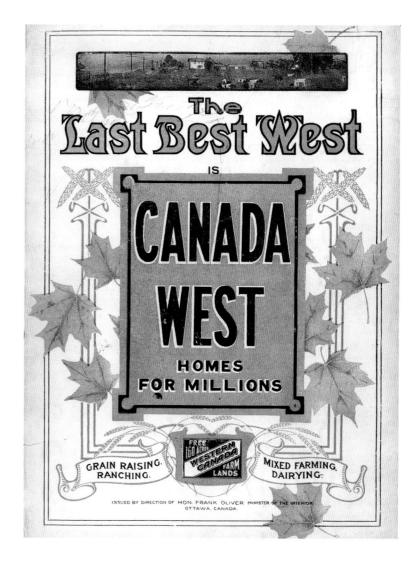

▲ With the availability of good agricultural land becoming a thing of the past in the United States, the lure of free homesteads in the Northwest earned the region the title of "Last Best West." JAMES E. LANIGAN COLLECTION

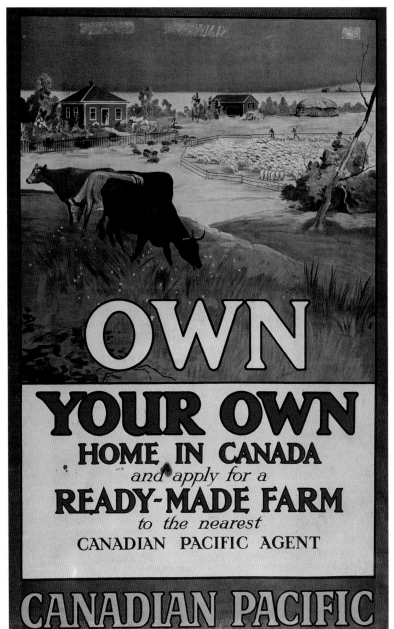

Ready-made for living

The campaign was formally launched by Shaughnessy, the third president of the CPR, described by London's *Daily Mail* as "an active member of the greatest railway system in the world, the Canadian Pacific Railway." Shaughnessy had just disembarked from the Cunard ocean greyhound *Lusitania* in the opening days of 1910 and was, according to the paper, "full of fresh plans for strengthening Anglo-Canadian relations."[13] Shaughnessy, the special correspondent informed his readers, was the "overlord of a vast system of transportation stretching from Liverpool to Hong Kong, China, with 14,500 miles [23,300 km] of track, 40,000 employees, several great lines of steamships, and millions of acres of land. He wields a power difficult to over-estimate."

Suggesting to the press that "the British people have not in the past availed themselves so fully of the opportunities of the West as they might," Shaughnessy had explained that "the American, even the wealthy American, will build himself a rough hut and live in it for a season or two while making a start. The Englishman does not like this, yet he wants land."

He laid out his solution:

Recently, when 1,600 small holdings were offered in England, there were 35,000 applicants. All of these could be accommodated by us. We propose to prepare land for this class of small holder. We will build his house, fence his holding, break part of the soil, and sow it, so that he can come and find all ready for him to settle down. This will be within reach of the English countryman who has 100 pounds capital to make a start.[14]

A similar plan had been suggested several years earlier by the CPR's first president, George Stephen, to Prime Minister Gladstone's secretary for Ireland, but nothing had come of it.[15]

The first emigrant party bound for "ready-made farms" in CPR's irrigation district sailed from Liverpool aboard the *Empress of Britain* in March 1910. Among them were Englishmen, Irishmen, Scotsmen, Welshmen, and even Australians. The steamship line listed their occupations as poultry farmer, veterinary surgeon, innkeeper, stock-raiser, army pensioner, coachman, and accountant, to name but a few. "All belong to the superior class of emigrant," said a newspaper account of the departure, "men with special knowledge of various kinds, strong, in good health, and of the kind that is bound to make headway even on land which is less ready than the fertile soil of the West to yield up its riches to the cultivator."[16]

The CPR assigned Archibald S. Walton from its colonization department to escort the party to the New World. *The Times* of London also sent two photographers to record the details of the ambitious adventure for its readers.[17]

CPR land in Alberta, on average, was now selling for $30 to $40 per irrigated acre ($74 to $99/ha) and $20 per non-irrigated acre ($49/ha). Settlers were expected to make an initial investment of $1,500 in their properties, while the railway would add an additional $1,000 in improvements to be repaid on easy terms.

The group arrived in Saint John, New Brunswick, with enthusiastic fanfare from railway officials who ushered the immigrants aboard an awaiting string of CPR colonist cars. An immigration agent from Canadian Pacific's colonization subsidiary accompanied them. Within five hours of landing at the pier, they were on their way West. "The commissary car attached to our train was well appointed, and the meals served of a standard appreciated by every member of the party," one immigrant recalled. It was a good start to the relationship between the settlers and their land-lords, which continued when the party reached Strathmore, Alberta, in the Western Section of the Canadian Pacific irrigation district.[18]

The train was shunted onto a siding, and the cars left at the disposal of the home-seekers. As alternative accommodations, the CPR had erected an immigration hall at Strathmore where the new arrivals could stay free of charge until they were settled. The first group to occupy the hall found it to be "very convenient and scrupulously clean."

As soon as they were settled, a number of the party were driven out over the land to choose from among the 80-acre (32 ha) properties that awaited them or, for those who were not going to occupy ready-made farms, to inspect other areas that the company had reserved for its British clients. "It is safe to say that we all reached our new home in a most enthusiastic frame of mind," the group's chronicler noted, "and from the general appearance that is everywhere in evidence, it appears that the question of success or failure rests entirely with the individual and not with the company."[19]

Paternalistic arrangements of this nature had been contemplated by the CPR even before its transcontinental line was completed through to the Pacific Coast. In 1885, vice-president Van Horne had corresponded with Keewatin Lumbering & Manufacturing and received illustrated pamphlets explaining the company's portable house system.[20] In 1894, when Van Horne had asked L.A. Hamilton, the railway's land commissioner in Winnipeg, to research the cost of establishing a farm, Hamilton itemized everything a farmer would need to begin homesteading immediately upon arrival in the Northwest. Beginning with a four-room house and a stable, his list came to include oxen, five cows,

poultry, pigs, and a miscellany of farming tools. It also anticipated preparing 20 acres (8 ha) of land and sowing seed. Altogether, the report came up with a figure of $1,145, and added a margin of $355 for unforeseen contingencies (see page 159).

"If you desire me to say anything on this … repayment of the loan within a certain term of years based only on the security of the homestead and the chattels," Hamilton told the boss, "I am afraid that I could not endorse it, as I do not think it possible for the farmer to start on a homestead saddled with a debt of $1,500. My own experience leads me to say that $500 would be the outside loan that would be safe to make on a security of that nature."[21]

His reservations, in part, were driven by the depressed state of the economy in the early 1890s. He reminded Van Horne that the Germans and Scandinavians already on the land in the Northwest, who had received modest financial considerations from the railway were, despite their frugal habits, having difficulties paying the interest on the loans. A decade and a half later, though, the economic conditions were very much different.

The CPR's ready-made farm program had its origins in a settlement plan sponsored by the Salvation Army, with the work of preparing the properties to be handled by the CPICC. In the fall of 1909, the Salvation Army had purchased enough land to settle one hundred and twenty settlers in a colony similar to those it had created in other parts of the world.[22]

The original proposal had contemplated thirty farms in a colony to be located near the town of Irricana—a contraction of "irrigation" and "canals"—which already boasted a post office, hotel, and general store. When the Salvation Army backed out of the plan, Dennis and his staff used the

A restored house from the CPR settlers' colony at Nightingale is among the most significant settlement exhibits at Calgary's pioneer village, Heritage Park. DAVID L. JONES PHOTO

site to prepare twenty-four 80-acre (32 ha) ready-made farms, which were all bought out in the first year they were promoted abroad. The cost of preparing these farms came in a little over $1,500 a piece, very close to Hamilton's estimate for a similar venture fifteen years earlier.[23] That first colony was known locally as the English Colony before being rechristened Nightingale in honour of Florence Nightingale. A nearby settlement was named Florence.

A newly arrived immigrant to Nightingale found himself invited to lunch with the unofficial mayor and mayoress of the community. His host had been a poultry farmer in Lowestoft, England, a coastal town on the North Sea in Suffolk County, before emigrating to Nightingale. "I learned that his hundred fellow citizens include a butcher, a veterinary surgeon, a pig breeder, a coal merchant, two engineers, a Scotch gardener with a large family, a clerk, a marine surveyor, a retired Indian Civil servant, a schoolmaster, a rural innkeeper, a mate of the Merchant Service, and a piano tuner," he later wrote in his reminiscences.[24]

Within months, CPR's Development Department had sent a party to the foothills of the Rocky Mountains to obtain evergreens and other trees for use in the irrigation block. The men returned with more than seven thousand trees, many of which were used around Nightingale "for the purpose of enhancing the charm of the surroundings of the various homesteads."[25]

Fifty acres (20 ha) on each property were cultivated before being sold. Because the CPR's colonization department was encouraging all settlers to supplement their agricultural pursuits with at least some dairy farming, and because the Nightingale colony was heavily invested in this endeavour, Dennis authorized the construction of bigger barns than were initially anticipated.

Three other colonies of ready-made farms were planned: the Cairnhill Colony, a short distance from Strathmore in the Western Section of the company's irrigation block; the Crossfield Colony, west of Irricana, also in the Western Section; and the Sedgewick Colony, outside the irrigation block and immediately adjacent to the town of Sedgewick on the CPR's Wetaskiwin line that ran east from the company's C&E. These three colonies would allow the CPR to put seventy-seven more ready-made farms on the market in the spring of 1911.

The first buildings at Nightingale were simple, two- or three-room houses, erected by the railway's bridge and building workers, along with small barns, storage sheds, and outhouses. The homes on the other three colonies were slightly more elaborate structures built by local contractors. The Alberta Construction Company built the houses and outbuildings at Sedgewick, while the Crown Lumber Company developed all of the structures on the fourteen farms at

WESTBOUND TRAINS Inferior Direction			IRRICANA SUBDIVISION		EASTBOUND TRAINS Superior Direction	
FIRST CLASS 515 Psgr. l Tues. Thurs. Sat.	Miles from Bassano	Telegraph Offices	STATIONS	Telegraph Calls	FIRST CLASS 516 Psgr. a Mon. Wed. Fri.	FOURTH CLASS 92 Freight a Daily ex. Sun.
12.35	.0	D N	BASSANO — YK	B A	17.15	14.20
			6.6			
f 12.53	6.6		GRANTA		f 17.00	13.53
			6.8			
f 13.11	13.4		MAKEPEACE		f 16.45	13.11
			7.6			
s 13.33	21.0	D	HUSSAR	H S	s 16.25	12.35
			8.1			
s 13.56	29.1	D	CHANCELLOR	C O	s 16.00	11.35
			6.7			
s 14.14	35.8	D	STANDARD	Y N D	s 15.38	10.30
			9.7			
s 14.44	45.5	D	TUDOR	D O	s 15.07	9.15
			5.3			
f 14.57	50.8		HAMLET		f 14.54	8.50
			1.8			
	52.6		* FLORENCE			
			2.3			
s 15.12	54.9	D	NIGHTINGALE	N G	s 14.43	8.35
			7.6			
f 15.33	62.5		SWASTIKA		f 14.21	8.00
			5.5			
f 15.47	68.0		CRAIGDHU		f 14.06	7.30
			4.5			
15.59	72.5	D	IRRICANA — YKC	R I	13.50	7.00
a Tues. Thurs. Sat. 515			* No Passing Track		l Mon. Wed. Fri. 516	l Daily ex. Sun. 92

Left CPR employee time-table, Alberta District No. 32, September 17, 1922. The CPR subdivision from Bassano to Irricana, opened in 1912, included stops at several fledgling settlements within the irrigation district that had ready-made farms. DOUGLAS R. PHILLIPS COLLECTION

Right Plan for a pre-fabricated farm building, southern Alberta, dated July 5, 1912, draughtsman unknown The first houses for ready-made farms were designed by engineers and draughtsmen in CPR's Department of Natural Resources and built by the railway's bridge and building workers. LIBRARY AND CULTURAL RESOURCES DIGITAL COLLECTIONS, UNIVERSITY OF CALGARY CU1110191

Crossfield.[26] One homesteader living in Lougheed, Alberta, just east of Sedgewick, later remembered seeing wagons of lumber going by his property on their way to the CPR farms.[27]

The ready-made homes may have looked modestly better than the shacks thrown up by nearby homesteaders, but they apparently offered small comfort when winter descended on the Northwest, as a settler who lived in one recalled: "These CPR cottages were frame structures, no insulation of any kind, 2 by 4 joists, tarpaper and drop siding on the outside; inside laths and plaster directly on the joists." The settler's son recalled family stories of banking barnyard manure to the level of the windows in winter to keep out the frost.[28]

Dennis informed Shaughnessy that the expenditure to prepare the farms in the colonies at Sedgewick, Cairnhill, and Crossfield had been several hundred dollars more than originally anticipated. "The question of obtaining a water supply for domestic purposes has proved to be a serious one," he reported. "Practically all the [government] homesteaders within three townships have left their claims owing to the want of water, but we have found by putting down a series of wells, that a first-class supply of water can be obtained at a depth of from 250 to 350 feet [76 to 107 m]."[29]

The background of the colonists reflected how the ready-made farm program was aimed at Britishers, and just how readily people from the UK had responded. The early settlers bore good Scottish and English names such as Stuart, Campbell, Southwell, Cornwell, Goodwin, Hilton, Davis, and Carlton. The CPR's targeted initiative got an enormous amount of coverage in the British press, and among those paying close attention was the Duke of Sutherland, who contacted the CPR in 1910 to make known his desire to purchase land in the irrigation block.[30]

The duke planned to develop twelve farms, varying in size from 80 to 160 acres (32 to 65 ha), where he would settle the sons of some of his tenants from his estate in Scotland. He and his wife would also spend a few weeks each summer on the colony's central farm. In keeping with his wishes, the CPICC erected all of the buildings and prepared the farms in much the same way it did other ready-made properties.

Irrigation manager Charles Walter Peterson, realizing the potential publicity value of the duke's colonization project, wrote to CPR's John Murray Gibbon, who at the time was the company's advertising agent in Britain, to ensure the plan was appropriately interpreted. In particular, he wanted to "remove the impression that the Duke is making the investment for the purpose of evading taxation in Great Britain (which I personally know he is not)." Peterson suggested "making it read as if it were for Imperialistic and sentimental reasons that his Grace is anxious to become actively identified with one of the colonies and to do his share in bringing out good English stock to the plains of Western Canada."[31]

The CPR sold the duke two sections of land just north of Brooks for what would essentially be his Canadian estate, not far from where the headquarters for the Eastern Section of the irrigation block would be. The price of the property was $35 per acre ($86.50/ha) for irrigable

land and $15 per acre ($37/ha) for non-irrigable land. The duke also paid cash for the necessary buildings and other improvements on the individual farms: $2,300 for the small ones and up to four times that for the larger ones.[32] The railway's illustrious supporter of colonization settled as many as thirty families on the land, and bought many cows, pigs, and chickens from the CPR in support of mixed farming. The duke's death in 1913 cut short further plans for expansion and development. For some years, CPR took over the care of his estate residence, and it is now maintained as an Alberta Provincial Historic Resource.

The homes built during the next couple of years for ready-made farms were, like the duke's Canadian enterprise, designed by CPR's own engineering staff and built

to higher standards than the initial prototypes. Calgary contractor Harden & Skene—"concrete and bridge work a specialty"—built 99 of the 150 ready-made farms completed in 1911. "Each included a four-roomed house with porch and a saltbox barn, both finished with coordinated trim and siding colours."[33]

The CPR got more publicity than it wanted that April when the *Empress of Ireland* steamed into the harbour at Saint John, New Brunswick. Among the fifty farmers heading for ready-made farms in Alberta was a woman dressed as a man. The discovery shocked the immigration agents, "who had heard of no such thing in this part of the world, where there are no suffragettes or anything of that kind."[34] "Masquerading as a man" was considered to be a crime in both Canada and the United States, and several women had been jailed in recent years in both countries for just such an offence.

One rural newspaper in Alberta, the *Gleichen Call*, took the whole thing in stride, suggesting that "the fact that she [the woman in question] adapted her attire to her work shows her good sense." Much column space was filled in subsequent days to tell the tale of the woman who gave her name as "Miss Jack May." May, whose real name was apparently Isobel, had been among those who had successfully applied for a CPR ready-made farm at Sedgewick. In addition to May's legal problems with the government, the railway's contract specified that the applicants were to be married men with agricultural experience. Despite this, May seems to have been accepted by everyone involved. After all, she had paid $16 an acre ($39.50/ha) for her property and had filled out all the necessary paperwork; she settled relatively peacefully in the Sedgewick Colony with her companion, Miss Louisa May Wittrick of Norfolk.[35]

◄ Poster images of ready-made farm colonies painted an idyllic picture of life in the Northwest, "close to schools, markets and churches." AUTHOR'S COLLECTION

Opposite, top The realities of early settler life on the bald prairie must have come as a shock to these residents of Namaka Colony, southeast of Strathmore. HARRY POLLARD, LIBRARY AND CULTURAL RESOURCES DIGITAL COLLECTIONS, UNIVERSITY OF CALGARY CU1173528

Opposite, bottom The Duke of Sutherland's Canadian estate near Brooks in the Eastern Irrigation Section. LIBRARY AND CULTURAL RESOURCES DIGITAL COLLECTIONS, UNIVERSITY OF CALGARY CU1133778

The other Sedgewick colonists were more concerned about a delay in taking possession of their land as a result of a legal wrangle. The CPR had charged them $3 per acre ($7.41/ha) more than the price quoted in England by the company agent, presumably resulting at least partly from the added expense of digging wells.[36]

As a boost to the CPR's advertising efforts being expended in Britain, and perhaps as a salve for bruised relationships with the colonists, Shaughnessy announced that he would present a silver cup each year to the most successful farmer on one of the company's ready-made farms. The settlers themselves would choose the winner. The CPR also announced its intention to extend the popular settlement scheme to emigrants from Northern Europe and the United States.[37] From London, Charles Peterson, now manager of CPICC, travelled to Holland, Belgium, and Austria to assess the advisability of extending the improved farm plan to those countries.[38]

The CPR constructed more than 400 miles (640 km) of new prairie railway lines in 1911 and spent no less than eight million dollars to extend the company's irrigation system to the Eastern Section of the irrigation block between Calgary and Medicine Hat. Mixed farming, particularly if it also included a few cows, was looked upon by both the governmental and the railway agricultural specialists as being much more sustainable than dedicated wheat farming—though the latter could be very lucrative in the short term, if all went well. The target tenant for a CPR ready-made farm was the settler who intended to run a diverse farming operation. Railway vice-president William Whyte was interviewed in 1911 by a Medicine Hat newspaperman on just that topic. He said that, while the Northwest had some of the best agricultural land in the world, the CPR had been

forced to import twelve million eggs from the US in the past year. Chickens to serve on the dining cars had to be brought in from Chicago.

"The trouble is that our farmers are wheat mad," he asserted. "They have made money with wheat; and they have not the labour which mixed farming involves. They can go away in the winter and leave the hired man to take care of the horses."

He also recognized what a downturn in the price of wheat on the world market, or a few consecutive years of bad weather, might bring to the single-minded farmer. "The loss which follows exclusive raising on the farm is universally recognized . . . He [the settler] is using the land not as a farm should be used, but as a miner uses a mine. He is taking all out and putting nothing back."[39]

Whyte's concerns about a lack of certain food stuffs, resulting from too little mixed farming being practiced in the Northwest, may have also been on CPR president Shaughnessy's mind the year before, when he voiced support for Georgina Binnie-Clark's agricultural training farm for English girls in Saskatchewan. Binnie-Clark was a British journalist who had immigrated to Canada as an independent farmer and purchased a quarter-section from the CPR, being ineligible for a free homestead. Against all odds, she succeeded and became a great advocate for settler and grain-grower rights. Shaughnessy suggested Binnie-Clark's pupils could provide the CPR with eggs and poultry.[40]

With both the odd-numbered and even-numbered sections owned by Canadian Pacific for 150 miles (240 km) east of Calgary, between the Bow and Red Deer rivers, land-seekers looking for free homesteads now had to go farther and farther afield. A resident of Claresholm, who was hoping to find a government homestead in his vicinity, ended up having to look as far north as Hanna. Back home he wrote down his thoughts about CPR's irrigation block, through which he had passed during his search:

There are thousands of sections through here with no sign of plow or habitation, not even horses or cattle grazing there. We are forced to ask each other the question: Is it right that the C.P.R. should hold this land out of use, with an upset price of possibly $22 to $30 per acre, while thousands of homesteaders were forced to go on, on, on, 'way beyond the Red Deer to find land to settle on?[41]

Demonstration farms and display trains

With land sales booming in both the irrigation district and surrounding areas, CPR agents were swamped with requests for advice on all manner of agricultural issues. Most of the settlers on newly irrigated land had little or no experience with this type of farming, and those outside the irrigation sections were struggling to become better

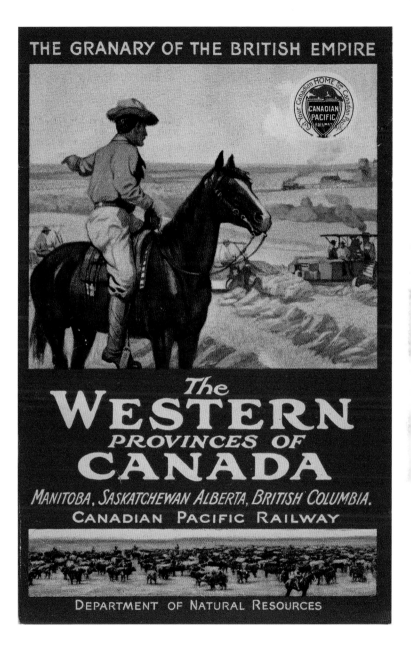

THE GRANARY OF THE BRITISH EMPIRE

The WESTERN PROVINCES OF CANADA

MANITOBA, SASKATCHEWAN ALBERTA, BRITISH COLUMBIA. CANADIAN PACIFIC RAILWAY

DEPARTMENT OF NATURAL RESOURCES

acquainted with dry-farming techniques. The land department promoted mixed farming among recent colonists, which generated innumerable questions about animal husbandry as well.

The notion of operating demonstration farms had been a component of CPR's settlement strategy since the company's dalliance with a series of experimental farms back in the early 1880s. This time, though, Dennis and his staff would go one better and establish a combined demonstration and supply farm that would serve as a laboratory for agricultural study, learning, and cooperation, while also providing fresh produce for the CPR's dining cars and mountain hotels.

Canadian Pacific firmly believed it was infinitely more valuable to put a productive settler on the land than it was to just sell a piece of property. The land department's own policies were clear that "when a parcel of land had been sold, the company interest in the transaction would not cease with the sale. In fact, it only commenced. The railway company was vastly interested in the success of every individual purchaser, who at once became a valued patron of the road."[42]

In 1905, CPR began to survey what would become the company's 2,500-acre (1000 ha) Strathmore Demonstration and Supply Farm, about 30 miles (48 km) east of Calgary, not far from the original hamlet of Strathmore, in the centre of the Western Section of the irrigation district. A few settlers were relocated, along with the existing cattle-loading corrals, a portable station, and a railway section house, to the new townsite from what had basically been a railway siding with a few modest structures, 4 miles (6.4 km) to the south at Eagle Lake.[43] The sidings and nascent villages at Cheadle to the west of Strathmore

◀ As the administrative hub of CPR's Western Irrigation Section, Strathmore grew by leaps and bounds to include a permanent station building, colonization office, grain elevators and numerous stores and homes. LIBRARY AND CULTURAL RESOURCES DIGITAL COLLECTIONS, UNIVERSITY OF CALGARY CU1109692

▶ To make up for the shortage of labourers in the Northwest, Canadian Pacific imported tens of thousands of harvesters from along the lines of its American subsidiary, Soo Line. AUTHOR'S COLLECTION

Top left The demonstration and supply farm at Strathmore would grow to become a famed North American showcase for the pursuit of excellence in all aspects of agricultural innovation and animal husbandry.

AUTHOR'S COLLECTION

Top right The headquarters of the Western Irrigation Section at Strathmore was a substantial structure, designed to impress and represent the solidity of the entire irrigation and colonization project. Dated June 28, 1912. LIBRARY AND CULTURAL RESOURCES DIGITAL COLLECTIONS, UNIVERSITY OF CALGARY CU192985 and Namaka to the east were also moved westward a few miles on the CPR main line. The new settlement of Strathmore was laid out beside a coulee near the CPR main line. It included a railway siding for unloading supplies and a stockyard for holding animals to be shipped east. A large fruit and vegetable garden was cultivated on the opposite side of the tracks.

Canadian Pacific forces began to develop the site and erect a number of small administrative and farming structures on what would be Strathmore's First Avenue in 1906.[44] Within a few years, several hundred acres on the demonstration farm had been sown with grain. In addition, the property boasted 10 acres (4 ha) of root crops, 40 acres (16 ha) of alfalfa, a large patch of strawberry plants, and a nursery that was already nurturing tens of thousands of saplings and young trees.[45] The townsite soon included a permanent railway station building, a couple of grain elevators, and a general store. The first CPR station burned down in 1909 and was replaced the following year.

To supervise the expanding agricultural activities at the farm, Dennis—who by now was assistant to Shaughnessy, the CPR president—hired William James Elliot, a graduate of Guelph Agricultural College and professor of agriculture in Montana. Whether or not Elliot's expertise was a factor, as 1910 came to a close, the *Canadian Gazette* said the produce from the farm was "the exemplification of what can be done under scientific irrigation, and the quality of the vegetables, chickens and dairy produce is best appreciated by those who use the hotel and dining-car services of the Western division of the C.P.R."[46]

Already the farm's function as a supplier of produce for the railway was in full form, particularly the dairy branch. More than one hundred head of dairy cattle produced 120 gallons (450 l) of cream every week for CPR dining cars. An abundant supply of hot water and steam was used to keep clean the new milking machines that gave "better results than by hand," while the buildings were lit by electricity. And the rich alfalfa, which was cultivated so extensively in the Bow River Valley—three crops a year under irrigation— "constituted in itself a salient factor in successful dairying," as it was among the most nutritious cattle feed anywhere.[47]

The agricultural staff at the demonstration farm were very keen on the promotion of alfalfa as forage for cattle and horses as well as a beneficial crop for human consumption, being low in calories while high in protein and nutrients. Alfalfa was particularly appropriate in areas prone to drought, as it could survive extended dry periods. Its deep and extensive tap roots meant that forty to 50 percent of the plant's mass was below ground, helping to reduce both erosion and soil compaction and building organic matter in the soil from year to year.

At Calgary, the provincial government ran the largest dairy station and cold storage in the West. Its output of butter alone had grown from 400 pounds (180 kg) in 1902 to nearly 2.5 million pounds (1.13 million kg) in 1909. There was an abundant market for dairy products in both Alberta and southern British Columbia as well as a rapidly growing market in Japan and China.[48]

In the early years of its operation, another important function of the Strathmore Demonstration and Supply Farm was, of course, to instruct settlers in the intricacies of constructing and maintaining efficient irrigation channels on their own properties and using the water made available to them to its best advantage.

If the land was soaked after a harvest, it would retain much of the moisture during the fall and winter. Spring

W.C. McKILLICAN.   T.N. WILLING.   Dr JAMES FLETCHER.   G.H. CLARK. SEED COMMISSIONER.   L.ANGUS McKAY.   S.A. BEDFORD.   JAMES MURRAY.

JOHN MILLAR.   A. MITCHELL.   PROF. GEO. HARCOURT.   HON. W.R. MOTHERWELL.   D.W. McCUAIG.   R. McKENZIE.   R.C. HENDERS.

FOR GOOD SEED AND CLEAN FARMS.

W.H. FAIRFIELD.   GEO. H. GREIG.   W.B. LANAGAN.   Wm WHYTE. SECOND VICE PRES. C.P.R. Co.   GEO. SHAW. TRAFFIC MANAGER. C.N.R.   J.A. MOONEY.   D.D. CAMPBELL.

THE TOPLEY STUDIO. OTTAWA.

1906
SEED SELECTION SPECIAL
MANITOBA · SASKATCHEWAN · ALBERTA

grain could be sown as early as advisable, depending on the variety; and winter wheat could be sown in August. The farm demonstrated that land irrigated in July or August could produce 40 bushels an acre (99 bushels/ha) of winter wheat without further irrigation or with no more than two inches (5 cm) of rainfall.[49]

During Elliot's tenure at the Strathmore farm, classes and lectures were held regularly for large groups of immigrants to gain knowledge about horticulture and animal husbandry. An article in a 1911 spring edition of the *Strathmore Standard* quoted the farm superintendent:

In opening up their lands in the great Canadian West, the Canadian Pacific Railway has taken every precaution to safeguard the interests of the settlers. These precautionary measures extend much further than the average individual would suppose. In fact, with ordinary and faithful application, it would be hard for the average settler to fail... We have all kinds of people coming from all kinds of agricultural conditions, and it certainly shows advanced ideas on the part of the C.P.R. when they do all in their power to help all the various classes of settlers to be successful right from the start.[50]

With a solid strategy in place for encouraging immigration from Britain, Dennis devised another incentive to appeal to the still large contingent of potential colonists from the CPR's most lucrative market.

"The American comes across the international border, sees for himself, and invests. He comes, he sees, he buys," said a special correspondent writing about the CPR's irrigation scheme. "The Englishman is slower to decide, and not unnaturally, considering the different geographical conditions, more difficult to interest."[51]

The CPR still had about 7 million acres (2.8 million ha) of unsold land and one of the best land sales forces on the continent in the United States. Building on its ready-made farm program, the company devised a similar "improved-farm" offer for American land-seekers that offered $2,000 loans to cover the cost of a house, barn, fencing, and a well, with an easy repayment plan spread out over 20 years. Settlers were limited to a maximum purchase of a half section, or 320 acres (130 ha), and they had to do their own cultivating and seeding. They also had to agree to occupy their property for at least six months each year.[52]

US settlers would, of course, have access to all of the railway's support staff, agricultural expertise, and aid with animal husbandry, which included the option to purchase or borrow stud animals as required. The American government showed little concern for the northward migration of its citizens on the prairies, but the US press had had the issue in its sights for a while. A Chicago editorial even placed the blame directly on the CPR's doorstep:

Our country has been despoiled of more than eighty thousand of its best citizens and of some $100,000,000 in cash... The principal agent of our despoliation is the Canadian Pacific Railway, and it has been able to accomplish much by clever advertising... Its agents, widely active, have found that the best way to make a fairly prosperous farmer leave a fairly satisfactory farm is to offer him a better farm, ready-made.[53]

While Dennis was establishing the demonstration farm at Strathmore, CPR vice-president William Whyte had submitted to the Dominion Department of Agriculture a proposition for a joint initiative between the railway and the government to impress upon grain growers the importance of sowing the best seed available. The initial approach soon led to a conference that also included representatives from the Canadian Northern Railway, the Manitoba &

Northwest Territory Grain Growers' Association, and the Northwest Territories' Department of Agriculture.

The outcome was an agreement to run demonstration or display trains, beginning in early January 1906, through Manitoba, Saskatchewan, and Alberta to instruct settlers about the importance of sowing good seed and how to secure it. Two cars were outfitted with cabinets filled with samples of grain sown under perfect seed conditions and others taken from fields where the seed had been allowed to deteriorate, with a corresponding loss in revenue per acre to the farmer. Samples of wheat pests would also be shown, along with practical information on how to eradicate them. The railways would supply and pay all expenses associated with the trains, and the Dominion government would be responsible for arranging and paying for lectures and live demonstrations as well as covering the cost of advertising.[54]

The first such initiative in Alberta—the "Seed Grain and Weed Special" train—opened in Cardston, Magrath, Raymond, and Lethbridge for eight or nine hundred farmers. Dominion seed commissioner G.H. Clark spoke about testing seed for vitality and how to make the proper selection; S. Bedford, the director of the government's experimental farm at Brandon, gave a lecture about smut and weeds. In another car, others instructed the visitors about growing wheat and alfalfa.[55] The seed and weed special was just the first of many instructional trains that would be operated throughout the following decade.

Beginning in 1911, CPR and the Canadian Northern in partnership with the provincial departments of agriculture operated "Better Farming" trains, which initially consisted of four demonstration cars with displays and lectures held at three different times during the day: one specifically for men, one for women, and one for boys and girls five years of age and older. Younger children were watched over by one or more female attendants in a nursery car. The trains travelled for four years, every July and August, and visited nearly 150 communities, while dispensing information on "new seeds, new methods, desirable breeds of farm animals, proven farm appliances and model farm buildings."[56]

In a similar vein, a jointly operated "Mixed Farming Special" train toured Alberta for five weeks in 1912. An editorial in the *Olds Gazette* noted that the farmers' wives were particularly taken with the poultry exhibit and the lectures given on that subject.[57]

To further promote the benefits of mixed farming that same year, "demonstration" or "illustration" farms were established by the CPR that were known by the name of the towns to which they were adjacent, such as the "Cochrane C.P.R. Mixed Farm." The company's *Staff Bulletin* gave a brief description of what those entailed:

Each of the farms selected is 160 acres [65 ha] in area and no effort has been made to secure the best land, the idea being to show what can be done on land of only average fertility. The farm stock will consist of four brood mares, four to six milch cows, six brood sows and ten to fifteen sheep. The farm buildings will be of substantial character and competent men will be placed in charge who will be paid a salary and a portion of the returns from each year's crop. An exact record of all work, sales, returns, etc., will be kept on each farm and given out without charge to applicants after the farms have been in operation one year.[58]

Twenty-six locations had originally been identified by the railway as potential sites for the illustration mixed farms, but that was quickly pared down to thirteen, twelve of which were developed: three in Manitoba, at Pierson, Pipestone,

► "Better Farming" trains were operated by the CPR and Canadian Northern in partnership with provincial departments of agriculture. Various on-board displays and lectures were aimed at men, women and even boys and girls five years of age and older.
AUTHOR'S COLLECTION

CANADIAN PACIFIC RAILWAY CO.
DEPARTMENT OF NATURAL RESOURCES
READY MADE FARM BUILDINGS
STANDARD BARN No 7

Scale 8 feet to One Inch.

2 Sheets Sheet No 1

Office of the Chief Engineer.
Calgary, Alberta
26th day of June 1912
A.S. Dawson
Chief Engineer.

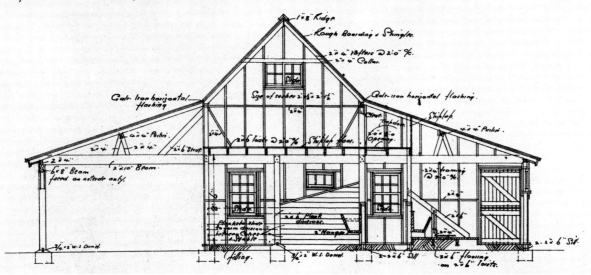

and Virden; four in Saskatchewan, at Alameda, Vanguard, Wolfe, and Wynyard; and five in Alberta, at Broxburn, Coronation, Sedgewick, Vulcan, and Cochrane.[59]

Another special train in 1912 was launched to encourage old settlers and new to buy all of their needs in Canada. The central message had its origins in the federal election the year before, when Canadian manufacturing interests abandoned Laurier, whose Liberal Party favoured reciprocity with the United States, for Robert Borden's winning Conservatives and their pro-tariff stance. The Canadian Home Market Association in partnership with the CPR organized a "Made-in-Canada" train to educate settlers about the importance of tariff protection.[60]

The special train steamed out of Montreal's Windsor Station on May 15 for a lengthy tour that included nearly one hundred stops on the prairies. When it opened to the public in Stavely, Alberta, on a Monday morning, all the stores closed "so that all would have the opportunity of visiting the exhibit."[61]

The rolling advertisement for Canadian goods featured more than eight thousand individual items displayed in ten railway cars. Each piece had been manufactured in Canada, including the train itself, which was outshopped from CPR's own Angus shops. Newspaper coverage mentioned rubber products, pianos, bicycles, motors, pumps, kitchen appliances, a two-ton safe, beds, paints, and plenty of farm supplies (including a miniature model of an automatic grain weighing machine and a kerosene power plant for lighting farm residences and barns).[62]

The tour was deemed such a success that the Made-in-Canada train took to the rails again in 1913. That was the last year for the special train, but the Canadian Manufacturing Association maintained the same theme for its advertising campaigns during the war years.

Two significant events in 1912 added considerable impetus to CPR's immigration and settlement activities in the Northwest. The first was the purchase of majority control of the Alberta Railway & Irrigation Company (AR&I), including irrigation works, railway operations, and colonization involvements. The second was the creation of CPR's Department of Natural Resources.

Peter L. Naismith, general manager of the AR&I, became the head of the natural resources department, reporting to J.S. Dennis. Augustus Nanton, the AR&I's managing director, whose firm Osler, Hammond & Nanton was heavily connected with the CPR, was named a director of Canadian Pacific two years after the takeover. The change of management gave CPR control of an additional 500,000-acre (200,000 ha) tract of land in southern Alberta.[63]

The CPR's ready-made farm program was extended to the Lethbridge area that same year. In May, Dennis announced that 17 ready-made farms of 160 acres (65 ha) each would be made available for occupation the following year. The farms in the Coaldale Colony would be built to the specifications on Department of Resources standard plans for houses and barns. The CPR supervised the development under the department's Land Branch.[64]

The Seventh International Dry Farming Congress was held in Lethbridge that year, attracting five thousand representatives from fifteen countries. Dry farming techniques used deep plowing, subsurface packing, repeated cultivation, and special machinery to preserve the soil's moisture during droughts. Dry land cultivation swept across the Northwest as it had in the US, with one historian describing the attendant enthusiasm as "a religious revival movement." CPR was keen to get on board, viewing the dry-farming methods as potential salvation during slow periods of irrigated land sales.[65]

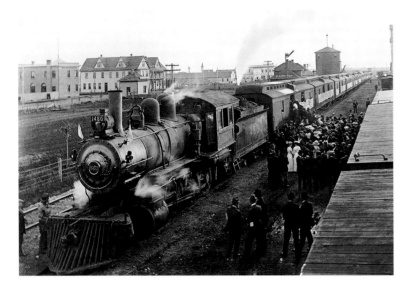

The formation of the Department of Natural Resources (DNR) in Calgary was an official acknowledgement that the vast majority of the company's land and resource activity had moved westward. As the name of the new department implied, it also satisfied Shaughnessy's desire for greater coordination of the company's vast and largely untapped sources of revenue. The Land Department in Winnipeg became a thing of the past, as did the CPICC. At first, the change of name caused some confusion about the function of the department. One enquiry from abroad came addressed to the "Department of National Racehorses."⁶⁶ But after a time, the new organization achieved widespread recognition.

The DNR was divided into branches for land, engineering, coal mining, treasury, and accounting, each with an organization of its own, but all reporting to Dennis, who in turn was responsible directly to the CPR president. The department's general townsite agent was also located in Calgary.

Under the Land Branch, company agencies were set up in Winnipeg, Saskatoon, and Calgary. At Lethbridge, a company agent was in charge of lands and town lots previously under the control of the AR&I. For the first time, the Calgary office would be in charge of administering all of the company's lands throughout the Northwest.

Along with its focus on land sales within the irrigation block, the company had turned its attention toward CPR lands tributary to the Canadian Northern Railway and the Grand Trunk Pacific. W.J. Gerow, the CPR's land department representative in Saskatoon, recommended that the company market four large blocks of land northeast of Lloydminster on the Canadian Northern. North of Bangor, Saskatchewan, along the Grand Trunk Pacific, there was also a block of land available in the midst of a Welsh community, a fact which Gerow used to attract more settlers of that nationality to the district. North of Biggar, on CPR's Wetaskiwin-Saskatoon line, he identified a good area for colonization by Russians, Germans, or other continental Europeans interested in mixed farming, as there was already a large German community in the area.⁶⁷

Government brochures continued to advertise primarily for farmers, farm labourers, and domestic servants, while specifically prohibiting the entry to the country of "idiots, imbeciles and feeble-minded persons, persons afflicted with loathsome diseases and persons engaged in any immoral occupation."

CPR went upscale with a special advertising campaign featured in fairly sophisticated publications such as *Popular Mechanics*, out of Chicago, and *Country Life*, a favourite with the British gentry.[68] The company continued to bring in colonists for its ready-made farms in the irrigation block near Strathmore and at Sedgewick and was preparing the grounds at several other locations. Many of the new immigrants who had entered the country under the ready-made farm plan had been described as members of "a very good class" in possession of from two to five thousand dollars when they entered Canada.[69] For other British arrivals of more modest means, the government soon dropped the requirement to have a minimum of twenty-five dollars when they landed if they were on their way to live with family members already resident in the country.

The settlers in ready-made farm colonies had numerous complaints about various details that the railway had failed to attend to or even mention during the initial land transactions. To achieve some bargaining power, they formed the British Ready-Made Farmers Association, with several committees in individual colonies. Very quickly, the lobby group managed to negotiate a better payment plan, requiring that they cover only the interest on their debts for the first three years of their residence. After that, they would be issued new contracts calling for the payment of principal and interest over twenty years rather than ten.[70]

At the end of 1912, 146 of the available farms, or just over 40 percent, were still vacant.[71] Some settlers defaulted, others found the going too hard, but the CPR kept building, advertising, and bringing immigrants into the country.

Dennis and his staff also took some hard knocks when President Shaughnessy's secretary, P.O. O'Farrell, was out west on a business trip. After dining with various business associates in Calgary, he passed on the local scuttlebutt to the boss. "The general staff in the Department of Natural Resources at Calgary have a very poor reputation," he reported, "and, as one man put it to me, 'they are all out for the graft.'"

O'Farrell followed up with a visit to the Strathmore Farm, and his reported assessment was not very flattering:

I went into the cow house while 60 cattle were being milked and to my amazement I saw that 50 of them were scrubs. I really thought that the Canadian Pacific would have nothing but first-class stock in their dairy farm, but all I could see were ten or twelve. The barn where they were being milked was fitted with unsuitable, utterly unsuitable stalls, and it was filthy and absolutely unworthy of any connection to C.P.R... They have a filthy yard where they wallow in the mire... The piggery is the worst exhibition of them all. It is the filthiest and most neglected institution of the kind I have ever seen, and, although there were about 200 hogs, young and old in the pens or wallowing in the filthy yard, there was not a single workman in sight to look after them. The poor things bear unmistakable evidence of neglect and disease for both pneumonia and, I think, cholera has attacked them.[72]

Dennis, of course, looked into the situation immediately and received a lengthy, somewhat contrite reply from J.G. Rutherford, who had only recently been appointed superintendent of agriculture and animal husbandry at the farm.

Without admitting that the criticisms of the dairy herd... are in any reasonable degree justified by the actual facts, it must be frankly acknowledged that there are on the farm at present a considerable

number of cows which cannot be classed as desirable... The dairy barn is certainly not up to modern standards either as regards construction and fittings, but for this the present management of the farm is in no way responsible. After what has been practically a life-long experience in visiting stables of all kinds, good, bad and indifferent, I have no hesitation in saying that the condition in which the dairy barn at Strathmore is kept is, in view of all the circumstances, very credible... So far as the pigs are concerned, I may say that I am personally rather proud of this year's showing. The piggery is certainly an ordinary inexpensive building, but the highest authorities agree that while pigs should be given fairly comfortable quarters, they need not in any way be luxurious... These animals are thrifty and so far as I can see in excellent health and condition, there being no evidence of disease among them, though a few young pigs from the sows recently brought in from Eastern Canada were lost from broncho-pneumonia.[73]

In any case, the stinging criticism was probably a good thing in the long run, as Strathmore farm soon gained a strong reputation for cleanliness and efficiency, winning several trophies and accolades for its dairy cows in particular.

By 1914, there were ready-made farms within the CPR irrigation block at colonies in Nightingale, Crossfield, Acme, Irricana, Namaka, Cluny, Carseland, Bassano, Rosemary, and Duchess, all of which developed into hamlets or towns. Other settlements of various sizes, from the 20,000 acres (8,100 ha) at Gleichen to the 400 acres (162 ha) at Cheadle, included ready-made farms, but not exclusively. Some smaller colonies within the irrigation block, which may have had at least some ready-made farms, but fell off the map altogether, include Cairnhill, Crowfoot, Strathmead, Strangmuir, Elwood, Mewasin, and Craigantler. And, of course, there was the town of Strathmore, which quickly acquired a relatively large population, without the need for a colonization strategy, by virtue of its designation as the CPR's preeminent demonstration and supply farm.[74]

Other ready-made farm colonies outside of the irrigation block were developed at Lethbridge, Coaldale, and Carmangay after CPR's acquisition of the Alberta Railway & Irrigation Company. East of the colony at Sedgewick, the railway constructed a few ready-made farms at Loughheed, and west of Red Deer a few more were built at Sylvan Lake. Other colonies founded in Alberta around the same time failed and disappeared from the map, such as Parsons, Morrison, and Glenrose.

CPR established three ready-made farm colonies in Saskatchewan, with the names Winona, Wolfe, and Wynyard, only the last of which evolved into a town. The company also developed a ready-made colony at Wardner, British Columbia, which still exists as a small, unincorporated town between Cranbrook and Fernie.[75]

Fairly stinking with blossoms

By 1910, most of the Western Section of the irrigation block was in operation, and about two-thirds of the land had been sold to settlers. In 1911, the federal Department of the Interior received a number of complaints from water users who made conflicting claims, on the one hand that CPR's canals were inadequate to supply water to the entire area identified as irrigable land, and on the other hand that the rainfall in the area was generally adequate for growing satisfactory crops without irrigation. There were also issues about whether some of the semi-arid lands requiring irrigation were located above the level of the railway's supply canal.[76]

As a result of the government's deliberations, the area in the Western Section identified by the CPR as irrigable land was reduced officially from 367,000 acres (149,000 ha) to 225,000 acres (91,000 ha). A study of the practicality of irrigation for the area was published in 1915, after a two-year government audit of the entire operation. The "Report on the Climatic and Soil Conditions in the Canadian Pacific Railway Company's Irrigation Project, Western Section" concluded that there was really no basis for any of the farmers' concerns.[77]

The western part of the Central Section was used largely as grazing lands for ranching, while the remaining area was incorporated into the Eastern Section. It was here that the CPR now turned its attention.

It would take four years to build what was then the largest irrigation project in North America, dwarfing the railway's earlier works. The most impressive and challenging engineering features were the 720-foot (220 m), concrete Bassano Dam, which raised the level of the Bow River to feed the network of canals, and the Brooks

Aqueduct, which stretched across a valley that is 2 miles (3.2 km) wide and 60 feet (18 m) deep, to maintain the flow from Lake Newell to the far eastern end of the irrigated lands. Lake Newell, itself a large man-made reservoir, was created during the construction of the irrigation works.

The Town of Bassano was the centre of activity during the early construction years, and the first incorporated village in the Eastern Section. Adopting the slogan "Best in the West by a Damsite," Bassano's population spiked to more than 1,200 persons. The town's namesake dam was designed by Hugh B. Muckleston, assistant to CPR chief engineer A.S. Dawson.[78] In 1911, more than five hundred

men were reported to be employed by the CPR on the dam and surrounding works, with the aid of 400 teams of mules brought in from Panama.[79] The railway built enormous wooden trestles across the Bow River and along the main canal to move and dump excavated earth and shuttle building materials.

A Danish immigrant, Johan Wulff, took the train from Calgary to Bassano in March of 1912 to take up work on the dam. In a letter home, he described his fellow travellers: "Half a dozen Canadian farmers, long-limbed and weather beaten, smoking and spitting all the time; two Chinese; a Japanese; three European immigrants travelling with a

uniformed inspector who was to show them where they could settle; and three Red Indians with long black plaits and silver coins in their ears. The guards [porters] were black, so that at least four continents were represented."[80]

For several months, Wulff lived in a camp with a dozen men, mostly Norwegians, mixing concrete for various structures associated with the irrigation canals. The camp leader was an American, and the cooks Chinese. The work day started at 1 AM and finished at 6 PM. Wulff wrote about seeing huge plows to dig the canals pulled by ten horses and carts drawn by mule teams delivering the earth to conveyor belts for removal. "In the intense summer heat," he said, "they were plagued by mosquitoes and had to wear gloves and a veil; the insects got in under sleeves and trouser legs in their hundreds and everybody was badly bitten."[81]

At the end of the summer, all of the workers were invited to the irrigation headquarters in Brooks for dinner and a singsong. "About thirty men sat down to a good dinner with beer and whisky," Wulff recalled, "and they sang, often two different songs at the same time." Despite making a good wage, "the uncertainty and primitive conditions of work in Canada" made Wulff decide to return to Denmark when his job was done.[82]

As the work on the dam neared completion, many of the workers moved eastward to proceed with the extension of the canal system and to finish other major structures such as the Brooks Aqueduct. The aqueduct was built to keep the supply of water at the desired level as it spanned a large north-south valley. It had two claims to fame: it was the longest aqueduct ever constructed to carry such a large quantity of water, and the first aqueduct in the world to make use of an "hydrostatic catenary" curve, or the natural shape a flexible material would take when filled with water and suspended between two level supports. The use of

Top More than 500 men and 400 teams of mules brought to Bassano from Panama would be put to work constructing what was at the time one of the world's largest dams. J.H. STILES, LIBRARY AND CULTURAL RESOURCES DIGITAL COLLECTIONS, UNIVERSITY OF CALGARY CU1107448

Bottom The concrete Bassano Dam, 720 feet long, raised the level of the Bow River to feed the network of irrigation canals. LIBRARY AND CULTURAL RESOURCES DIGITAL COLLECTIONS, UNIVERSITY OF CALGARY CU1133420

Top left The CPR cookhouse near Bassano required a large contingent of kitchen workers to feed the construction forces employed on the massive dam project. RESTON AND HENRY, LIBRARY AND CULTURAL RESOURCES DIGITAL COLLECTIONS, UNIVERSITY OF CALGARY CU180505

Top right The Brooks Aqueduct was built to keep the water supply at the desired level as it spanned a large north–south valley on its way to irrigation ditches in the Eastern Section. AUTHOR'S COLLECTION

Bottom left Steam shovels dig main canal "B" on the Eastern Section of the CPR's irrigation project, near Bassano. HARRY POLLARD, LIBRARY AND CULTURAL RESOURCES DIGITAL COLLECTIONS, UNIVERSITY OF CALGARY CU1173475

reinforced concrete was innovative for the time, as was the design of the unique inverted syphon which carried water below ground at the point where the aqueduct crossed the CPR's main railway line.[83]

The aqueduct was plagued with problems from the beginning, including constant leaks and excessive maintenance costs, causing some local critics to refer to the already unpopular, monopolistic CPR as "Canadian Pathetic."[84] But the innovative and picturesque landmark structure brought enormous quantities of water to moisture-starved lands for more than sixty-five years without a major failure.[85]

The availability of abundant agricultural land close to railway lines in Alberta, and the general buoyant health of the national and world economies, made 1912 and 1913 two of the best years for Canadian immigration ever. It was beginning to look good for Van Horne's prediction that the entire irrigation district would soon "fairly stink with blossoms."[86]

Northwest of Bassano, on the railway branch line to Irricana, a local syndicate known as the German-Canadian Farming Company, purchased a large tract of land from the CPR in the range land that had been part of the former Central Section of the irrigation block. The hamlet established there was named Hussar in honour of one of the company founders, who had been a lieutenant of a German Hussar regiment.[87]

The first settlers in the Eastern Section arrived by rail at Bassano in 1914 to take up farms northwest of Brooks, at Gem. Brooks became the hub of the district and was incorporated as a village as early as 1910. The CPR set up administrative offices and staff residences there for irrigation workers. It was also the location of one of three demonstration farms in that part of the irrigation block

Top The reinforced concrete aqueduct was the first in the world to be built with a "hydrostatic catenary curve." AUTHOR'S COLLECTION

Bottom A unique syphon propelled the aqueduct's flow of water down and under the CPR main line, and back up again on the other side. LIBRARY AND CULTURAL RESOURCES DIGITAL COLLECTIONS, UNIVERSITY OF CALGARY CU1107030

where experimental work with both crops and livestock was carried out, the others being at Tilley and Cassils.

With war clouds on the horizon, 1914 brought one more large land sale for the CPR. The railway covered the expenses of a delegation of Russians from San Francisco to travel to Bassano, where the group found the prairies of southern Alberta to be very much like the countryside they knew in southern Russia. They soon selected three tracts of land in the neighbourhood of Rosemary: one consisting of forty-two sections, a second of twelve sections, and a third of four sections, totalling 37,120 acres (15,00). The average price they paid was $50 per irrigated acre ($124/ha) and $25 per acre ($62/ha) of non-irrigated land. An article in the Russian-language newspaper that covered the transaction claimed that the same quality of lands in California would have cost $200 to $300 an acre ($494 to $741/ha).[88] Dennis, who, as both chief of the Department of Natural Resources and assistant to the CPR president, was the most influential powerbroker in the Northwest, buttered up the delegates when they came through Calgary, telling them that "it was the first time in his experience to meet

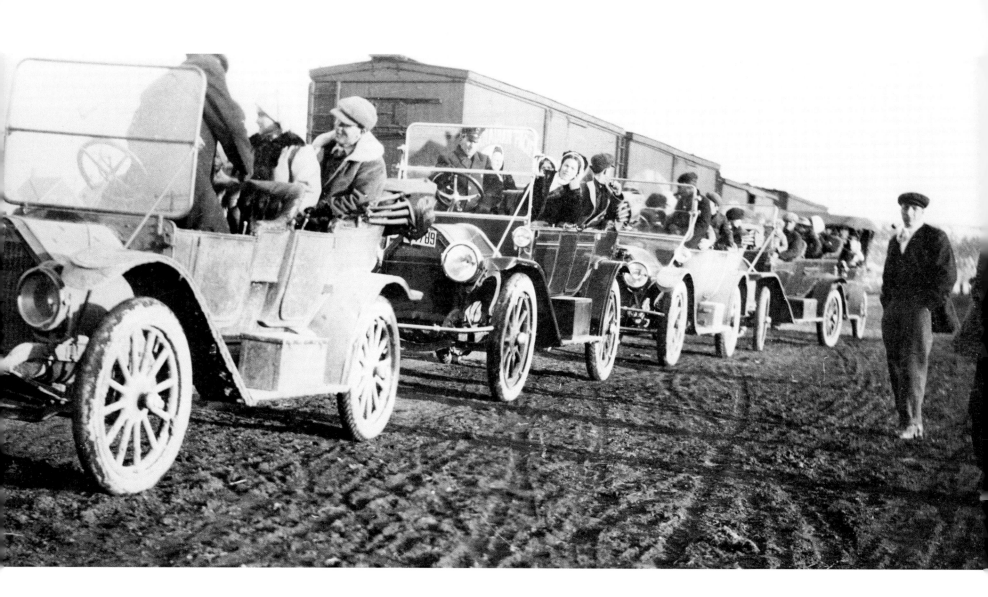

farmers arriving to look for land, who knew what they were looking for."[89]

The CPR had by now spent more than eighteen million dollars to adapt the semi-arid lands in Palliser's Triangle to intensive cultivation. The company had been confident that land sales within the irrigation block would more than cover the cost of development, and the traffic it created for the railway would be an ongoing benefit. However, as had been the case during the doldrums of the late 1880s and early 1890s, this proved to be overly optimistic. Recruiting farmers unfamiliar with irrigated farming would require ongoing assistance in the form of loans, agricultural expertise, and even more on-site guidance.

Despite the challenges the railway faced in implementing its colonization and settlement plans, however, the number of immigrants taking up residence in the Northwest continued to rise throughout the first decade and a half of the twentieth century. Then came the First World War, and the bottom dropped out of the land sales market.

10 A WORLD IN DISARRAY

The Austrian misadventure

The advent of the twentieth century was accompanied by the ascendency of the ethnic nation state and the accompanying exclusionary attitudes of increasingly xenophobic citizens. The first to pass strong legislation controlling the racial makeup of those immigrating to their country were the Australians. Their Immigration Restriction Act of 1901 not only excluded non-Europeans from entering the country, it also granted Australia's immigration officials sweeping powers to test the language skills of would-be newcomers and deport illegal or undesirable immigrants.

Other countries, including Canada and the United States, also considered tightening up their immigration regulations. Canada already had a lengthy list of prohibited classes, and there were those who suspected even England, which released more emigrants than any other country, was using North America as a clearing house for dumping its most unsavory elements. As a result, the major steamship companies on either side of the Atlantic were employing extra vigilance to exclude passengers who would likely be refused admission at the ports of entry they served, resulting in added expense for the ship owners.

In many European countries, more controls on both immigration and emigration were being considered. In most of the nation states, it was becoming common practice to compel emigrants to secure a passport or other specified legal identification before leaving. An estimated twenty million people had emigrated to North America in recent decades from Germany, Scandinavia, Denmark, Holland, and France, the majority of whom had been welcomed as just the type of thrifty, industrious, and intelligent citizens required in the New World; but now those same nations were demanding that every citizen of age should perform military service before leaving their home countries.[1]

Some of the most promising hunting grounds for new Canadian immigrants were being closely watched by the authorities. Emigration was tightly controlled in Holland, Denmark, and Scandinavia. German law forbade the emigration of any of its citizens who had not fulfilled their military duties. The Russian government also maintained strict control, but illegal emigration increased markedly in 1904, after the beginning of that country's war with Japan. Thousands were smuggled across the border and taken by railway to the German ports of Hamburg and Bremen, from which they embarked for North America.[2]

At the same time that the propaganda efforts of Canadian government and railway agents were being closely watched, a representative of the Austrian State Railways approached CPR's agent in Vienna for tips on boosting tourism revenues

out of the newly opened port of Trieste, thereby enabling the Austrian authorities to keep a check on emigrants leaving the country. They had become increasingly concerned about the number of male emigrants leaving uncontrolled through other ports monopolized by the North German Lloyd and Hamburg America steamship lines. This agreement—with CPR ships *Lake Champlain* and *Lake Erie*, from the former Elder Dempster Beaver Line service, renamed *Ruthenia* and *Tyrolia*—was inaugurated in 1913, making ten trips out of Trieste and carrying 6,415 passengers to Canada.[4]

The German steamship lines took great exception to the incursion and started a campaign in the Austrian newspapers against the *menschenfresser* [man-eaters] who "were out to devour the poor Austrian peasants." But the CPR held its ground, as reported in the London *Financial Times*:

The Canadian Pacific Company will not give way, but are ready to agree to any reasonable terms put forward by their competitors so long as they retain their foothold in Trieste. This company occupies the advantageous position that it is able to recoup a portion of any loss incurred in connection with its ocean business through the additional traffic in which it is engaged in transporting on its own railway. The German companies are not similarly situated.[5]

Nevertheless, the German interests were relentless, with steamship magnate Albert Ballin of the Hamburg America Line leading the charge. The situation worsened rapidly, the Austrian government closed the Canadian Pacific offices, and the company's staff members were taken into custody before being released on bail.

The news was a major scandal, covered by the international press and followed closely in North America.

The current boundaries of Manitoba were set in 1912, when Quebec, Ontario, and Manitoba were all extended north to Hudson Bay. In 1927, the boundary disputes between Quebec and Labrador were resolved, and in 1949 Newfoundland joined the Canadian federation, with the name of the province changing to Newfoundland and Labrador in 2001. BREATHE COMMUNICATIONS, AUTHOR'S COLLECTION

within that country. The agent's recommendation that observation cars similar to the ones operated by the CPR be attached to the trains operating through the scenic Tyrol region led to an Austrian delegation paying a reconnaissance visit to Canada. As a result of collaborative negotiations, CPR ended up designing and operating eight such custom-built railway cars on the tourist routes of the Austrian State Railways, the first three of which went into service between Vienna and Innsbruck in August 1912.[3]

During the formation of this business arrangement, Canadian Pacific persuaded the Austrian government to allow the Canadian company to operate a steamship service

Shaughnessy, the CPR president, admitted that Canadian Pacific had made a tactical error in its rush to obtain the new business:

The company made a faux pas by allowing the transportation of Austrians who had not completed military service. The Austrian government is very strict regarding these regulations. Our representatives at Vienna have been cautioned to respect the wishes of Austria in this matter, but, of course, it was impossible for the agents to detect all frauds which men anxious to leave the country might perpetrate.[6]

The trial that followed, in the words of CPR public relations man John Murray Gibbon, "had all the elements of a Gilbert and Sullivan comedy, though without the music." Canadian Pacific was accused of "having enticed six hundred thousand Austrians of military age to emigrate to Canada in 1911, the inducement being free land with two buffalo to work the farm."[7]

In its defence, the CPR lawyers showed that many of the names of the supposed emigres had been purchased from a national registration bureau. While none were shown to be strictly fictitious, they included the names of Austrians long since dead, children who had died in infancy, and other improbable sources for potential colonists.[8] Little or nothing was said about the buffalo.

The case dragged on in the courts, but before a judgement was reached, the Archduke Franz Ferdinand, who was the heir apparent of the Austro-Hungarian Empire, was assassinated in Sarajevo, beginning a deterioration in European affairs that would soon culminate in the outbreak of the First World War.

Top The CPR shops provided eight custom-built railway cars to Austrian State Railways. AUTHOR'S COLLECTION

Bottom The first cars built by Canadian Pacific for Austrian State Railways, featuring swivel chairs in large, open observation areas, went into service between Vienna, the capital city in the east, and Innsbruck in the west. DOUGLAS R. PHILLIPS COLLECTION

ALLAN LINE

H.M.S. ALSATIAN, FLAG SHIP MERCANTILE CRUISER SQUADRON

St. Lawrence Sailings
Season 1915

Montreal - Quebec to Liverpool
(ROYAL MAIL SERVICE)

From LIVERPOOL	STEAMERS	From MONTREAL		From LIVERPOOL	STEAMERS	From MONTREAL
Fri. April 30	GRAMPIAN	Fri. May 14		Fri. Aug. 6	HESPERIAN	Fri. Aug. 20
Fri. May 14	HESPERIAN	Fri. " 28		Fri. " 20	GRAMPIAN	Fri. Sep. 3
Fri. " 28	GRAMPIAN	Fri. June 11		Fri. Sep. 3	HESPERIAN	Fri. " 17
Fri. June 11	HESPERIAN	Fri. " 25		Fri. " 17	GRAMPIAN	Fri. Oct. 1
Fri. " 25	GRAMPIAN	Fri. July 9		Fri. Oct. 1	HESPERIAN	Fri. " 15
Fri. July 9	HESPERIAN	Fri. " 23		Fri. " 15	GRAMPIAN	Fri. " 29
Fri. " 23	GRAMPIAN	Fri. Aug. 6		Fri. " 29	HESPERIAN	Fri. Nov. 12

Montreal - Quebec to Glasgow

From GLASGOW	STEAMERS	From MONTREAL		From GLASGOW	STEAMERS	From MONTREAL
Sat. April 24	PRETORIAN	Sat. May 8		Sat. Aug. 14	CORSICAN	Sat. Aug. 28
Sat. May 8	SCANDINAVIAN	Sat. " 22		Sat. " 28	SCANDINAVIAN	Sat. Sep. 11
Sat. " 22	CORSICAN	Sat. June 5		Sat. Sep. 11	CORSICAN	Sat. " 25
Sat. June 5	SCANDINAVIAN	Sat. " 19		Sat. " 25	SCANDINAVIAN	Sat. Oct. 9
Sat. " 19	CORSICAN	Sat. July 3		Sat. Oct. 9	CORSICAN	Sat. " 2:
Sat. July 3	SCANDINAVIAN	Sat. " 17		Sat. " 23	SCANDINAVIAN	Sat. Nov. 6
Sat. " 17	CORSICAN	Sat. " 31		Sat. Nov. 6	CORSICAN	Sat. " 20
Sat. " 31	SCANDINAVIAN	Sat. Aug. 14				

Sailings from St. John, N.B. and Halifax, N.S. to Liverpool

From ST. JOHN	STEAMERS	From HALIFAX		From ST. JOHN	STEAMERS	From HALIFAX
Wed. Mar. 24	HESPERIAN	Thu. Mar .25		Wed. Apr. 21	CORSICAN	Thu. Apr. 22
Fri. April 2	SCANDINAVIAN	Sat. April 3		Fri. " 30	HESPERIAN	Sat. May 1

Tickets for Sale Here

Wartime reconfiguration

Although Britain and her Commonwealth allies did not formally declare war on the Central Powers of Germany, Austria-Hungary, and the Ottoman Empire until well into 1914, the year brought less than half the immigrants to Canada than had arrived in 1913. For the next four years, immigration from Europe would be at a standstill, while the flow of US immigrants was reduced to a trickle.

Since the Industrial Revolution of the mid-nineteenth century, the British authorities, together with charitable societies, had carried out a child migration scheme to other countries in the Commonwealth to relieve the social problem of orphaned, abandoned, or otherwise unwanted offspring putting a strain on the social system. Because there was no welfare safety net at home, many children were sent overseas to work on farms or elsewhere, often never to see their families again. The fresh air of an Australian or Canadian farm was seen to be infinitely better than the alternative of living in a squalid urban slum.

In the months immediately preceding the war, these cast-offs were joined by "guest children," who were evacuated to Canada from dangerous areas in Britain that were deemed highly susceptible to enemy attack and bombardment. Parents were relieved that their offspring would be out of harm's way among the cowboys, mounted police officers, and lumberjacks across the pond. Some were eventually adopted by Canadians, some returned to Britain after the war, and others chose their own destiny upon reaching adulthood, perhaps working as a cowboy or in some other romantic trade, but in all likelihood taking a position in the city or on a farm like the ones on which they had been raised.

◀ During the first years of the war, immigration ground to a near standstill, though the CPR's Allan Line steamships kept up a basic service from Liverpool and Glasgow to Quebec City. AUTHOR'S COLLECTION

Opposite, left The cabin-class steamer *Melita*, built by Barclay, Curle & Company of Glasgow, initially was intended to go into service with the Hamburg America Line, but was acquired by the CPR before the end of the war. AUTHOR'S COLLECTION

Opposite, right Though ownership and control remained with the railway, the company's steamship operations on the Atlantic and Pacific were amalgamated under the new name, Canadian Pacific Ocean Services. AUTHOR'S COLLECTION

The CPR had just recently assigned matrons to look after women and unaccompanied girls on transatlantic crossings of its Empress steamships and the *Lake Manitoba*. Now those same women would also keep an eye on all of the relocated children headed for Canada.

After the declaration of war, the British Admiralty quickly requisitioned the larger steamships in Canadian Pacific service. Of the fifty-two ships with which Canadian Pacific entered the war, a dozen of them were lost to enemy action, ten were sold to the Admiralty, and only twenty-seven came through relatively intact.[9] During the war years, a skeletal service was maintained between Canada and the continent almost entirely for freight and war materiel.

In February 1915, Shaughnessy made an unexpected announcement about changes in the administration of CPR's ocean-going steamships, leaving control of its Pacific Coast and inland vessels basically as it was:

The ownership and control of the steamship company will remain with the Canadian Pacific Railway Company, but the management and operation of the [ocean] steamship lines will be vested in the Board of Directors of the Canadian Pacific Ocean Services Ltd. It is only another step in the direction of eliminating from the direct operation of the railway company of items that do not relate to the railway property itself.[10]

Before the war, Canadian Pacific had recognized the need for an upscale immigration service, at the same time that demand for first-class accommodation was falling off. To meet that need, the company had advertised the *Lake Champlain* and *Lake Manitoba* as "one-class cabin steamers," and on the brink of war had designed and launched the *Missanabie* and *Metagama*, as cabin-class vessels. Two other cabin-class steamers, the *Melita* and *Minnedosa*, that had originally been intended for the Hamburg America Line, were acquired by Canadian Pacific toward the end of the war.

The role of the steamship department—and now the new Canadian Pacific Ocean Services (CPOS)—in securing immigrant traffic was an important one. Steamship agents maintained close relationships with numerous overseas colonization boards, societies, and charitable organizations.

In the first nine months of 1915, there was a net decrease of 6,741 homestead entries over the previous year. A report filed by CPR's Department of Natural Resources showed that seventy vacant ready-made farms were cultivated, and more than six thousand cattle, three thousand sheep, and thirteen hundred swine were supplied to farmers on easy terms. Ten of the company's "illustration" mixed farms made a profit that year, while three carried a loss. The department had added a thirteenth farm to the twelve established before the war, at an Alberta location called

Willems. The four demonstration farms in the irrigation block, at Strathmore, Brooks, Cassils, and Tilley, also operated with a small profit.[11]

The CPR closed some of its offices in the United States and reduced staff in the three that stayed open in New York, St. Paul, and Denver. All the offices in Great Britain were shuttered except London, which was used as a centre to handle intended settlers. However, it operated on a shoestring, for most of the staff from the London office had joined the British Army. One after another, the offices on the European continent were besieged, and company staff fled from the strategic centre of Brussels as well as from The Hague, and even the sub-agency in Paris. The office in Oslo was maintained throughout the war.[12]

The CPR continued to distribute immigration literature in the United States and participate in major fairs, such as the Panama–Pacific International Exposition in San Francisco that remained open for most of 1915. The world's fair was conceived to celebrate the opening of the Panama Canal and showcased technological advances in thirteen different categories, each with its own pavilion or "palace." Dozens of other countries participated, with displays in the various exhibition palaces or with national pavilions of their own. Canada was represented in a number of the palaces and also hosted its own massive colonnaded pavilion.

Canadian Pacific was one of only a handful of private companies to erect their own building at the popular exposition. Among the main attractions therein was an impressive working model of Bassano Dam. Daily illustrated lectures, complete with motion picture shows, were delivered by CPR representative L.O. Armstrong and his assistants.[13] The exposition was such a success that it was held over for the next year.

Opposite, top The Canadian Pacific office in Oslo, Norway, was one of the few maintained by the company throughout the First World War. AUTHOR'S COLLECTION

Opposite, bottom Canadian Pacific built an elaborate pavilion for the Panama-Pacific International Exposition (1915) that celebrated the opening of the Panama Canal. LIBRARY AND CULTURAL RESOURCES DIGITAL COLLECTIONS, UNIVERSITY OF CALGARY CU1296896

A similar but smaller fair, the Panama–California Exposition, also drew large crowds in San Diego and was another good opportunity for disseminating CPR immigration and colonization propaganda materials. In a special census conducted on the prairie provinces in 1916, the population of the area was recorded as 1,698,220, up nearly 30 percent from 1911. In Manitoba, Saskatchewan, and Alberta, 132,649 people reported birthplaces in Germany or Austria-Hungary, 7.8 percent of the total population of the Northwest. The largest single group in this category were people from Ukraine, who were generally referred to as Ruthenians, the German name for all Ukrainians, or Galicians, from the province of Galicia. Others had arrived in Canada from German communities in Russia, Romania, and the United States.[14]

The war created problems regarding the naturalization of these people. They were susceptible to accusations of sedition and were often strongly opposed to conscription. Identified as "enemy aliens," many had been required to register at special offices opened by November 1914 but were told they would not be disturbed "so long as they quietly pursue their ordinary avocations" and did not spy, engage in hostile acts, or violate the law.[15]

In the first month of the war, Shaughnessy had suggested to the government that detention camps be established to take care of unemployed German and Austro-Hungarian immigrants, where they could voluntarily register themselves. But the federal solicitor-general, Arthur Meighen, believed such camps would be looked upon as "lazy man havens."[16] Not long afterward, the Canadian Northern Railway discharged a number of its workers, who were recent German immigrants, adding to the ranks of the group in question.[17]

During the war years, 8,579 male prisoners were interned, along with 81 women and 156 children. Western internment stations were located in Winnipeg at Fort Garry; exhibition buildings at Brandon and Lethbridge; the Parks Building at Banff; a tent camp at Castle Mountain, Alberta; and old railway coaches and boxcars at two locations on Canadian Northern Railway tracks, first at Munson, Alberta, north of Drumheller; and then at Eaton, Saskatchewan.[18] While in cars on railway sidings at Munson and Eaton, the internees were put to work as labourers on the Canadian Northern.

By the spring of 1915, Dennis, with the DNR, was devising a postwar strategy for immigration and colonization and filing detailed memoranda for the CPR president as well as for the up-and-coming Edward Beatty, who was company vice-president and general counsel.

As a result of the competitive building of railway tracks in the previous decade, the Northwest had, by this time, more railway mileage per capita than anywhere else in the world, one mile per 110 persons (1 km per 68 persons). The rail lines had been built in advance of settlement, and urban development had proceeded ahead of agricultural development, leaving many unsold or unused sections of land outside of the cities, towns, and villages.

Some, including William Pearce, blamed the lack of activity on lands surrounding urban areas on a lack of government diligence in ensuring residency requirements were met by those who applied for homestead entries. "Those responsible for the Homestead Act and the administration thereof seem largely, if not wholly, to have lost sight of the fact that a homestead was intended as a home, not as a gift of 160 acres [65 ha] to a man coming into the country," Pearce wrote in his memoirs. "Thus around all

Top The Duke of Connaught walks in front of a group of inmates, as he inspects the First World War labour camp at Castle Mountain, Alberta. CRHA/EXPORAIL CANADIAN PACIFIC RAILWAY FONDS NS-3270

Bottom A couple of railway cars placed on a siding at Munson, Alberta, housed internees who were put to work on the Canadian Northern Railway during the war. AUTHOR'S COLLECTION

► Wartime posters for the CPR's Department of Colonization and Development employed imagery similar to what the Russian Soviets presented on their propaganda materials. AUTHOR'S COLLECTION

THE BUREAU OF CANADIAN INFORMATION
DEPT. OF COLONIZATION & DEVELOPMENT
CANADIAN PACIFIC RAILWAY
MONTREAL — LONDON — NEW YORK — CHICAGO

our towns and villages under the Act, all the lands were taken by people who lived in them [the towns], not on the homestead."[19]

The population of the Western provinces was about half rural and half urban, an "unsound condition of distribution" in Dennis's view. He was still looking to the US as the best field for obtaining suitable immigrants, as it had a "vast population living on rented or high-priced farms, who can be attracted to lower priced virgin land in Canada." The supply of good agricultural colonists had been tapped out in Britain, so he recommended stepping up recruitment efforts in Belgium, Holland, Denmark, Norway, Sweden, Germany, the Baltic provinces of Russia, and Austria-Hungary—while cautioning that only in the first four could the company legally engage in any immigration propaganda.[20]

Dennis suggested to his superiors that they influence the federal government to scrap the Immigration Branch of the Department of the Interior and form a new separate Immigration and Colonization Department. He was apparently unimpressed with government efforts in that domain, for he stated bluntly that the present government staff should be reorganized to eliminate "dead wood," and be replaced by "thoroughly qualified men." And CPR influence or not, within two years the government did exactly that.[21] James Alexander Calder was the first federal minister of immigration and colonization. He became a close friend and colleague of Dennis.

In 1916, CPR had created its own Department of Colonization and Development, with headquarters in Montreal, which took over all of the company's colonization activities, chief among them securing settlers, something formerly carried out by the DNR. The latter department's publicity and industrial branches were also moved to the new department. Dennis would be its first chief commissioner. The DNR retained responsibility for selling railway lands, but would now be focused, as its name implied, largely on the development and exploitation of the many resources owned by the company.

Railway vice-president Beatty was generally in agreement with the views Dennis had on immigration, with one caveat: "I do not think German or Austrian settlers (whether Galicians or not) should be sought after," he replied. "For some years after the war is over these men will be regarded as enemies. They will not mix easily or naturally with the rest of the population of Western Canada and it is extremely doubtful whether we will want them there until some years after normal international conditions are established."[22]

Dennis became well versed in wartime economics and the challenges of moving military men from one theatre to another when he was given the rank of colonel, in charge of the British-Canadian recruiting mission in the United States, for which service he was made a Companion in The Most Distinguished Order of Saint Michael and Saint George (CMG). The next year, he was with the Canadian economic commission and military contingent in revolutionary Siberia, where he was responsible for transportation logistics. Dennis was also commissioner of the Canadian Red Cross during the latter part of the war. For the remainder of his career, he was known publicly as Colonel Dennis.

The question of returning Canadian soldiers was an ongoing occupation of CPR senior management, noting that it had been an acute problem following all wars, and that Canada's earliest colonization to Manitoba had consisted of discharged soldiers following the Napoleonic wars in Europe. Two or three hundred thousand Canadian men deactivated from service in the First World War were expected to soon require rehabituating to civilian life.[23]

Within a few months of the war's end, it was obvious that a lot of planning in this area had been carried out by both the federal government and the CPR. Arthur Meighen, minister of the interior, speaking to the Calgary Board of Trade in the summer of 1919, stated that Canada had already put more soldiers back on the land than had Australia, New Zealand, Great Britain, and the United States combined. The government's Soldier Settlement Board had received nearly 26,000 applications for homestead lands, of which more than 20,000 had been approved. The program had been expanded to include soldiers of the British Army as well as sailors not formerly resident in Canada. The CPR's Returned Soldiers' Land Colonization Scheme operated under the same parameters, with a 20 percent reduction in the price of company lands sold to soldiers.[24]

Canadian Pacific's postwar service from Liverpool to Saint John, New Brunswick, was inaugurated in December 1918 when the *Minnedosa* sailed with 500 cabin-class passengers, and another 1,500 in temporary steerage space.[25] To accommodate the large numbers of troops and their dependents returning to Canada, as well as new immigrants, all of the company's cabin-class steamships were modified to hold more passengers. Freight service between Montreal and Antwerp was resumed by CPOS steamer *War Beryl* in June 1919, after a five-year interruption, with more than 10,000 tons (9,071 tonnes) of grain from the Northwest on board as well as 230 head of cattle. Built to the specifications of the British Ministry of Shipping, the vessel was purchased by CPOS, along with sister ship *War Peridot* after the armistice was signed.[26]

Opposite, left A postwar service from Liverpool to Saint John, New Brunswick, was inaugurated when the CPR steamship *Minnedosa* sailed with 500 cabin-class and 1,500 steerage passengers aboard. Package delivery was handled by the Canadian Pacific subsidiary, Dominion Express, through its more than 8,900 agencies. CRHA/EXPORAIL CANADIAN PACIFIC RAILWAY FONDS NS9016

Opposite, top right After a refit, the Allan Line steamship *Alsatian* was renamed *Empress of France* to serve as Canadian Pacific's premier passenger liner. AUTHOR'S COLLECTION

Opposite, bottom right One of three ready-made settlements for returning military men was the CPR's Anzac Colony at Chancellor, Alberta. LIBRARY AND CULTURAL RESOURCES DIGITAL COLLECTIONS, UNIVERSITY OF CALGARY CU1194404

After a refit, the former Allan Line steamship *Alsatian* (built in 1913) became the premier ship of Canadian Pacific's fleet. On her maiden voyage under her new name of *Empress of France*, she made a record run from Liverpool to Quebec in five days, twenty hours, and six minutes, carrying three classes of passenger to Canada, including many immigrants.

While the war was still raging in Europe, the railway had established three ready-made farm colonies in southern Alberta for returning military men: the Van Horne Colony southeast of Coaldale, near Lethbridge; the St. Julien Colony, near Tilley on the CPR main line; and the Anzac Colony at Chancellor, north of Bassano. The first two had 25 and 50 irrigated farms, respectively, each on 80 acres (32 ha), with equal adjacent acreage as an option, while Anzac had 25 non-irrigable farms each on 160 acres (65 ha).[27]

The Lethbridge Board of Trade had lobbied the CPR in a telegram to Shaughnessy, suggesting to the railway president that one of the veterans' colonies should be established "on your company's irrigated lands near Lethbridge, where intensive farming is being successfully carried out."[28] Construction on the first buildings at Coaldale had begun in May 1916 and at the other two sites soon after.

In each of the CPR colonies, a central farm for control and administration was set up with a competent, experienced farmer as superintendent to help the settlers in all

matters of farm development and care of livestock. These control farms also served as supply depots for stud animals and shared farming implements such as drills, mowers, binders, and threshers.[29]

The CPR also opened what were to be known as Bureaus of Canadian Information in New York, Chicago, and London to disseminate reliable information about agricultural and industrial opportunities in Canada and to stimulate interest in the country's undeveloped resources. An official crest and slogan was adopted that featured the company's standard beaver shield with the tag line, "For all information about Canada, ask the C.P.R." Management sent out a decree to the railway's offices around the world to use the new advertising logo unsparingly, on office doors and windows as well as on stationery and company publications.[30] The slogan surrounding the crest went through a number of iterations, including the directive to "Get Your Farm Home from the Canadian Pacific," but was soon simplified to the all-encompassing "Ask the Canadian Pacific about Canada." It served the company well for many years.

The competition goes bust

The unsustainable construction of myriad railway lines in the Prairie provinces in the first two decades of the twentieth century put a strain on the annual balance sheets of the Canadian Pacific Railway and drove its competitors to the brink of financial ruin. In 1918, the federal government assumed majority control over the near bankrupt Canadian Northern Railway and appointed a board of management to oversee the company's operations. At the same time, other companies managed by the crown corporation

Top A new slogan served the company well, while land sales were a priority. AUTHOR'S COLLECTION

Bottom After a few iterations, an all-inclusive slogan graced Canadian Pacific stationery and office doors for many years. AUTHOR'S COLLECTION

► At the end of the First World War, there were still about thirty million acres of good farmland available within fifteen miles of prairie railway lines and ready access to market. AUTHOR'S COLLECTION

CANADIAN PACIFIC

TO THE CANADIAN FARM
INSIST ON TRAVELLING BY C·P·R
For Particulars as to Rates, Sailings & Opportunities for all - Apply:-

Canadian Government Railways (CGR)—Intercolonial Railway of Canada, National Transcontinental Railway, Prince Edward Island Railway, and Hudson Bay Railway—were placed under the oversight of the Canadian Northern's management group. Another of CPR's competitors, the Grand Trunk Pacific, also came under government control when its parent company, the Grand Trunk Railway of Canada, defaulted on construction loans.

On December 20, 1918, the federal government created Canadian National Railways (CNR) as an umbrella company for all the government's railway holdings. The next year, the newly incorporated company officially took over "the railways, works and undertakings of the Companies comprised in the Canadian Northern System," with a provision for the later inclusion of any additional railway acquisitions by the government.[31] By the spring of 1920, the Grand Trunk and the Grand Trunk Pacific were also under the control of the CNR and were fully acquired by that company in 1923.

Recession and a shaky recovery

At the end of the First World War, there were still about 128 million acres (52 million ha) of unoccupied, surveyed land in Manitoba, Saskatchewan, and Alberta well suited for either mixed farming or grain growing.[32] About 30 million acres (12 million ha) were within 15 miles (24 km) of a railway line and ready access to market.[33] CPR had managed to sell more than 300,000 acres (121,00 ha) of its own irrigated holdings and still held more than 5 million available acres (2 million ha) of agricultural land—irrigated and non-irrigated—in the three Prairie provinces.

CANADIAN
PACIFIC

COLONIZATION
AND
DEVELOPMENT

ASK US
ABOUT
CANADA

The shutdown of war-related industries took a toll on the national economy, exacerbated by the return of a quarter million soldiers from Europe who needed to be reabsorbed into the job market. Rising prices and growing unemployment were the order of the day. In response, the federal government made amendments to the Immigration Act to expand the grounds on which a person could be deported from or denied entry to Canada.[34] But the reactionary moves would not be without their opponents.

"Colonization is the most important problem with which we are today faced in Canada," said Dennis, the CPR immigration commissioner, to the annual convention of the Alberta Industrial Development Association in June 1920. "By colonization, I mean not only obtaining of the farmer to cultivate our vast unoccupied area of good agricultural land, but the increasing of our population by the immigration of desirable citizens who will undertake the development of all our other natural resources by providing the necessary capital and labour."[35]

"What we need is more cooperation and concentrated effort on the part of governments, corporations and individuals," Dennis asserted. "In this connection it is, I am sure, gratifying to us all to note that the movement which originated with this Development Association last year, has now resulted in the organization of the Western Canada Colonization Association (WCCA)."[36]

The founders of the new, expansive organization hoped it would operate as a citizens' movement, and many leading citizens in Eastern and Western Canada were among the founders. The government was not asked to be an active participant, nor were the railways part of the original administration. This arrangement, of course, was completely unproductive, and within a year it was rebranded as the Canadian Colonization Association (CCA), after having

◄ The CPR's immigration commissioner, J.S. Dennis, insisted that colonization was the most important issue facing Canadians. AUTHOR'S COLLECTION

Opposite, left After the war, a new Canadian Pacific travelling van, seen here in London's Trafalgar Square, was back on the road promoting immigration, steamship, railway, and express services. AUTHOR'S COLLECTION

Opposite, right Major A. Ewan Moore, left, manager of CPR's Department of Colonization and Development, and E.R. Bruce, director of the Exhibits Branch, inspect the contents of the company's travelling promotional van. AUTHOR'S COLLECTION

been taken over by Canadian Pacific, CNR, and the Dominion government—with the government covering 50 percent of the expense and the railways 25 percent each.

Federal immigration minister James Calder had travelled to England and Scotland early in 1920 to assess shipping conditions across the North Atlantic, only to find that agents in Europe were exercising caution, carefully scrutinizing applicants seeking passage to Canada to avoid bringing unsuitable candidates.[37] Not only did the government prohibit "idiots, imbeciles, feeble-minded persons, epileptics, insane persons and persons who have been insane at any time previously," it now also deemed undesirable people with contagious diseases, immoral persons, "professional beggars or vagrants," anarchists, and

immigrants who were nationals of Germany, Austria, Hungary, Bulgaria, or Turkey.[38]

To add to its promotional arsenal, in 1920 Canadian Pacific formed a film production company, Associated Screen News (ASN), to create and distribute newsreels to three or four thousand theatres in Canada, the United States, Britain, Australia, and South America. Along with luring and entertaining tourists and sparking interest in Canadian industry, ASN's products were often crafted as promotional tools for the railway's immigration agents.[39]

The most promising development that year occurred when a large group of Norwegians in the United States expressed an interest in relocating to some of the 400,000 acres (162,000 ha) of unsold land west of the CPR's

CANADIAN NATIONAL RAILWAYS
Departments of COLONIZATION AND AGRICULTURE
CANADIAN NATIONAL LAND SETTLEMENT ASSOCIATION

Calgary and Edmonton line. A good portion of these lands were timbered and could not be colonized by settlers from Great Britain, who were unused to clearing brush and trees. An easy payment plan was offered, whereby the purchaser could pay 20 percent down and the balance in nineteen annual instalments.[40]

Western Canada, along with much of North America, suffered through a depression in 1921 and 1922 that was accentuated by drought, crop failures, and low prices for farm products. After a two-year, postwar boost in immigration, the number of colonists coming to the New World dropped precipitously. Many that had already settled in the Northwest pulled up stakes and left for the United States.

The disturbing trend of eastbound transatlantic steamship sailings carrying more passengers than the westbound ones was curbed temporarily when two thousand immigrants arrived in a single day, August 2, 1921, at the port of Quebec. Arriving on three CPOS liners, they included Danes, Poles, Ukrainians, Czechs, Russians, Swiss, and Italians.[41] CPR service to Italy, handled by the steamship *Montreal*, was cancelled soon afterward, due to lack of interest and an attendant paucity of bookings.

Despite the slowdown in traffic from Europe, Canadian Pacific took a tentative step toward expanding its operations on the continent with the 1922 opening of a new agency and ticket sales office in Cherbourg, Normandy, which the company shared with the Furness Line, a UK steamship company with service to ports in the United States.

In March 1922, the Japanese government welcomed the world to the Tokyo Peace Commemorative Exposition to celebrate the fourth anniversary of the end of the Great War. Earnest Robert Bruce, CPR's director of exhibits, and his staff in the Department of Colonization and Development designed, constructed, and showcased an enormous, illuminated map, showing the locations where eighty different raw materials in Canada could be extracted and exploited. The outsized map also detailed Canadian Pacific steamship and railway routes, and the country's general areas of timber, fisheries, and agricultural lands. Canada's trade commissioner in Yokohama, A.E. Bryan, reminded all business interests in the Dominion that Japan was a market of sixty million people, ready to purchase Canadian goods or acquire land holdings.[42]

The CPR, in partnership with the CNR, once again reassembled the Better Farming train, comprising four livestock cars, a field crop lecture car, a field crop exhibit car, a poultry and dairy lecture car, a machinery exhibition car, a boys' and girls' magic lantern car, a household science car, and a nursery car. Its popularity was said to be matched only by that of the "circus train" that toured from the United States.[43] Other demonstration specials that the railways operated during the 1920s, as necessary, were Better Livestock trains and Livestock Improvement trains.

After a couple hard years, however, what farmers wanted more than instruction was a break in their financial arrangements from their bankers and from the CPR. Settlers on CPR lands in the Hussar, Wayne, and Wintering Hills districts were particularly unsettled. While the farmers were finding it difficult to meet their financial obligations in the short term, it was reported that they "had faith in ultimate recovery from present conditions" and believed that "the natural farming advantages here found will eventually ensure success and a prosperous community if the farmers be given immediate relief and some encouragement to stick."[44]

The farmers had in fact listened to the advice of the bankers and the CPR and had gone into mixed farming. They had subsequently watched the bottom drop out of the market for cattle and horses, hogs, poultry, eggs, and butter, as well as grains and just about every other thing they owned or produced.

To deal with the situation, Canadian Pacific cobbled together a new contract plan in the fall of 1923 for more than thirty thousand land holders in Western Canada, offering to consolidate their indebtedness and issue new contracts on an amortization plan that would extend payments over a period of thirty years.[45] Two days before a CPR-imposed deadline for settlers to make a decision, farmer delegates held a mass meeting in Calgary to consider the company's distributed circular.

"About one hundred all told attended meeting last night and listened to considerable Bolshevik talk by several agitators," DNR manager Naismith said in a telegram to Augustus Nanton. "Nothing was done and they decided to take no further action until action was taken by Company."[46] Nevertheless, newspapers reported the next day that the delegates had rejected Beatty and the CPR's offer.[47]

Despite the vociferous solidarity campaign waged by some of the farm associations and their more radical leaders, a significant portion of CPR contract holders signed a joint statement confirming their satisfaction with the railway's new amortization scheme.[48] In response, W.D. Trego, secretary of the CPR Contract Holders' Association, and a major agitator, threatened to leave the Northwest with farmers who were unhappy with the CPR and start a new colony in South America if the railway did not accede to their demands.[49]

Despite the sensational headlines in the popular prairie press, most CPR land holders quietly acquiesced to the new contract terms and signed up for the long term. By March 1924, Canadian Pacific was advertising the "Amazing new farm offer!" Prospective new purchasers were offered "payments so small you will have a surplus for comfortable living," with "payments extended over 35 years."[50]

The federal government had bailed from their commitment to the CCA in 1923, leaving the CPR and CNR to take up the slack. The following year, the CNR also decided to go its own way by establishing a land branch of its own, the Colonization and Agriculture Department. Its Canadian National Land Settlement Association would go on to assist more than 27,000 immigrants to settle, mostly on government homestead lands and CPR holdings.

Sir Henry Thornton, president of the CNR, weighed in on immigration issues when he spoke to the Quebec branch of the Canadian Manufacturers' Association on May 15, 1923:

No immigrants should be admitted, unless they are physically and mentally sound. The immigrants should be made to understand that they must respect the laws and customs of the country; in other words, the new immigrant must be such that he is no danger of

▶ The international exhibition was an opportunity to showcase Canada and Canadian Pacific's leading roles in the colonies and dependencies of the British Empire. AUTHOR'S COLLECTION

becoming a burden upon the community. Finally, every new citizen should be of the Caucasian race. We do not want a colour problem like they have in the republic to the south of us.[51]

Thornton and his new Canadian National Land Settlement Association may have been singularly focused on a Caucasian clientele, but in the summer of 1924, Canadian Pacific was helping to host the world at the British Empire Exhibition in Wembley Park, London, to foster trade with and immigration from among not only the British public but the colonies and dependencies of the British Empire as well.

A budget of $100,000 had been allocated to CPR's Publicity Branch, half to construct an eye-catching pavilion and the other half to fill it with exhibits extolling the merits of the Canadian West. The two-storey Canadian Pacific building was one of the foremost showpieces at the fair, featuring more than 5,400 square feet (500 m²) of display space on the main floor alone. Upstairs, a three-hundred-seat theatre lured curious audiences to continuous showings of CPR-sponsored films, enlivened by commentary and engaging anecdotes from distinguished lecturers.[52]

The Empire Exhibition was open for six months in 1924, attracting an estimated twenty-seven million attendees, and again in 1925 for another half-year run. In the second season, E.R. Bruce, CPR's director of exhibits, said it was a mistake to think the railway's displays would be merely a rehash of the previous year. Among the "innovations and elaborations" he cited—of particular interest to immigrants going to Canada by steamship—was an illuminated mechanical model of the harbour at Saint John, New Brunswick.[53]

Sea changes and displaced people

On September 8, 1921, CPR had again changed the name of its shipping arm, on this occasion from Canadian Pacific Ocean Services to Canadian Pacific Steamships (CPSS).

Among the ships acquired by the company to replace losses suffered during the war was the *Empress of Scotland*. The ship had been built and launched by the Hamburg America Line as the *Kaiserin Auguste Victoria* and, as flagship of that line, had sailed in service between Hamburg and New York. After the First World War, Cunard had received the liner as reparations and in 1921 sold it to Canadian Pacific.

The "Empress" designation was still the mark of the company's express service, carrying all classes of passenger. On January 22, 1922, the *Empress of Scotland*—with a capacity of 460 passengers in first class, 470 in second class, and 530 in third class—sailed on its maiden voyage from Hamburg to Halifax and New York. After a 74-day winter cruise around the Mediterranean, the *Empress* inaugurated a regular transatlantic service between Hamburg and Quebec City via Southampton and Cherbourg. The *Empress of France* joined the *Empress of Scotland* in the Hamburg service, after also completing her first cruise of the Mediterranean, in April 1922.

The following year, Southampton became the home port of the Empresses, with some sailings calling at Cherbourg. Sailings from Glasgow were on occasion routed via Belfast, the *Tunisian* making the first call on March 25, 1922.

More of the company's cabin-class ships were given the "M" designation: *Marburn*, *Marglen*, *Marloch* and *Marvale*. Three CPSS ocean liners with "Mont" names—*Montclare*, *Montcalm* and *Montrose*—entered the Liverpool run in 1922,

The company pavilion was among the foremost showpieces at the Empire Exhibition in 1924, featuring more than 500 square metres of display space. AUTHOR'S COLLECTION

Top left The Canadian Pacific pier and CPR tracks were located efficiently alongside the Quebec immigration reception hall. *CANADIAN PACIFIC STAFF BULLETIN*, IT 179, DECEMBER 1, 1923

Bottom left European emigrants get some fresh air on the deck of the *Empress of Scotland* on their way to Canada. AUTHOR'S COLLECTION

Top right The *Empress of Scotland* had been launched as the *Kaiserin Victoria* by the Hamburg America Line. It was received by the Cunard Line as war reparations, and later sold to Canadian Pacific. AUTHOR'S COLLECTION

CANADIAN PACIFIC

MONTCALM · MONTROSE · MONTCLARE

SOUTHAMPTON to CANADA & U.S.A.

and the following year this service was extended to call at Greenock, Scotland, and occasionally Belfast.[54]

The "Monts" were very popular with emigrants, despite their somewhat spartan accommodations, and as their passenger numbers began to climb later in the decade—as a result of Canadian Pacific's efforts, if not the federal government's—the ships were filled to capacity with new settlers.

"My mother Dorris Pirra was a stewardess/interpreter for the immigrants—English, Italian, French, and German, mainly on the 'Monts,'" recalled one sailor. "They were wet boats due to a long working alleyway on the main deck, which was awash in the Atlantic winters, most of the time. The ships were cold with no heating, and it was a long walk to the toilets."[55]

In the fall of 1922, as the *Montclare* was steaming toward Canada with about seven hundred passengers, mostly immigrants in third-class, a case of smallpox was detected onboard. Captain Robert Gilmore "Jock" Latta

immediately isolated the sufferer and made for the quarantine station at Grosse Isle, just downriver from Quebec City.

About two hundred and forty passengers were deemed to have been in some danger, however small, of having been exposed, and were brought ashore for further isolation, vaccination, and observation. A considerable amount of clothing, bedding and such was fumigated on the docks. Despite the inconvenience and discomfort, the ship's staff organized things so thoroughly that one passenger later said the meals served in the spartan quarters at the quarantine station were quite up to the standard of the ship's dining room. Normally, the isolation period for smallpox was fourteen days, but with no further cases erupting, the first hundred passengers were allowed to return to the ship after six days, with the rest following a few days later.[56]

Canadian Pacific's expanded fleet of good, solid emigrant vessels would be put to extensive use in the conveyance of postwar displaced persons. In addition, the Russian revolution and that country's subsequent civil war had left tens of thousands of peasants and farmers homeless, and some ethnic groups considered emigrating.

One of these groups were German Mennonites, and more than twenty thousand came to Canada in the 1920s to escape widespread persecution and deprivation. J.S. Dennis had begun negotiations as early as 1919, with the aid of David Toews, the chairman of the Canadian Mennonite Board of Colonization, and A.R. Owen, the railway's agent in Moscow. By 1922, A.M. Evalenko, the publisher of the *Russian-American* magazine and a former immigration commissioner for the US Santa Fe Railroad, had been dispatched to Petrograd by the CPR to negotiate an agreement with the Soviet government. That same year, a contract was signed between CPR and the Mennonite Church of

Canada to bring the first group of 3,000 emigrants to their proposed new home outside Rosthern, Saskatchewan, just north of Saskatoon.[57]

Twenty-five percent of the $400,000 negotiated fee would be paid up front by the church and its North American supporters, with an additional 25 percent due in three months and the balance in six months. Two Canadian Pacific steamships were to embark with the Mennonites from the Black Sea port of Odessa, but a major obstacle was encountered. While the group managed to assemble dockside for departure in the fall of 1922—complete with passports granted by the Soviet authorities—Odessa was quarantined by an outbreak of cholera.[58]

Though all of the arrangements went into sudden abeyance, an alternative route was arranged for the following year. The general manager of the CCA, Traugott Otto Francis Herzer, was sent by the CPR to work out a new plan with the distressed group and was successful in arranging a special through fare from the Baltic port of Libau, Latvia, to Saskatoon, Saskatchewan.[59]

Many delays occurred, with Soviet officials unwilling to allow Canadian medical and civil examiners to clear the Mennonites for emigration. However, after several months of negotiation, they were allowed to leave Russia and were brought to the Latvian port for inspection and clearance.[60] In 1923, the Canadian Pacific steamship *Bruton* made three trips from Libau to Southampton with several thousand Mennonites aboard. There the refugees were processed at a quarantine camp known as Atlantic Park, in Eastleigh, after which they proceeded to Canada on CPSS "Mont" ships.[61]

In Canada, the CCA worked closely with the Canadian Mennonite Board of Colonization. Thankful for the railway's ongoing efforts to resettle the Russian emigrants,

► After several months of negotiation, CPR representatives were able to arrange for Mennonite refugees to leave Russia aboard the company's steamship *Bruton*. CRHA/ EXPORAIL CANADIAN PACIFIC RAILWAY FONDS A15400

Top left The CPR train departs after delivering a large group of Russian Mennonites to their new home in Rosthern, Saskatchewan. LIBRARY AND CULTURAL RESOURCES DIGITAL COLLECTIONS, UNIVERSITY OF CALGARY CU1124773

Top right In the midst of the Depression, the Mennonites of Coledale, Alberta, invited CPR president Edward Beatty to their church to personally thank him for his humanitarian work on their behalf. CRHA/ EXPORAIL CANADIAN PACIFIC RAILWAY FONDS A34730

Bottom right A piper parades on Lochboisdale Pier on the Island of Uist, in Scotland's Outer Hebrides, prior to the embarkation of a group of emigrants to Canada. AUTHOR'S COLLECTION

the Mennonite board was eager to locate its people on CPR land in the Northwest. The first group in 1923 was greeted at the Saskatoon CPR station by a veritable fleet of Studebakers, Chevrolets, and Model T Fords—450 of them by one account—as well as horse-drawn buggies and wagons.[62]

In 1924, thousands more Mennonites came to Canada by the CPSS steamship *Marglen,* via a quarantine station in Antwerp. Over the next three years, Edward Beatty, who had succeeded Shaughnessy as CPR president in 1918, authorized more than $1,750,000 in credit to 1,138 Mennonite families who had settled on railway land, all of which was duly paid back within a few years by the conscientious and productive immigrants.[63] The largest settlement was at Coaldale, on irrigated lands previously owned by the AR&I, but others purchased land south of Lethbridge at Raymond, Magrath, and elsewhere. A group of Hungarian colonists settled in Magrath around the same time.

The Mennonites were able to take advantage of the Lethbridge Experimental Farm established by the federal government in 1906 to demonstrate farming practices under irrigation. They also had access to the CPR demonstration farm at Coaldale, where a herd of shorthorn cattle was being raised. Settlers in the Coledale improved-farm colony worked with agriculturists to cultivate sugar beets, a pursuit that proved to be highly successful and developed into a thriving industry in the coming years that employed many Mennonite workers. Just east of Lethbridge, another CPR demonstration farm at Chin specialized in the raising of Aberdeen Angus cattle, a Scottish breed of beef cattle.

Another large displacement of struggling people began on the island of Lewis in the Scottish Hebrides. "In a century in which the mass media would become all-pervasive," wrote one Dundee historian, "the emigration of 21 April 1923 was the island's first mass-media event."[64]

On that day, the CPSS steamship *Metagama* sailed from Stornoway—the capital of Lewis and Harris, and by far the largest town in the Hebrides—with more than three hundred Lewis emigrants on board, all but twenty of them young men eager to seek a new life in Canada. The embarkation made for a bittersweet event on the crowded docks, as the authorities conducted medical examinations, town councillors and other leading citizens made speeches, and the Ladies' Highland Association distributed Gaelic bibles to the departing pilgrims.[65] Though these young emigrants were not fleeing starvation and landlessness, they did feel that the Hebrides held little hope for their future. The boisterous send-off was covered extensively by newspapers on both sides of the Atlantic.

The *Metagama* had dropped anchor about a mile (1.6 km) from the pier, and the tender *Hebrides* ferried the Stornoway passengers to the liner, which already had about one thousand other emigrants aboard who had embarked

from Glasgow the day before. Many of the ship's complement were headed for the Canadian West, but the majority of emigrants in the Stornoway group was going to destinations in Ontario.

A week earlier, another contingent of Hebrideans families had departed Lochboisdale, on the island of South Uist, aboard the CPSS liner *Marloch*. Those emigrants were headed farther west, to the Red Deer area of Alberta.[66] The *Marloch*, *Metagama*, and a third CPR ship, *Montcalm*, all docked in Saint John, New Brunswick, within days of one another, with many a Scot on board.[67]

Hundreds more would follow over the next couple of years, mostly settling in the Red Deer and Edmonton districts. Western newspapers expressed the delight with which the new arrivals were greeted. "Cheerful Hebrideans Pass Through on Way to New Homes," read one headline, while the immigrants, from a three-month old baby to the oldest adult, were described as "bright, healthy, intelligent persons," who all spoke good English, "diverting to Gaelic occasionally."[68]

The settlement of Scottish settlers in the 1920s was greatly aided by the efforts of Father R. Andrew MacDonell, a priest who had served during the war as chaplain with the Western Scots regiment in France. He subsequently became intimately involved in settlement schemes to provide Scottish families with farms in Canada. While in Canada, MacDonell organized the Scottish Immigrant Aid Society, with General Stewart of Vancouver as president; Colonel John S. Dennis, CPR's chief commissioner of immigration, as vice-president; and himself, as general manager. They would take advantage of terms laid out in the British government's Empire Settlement Act of 1922, which included subsidies for transportation costs and agricultural training as incentives for settlers emigrating to Canada.

Top This extended family of Scottish immigrants was proud to announce its affiliation with the crofters from their native country's highlands. AUTHOR'S COLLECTION

Bottom The railway arranged for an appropriate welcome for these Scottish Hebrideans when they arrived in Edmonton. MCDERMID STUDIO, LIBRARY AND CULTURAL RESOURCES DIGITAL COLLECTIONS, UNIVERSITY OF CALGARY CU156032

► A large tour group of about eighty-five people with the American Agricultural Editorial Association arrived in Brooks for an automobile tour of the irrigation district, sponsored by the CPR. LIBRARY AND CULTURAL RESOURCES DIGITAL COLLECTIONS, UNIVERSITY OF CALGARY CU1123098

Through his close and productive working relationships with several key CPR officers, MacDonell was able to travel back and forth at favourable rates between the Hebrides and the Red Deer area.

Canadian Pacific made every effort to provide comfort and assistance to new settlers, both on board its ships and during the trip across the continent. Immigration agents and, where required, translators met incoming ships at the wharves to get colonists and their baggage sorted and safely aboard westbound railway cars. The railway's travelling passenger agent from Calgary routinely boarded the emigrant trains at Medicine Hat and went through to Red Deer with the various groups to smooth out any wrinkles in their arrangements.

The land agents were now spending a good deal of time between Calgary and Edmonton, as that CPR corridor became the chosen destination for more of the new arrivals. The railway's agricultural specialists made as many tours up and down that railway line as they did around the more established colonies in the irrigation block.

11 SPANNING THE WORLD

Immigration cooperation and expansion

By the middle of the decade, the overall results of recent immigration efforts had been disappointing, with the number of new arrivals in Canada declining from 124,164 persons in 1924 to just 84,907 in 1925.[1] To promote efficiency, the CPR and the CNR urged the federal government to foster closer collaboration between the country's two largest railways and the country's many immigration agencies and charitable societies. The result was the Railway Agreement of 1925, which initially was to be in effect for two years.

By the terms of the agreement, the Canadian Department of Immigration and Colonization would deal exclusively with immigrants from "preferred" countries, primarily British, Americans, and northern Europeans. Meanwhile, the railways' own formidable immigration and colonization administrations continued their work in those countries but also made a concerted effort to process appropriate candidates from "non-preferred" countries in Central and Eastern Europe and elsewhere.

The intent of the new arrangement was to reduce duplication of effort and expense, on the one hand, while on the other hand narrowing the focus from an open-door policy to one that would attract settlers to specifically take up unoccupied lands in the Northwest and become productive farmers. Ironically, preferred immigrants had a distinct tendency to avoid the menial labour offered on farms. In many ways, the Railway Agreement was a means of asserting the old preference for experienced agricultural workers and domestics with a view to reducing the number of immigrants who migrated to the cities for work. This time, the railway immigration agents would look farther afield.

More than 700,000 immigrants entered the country in the latter half of the 1920s. As many as 185,000 of them came from central Europe, as a result of this new strategy.[2] Railway agents were given discretionary powers to choose which individuals and nationalities constituted acceptable immigrants under the agreement, while government officials conducted medical checks and issued visas, with fewer prejudices coming into play.[3] CNR officials even had some success in urging government bureaucrats to use the more acceptable term "European agriculturalist," in place of "non-preferred immigrant," in their pamphlets, which must surely have been more agreeable to that audience.

Successful applicants from central and southern Europe were issued "certificates of immigration," with a portrait photograph and family details on one side and a warning

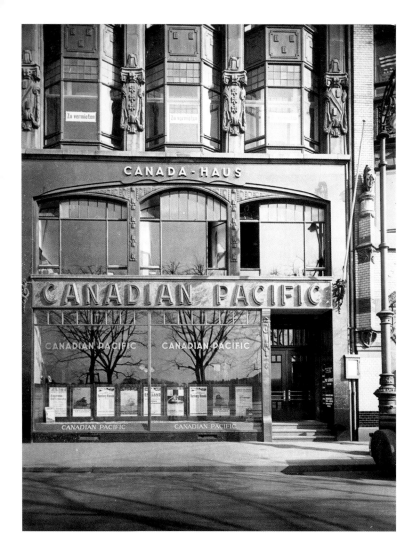

▲ Canadian Pacific's Hamburg office was the central location for readying North Europeans for the ocean crossing. AUTHOR'S COLLECTION

► Canadian Pacific steamships continued to serve Hamburg, in the "preferred" country of Germany. AUTHOR'S COLLECTION

on the reverse that the holder was coming to Canada to do farm work and would risk deportation if he failed to do so.

The move to broaden the field of acceptable settlers would meet resistance from organized labour, which warned Canadians of a capitalist plot to reduce wages for workers, and from religious groups that railed against the dilution of the British character of the country. The new, more tolerant immigration policy would cause a rising tide of nativism among groups such as the National Association of Canada, the Native Sons of Canada, and the infamous Ku Klux Klan, which was having a revival in the United States and had spread across the border "to defend a white Anglo-Saxon 'Kanada' against the influx of 'foreign scum.'"[4]

The branch of the Canadian Legion in Vermilion, Alberta, passed a resolution on April 6, 1928, expressing its concern about the undesirable nature of the immigrants from Central and Eastern Europe who were now being allowed to enter the country. The Reverend George Exton Lloyd, bishop of Saskatchewan, gave an hour-long speech at the Grand Orange Lodge in Edmonton on July 26, arguing that the Railway Agreement should be rescinded and a quota system imposed to ensure the British nature of Canadian society.[5]

Despite the overt biases in Western Canada, however, there remained a less vocal but effective wellspring of underlying generosity. With the support of the federal Department of Immigration and Colonization, ethnic communities throughout the western provinces established dozens of local colonization boards, composed of farmers, merchants, bankers, and other public-spirited citizens to take advantage of settlement opportunities for additional emigration from their countries of origin. The CPR's Canada Colonization Association (CCA) worked closely with

many of the groups to good effect, as it had earlier with the Canadian Mennonite Board of Colonization and the Scottish Immigrant Aid Society.

Canadian Pacific maintained its own offices in England, Scotland, Ireland, Belgium, France, Germany, Austria, and Russia as well as agencies and sub-agencies in a number of other countries. The CNR had colonization officers in France, Belgium, Poland, Czechoslovakia, and Croatia.

Among the countries that received increased attention from the railway's immigration agents was Hungary; the number of successful Hungarian settlers had been growing over the years. "What surprised me in my trip across Canada is your almost endless track of Hungarian settlers," declared Baroness Orczy, the author of the

A thriving emigration business in Bucharest was a testament to the expansion of Canadian Pacific's activities to "non-preferred" countries in Eastern Europe. AUTHOR'S COLLECTION

Canadian Pacific had sold land to Hungarians at several locations across the Northwest, in cooperation with the Atlantis Hungarian Board, and settled a large colony in the 1920s along the Lacombe & Northwestern Railway line, which connected with the CPR's Calgary-to-Edmonton branch line at Lacombe, Alberta.

Newly formed Czechoslovakia was also a prime hunting ground for immigration recruitment. The country had achieved independence with the postwar break-up of the Austro-Hungarian Empire. After Jan Mies had completed his mandatory military service in Czechoslovakia, local Canadian Pacific agents promised to find him work on a farm in Western Canada. He shipped out aboard the CPSS steamship *Montnairn* on May 4, 1927, with $25 in his pocket. Of the 517 passengers headed to Canada on the same vessel, nearly 200 were from impoverished villages and cities in Czechoslovakia. Mies had been assigned to a farm in Alberta, but through some miscommunication, his contact did not appear at the train station to meet him. Nevertheless, with the aid of local CPR immigration representatives, the determined Czech was successful in securing a job where he was not paid a salary but had his room and board covered and was able to learn English. Subsequently, he worked at farms in Wetaskiwin, near Edmonton; St. Paul, in northern Alberta; and Luseland, Saskatchewan, earning enough to assist his two brothers with their subsequent passage to Canada, the oldest of whom sailed aboard the CPSS steamer *Melita*.[7]

Father MacDonell and the Scottish Immigrant Aid Society once again made good use of their contacts at the CPR to secure more land, this time northwest of Lloydminster near the village of Vermilion, where they planned to establish a colony. In the spring of 1926, Scottish and Irish families—many coming from the Red Deer area and other parts of Alberta, and others from the old country— were placed on farms that had been prepared for their arrival. Beatty, the CPR president, advanced the colonists $100,000 for buildings and farming equipment, under a long-term amortization plan. CPR engineers and builders helped them to get settled in 100 houses initially, and more than 160 ultimately, all of which had barns, outhouses, fencing, and other features, not unlike the railway's earlier ready-made farms.[8] The new settlement became known as the Clan Donald Colony, after the highland Scottish clan to which many of the original settlers belonged.

By November that same year, a CPR field supervisor reported that as soon as the settlers set up their houses and were accustomed to their horses, they began to break ground, in some cases up to 50 acres (20 ha). A great many of the colonists were raising chickens and turkeys, and they had the use of two pure bred Holstein bulls loaned to them by Pat Burns, the Alberta rancher and entrepreneur who grew rich in the beef-cattle business. In addition to their agricultural pursuits, many settlers earned wages on road construction in the area as well as on a nearby CPR railway grade.[9]

More unexpectedly, disaffected parties of Russians had begun to land by steamship on the West Coast, the first group having arrived in Victoria on the Japanese liner *Shidzuska Maru*, on April 28, 1926. The twenty-two Russian passengers from Harbin, China, were detained for a

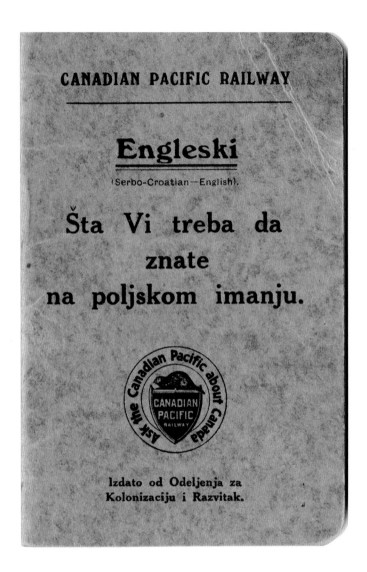

CANADIAN PACIFIC RAILWAY

Engleski

(Serbo-Croatian—English).

Šta Vi treba da znate na poljskom imanju.

Izdato od Odeljenja za Kolonizaciju i Razvitak.

debriefing from the immigration authorities, who were told that Western representatives of the CNR and the American Dollar Line steamship company were carrying on an active propaganda campaign to bring former Russian citizens over to North America. A Mr. Hawreliak was also identified as a representative of Canadian Pacific, although he was officially an officer of the Ukrainian Colonization Association, a sub-agency of the CPR.[10]

An article in the Russian paper *New Word*, published in Harbin, revealed that while Hawreliak had apparently placed an ad seeking "Farmers for Canada" and claimed there was a "specially reserved Russian colony in the Province of Alberta," he had been only authorized to solicit steamship passenger traffic for the CPR and had nothing to do with land sales. The news coverage went on to identify the CPR as a "powerful, well-known, famous company," and the Ukrainian Colonization Association as an "insignificant, very little known and unworthy organization."

Three months later, when a second party of Russians arrived by the CPSS steamship *Empress of Japan*, the CPR was ready to provide them with colonist cars to make their way to Ponoka, halfway between Red Deer and Edmonton as well as to Homeglen, just to the west. These immigrants were originally from the Ural district of Russia. After the revolution, they had been driven east to Kamchatka by the Bolsheviks before seeking refuge in Japan. They apparently had an inside tip from their fellow countrymen on where to locate, which was fortunate, considering their English-language skills were reported to be virtually non-existent. More Russians from China arrived that summer on the *Empress of Canada*.

A former Russian imperial officer explained to Colonel Dennis that the immigrants were loyal to the old regime and anxious to escape the Bolsheviks to find peace and happiness in a country with similar climate and soil conditions to their own. The Soviet government was not in favour of a wholesale exodus of their citizens and made it very difficult for them to obtain passports for overseas immigration. However, there was no objection to Soviet citizens leaving for China, so a number of Russians congregated there until they could get permission to come to Canada. Many of these immigrants thrived in their new country through hard work and perseverance. Others with no farming experience were also keen to learn how to succeed on the land. An employment firm in Vulcan, Alberta, sent a letter to CPR on behalf of some of the persecuted refugees:

We are in touch with a number of Russians of keen and good appearance, some of them former officers in the Csar's Army, who are desirous of securing employment on farms with a view to gaining experience in farming before taking up land of their own. They have some means and all of them are accustomed to handling horses. They are ready and willing to do any kind of farm work, and are anxious to learn. I can recommend them to anybody who will be willing to employ them.[11]

In the fall of 1926, CPR president Edward Beatty and Colonel Dennis arranged for Dr. Erich Koch (later Koch-Wesser), former vice-chancellor of the German republic, to meet German colonists in Canada and investigate the possibilities for aiding more of his countrymen to follow their lead. Beatty asked Dr. Otto Klaehn, chairman of the Lutheran and Immigration Board, to meet Koch upon his arrival in Quebec aboard CPSS *Empress of Scotland* and accompany the vice-chancellor on his Western tour. CPR also worked closely for a few years with Der Volksversein Deutsch-Canadischer Katholiken [Association of German-Canadian Catholics] or VDCK, one of the largest German-Canadian

CANADIAN PACIFIC RAILWAY

Anglicky

(Czech—English).

CO POTŘEBUJETE NA FARMĚ VĚDĚTI.

VĚNOVÁNO ÚŘADEM PRO KOLONISACI A ROZVOJ.

religious societies in Canada involved in immigration and cultural affairs.[12]

CPR agents in the United States also facilitated the emigration of twenty families of Dunkard Brethren, an ultra-conservative protestant sect that had recently broken away from the German Church of the Brethren. They bought railway land in the North Battleford Block.

With the expanded terms outlined in the Railway Agreement of 1925 now in effect for more than a year, Dennis sent a lengthy memorandum to Robert Forke, federal minister of immigration and colonization, to inform him, among several other issues, of the difficulty of interesting families in the "non-preferred" countries of Eastern and Southern Europe, on short notice, to dispose of their holdings and make all the preliminary arrangements to sever ties and undertake a long journey to an unknown land. For that reason, Dennis suggested extending the two-year trial period for the agreement, and he wondered if the minister might consider, in addition, that labourers and skilled mechanics be allowed to join agriculturalists and domestics on the list of acceptable immigrants from those countries.

In a covering letter to Forke marked "personal," Dennis mentioned that he had hoped that Dr. William John Black of the CNR's immigration department would see fit to co-authoring his attached recommendations, but he found his counterpart had "divergent views on some of the matters dealt with." In any case, the CPR's arguments for extending the official duration of the Railway Agreement were accepted by the minister, and it was extended to a five-year term.[13]

In short order, Dennis and the CPR were criticized when it became apparent that the railway was taking advantage of the looser definition of "acceptable immigrant." Despite having certified that most of the newcomers were intended for farm work, in many cases the railway employed the men on section gangs or in other railway jobs. In 1927, the federal government's Land Settlement Branch reported that 75 percent of the Continental European immigrants who had arrived that year in Calgary under the terms of the Railway Agreement had been given jobs with the CPR.[14]

Smooth sailing with assisted passage

The postwar tightening of North American regulations had caused a precipitous end to the immigration boom, with the number of newcomers entering Canada in 1925 about 40,000 lower than the previous year. To compensate, Canadian Pacific converted some of the third-class space on its ships to "tourist class," in an attempt to lure settlers from Europe to visit their home countries. Some small upgrades were made, but the change was one of perception more than substance.

The governments of Canada and the United Kingdom did, however, manage to facilitate the immigration of more than 18,000 Britishers between 1924 and 1940, under one of the plans made possible by the terms of the Empire Settlement Act. The initiative known as the "3,000 Family Scheme" aimed to settle immigrants in Canada on farms provided by the Dominion authorities, with machinery and livestock supplied by the British government.

Under the plan, which was launched in 1926, government officials on both sides of the Atlantic had negotiated reduced third-class steamship fares for settlers in Canada. The rates were as low as two pounds per person from British ports to Halifax and Saint John, with free passage for children under seventeen years of age. Sailings from Antwerp were dropped, and Liverpool became the primary

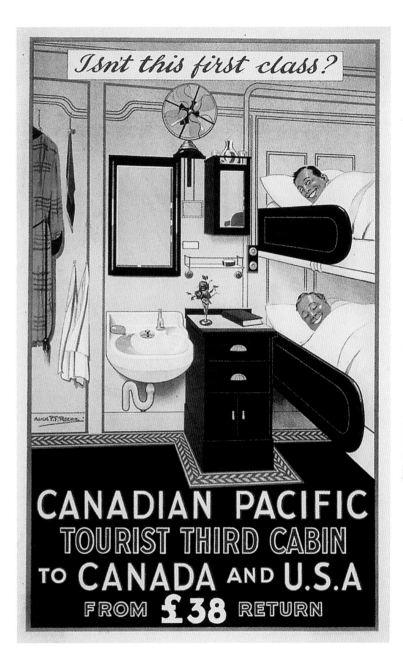

Isn't this first class?

CANADIAN PACIFIC
TOURIST THIRD CABIN
TO CANADA AND U.S.A
FROM £38 RETURN

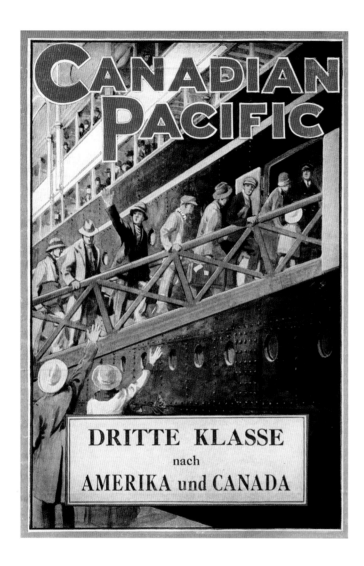

CANADIAN PACIFIC

DRITTE KLASSE
nach
AMERIKA und CANADA

Opposite, left Third-class accommodations from Germany to Canada and the United States were advertised in attractive, colourful booklets. AUTHOR'S COLLECTION

Opposite, top right Dining was communal, but stylish. AUTHOR'S COLLECTION

Opposite, bottom right Lounges were for smoking and reading the newspapers AUTHOR'S COLLECTION

Left Nurseries came with female attendants. AUTHOR'S COLLECTION

Right The rates for third-class passage were as low as two pounds Sterling per person from British ports to Halifax and Saint John, and free for children under the age of seventeen. JAMES E. LANIGAN COLLECTION

port, with calls at Greenock and Belfast. Canadian Pacific steamships sailed weekly with passengers eligible for this scheme, from Liverpool, Glasgow, Southampton, and Belfast. Upon arrival in Canada, low, subsidized railway rates were also offered to various points in the Northwest on the CPR main line.[15]

In the mid-1920s, Canadian Pacific embarked on its biggest ship-building program to date, including five cargo liners and, significantly for the immigrant trade, four "Duchess" ships, the most up-to-date cabin ships of their period. The new vessels—the *Duchess of Bedford* and the *Duchess of Atholl* launched in 1928, followed by the *Duchess of Richmond* and the *Duchess of York* in 1929—were the company's "mini-Empresses." The well-appointed, 20,000-ton (18,000-tonne) ships, with their relatively flat-bottomed hulls, were the largest ships able to sail up river to dock at Montreal. Unfortunately, the same hull design that allowed them to negotiate the shallower passage from Quebec City to Montreal also caused them to roll from side to side more readily in rough ocean conditions,

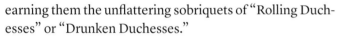

earning them the unflattering sobriquets of "Rolling Duchesses" or "Drunken Duchesses."

One immigrant who came to Canada on the *Duchess of Bedford* in 1929 later recalled the misery of his transatlantic passage. "One boy never ate a meal on the whole trip except the Friday supper," he wrote. "If the ship had sunk he would have been happy. The second or third day out the smell below decks was horrible—not really the vomit, but the disinfectants. However, as long as I could remain on deck I was fine. But I was always thankful to get away from my cabin, which was away, away down."[16]

Despite a few inconvenient shortcomings, however, the Duchesses were very popular with travellers of all stripes, each providing space on board for 580 cabin, 480 tourist, and 510 third-class passengers. Meals had become much more sophisticated for all classes. Cabin passengers chose their food à la carte, a menu that allowed them to order separate items at individual prices in whatever combination they chose, rather than being confined to a set list of meals. They also had access to a large cold buffet. Tourist

passengers ordered in much the same way, but from a somewhat reduced menu. The fare for third-class passengers wasn't quite as fancy, but it was a considerable improvement over the boarding house meals served on emigrant ships of the past. These passengers chose from a short list on a table d'hôte menu of multi-course meals at a set price.

Another Canadian Pacific liner entered transatlantic service on June 25, 1927, on its much-ballyhooed inaugural voyage with Prince George, Duke of Kent, and the British prime minister, Stanley Baldwin, and his wife on board. The former Hamburg-America steamship *Tirpitz*, now sailing as the *Empress of Australia*, was bringing its noteworthy passengers to Canada to take part in the Diamond Jubilee celebrations of Canada's federation. The luxurious ship that could accommodate 400 first-class, 150 tourist-class, and 635 third-class passengers then settled in as a regular carrier of immigrant and other traffic from Southampton to Quebec.

The Canadian Ministry of Labour, in cooperation with the British Colonial Office's Overseas Settlement Committee, arranged an unprecedented number of schemes to get young men aboard Canadian Pacific steamships on their way to jobs on Canadian farms. CPR encouraged settlers to apply to the railway's Farm Labour Service for help with any tasks associated with their livelihood. The farmers took care of the young men's food and lodging, while the railway paid them a small monthly stipend.

Booking agents in Canadian Pacific offices throughout Britain were authorized to arrange for the placement and training of boys between the ages of fourteen and seventeen on specially selected farms in Canada. Approved applicants were carried by CPR, free of charge, and assigned to needy settlers as farm hands, where they could help

CANADIAN PACIFIC
EMPRESS OF AUSTRALIA
EUROPE · CANADA · U.S.A.
APPLY—
PICKFORDS LTD.,
95 QUEEN'S ROAD, BRIGHTON.

sponsoring families become independent, productive colonists, while preparing themselves to own and work their own farms. In their adoptive land, they were regularly visited by government inspectors, who saw to it that the boys were comfortable and happy in their support role.

Macdonald College, an educational institution associated with Montreal's McGill University—where CPR's president, Beatty, served as chancellor from 1920 to 1943—also provided an opportunity for young men between the ages of seventeen and twenty-five to get agricultural training with no tuition fees. Interested parties in Britain could get full particulars at Canadian Pacific offices, and successful applicants were eligible for reduced steamship fares. As an alternative, students who could afford $30 a month for room and board could choose to attend one of the Alberta Provincial Agricultural Schools at Olds, Claresholm, or Vermilion, where their training was paid for jointly by the Alberta and British governments. During the summer months, students were placed on farms in the province to gain hands-on experience.[17] Beatty arranged for the students with top marks at each school to get jobs at the CPR's demonstration and supply farm at Strathmore.[18]

Strathmore had grown into the most prestigious operation of its kind, with the largest herd of Holsteins on the continent. Among its 600 head of cattle was a two-year-old female Holstein that had just been named grand champion at a large annual fair in Edmonton. The farm's 3,000 hens were each producing more than twenty-one dozen eggs per year for CPR dining cars and hotels as well as collectively hatching seven thousand chicks.[19]

Though the supply of able young men was being adequately met, the demand for more and more young women never seemed to diminish. While awaiting railway connections, women travelling to Canada under the reduced steamship rate were encouraged by government and railway agents to take advantage of a day's free room and board at local women's hostels, often located across the street from, or in close proximity to, CPR stations.

James Colley, CPR's assistant superintendent of colonization, was instrumental in the establishment of the Central Women's Colonization Board in Calgary. The board placed immigrant girls or women from various European countries in domestic employment. "Most of these girls cannot speak English when they first arrive," a board member informed an interested party in 1927, "but our experience in placing large numbers of them during the past year has shown that if the employer will have a little patience at the beginning, the girls soon acquire a working knowledge of English and they soon adapt themselves to Canadian ways."[20] While there was a decided preference among householders for Swedish, Norwegian, or Danish girls, those looking for help were usually willing to take a chance with other girls or women from Czechoslovakia, Estonia, Hungary, Lithuania, Poland, and Yugoslavia, mostly recruited by Canadian Pacific agencies.

When the Women's Board was accepting large numbers of domestics recruited by CPR European immigration agents in the latter part of the 1920s, occasional problems arose with underqualified applicants. "I have been asked specially to draw to your attention the need for careful selection of the girls on the other side," Colley advised his boss, Chester Allan Van Scoy. "Some of the girls last year were very hard to place because of incompetence. One unsuitable girl can cause as much work as thirty or forty competent ones and they also help to create a prejudice against foreign girls."[21]

Opposite, left Booking agents in Canadian Pacific offices throughout Britain could arrange placement and training for boys on specially selected farms in Canada. AUTHOR'S COLLECTION

Opposite, right CPR president Edward Beatty took a personal interest in the well-being of boys undergoing training at Quebec's Shawbridge Boys' Farm, as well as at three Alberta Agricultural Schools. CHRA/EXPORAIL CANADIAN PACIFIC RAILWAY FONDS NS12010

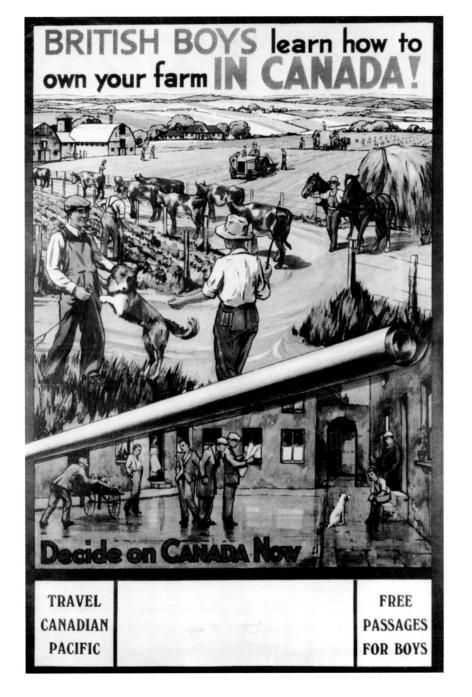

CANADIAN PACIFIC

WANTED

GIRLS & WOMEN

USED TO HOUSEHOLD WORK

FOR ASSURED POSITIONS

AT GOOD WAGES IN

CANADA

Meet and Have a Talk with
Mrs. WAITE, Supervisor,
CANADIAN PACIFIC WOMEN'S BRANCH
who Knows Canada's Kindly conditions of
Work, Wages and Welcome for Girls and
Young Women.

ASK FOR HER.

APPLY WITHIN

SPECIAL CONDUCTED PARTIES EACH WEEK BY
CANADIAN PACIFIC The Easy Way TO CANADA

£10

OCEAN
FARE

WILL

TAKE
YOU
TO

CANADA

AND THE ASSURANCE OF

WORK at GOOD WAGES

on Canadian Farms

(Above applies to Persons of British Nationality, resident in Gt. Britain and N. Ireland, irrespective of Occupation)

Assisted **Passages** available for **Approved Families** going to Farm Settlement,
Women for **Household Work, Boys under Nineteen** as Farm Learners,
and for the **Wives and Children of Men** satisfactorily Settled in Canada

FURTHER PARTICULARS FROM THE

CANADIAN PACIFIC

APPLY HERE

SUTTLEY & SILVERLOCK, Ltd., Blackfriars Road, London, S.E.1

Opposite, left The demand for more and more women never seemed to diminish. AUTHOR'S COLLECTION

Opposite, right Women and boys, in particular, were encouraged by government and railway agents to take advantage of low ocean fares to come to Canada to work. AUTHOR'S COLLECTION

▶ A group of women at a Regina women's hostel arriving to take jobs as domestics. Newcomers to the country could be deported for such offences as living with a man out of wedlock or contracting a venereal disease. AUTHOR'S COLLECTION

Van Scoy, CPR's superintendent of immigration at Winnipeg, had a lot of control over where women and boys recruited overseas by company agents were sent to work in the Canadian West. Colley, from his vantage point in Calgary, had more to report to Van Scoy on the subject:

Another cause of dissatisfaction has been that a number of the girls have friends in the East or in the United States and are constantly wanting to join these friends who hold out the lure to the girls of higher wages than are paid in domestic service in this territory. It would be well to have the representatives in Europe and their staff instructed to inform all domestics that they are expected to take up the positions the board finds for them and to stay in these positions for a reasonable time (at least six to twelve months), and that they will run the risk of deportation if they attempt to leave for the United States or Eastern Canada without the consent of the board ... It should also be made clear that girls without a knowledge of English cannot reasonably expect more than $15 a month to begin with. As soon as they acquire some knowledge of English and show themselves capable, employers will generally increase the wages very quickly.[22]

Within a month, Colley was already reporting that the situation had improved. He informed Van Scoy that the Women's Board was doing everything possible to make the girls happy and contented: "In cooperation with the Y.W.C.A. and the hostel of the Catholic Women's League, clubs have been formed whereby the girls come together and spend the afternoons they have off duty, and opportunities are given to them to learn English."[23]

According to records of the Women's Division of the federal Department of Immigration and Colonization, Canadian government representatives had more problems than just language and wage issues. Nearly 700 British

domestics were deported between 1926 and 1931 for such offences as living with a man out of wedlock, having more than one sexual partner, bearing illegitimate children, or contracting a venereal disease.[24] But more than 88 percent of the young women stayed in their adopted land and integrated into Canadian society.[25]

The decade had been a busy one, mostly as a result of the reduced transportation costs to come to Canada under the terms of the British Empire Settlement Act. Yet another immigration scheme was introduced in 1928 through a cooperative effort between His Majesty's Secretary of State for Dominion Affairs, a British government department commonly known as the Dominions Office; the Canadian

CANADIAN PACIFIC

THE BEST WAY TO

YOUR OWN FARM IN CANADA

FREE
PASSAGES
FOR
CHILDREN

BRITISH
SETTLERS
ON THEIR
CANADIAN
FARMS.

LOANS
FOR THE
PURCHASE
OF FARMS

SPECIAL FARES TO CANADA

From British Ports to the following Canadian Pacific Centres

Halifax, Nova Scotia	- £3 : 0 : 0		Saskatoon, Saskatchewan	- £6 : 0 : 0
Saint John, New Brunswick	3 : 0 : 0		Regina, Saskatchewan	- 6 : 0 : 0
Quebec - - - -	3 : 0 : 0		Moose Jaw, Saskatchewan	- 6 : 0 : 0
Montreal - - - -	4 : 0 : 0		Edmonton, Alberta	- 6 10 : 0
Toronto, Ontario - -	4 10 : 0		Calgary, Alberta	- 6 10 : 0
Winnipeg, Manitoba -	5 10 : 0		Vancouver, British Columbia	9 : 0 : 0

For further Particulars **APPLY WITHIN**

Pacific Railway; and the Governor and Company of Adventurers of England Trading into Hudson's Bay (the HBC). The HBC was still a significant holder of available land in the Northwest and ready to carry out a joint immigration scheme with other serious players.

The plan was aimed at families, generally defined a man and his wife with at least one child, in possession of at least fifty pounds, and eligible for passage assistance. The two companies agreed to provide two hundred ready-made farms, complete with the necessary buildings, fencing, and cultivated acreage.

They would also advance loans for livestock and farm equipment. Payment was to be amortized over a twenty-year period. The CPR and the HBC would also send representatives to meet colonists upon their arrival in Canada and shepherd them through the settlement process. The Dominions Office was contractually obligated to cover 50 percent of the cost of the advances for the settlers' land, livestock, and equipment.[26]

The colony was established close to where many Russians had settled in recent months, outside the village of Vermilion, Alberta. Each of the farms was 160 acres (65 ha) and came equipped with a furnished cottage and all of the other promised amenities. The families that were selected for the settlement scheme had on average three children, and the parents had at least some farming experience. The settlers were coached on all aspects of their new undertaking by CPR supervisors, and farm hands were provided initially at little or no cost.[27]

In support of the various emigration schemes, the British government established at least three training camps in Bedfordshire, England, to prepare young men for employment in the colonies. To augment this work, and direct as

▲ Using the slogan "World's Greatest Travel System" to good effect, Canadian Pacific steamships catered to the tourist market as much as to immigrants. AUTHOR'S COLLECTION

many immigrants as possible onto their ships and toward their land holdings, the CPR, Cunard, and the HBC also ran a joint training farm for a brief period of time at Bedfordshire's Brogborough Park. The CPR placed more than 2,500 men from the government training stations on farms in the Northwest, and more than 120 from the private centre.[28]

Harvesting discontent abroad

Every year since 1891, Canadian Pacific had been bringing more and more workers to the Northwest to help bring in the grain harvest. Before the advent of combines and modern farming equipment, every field of wheat planted by one man required ten men to harvest it. If grain was not cut, threshed, winnowed, and delivered to elevators in a timely manner, the crop could be ruined by an overabundance of rain, or even snow.

The railway brought thousands of harvesters out west every year, many from the eastern provinces, and often from overseas. At the urging of the Canadian government, in 1918, Great Britain rounded up ten thousand unemployed men from mining areas around the country to work the fields.

"What will be the reaction to all this?" asked an editorial in the *Montreal Star*. "That depends almost entirely upon us in Canada. If we are wise, we shall leave nothing undone that lies within our power to ensure that of those ten thousand men, by far the greater number who return do so with words of praise rather than disparagement for this country."[29]

A large contingent of those harvesters would be in the hands of the CPR, as many would arrive by the company's steamships and join others travelling across the country in

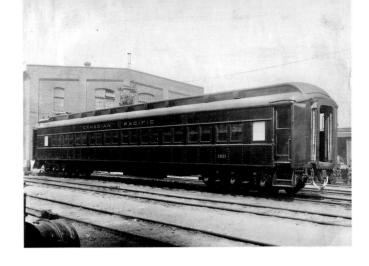

Opposite, top Every year, Winnipeggers saw increasing numbers of men at the CPR station heading for the wheat fields of the Northwest to help with the harvest. AUTHOR'S COLLECTION

Opposite, bottom Well-dressed harvesters on the CPR steamship *Montclare* would soon don their coveralls for a hard day's work. AUTHOR'S COLLECTION

Left Whether immigrating to the Northwest or coming temporarily to help bring in the annual harvest, railway passengers could take advantage of new steel-sheathed colonist cars to make the trip in comfort. DOUGLAS R. PHILLIPS COLLECTION

Right The immaculate interiors of the new generation of colonist car would lose some of their gloss when hundreds of rowdy harvesters clambered aboard on their way to employment in the Northwest. DOUGLAS R. PHILLIPS COLLECTION

CPR and CNR colonist cars. During one eight-day period in August, five CPSS liners arrived in Canada with more than 2,700 British men heading for the wheat fields.[30] The government and the railway had agreed to a through rate to Winnipeg of 12 pounds sterling per man, with an added charge of a half cent per mile (1.6 km) to get to the specific prairie stations where their employers awaited.

One CPR agent in the Dominion Express Company office at Vauxhall, Alberta, informed the railway's immigration people in Calgary that men were showing up by train claiming to have no money and nothing to eat. The agent reported that the town's railway foremen had grabbed a few of them, fed them, and put them to work on his gang; the local "Motion Picture man" opened his hall free to the men for a few days; and he himself had arranged with a restaurant to furnish them with three meals a day. The agent distributed meal tickets to each man until they got squared away on the farms to which they had been assigned.[31]

In September, Colley complained to Van Scoy that he had had to put some of the harvesters on a train back to Winnipeg, as they were causing trouble in Calgary, claiming to have been underpaid for work that was too hard.

"More than half of these men had come over the lines associated with the Canadian National," he reported, seemingly blaming the majority of his problems on CPR's rival. "All of these men soon found sympathizers with the Communist Party here, and the greater part of their time was spent in Communist Hall." He did concede that his CNR counterpart had helped him to banish the troublemakers.[32]

As it turned out, there was quite a bit more to it than a few rabble-rousers in Calgary, and 1928 ended up being a watershed year for bringing harvesters to the West. In future, mechanized farming would reduce the need for such large numbers to bring in the crops; judging by the public hand-wringing after that fateful harvest season, it was just as well.

Before the last of the harvesters had even arrived on the Prairies, a large number had already quit their jobs and were requesting to be sent back to Britain. By the end of September, more than three hundred men were back in Winnipeg, penniless and seeking shelter in immigration halls. However, the CPR had handled all of the men it had brought over to Canada through its own colonization department and had sent each man to a specific farm from its Winnipeg office. As a result, fewer of these workers were displeased with their placement, and fewer quit.

There was still plenty of displeasure to go around among the imported harvesters. They railed about filthy conditions in the immigration halls. They complained that, at five dollars a day, they were being underpaid. They weren't keen on the weather. They were homesick and travel weary. They said farmers pulled guns on them, underfed them, and made them sleep on beds with no blankets. And they reported that all Canadian farmers were foreigners who, as soon as they were able, would get rid of the hired stranger in favour of one of their own.

A writer who had come to Canada with harvesters from Ulster later wrote that Van Scoy had shown him a large file of letters from farmers asking for more of the miners. He also had notes of thanks from some of the men themselves telling of their good fortune and their happiness with the work.

Most of the coverage on either side of the Atlantic, however, presented the entire affair as a fiasco. The newspapers wanted to know who was responsible, and government officials for the most part pointed their fingers at the railways. Leo Amery, the secretary of state for Dominion affairs, attempted to explain to readers of the *Colonizer* how the initiative came about:

The Canadian government stated that they could accept 10,000 harvesters from Great Britain provided that the responsibility for harvest and winter farm placement rested with the Canadian railway companies [that] . . . undertook to give a reduced fare outwards and inwards, to place the men in work and to bring back those who were not placed. The Canadian government agreed to cooperate with the railway companies in finding winter employment for those who chose to stay.[33]

Amery went on to say that 25,000 unemployed men, "many of whom had not worked for years and to whom a 5,000-mile trip at someone else's expense looked like a pleasant break in the routine of life," had clogged the civil and medical inspection arrangements "past all hope of a reasonable weeding out." Consequently, he estimated that about a quarter of the men who were sent by his government to Canada "were not satisfactory material."[34]

One of the men who came back to Britain with the first party of returning harvesters frankly admitted that he had failed to mention to recruiters that he had been discharged from the navy as an invalid. As a result, he had apparently found it difficult to put in a full day's work on a farm overseas. He did state, however, that he would like to come back to Canada when his health improved. Another farm hand, described as a "sturdy, six-foot Scot from Lanarkshire, ruddy with good health," had been happy to make four dollars a day on a farm in Souris, Manitoba, until he heard some American harvesters were getting five dollars a day. He induced eleven other workers to leave with him when he quit.[35]

Sensationalism aside, some good did come from the overseas pilgrimage. Of the 8,449 harvesters who came to Canada, 1,573 remained in the country to take up farming on their own terms.[36] One farmer near Winnipeg said that, as a result of hiring a farm-trained labourer from among the imported harvesters, "his horses had never taken on such gloss and the work about the barns gone so smoothly." The wife of another farmer near Regina was even more effusive with her praise for an Irish farm hand from Britain: "I never had anyone I liked better; he was so handy with everything," she said. "This chap was willing and cheerful and most adept if shown how to carry on with the

Canadian implements of the soil, and he was well versed in the care of stock." [37]

Homogeneity or diversity?

By the latter part of the 1920s, there were still fewer than two and a half million people living in the three Canadian Prairie provinces, three-fifths of them of British origin, including transplanted Americans of Anglo-Saxon ancestry. The remaining two-fifths were largely from Germany, Scandinavia, Holland, Russia, Poland, and Ukraine. In recent years, migrants from Britain had been greatly outnumbered by newcomers from Central and Eastern Europe, which started a public debate about whether the Canadian West should be a "mosaic" of people from a multitude of nationalities, or should attempt to remain mostly Anglo-Saxon, as Australia had.

GREAT·WEST CANADIAN
FOLKDANCE ~ FOLKSONG
HANDICRAFTS FESTIVAL
CALGARY ~ ~ MARCH 19-22
CANADIAN PACIFIC

HIGHLAND GATHERING
BANFF SPRINGS HOTEL · AUG 29th · SEP 1st
CANADIAN PACIFIC

In general, it was recognized that the more "foreign" elements were industrious citizens who were making a contribution to Canadian culture by preserving their native handicrafts, songs, and dances. CPR's publicity agent, John Murray Gibbon, was widely lauded for organizing and staging folksong and handicraft festivals in several of the company's major hotels—including the Palliser in Calgary; Hotel Saskatchewan in Regina; and Banff Springs in Banff—to encourage immigrants to showcase and celebrate their ethnic traditions. If the festivals also served to maintain the railway's paternal relationship with these groups, well, that was good, too.

Negative attitudes arose from the tendency of some of these immigrants to segregate themselves in communities where the mother tongue from the Old Country prevailed. There was little intermingling and even less intermarriage between the British and the "others." Canadian organizations of the ultraconservative or hyper-religious persuasion openly campaigned against the threat of what they viewed to be a "mongrel Canada." Extreme examples like the resurgent Ku Klux Klan were unapologetically nativist, anti-foreign, anti-Semitic, and anti-Catholic.

The Canadian federal government had extended by three years the railways' mandate to recruit settlers from a wider swath of Europe, but as the decade was coming to an end, the door was closing fast, as was made clear from a statement to the newspapers from the deputy minister of immigration and colonization:

Unquestionably there is a very strong feeling against the unduly large proportion of foreigners as compared with British immigrants, shown in the immigration statistics of the last few years. The movement under the railways' agreement is very largely responsible for

CANADIAN PACIFIC RAILWAY

ORDER YOUR FARM HELP NOW

FOR 1927

To be of help to **WESTERN CANADIAN FARMERS** and assist in meeting their needs in securing competent farm help, the **CANADIAN PACIFIC RAILWAY** will continue its farm help service during 1927, and will include in this service, as last year, the securing of women domestics and boys.

Through experience in securing this farm help during the past few years, the Company is now in touch, through its widespread European organization, with good farm laborers in Great Britain, Norway, Sweden, Denmark, France, Holland, Switzerland, as well as in Poland, Czecho-Slovakia, Hungary, Jugo-Slavia, Roumania and Germany, and can promptly fill applications from Canadian farmers for farm help.

In order to have this help reach Canada in ample time for spring farming operations, farmers must get their applications in early to enable us to get the help needed.

Blank application forms and full information may be obtained from any C.P.R. agent or from any of the officials listed below.

THE SERVICE IS ENTIRELY FREE OF CHARGE

THE CANADIAN PACIFIC RAILWAY COMPANY
DEPARTMENT OF COLONIZATION AND DEVELOPMENT

WINNIPEG - - -	C. A. VanSCOY, Supt. of Colonization
	THOS. S. ACHESON, General Agricultural Agent
	CANADA COLONIZATION ASSOCIATION
SASKATOON - -	W. J. GEROW, Land Agent
	JNO. A. WILLIAMS, Asst. Supt. of Colonization
REGINA - - -	G. D. BROPHY, District Passenger Agent
CALGARY - - -	JAMES COLLEY, Asst. Supt. of Colonization
EDMONTON - -	J. MILLER, Asst. Supt. of Colonization
VANCOUVER - -	H. J. LOUGHRAN, Land Agent
MONTREAL - -	J. DOUGALL, General Agricultural Agent

J. N. K. MACALISTER,
Asst. Commissioner

J. S. DENNIS,
Chief Commissioner

Left The railway company did everything possible to ensure farmers in the Northwest had adequate help, recruiting women and boys from across Europe for that purpose. LIBRARY AND CULTURAL RESOURCES DIGITAL COLLECTIONS, UNIVERSITY OF CALGARY CU186795

Top right Prospective emigrants gather around the front entrance of the Canadian Pacific ticket and emigration agency in Veliki Beckerek, Yugoslavia, now Zrenjanin, Serbia. CRHA/EXPORAIL CANADIAN PACIFIC RAILWAY FONDS A8074

Bottom right An immigration poster in Cyrillic script advertises ocean passage on the CPR's *Empress of Australia.* AUTHOR'S COLLECTION

bringing about this condition. The agreement itself was intended to encourage a movement only of the agricultural class, but after three years' experience it has become evident that out of the total arrivals probably not more than 30 percent have made any real effort to remain on the land.[38]

Despite the best efforts of the CPR president, Beatty, and the CNR president, Henry Thornton, to sway the outcome, the government announced that immigration from non-preferred countries—Austria, Czechoslovakia, Hungary, Lithuania, Estonia, Latvia, Romania, Poland, Yugoslavia, and the Russian republic—would be restricted to 30 percent of the number of these immigrants who had come to Canada in 1928. There were no such restrictions on Britishers, though, and the powers that be kept coming up with fresh schemes to entice people in the UK. Early in 1929, the British government and Canadian Pacific launched a joint project aimed at English-speaking farmers under forty years of age with "a wife a little younger, and a couple of children or three, all healthy and vigorous," to move to a cottage in the Canadian Northwest.

The CCA would lease 2 acres (0.8 ha) of land for each family from established farmers across the Prairies and build fully furnished cottages for them. Each family would also be provided with a cow and twenty-five hens of their own. The husbands would be given work on the farm on which his cottage was erected or on another close by. The wife would look after the household and do a little extra work here and there, where possible. The rent for one cottage was four dollars a month, and it was thought that after a year or two, the families would be acclimatized and ready to take up their own farms. In very short order, twenty of these farm-cottages had been built in Manitoba, thirty in

Saskatchewan, and forty-seven in Alberta. The other three homes in what was sometimes advertised as the "Hundred Cottage Scheme" were in BC.[39]

The other massive joint program of the CPR and the Dominions Office was the so-called One Thousand Family Movement. Under this 1929 plan, the UK was to settle impoverished British families in Canada within a period of five years, also through the agency of the railway's settlement arm, the CCA. Unemployed miners and their wives and children made up a large portion of those to be assisted.

As with most of the schemes hatched under the terms of the Empire Settlement Act of 1922, farm structures would be erected in advance of the settlers' arrival. Colonists would receive assisted passage to Canada and advice on all agricultural matters, and financial aid would be provided by railway and government for equipment, livestock, and other necessities. As many as 350 families were settled in Alberta the first year, mostly along the C&E railway line and some in the newly opened Peace River country north of Edmonton.[40]

"The dawning of a really progressive era for the Peace River country was heralded when the Canadian Pacific Railway took over for operation the Edmonton, Dunvegan & British Columbia Railway, which penetrates the southern section of the property," the CPR's monthly publication *Agricultural and Industrial Progress in Canada* informed its readers in January 1924. "Since that time [the CPR lease ran from July 1920 to November 1925], there has been a fairly steady influx of settlers and a certain definite agricultural development. Many United States ranchers have become interested in the cattle-raising possibilities of the area and cattle shipments into Edmonton have become a regular feature."[41]

◄ Canadian Pacific, in partnership with the British and Canadian governments entered into a number of schemes throughout the 1920s to bring British families to Canada. AUTHOR'S COLLECTION

Opposite, top The Edmonton, Dunvegan & British Columbia Railway (later Northern Alberta Railway) depot in Peace River, Alberta, in 1917. CRHA/ EXPORAIL CANADIAN PACIFIC RAILWAY FONDS, A6739

Opposite, bottom Throughout the mid-1920s, there was a steady influx of settlers to the Peace River country, many of whom bought land through the Grande Prairie Land Company. LIBRARY AND CULTURAL RESOURCES DIGITAL COLLECTIONS, UNIVERSITY OF CALGARY CU1101984

In 1929, the provincial government created Northern Alberta Railways (NAR) to amalgamate the Edmonton, Dunvegan & British Columbia Railway with three other struggling railways. A year later, the NAR was turned over to the CPR and the CNR to jointly operate, which spurred the opening up of vast tracts of land in the north to settlement. Western newspapers described the flood of settlers entering the Peace River District, straddling the Alberta-British Columbia border, as a "flight from Egypt," and a great "trek of the land-hungry." Grande Prairie, Alberta, alone had already attracted a population of 1,800—almost as many as the entire population of the Peace River country in 1911, and, as reported, "there isn't a vacant house in the whole town, in fact, people are demanding houses when none are to be had."[42] As many as ten thousand were expected to take up farming in the region in the next few years.

The Peace River District in British Columbia would get a population boost in the following decade, when Hitler's regime took over the Sudetenland portion of the Czechoslovak Republic in October 1938. The CCA and CPR settled nearly 600 Sudeten German refugees—Christians and Jews—in eastern British Columbia, about 300 miles (500 km) west-northwest of Edmonton, near Tupper in the Tomslake area just south of Dawson Creek; CNR settled about the same number near St. Walburg, Saskatchewan. Aided in their plight by the British Labour Party, with money from the Czechoslovakian government, the first of the displaced settlers left Southampton aboard CPSS's *Montcalm* on April 8, 1939. The last sailing left on July 28, Canadian Pacific's *Duchess of York*.

Harking back to the days of the imperialist estate-owners who promoted emigration, CPR chief commissioner Dennis announced that W.H. Askew, the Laird of Ladykirk, near Berwick-upon-Tweed, Scotland, would provide the "munificent gift" of one thousand dollars for each family he would sponsor from the border region of England and Scotland to "engage in agricultural work" in Canada.[43]

Forty families set sail on CPSS *Melita* in the spring of 1929, personally conducted by a Canadian Pacific agent. More than half of the "staunch and sturdy border stock" were settled by the company subsidiary, the CCA, on railway lands, some on the farm cottages recently erected and some on other properties prepared by the CPR under agreement with the Overseas Settlement Committee. "I have no hesitation, whatever," said Dennis, "in saying that Mr. Askew's magnificent action is a strong reminder that the whole matter of movement of British colonists to Canada calls for special efforts on the part of organizations and individuals who are in the position to speed up the important task in question."[44]

Dennis, always on watch for a new ally, made it a point to sign an agreement with the Imperial Order Daughters of the Empire (IODE) to "avail ourselves of the welcome and welfare services offered by your order, on behalf of the British settlers in Canada." Founded in 1900, the IODE was and still is a charitable organization of like-minded women who work to "improve the quality of life for those in need"—particularly if they were British. A list appended to the agreement included 133 IODE chapters in the Canadian Northwest.[45]

Meanwhile the CPR was still bringing in Eastern Europeans, smoothed over with a healthy dose of public relations pronouncements. "The type of newly arrived settlers to be found on the C.P.R. lands southwest of Leduc is distinctly superior to certain other types of European immigrants,"

the *Calgary Herald* asserted. "The men are strong, intelligent and contented, while the women are the home-making type of the better class of European peasants. Thoroughly accustomed to hard work and long hours in their native land, they are the best possible class of immigrants for the arduous work of clearing Alberta's brush lands."[46]

The CPR's James Colley, assistant superintendent of colonization, informed newspaper readers that "we know they will stick it out because your Hungarian will not be enticed away from his land with offers of a job because it is his greatest ambition to own producing land for himself."[47]

A staggering contribution

"One of the most amazing statements I have heard for many a day was that of an official of the Canadian Pacific Railway, who assured me that his Company has expended over 75 million dollars in all in the development of migration to Canada." It was the summer of 1928, and the amazed British newspaper reporter had been trying to get a handle on the contribution of the CPR in promoting emigration from his country to the Canadian Northwest. He was most impressed by what he deemed to be the "staggering total."[48]

The same reporter estimated that Britain could comfortably support a population of about fifty million people, while Canada's limit was—"well, nobody can say." His disclosure about CPR's tremendous contribution to Canada's settlement and development, he concluded, "might almost put to the blush the Governments of both Britain and Canada."

The CPR had sold 50 percent more farmland in Western Canada that year than it had in 1927, greater than any year since 1921.[49] But Canadian Pacific was beginning to look at the Canadian economy—and its own future prospects—through a wide-angle lens.

The first Western paper mill had recently begun operations in Manitoba, and during the twenties the production of newsprint had become the country's second largest industry, next to agriculture. Alberta had its oil and gas, Saskatchewan its lignite coal. Train tracks and telegraph wires criss-crossed the land in profusion. One of the era's most popular songs may have maintained that "Yes, we have no bananas," but as a country, Canada had just about everything else. And the CPR's Department of Natural Resources had its fingers in every pie. It remained to be seen if the nation would have the people it needed to exploit those riches or if it would require a continuing influx of foreign workers to meet the challenge.

◄ Chocolates, tobacco, cigarettes, and other little luxuries were in the packages dispensed by Mrs. W. N. Askew, wife of the Laird of Ladykirk, Scotland, to prospective colonists leaving for Canada on the CPR steamship *Melita*. AUTHOR'S COLLECTION

12 DARK, DREARY, AND DEADLY DAYS

Too much and not enough

The stock market crash of October 1929 set the scene for what would be called the "Dirty Thirties" or the "Hungry Thirties." The decade put an end to the long period of prosperity that had inspired Prime Minister Wilfrid Laurier to claim that the twentieth century would belong to Canada and caused settlers in the Golden Northwest to abandon their dreams as rapidly as they had once conjured them up.

The twenties had been a decade of expansion for Canada. Farm production reached unprecedented levels. Forest products and manufactured goods grew by leaps and bounds, largely driven by cheap credit. But with the stock market crash, optimistic growth turned to frightened panic, and the era of prosperity came to an abrupt end. To make matters worse, a particularly harsh drought descended upon the prairies, and the winds of desperation carried away the livelihood of many a farmer as the once fertile topsoil turned to dust.

Thousands of immigrants and seasonal workers who were still in the Northwest when the economy collapsed were now unemployed and straining the limited resources of government relief programs and private charitable organizations. Immigration policy, always a controversial topic in the West, became a critical matter for a country that still needed to put more productive agriculturalists on the land.

Senator Robert Forke, the former federal minister of immigration, made three relevant points in a 1930 speech to the United Farmers of Manitoba. First, he opposed assisted immigration, as he felt that those who made their way to Canada on their own had more of a stake in succeeding; secondly, he considered the situation satisfactory in regard to welcoming Central and Eastern Europeans, who would open up bush lands and "scrub-grown areas" where Canadians and Britishers would not go; and thirdly, he did not think the country was encouraging too much immigration, but that it *was* suffering from the seasonal nature of much of the work.[1]

In 1930, CPR's Department of Colonization and Development became the Department of Immigration and Colonization to reflect its specific focus on populating the land, particularly in the Northwest. It was headquartered in Montreal. While the new department pursued its singular goal, all aspects of the country's ongoing development would fall within the purview of the Calgary-based Department of Natural Resources.

"The future of Canada depends largely on how courageously the problem of immigration and colonization is faced," said Ashley Edwards, editor of publications for

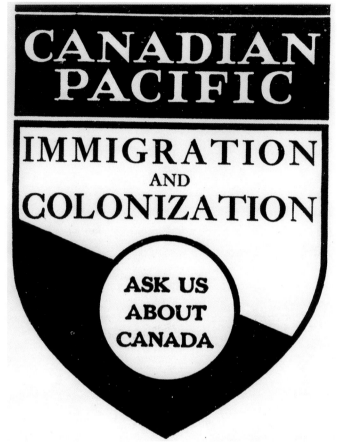

CANADIAN PACIFIC

IMMIGRATION AND COLONIZATION

ASK US ABOUT CANADA

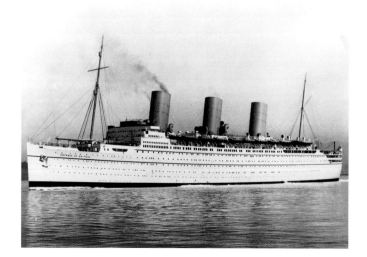

Top, left The winds of desperation carried away the livelihood of many a farmer, as the once fertile topsoil turned to dust. LIBRARY AND CULTURAL RESOURCES DIGITAL COLLECTIONS, UNIVERSITY OF CALGARY CU1154941

Middle, left Horse-drawn conveyances, converted from what were once motor vehicles, were scornfully referred to as "Bennett buggies," as the blame for the Depression was laid by much of the public at the feet of the federal government. LIBRARY AND CULTURAL RESOURCES DIGITAL COLLECTIONS, UNIVERSITY OF CALGARY CU195264

Bottom, left Settlers like Mr. & Mrs. Gregorz Polasczuk and their children, after building a rough home near Seba, Alberta, had the option of staying on their land by paying down debts with a portion of their crops rather than with cash. LIBRARY AND CULTURAL RESOURCES DIGITAL COLLECTIONS, UNIVERSITY OF CALGARY CU111003 OPPOSITE, 1

CPR's newest department, to the St. George's Men's Fellowship Club in Montreal. If Canada did not acquire many times its current population, he believed, the country's natural resources and its economic possibilities would remain unrealized:

With the amazing natural resources that Canada possesses—forests, mines, water power, fisheries and the rest, her manufacturing activities have increased so rapidly that, while the agricultural foundations must continue to be broadened, there is every reason to believe that the industrial life of Canada will continue to steadily grow. The growth of industry depends, of course upon the securing of capital.[2]

He went on to say that the CPR worked continuously to secure the right class of settler and to attract capital from other countries, "helping hundreds of thousands of worthy citizens to realize opportunities that otherwise they could not have found, not only to accelerate the economic growth of the country but to cultivate and develop the natural resources of mind and character."

During this depressed state of world trade, agents with the CNR reached an agreement with the CPR to sell passenger tickets for Canadian Pacific Steamships to and from Atlantic ports, even if that sometimes meant losing railway traffic once the ships had docked. CP passenger ships sailing to and from Saint John, New Brunswick, would call at Halifax, both westbound and eastbound.[3]

The largest steamship ever owned by Canadian Pacific, the *Empress of Britain II*, had been launched in the John Brown shipyard in Clydebank, Scotland in June 1930. At the time, it was the fastest and most luxurious ship to sail between Canada and the United Kingdom. With space for 470 third-class passengers, along with more than 700

in first-class and tourist cabins, it had a brief career as an effective carrier of immigrants to the New World before being requisitioned for troop transport in November 1939.

The last direct CPSS sailing from Glasgow was made by the *Montclare* on August 21, 1931, after which most voyages left from Liverpool and were routed via the Clyde and Belfast.[4] By 1932, the number of settlers taking the eastbound passage on company ships had dwindled to 6,882. There were more emigrants than immigrants that year, as many who had come to Canada returned to their former homes in Europe.[5]

The worst years of the Depression were 1931 through 1933, and plunging Canadian immigration statistics would reflect that, recording 165,000 new arrivals in 1929 and just over 14,000 in 1933.[6] A downsizing of the "trainee" movement from Great Britain, which had resulted in some 3,000 youths coming to Canada in 1929, introduced much more rigid standards and thinned out numbers substantially.[7] The price of a bushel of wheat fell to forty cents and the value of Canada's agricultural exports dropped by two-thirds. Swarms of grasshoppers inflicted heavy damage to crops.

On a positive note, the CPR's demonstration and supply farm at Strathmore still had the largest dairy herd in Canada, with at least 550 head of Holstein cattle that supplied fresh dairy products daily for CPR hotels and dining cars. Just as the Canadian economy was rapidly shrinking, Strathmore's prize cows were setting records for butter and milk production. The farm also bred outstanding Percheron horses, sheep, and Angus cattle, winning many awards at national shows.

Strathmore drew visitors not just from farms in the surrounding area, but from all parts of the world: Australia, New Zealand, India, Japan, Great Britain, Holland,

Denmark, Argentina, Mexico, and the United States. All the prize-winning horses, cattle, and sheep were home bred.[8]

In later years, Professor W.J. Elliot, the superintendent at Strathmore, said that CPR had taken every precaution to safeguard the interests of farmers and ranchers. By the end of the 1920s, the railway had already sold to the settlers, on credit, more than ten thousand cattle, one thousand horses, thirteen hundred swine, and about seven thousand sheep. "When times became tough in the thirties," Elliot said, "the C.P.R. cancelled all debts against the livestock and machinery purchased by these farmers. Without this they never would have made it."[9]

The arboretum at Strathmore had also proved to be a great success, providing bushes and trees for thousands of properties in the railway's irrigation block and other lands in the Northwest. In retrospect, Rhey C. Bosworth, CPR's superintendent of colonization in Winnipeg, gave much of the credit for the resulting lush groves to Don Mark, superintendent of the Irrigation Development Branch, at Brooks. Bosworth said the trees contributed to the overall well-being of settlers:

I consider a farm home with an attractive grove to be worth at least fifteen hundred to two thousand dollars more than a farm without a grove. From my personal experience, I know that farm homes with an attractive grove of trees greatly lessens the mortality among settlers. In other words, the entire family is more contented to remain on their farm if an attractive grove surrounds their home.[10]

Throughout the 1930s, the CPR demonstration farms at both Tilley and Bassano bred prize Hereford cattle, sheep, and Percheron horses. Bassano continued to experiment with various types of grain as well as hemp, and Brooks had a bountiful fruit plantation.

Top The interior of the dairy barn at Strathmore was staged to showcase the one-year output of "Strathmore Sylvia." The farm's most productive cow supplied the CPR with more than 29,000 pounds of milk and 1,200 pounds of butter over a twelve-month period. LIBRARY AND CULTURAL RESOURCES DIGITAL COLLECTIONS, UNIVERSITY OF CALGARY CU1194288

Bottom Now a world-famous agricultural institution, the Strathmore Demonstration and Supply Farm could boast sunflowers that grew to twice the height of a man. LIBRARY AND CULTURAL RESOURCES DIGITAL COLLECTIONS, UNIVERSITY OF CALGARY CU1194261

► The demonstration farm at Tilley, one of three in the CPR irrigation district, bred prize-winning cattle, sheep, and horses. LIBRARY AND CULTURAL RESOURCES DIGITAL COLLECTIONS, UNIVERSITY OF CALGARY CU1194399

The CPR's Exhibits Branch pursued its mandate to advertise Canada's natural resources and the company's lands in Western Canada through the maintenance of display cases throughout North America and more comprehensive exhibits at agricultural and land shows across the country and abroad. In 1930, the branch's staff had installed a CPR exhibit in the Canada Building at the Antwerp Exhibition, and the next year moved it to the British Empire Trade Exhibition in Buenos Aires. They also created a joint display with the CNR and the federal government at the 1933 "A Century of Progress" Exposition in Chicago, attended by about twenty million people. The same year, Canada hosted the first World Grain Exhibition and Conference, in Regina, where the Exhibits Branch installed a major display. Every year, CPR played a leading role in the development of displays for the Railway Building at the Canadian National Exhibition in Toronto.[11]

"Don't emigrate to the Dominion at present," said the president of the British United Press at the outset of the Depression. C.R. Crandall warned his readers that "while

Top left An animal husbandry specialist shows off a prize-winning Hampshire ram at the CPR's demonstration farm at Tilley, Alberta.

Bottom left These Scottish girls (from left, Lily Kappelle, Marjory Robson, Margaret Menzie, and Isabel Paterson) sailed to Canada in search of employment, just before immigration from Europe was temporarily discontinued as a result of the war.

we know that emigration is encouraged by the great shipping companies ... the conditions of the workless man in Canada, unless he has some savings to fall back on, is far worse than that of the unemployed man in Britain ... Unlike this country, there is no 'dole' so that, apart from charity, a man out of work in Canada is faced with starvation."[12]

As early as mid-August 1930, the federal government had announced the discontinuation of all immigration from continental Europe, with the exception of "experienced farmers of suitable type, who are in possession of ample means to immediately establish and maintain themselves on farms," and the "wives and children of persons already established in Canada." The authorities hoped that the policy would remove some of the pressure from the unemployment situation, or at the very least would not contribute to it.[13]

For settlers already on the land but struggling with finances during the Depression, T.O.F. Herzer, the manager of the CCA, launched the Colonization Finance Corporation to coordinate the work of fourteen of the largest insurance and mortgage companies in Canada, with a view to saving money on administrative costs and making the properties of absentee land owners more productive, to the advantage of the entire community.[14] Beatty, the CPR president, said the new financial institute would help "borrowers, who, through the combination of low prices for agricultural products and losses resulting from improper farming methods, find themselves going backward in their farming operations and have become financially embarrassed."[15]

The policy that the CPR had used from time to time, of accepting a portion of settlers' crops in lieu of cash payments, was instituted more broadly during the Depression than it had been previously. Beginning in 1932, the railway

▲ The theme of the 1933 World's fair in Chicago was "A Century of Progress," giving the CPR an opportunity to run special trains to the event, and to showcase the company's achievements in settling the Northwest. CRHA/EXPORAIL CANADIAN PACIFIC RAILWAY FONDS A6256

began to accept just one-quarter of the harvest as payment, rather than one-third. Nevertheless, many farms were abandoned and others went unsold. In some cases, in an effort to avoid paying taxes on unused land, CPR offered unsold lots to adjacent towns. As early as 1930, the railway had proposed a sale to the town of Gleichen of 144 lots for three dollars apiece, but the offer had been rejected. Lots in Consort, Sedgewick, Macleod, and a dozen other locations were unloaded for one dollar or best offer. Some properties were turned over to holding companies to reduce the CPR's tax liability.

In the middle of the decade, the farmers and ranchers in the Eastern Section of CPR's irrigation block established a formal water users' group and began discussions with the railway company to take over all the district's unsold lands, the entire water delivery system, and responsibility for its operation and maintenance. Within a year, the settlers in the Eastern Section would take full ownership of the land and all its resources and have complete control of their own future prospects. In April 1935, the negotiations resulted in the creation of the private Eastern Irrigation District (EID), with a mechanism for electing a board of trustees from among the water users. CPR turned over to the EID about 1 million acres (405,000 ha) of land within the region, the entire infrastructure of the irrigation system, and a cash reserve fund of $300,000 to assist with the start-up costs of the new organization.[16]

In 1933, not long after taking power, the National German Socialist Workers' Party (Nazis) announced a nationwide plan to depopulate German's big cities in an unprecedented "back to the farm" movement. Through their elaborate scheme, the Nazis hoped to make the country self-sufficient as far as foodstuffs were concerned. In

Top The CPR turned over about one million acres of land, along with the entire infrastructure of the eastern irrigation system, and a cash reserve fund of $300,000, to the newly formed, farmer-owned Eastern Irrigation District. LIBRARY AND CULTURAL RESOURCES DIGITAL COLLECTIONS, UNIVERSITY OF CALGARY CU191185

Bottom Jan Huba's family arrived in 1930 with a group of Czechoslovakian settlers in Onaway, Alberta, with $2,400 to get started in the Northwest. The two adults and three children had taken advantage of inexpensive ocean fares on the CPR steamship *Montcalm* to get to the New World. LIBRARY AND CULTURAL RESOURCES DIGITAL COLLECTIONS, UNIVERSITY OF CALGARY CU1110214

Polish settlers, like this group who arrived in Sundance, Alberta, by the CPR steamship *Empress of Scotland*, were experienced farmers and quickly adapted to their new environment. LIBRARY AND CULTURAL RESOURCES DIGITAL COLLECTIONS, UNIVERSITY OF CALGARY CU1110039

the first year alone, they intended to create five thousand new homesteads and more than one hundred villages, mostly in barren districts within the provinces of East Frisia, Hanover, Pomerania, and Silesia. Officials estimated that it would take twenty years of hard work to achieve the party's goals.[17]

The next year, the CPR and CNR reached an understanding with the federal government that each railway could recruit seventy-five families for agricultural settlement in any part of the Dominion, provided they were experienced agriculturists. To ensure that settlers selected by the railway had sufficient resources to not become a burden on the state, the government required the head of each family to deposit with the railways' colonization departments at least one thousand dollars at the time of their entry. Those funds would later be applied to the purchase of

their farms. Colonel Dennis had recently retired, so negotiations with the government were conducted by CPR's new chief commissioner of immigration, J.N.K. Macalister. The agreement specified that the families could come from Denmark, Norway, Sweden, Holland, France, Belgium, Switzerland, Poland, Hungary, Czechoslovakia, and Germany. Families of German ethnic origin from any country of Europe were also eligible.[18]

Within two years, CPR agents were dealing with nearly eight hundred families, with a minimum of one thousand dollars cash each, as prospective immigrants. Fifty-three families from a variety of European countries had already been settled on farms. More than half remained in the East rather than heading for the Northwest. None were German.[19]

By 1935, the passage of the Nuremberg Laws in Germany had left Jewish people disenfranchised and unprotected,

their citizenship revoked, and their businesses destroyed. By the time Nazi troops marched into the Sudeten region of Czechoslovakia, in October 1938, Denmark, Belgium, Holland, and the port of Antwerp were already filled with—among others—Jewish refugees from Germany, Austria, and elsewhere in Europe looking to escape persecution. Although some had farming experience and many were well off financially, steamship agents informed them that Canada was not accepting entry applications from Jews.

Canada's list of "non-preferred" immigrants had long included Jews, along with Asians and Black people, but individuals from all of these groups had been unofficially tolerated in out-of-the-way occupations, "risking life and limb in the mines and smelters of the west and north, holed up in lumber camps deep in the forest, or farming the more marginal areas of the western wheat frontier."[20] The onset of the Depression, however, had led to a total ban on these settlers.

With immigration taking a backseat in Canadian government affairs during the Depression, responsibility for that function was housed with the Department of Mines and Resources. After the 1935 defeat of Prime Minister Robert B. Bennett's Conservatives by William Lyon Mackenzie King's Liberals, Charles Blair took on the role of director of the Immigration Branch. Blair did not think that Jews made good agriculturalists.

Among the Canadians who passionately disagreed with the government's position in the matter was Mark Sorensen, a Danish immigrant who had settled in Western Canada and worked his way up to becoming CPR's agent in Copenhagen. Sorensen was horrified by what he saw as Canada's inhumane policy toward the Jews, and on a practical level, he wondered how the country could turn away

Top Immigrants who left Europe after Nazi troops marched into the Sudeten region of Czechoslovakia, in October 1938, pose two years later in front of their home in the Tupper/Tomslake area of British Columbia. Many other Sudeten refugees settled on the Prairies and in Ontario. LIBRARY AND CULTURAL RESOURCES DIGITAL COLLECTIONS, UNIVERSITY OF CALGARY CU1122674

Bottom Thomas Cook & Sons, working with the Children's Overseas Reception Board (CORB), brought this group from Britain to Canada during the early months of the war. The CP steamships *Duchess of Atholl* and *Duchess of York* were among the vessels used to convey the children to safety. LIBRARY & ARCHIVES CANADA A142400

potential immigrants who had both needed skills and huge amounts of capital to invest.

Sorensen's contempt for Canada's immigration policies was echoed by the CPR's European colonization manager, Henry C.P. Cresswell, who felt that many applicants of merit were being rejected out of hand by misguided government officials. The people being abandoned to their fate, he insisted, at any other time—and had they not been Jewish—"would have been welcomed with open arms."[21]

In the late spring of 1940, the CPR ordered Sorensen to abandon his office in Copenhagen and relocate to London. For the remainder of the war, he lamented Canada's lack of decency, which he viewed as "stark raving mad." The frustrated immigration agent wrote to his superiors in no uncertain terms:

The day will come when Immigration will be under debate, and then the Ottawa Immigration Service will be judged by [its] records. For us it will not be important to have these records at our fingertips. They shall then find us as their bad conscience.[22]

A long and bitter struggle

In September 1939, Britain and the Commonwealth countries had declared war on Nazi Germany and its allies. Five days later, convoys of merchant vessels under the protection of warships were already sailing between Canada and the mother country in support of the life-or-death struggle that would consume the world for the next six years.[23]

Most of CPR's ocean liners were quickly requisitioned by the British Admiralty for war duty, and immigration from Britain and the European continent was virtually discontinued. Some CPR ships, being British-registered, had already been taken over in anticipation of war, following the Molotov-Ribbentrop pact, negotiated between the Soviet Union and Germany, prior to hostilities breaking out.

The CPR continued to offer land for sale in the provinces of Manitoba, Saskatchewan, and Alberta throughout the conflict, but the only takers would be settlers from the United States or existing Canadian farmers wishing to expand their operations. Arrivals in Canada from all parts of the world fell from the already low levels experienced during the 1930s to fewer than ten thousand newcomers annually from 1941 through 1943. The country's population was now between eleven and twelve million.

Demand for new water contracts in the Bow River irrigation district had decreased during the 1930s and all but collapsed during the war. By 1940, the cost of maintaining the infrastructure had reached three times earnings, and on May 1, 1944, the remaining assets of CPR's Western Section were turned over to a newly formed landowners cooperative, the Western Irrigation District, under the auspices of the Alberta provincial government.[24]

The terms for purchasing available CPR's improved farms or partially improved farms were modest: 8 percent down and the balance arranged by crop share at 6 percent interest, with no payments due in the first year. For unimproved land, purchasers paid 8 percent down and the remainder in equal installments extended over a twenty-one-year period. Obtaining Canadian or British citizenship was not a requirement for owning land in Canada, and all property holders were entitled to vote in municipal and school elections.[25]

The war years were a time for Canada to re-examine immigration policy and help existing settlers consolidate

their holdings and remain productive. "When this war is over it is probable that we shall have to face problems in connection with immigration into this country that are altogether different from those we have had to meet in the past," wrote James Colley of CPR's Department of Immigration and Colonization. He then went on to list most of the same considerations that had always shaped Canadian immigration policy, including the general preference for Britishers over Central and Eastern Europeans, the need for agriculturalists over urban workers, and the tendency of people who were already settled to be largely unwelcoming of newcomers.[26]

The former Canadian prime minister, R.B. Bennett, now Viscount Bennett, suggested to the British House of Lords in 1943 that, after the war, the two countries should engage in "community emigration," by which people from the same districts in the UK would go overseas together, preventing loneliness and promoting cooperation among new Canadian settlers. The Duke of Devonshire, chairman of the Overseas Settlement Board, spoke up for reinstating assisted emigration to countries within the Empire, even though the practice had fallen out of favour in the host countries.[27]

Four years after the start of the war, the CPR's immigration staff were excited by the prospect of "good stock" emigrating to Canada. A number of men from the UK who had come to Canada to participate in the British Commonwealth Air Training Plan returned to Canada after being discharged from the armed forces. In addition, more than sixteen thousand Canadian soldiers were expected to take their English and Scottish brides home with them at the cessation of hostilities. Clearly, the lads had been busy with more things than combat.[28]

Top A CPR reservation card for a Canadian soldier returning home from the theatre of war in Europe. Many servicemen brought their British brides with them at the cessation of hostilities. AUTHOR'S COLLECTION

Bottom A meal ticket issued by the CPR and the Canadian Department of National Defence to returning soldiers, to be redeemed in any railway dining car or restaurant operated by Canadian Pacific or Canadian National. AUTHOR'S COLLECTION

The Canadian Institute of Public Opinion, in Toronto, surveyed the Canadian public on their attitudes about post-war immigration:

The atmosphere of war, in which antagonisms are at their height, is admittedly not the time to obtain the calmest or most unbiased opinion on such matters as immigration, but the prospect of a large post-war influx has been widely discussed, and it is significant that, despite the war atmosphere, only 21 percent of those Canadians interviewed favoured a completely closed door on immigration matters.[29]

The survey showed that nearly three-quarters of Canadians favoured selective immigration after the war. The greatest receptiveness to immigration was in Ontario and the Prairie provinces, and the least in Quebec. Canadians of French origin predominately favoured a complete ban on immigration, while nationalities other than British or French showed a much greater enthusiasm for an open-door policy. Seventy-eight percent of those interviewed thought that Japanese nationals should not be allowed into Canada, and 58 percent voted against admitting Germans.[30]

In the summer of 1943, Alberta Premier Ernest Manning convened a meeting with representatives from the CPR and CNR to discuss postwar settlement in the Northwest. Among other matters, Manning proposed to the railways' colonization people that the large body of American soldiers and civilians assisting the war effort from bases in the Northwest should be encouraged to take up residence in Canada after the war.[31]

After thirty-seven years' service with CPR, Macalister retired as chief commissioner of the company's Department of Immigration and Colonization and was succeeded by Henry Cresswell, formerly Canadian Pacific's European colonization manager, based in London, England.

13 TO CANADA BY SEA AND BY AIR

War-torn countries and logistical challenges

As many as twenty million Europeans were displaced by the war, no longer having homes, livelihoods, or anywhere to go. Most continental European countries were crowded with refugee camps, as was the United Kingdom, where countless exiles had sought sanctuary during the conflict. As well, many asylum-seekers had been abandoned in the defeated nations of Germany, Austria, and Italy.

Shortly after the war ended, the CPR's Department of Immigration and Colonization was reactivated in Montreal, with a sub-headquarters in London. The company redeployed representatives throughout Britain, continental Europe, and the United States to identify qualified settlers from among the refugees.

The CPR's western affiliate, the Canada Colonization Association, continued to help immigrants become successful settlers. From 1925, when the CPR had taken over full ownership of the CCA, to the fall of 1947, the company's agents established 9,435 families on farms in Western Canada, with a total acreage of nearly 2.5 million (1 million ha).[1]

Prior to 1939, railway agents had nominated potential candidates for settlement, and the governments of the countries from which they originated would issue licences or other papers authorizing the settlers to emigrant. Representatives of either the CPR or CNR were then assigned to handle the arrangements, depending on which company had done the recruiting. Many of the countries involved had passed emigration acts between the two world wars to ensure that emigrants received reliable information about the process and were dealt with fairly as well as to control the economic aspects of transportation from country of origin to the New World.

After the war, Canada opened visa offices in most European countries. These were manned by immigration officers, along with officers from the RCMP, for security purposes, and doctors to sign off on health certification. The two national railways were no longer the major, or sole, organizations engaged in recruiting potential emigrants, but they still worked very closely with government authorities to find and settle farmers, farm workers, and domestics. The state passport became a near universal form of identification.

As was the practice before the war, the railways assigned experienced settlement officials, including interpreters and travelling colonization agents, to meet steamships at Canadian ports. The chief activity of the immigration and colonization departments was still the placement of farm

THE SEAS ARE FREE AGAIN...

Canadian Pacific ships carried men and machines to war.....
Now, they move the Service personnel home, victorious.
Soon they will serve you again in peacetime travel and trade

Meantime, inquire here for overseas travel regulations.

Canadian Pacific Steamships

families and single men, either in agricultural employment or on farms of their own. Increasingly, however, that was supplemented by the effort to assist the federal government in settling skilled personnel in new or expanded industries.

Shipping was in disarray in the early postwar years. Only five of seventeen CPR passenger liners that had been requisitioned by the British Admiralty returned to peacetime service. The Norwegian America Line and the Swedish America Line resumed service to New York City shortly after the war, each using two vintage liners. Both steamship lines made calls at Halifax to disembark emigrants for Canada. The Holland America and Cunard lines were also back in the North Atlantic trade before Canadian Pacific Steamships resumed sailings to Montreal in the summer of 1947, with the reconditioned *Empress of France* and *Empress of Canada*, formerly the *Duchess of Bedford* and *Duchess of Richmond*, respectively.

After their release from war service, the two CPSS liners had been upgraded from their former cabin-class "Duchess" designation to a first-class role in the company fleet. However, for the first several postwar years, the ships carried mostly refugee and immigrant traffic westbound.

Most countries suffered a shortage of labourers to help with reconstruction, and severe restrictions were enforced on the amount of capital that could be carried outside their borders. The country most favoured for early recruitment efforts by CPR's chief commissioner of immigration, Cresswell, was Switzerland.[2]

"The need for a sound immigration flow was never more apparent," said CPR's chairman and president, William N. Neal, appointed to the position in 1947. Edward Beatty had died in 1943, after serving as the CPR president for thirty-four years, and Dalton Colman had served in

◄ In the aftermath of war, the thoughts of displaced Europeans turned once again to the possibility of relocating overseas. AUTHOR'S COLLECTION

► The CPSS Duchess cabin steamships were renamed and upgraded to a first-class role in the company's fleet. As the *Empress of France*, the former *Duchess of Bedford* resumed sailings to Montreal, along with the reconditioned *Empress of Canada*. AUTHOR'S COLLECTION

the interim, while Neal was being groomed for the top post. "This country, from one end to the other, and on the new frontier of the northwest, is in desperate need of the same kind of manpower which pressed its development in the early years of this century."[3]

Representatives from both of Canada's transcontinental railways testified before a Senate committee on immigration in 1946. Those who spoke for the CNR were optimistic about postwar economic expansion and called for an aggressive immigration policy, while the CPR speakers urged the

country's politicians to follow Australia's ambitious lead, stating that Canada should aim to double or triple its population.[4]

The Canadian Christian Council for Resettlement of Refugees (CCCRR) was formed in 1947 by the CPR, the CNR, and the CCA. The council worked closely with the Dominion immigration authorities as well as with such organizations as the Canadian Mennonite Board of Colonization, the Baptist World Alliance Immigration Service, Canadian Lutheran World Relief, and the Catholic Immigrant Aid Society.[5]

The CPR had just announced its acquisition of a former German submarine depot ship under reparations settlements. The converted *Huascaran* would re-emerge from the shipyard at Sorel, Quebec, as the *Beaverbrae*. The ship was mostly intended to carry large numbers of emigrants from Europe to Canada. It was the only CPR ship to carry only passengers on its westbound voyages and cargo eastbound. With a crew of one hundred and sixteen, the ship could accommodate 74 passengers in cabins and a further 699 in specially outfitted dormitory spaces.[6]

Working with CCCRR representatives, CPR agents helped to move emigrants from collection depots in Europe to the dispatching centre in Bremen, Germany, on the North Sea. The CCCRR brought 15,000 immigrants to Canada by the end of 1950. Many came from the Occupied Zones of Germany, though their countries of origin were often the Baltic states, Romania, Poland, Czechoslovakia, Ukraine, and the USSR.[7] Documentation and embarkation arrangements were handled by CPR agents in the company's Bremen office.[8]

The *Beaverbrae* made an average of one sailing per month, with between 500 and 700 passengers onboard, of whom about one-fifth were children. The immigrant ship completed 52 Atlantic voyages and carried more than 38,000 refugees, before leaving Bremen with her last party on July 28, 1954.[9]

The CPR usually had two trains at the port awaiting the arrival of ships, one for destinations in the East and the other for those heading for Winnipeg and all points west. Each train had a special three-car unit to feed the refugees: a kitchen car; a dining car, which served as a sleeper for the crew at night; and a third car, a combination dining and recreation car for the passengers. Church services were

Top The CPR steamship *Beaverbrae* carried large numbers of emigrants from Europe to Canada, many in specially outfitted dormitory space. AUTHOR'S COLLECTION

Bottom Separate CPR trains met incoming ships at the ports of Montreal in summer and Saint John, New Brunswick, in winter, one for passengers going to eastern destinations and another for those heading to Winnipeg and farther west. Here, the westbound train No. 7, the Dominion, departs Winnipeg, December 1, 1950. DOUGLAS R. PHILLIPS COLLECTION

sometimes held in the combination car as well. The CPR introduced two new "restaurant counter cars" to the immigrant service in 1952 and expected that more than 50,000 passengers would be served in them that year alone.[10]

In 1950, the Canadian government had opened a new customs and immigration terminal building in the port of Saint John, New Brunswick. The CPR liners *Empress of France* and *Empress of Canada*, now in regular North Atlantic service, were the biggest users of the port facility. Replacing several old buildings that had been destroyed by fire in 1931, the new terminal provided everything from a day nursery to a small theatre.

The port facilities were said to compare favourably with the modern terminal at Southampton in Britain. They included a kitchen and cafeteria; administration offices, with a large waiting room for disembarking passengers; a recreation room; dormitories for men and women, each with baths, showers, and toilets; hospital rooms for sick passengers, with a dispensary and quarters for doctors and nurses; storerooms; guards' rooms; and detention quarters, with an exercise yard on the roof.

Adjoining the customs room were the CPR and CNR ticket offices. Passengers arrived there wearing the lapel tags issued by the ship's purser, showing their names and destinations to help port staff handle them efficiently.

An 80-year-old Lithuanian widow aboard the *Beaverbrae* in 1950 was celebrated as the fifteen-thousandth immigrant brought to Canada by the Canadian Christian Council for Resettlement of Refugees. After another voyage of the *Beaverbrae*, a Polish immigrant heading for Winnipeg, Mrs. Alfred Jaschke, was about to give birth as her CPR train arrived in Schreiber, Ontario. The expectant mother was rushed to the hospital in nearby Terrace Bay to deliver

the child. To commemorate the location of the somewhat premature but happy event, she subsequently named her baby boy Manfred Terry (for Terrace Bay) Jaschke.[11]

A Danish woman who arrived in Canada by the government-chartered RMS *Aquitania* received a surprise while travelling on a colonist car to Lethbridge:

When we had settled in our car, the porter came in. He was a Negro. I had never seen one before and was overcome with curiosity. I was so stunned, I couldn't say anything. In the next few days, during all the time we were on the train, he was very kind to us... [when] we arrived at Lethbridge, the porter helped us get our luggage out, but when we tried to give him some money for being so kind to us, he wouldn't take it.[12]

Immigration takes to the skies

In early 1951, Henry Cresswell toured Europe to assess the future prospects for CPR's Department of Immigration and Colonization. The chief commissioner of immigration knew that the wide-scale establishment of government visa offices across the continent had been the beginning of the end for the involvement of Canadian railways and the major steamship companies in immigration matters. To make matters worse, Cresswell determined that most of the northern European countries, from which the CPR had previously been so successful in recruiting potential settlers, faced acute shortages of labour, and nearly all the nation states severely restricted the amount of capital that could be transferred out of country.[13]

Restrictions on the transfer of currency was one of the reasons Cresswell identified for the decrease in immigration from the United Kingdom, along with high ocean fares,

scarcity of immigrant ships, lack of Canadian publicity, and—most particularly—competition from Australia as an immigrant-receiving country. Britishers could go "down under" with no limits on transferring their capital assets, and they could still get government-assisted, reduced transportation costs.[14]

Despite the challenging situation in Europe in the early 1950s, Marius Holmgren, the CPR agent in Copenhagen, and his Canadian government counterpart, visa officer Vic Horan, toured the Scandinavian countries to give presentations and show films about opportunities in Canada. Two of the movies, in full colour and with sound, were produced by a Canadian Pacific subsidiary, Associated Screen News. At public schools and in public halls for special interest groups, either movie, *Across Canada* or *Canadian Pattern*, was usually the featured film, though other National Film Board productions were used as well. Several films were dubbed in various languages to reach a broader audience. Local groups like Bennett's Travel Bureau in Oslo and the Swedish State Railway Travel Bureau in Stockholm helped with the presentations.[15]

A request from the Canadian government to British steamship companies for 23,000 reservations for British immigrants to come to Canada in 1951 went unfilled, as the steamship lines were unable to guarantee enough sailings to meet the demand. As a consequence, Canadian immigration officials made an exclusive arrangement with the Cunard Line to charter its liner *Georgic* for a number of voyages the following spring and summer. To supplement the efforts of the shipping companies, they reached an agreement with Trans-Canada Air Lines to carry immigrants at reduced rates, with the government paying the subsidy. The flights were offered at a sum equivalent to tourist first-class passage by sea: $160 charged to the immigrant, with the airline receiving an additional $215.50 from the government.[16]

One of the first passengers to fly out of Amsterdam on the Canadian Pacific Air Lines (soon to be Canadian Pacific Airlines) "polar route" to Canada, inaugurated in May 1955, was a fifteen-year-old farm worker on his way to take up farm work in Innisfail, Alberta.[17] In little more than a decade, the company's steamship service would be out of the business of immigration. Newcomers would still arrive in Canada by sea, but they would be few and far between, and they would pay the same steamship and railway fares as the tourists.

Midway through the Second World War, Canadian Pacific had consolidated ten regional airlines into a comprehensive network, which initially served mostly the northern and western regions of the country. Beginning with routes to the Far East, the new airline soon expanded its intercontinental offerings with flights to destinations in Europe.

After 1955, for several years Canadian Pacific Airlines (CPA) was in partnership with the federal government to bring immigrants to Canada and process them for citizenship. The polar route to Amsterdam was the initial gateway, but it was later supplemented by other routes. "In view of the extension of Canadian Pacific Airlines service to Rome," said the vice-president, G.F. Buckingham, at the time, "the colonization department is promoting the use of this route by sponsors of immigrants moving from the Mediterranean area."

Canada Pacific Airlines entered the immigration business in a highly publicized way when the Canadian minister of citizenship and immigration, Jack Pickersgill, announced on November 6, 1956, that all eligible Hungarian applicants would be at the front of the line to take advantage of an assisted-passage loan scheme. An invasion of Hungary the month before by the Soviet army had resulted in more than 200,000 of the country's citizens fleeing their homeland for Austria and Yugoslavia. Canada was among the Western countries that opened their doors to the refugees who sought freedom from communism.[18]

Grant McConachie, president of CPA, signed a charter contract with the Canadian government to airlift Hungarian refugees from Vienna, Austria to Vancouver, in the company's Super DC-6B aircraft. In all, CPA brought 326 of the displaced Hungarians in a series of flights dubbed the "Operation of Compassion." The company also carried more than 36,000 pounds of medical supplies, food, and

clothing back to Vienna, a city congested with thousands of the refugees.

In working out the logistics for the "freedom flights," CPR district manager Bill Murphy was aided by employees of KLM Royal Dutch Airlines and a 24-year-old Hungarian girl who had escaped from her homeland only two weeks previously. Maria—whose last name was kept confidential because her relatives were still in Hungary—sought out and identified her countrymen who were scattered in refugee camps throughout Vienna.[19]

Another Canadian Pacific initiative launched in 1955 would be among the last gasps of the company's immigration campaigns as well as a serious effort to jump start postwar tourism from Europe to Canada. The newly built *Empress of Britain III* inaugurated a fully modernized transatlantic service and would soon be followed in that endeavour by sister ship *Empress of England* and, finally, a new incarnation of the *Empress of Canada*. The sleek, photogenic "White Empresses" were launched in response to the dramatic increase in postwar immigration, and they would be the latest word in passenger comfort for all classes. There were nearly two hundred first-class state rooms on board the *Empress of Canada* as well as accommodation for more than 850 tourist passengers. Seventy percent of the tourist cabins, for which most European immigrants opted, were said to have had their own private toilets, a considerable improvement from what her competitors were offering.[20]

The Empresses would make several hundred crossings over the next decade and a half, carrying thousands of immigrants to Canada, but inevitably, they became economically unviable and were withdrawn from service and sold off.

In December 1957, Norris R. Crump—president of the CPR since 1955—announced the formation of a new Department of Immigration and Agricultural Development to

Top The *Empress of England* was virtually identical to its sister ship, *Empress of Britain III*. AUTHOR'S COLLECTION

Bottom A room reservation card stamped an immigration officer, for ocean passage to Canada from Liverpool on a Canadian Pacific steamship. AUTHOR'S COLLECTION

► The new *Empress of Canada* was the last passenger steamship to be built for Canadian Pacific's Liverpool-to-Montreal service. AUTHOR'S COLLECTION

Canadian Pacific

THE NEW EMPRESS OF CANADA

LATEST ADDITION TO THE WHITE EMPRESS FLEET

consolidate the functions of the former Department of Immigration and Colonization, the CCA, and the company's general agricultural agents in Toronto and Winnipeg. It was one more move away from the business of colonization and settlement. Although a nominal nod to immigration remained inherent in the name of the new department, its manager, Frank Wolfe, would report to CPR's vice president of traffic.

Canadian Pacific had sold most of its agricultural land in proximity to its railway lines and began maximizing the value of its remaining urban lots with planned development and real estate partnerships. After the high-water mark of 282,164 new arrivals in Canada in 1958, immigration numbers dropped off by more than half the following year and would not reach that lofty level again until the twenty-first century. As a result, the company's emphasis was no longer immigration and land sales but the diversification of farming, improved land use, and the further development of the livestock industry.

The new Department of Immigration and Agricultural Development had twelve offices across Canada, staffed by highly trained agriculturists, appraisers, and farm supervisors, to ensure that all farms adjacent to CPR railway lines had access to modern practices. Consulting services were made available to farmers, shippers, or anyone engaged in agricultural pursuits. The department's specialists studied and offered advice about disease and pest control, livestock production, marketing, and processing.

Outside of Canada, the company still flew its house flag at twenty-one offices in Europe, increasingly to sell its new airline routes alongside its traditional steamship services. Apart from offices in the principal UK centres, it maintained a strong presence in France, Belgium, Holland, Germany, Denmark, Switzerland, Italy, Spain, and Portugal.

A new Department of Immigration and Agricultural Development with a staff of highly trained agriculturists, appraisers, and farm supervisors organized tours of Western farmlands. The windows in the company's offices and foreign agencies now focused primarily on tourism. AUTHOR'S COLLECTION

The nerve centre of the network was the Trafalgar Square building in the heart of London. The chief European destinations on CPA routes were Amsterdam, Rome, Lisbon, Madrid, and the Azores.

By 1960, its Department of Immigration and Agricultural Development was deeply involved in helping the Soviet-satellite countries of Romania and Bulgaria, as well as the communist state of Yugoslavia, to develop thriving cattle industries. Company agents organized the shipment of hundreds of heifers, bulls, and rams from Brooks and Medicine Hat, in Alberta, to CPR's eastern public livestock market in Montreal. The global exchange had begun early in the year with a scouting tour by members of Romania's diplomatic staff in Washington, DC. The cattle were shipped across the North Atlantic and the Mediterranean and through the Bosporus Strait to the Black Sea.[21]

Canadian farmers wanting to learn about agricultural methods in England and Scotland got the chance to find out for themselves when the Department of Immigration and Agricultural Development organized a special tour of Canadian farmhands, drawn from coast to coast. In partnership with the Canadian Federation of Agriculture, the National Farmers' Union of the UK, and the authoritative publications Scottish Farmer and Hereford Herd Book Society, the CPR booked the group's passage from Montreal to Greenock on the Empress of Britain, departing October 4, 1960.[22]

The Canadian agriculturists were shown how they handled turkeys in Ayrshire, saw the manufacturing and testing of British-made farm implements, attended the famed London Dairy Show at the Olympia Exhibition Centre, and visited both the Scottish Highlands and English meadows that their forefathers cultivated. In exchange, fifteen British farm boys were brought over to Canada on the Empress

of France, under the sponsorship of the Fairbridge Society, to apply their skills in Canadian fields. The tours proved to be very popular and were organized annually for the next three years. In 1962, a tour of Canada was added for British farmers, but it was confined to the eastern provinces and did not include a visit to the Northwest.[23]

By the end of 1962, CPR had wrapped up all of its emigration activities in Europe. Effective January 1, 1963, the company created the new Department of Industrial and Agricultural Development, eliminating "immigration" from its name to reflect the new reality. By December 1966, all of the Canadian Pacific passenger offices in Europe, other than the Trafalgar Square headquarters in London, were turned over to the airline, as they were no longer required to promote the company's railway and steamship passenger services.

During CPR's expansion in the early years of the twentieth century, the company's initial land grant of 25 million acres (10 million ha) had grown to about 36.4 million acres (14.7 million ha), with the acquisition of other lines and their accompanying holdings. To succeed as a viable business, it was necessary for the CPR to take the lead in fostering settlement and agricultural production throughout the Prairie provinces, the area in which the vast majority of the company's lands were granted and from where a good portion of its traffic would originate. In addition, much of CPR's initial effort had been directed at settling the "homestead" lands that were offered essentially free to would-be settlers before the railway's lands could be easily sold.

Of the lands granted to the CPR and acquired with the purchase of other railways, some 23 million acres (9.3 million ha) were marketed to the public over the years, mostly for agricultural settlement and exploitation. Of the

remainder, 6.8 million acres (2.8 million ha) were returned to the federal government in 1886 to settle the company's indebtedness from the construction of its transcontinental main line. Another 3.7 million acres (1.5 million ha) of land granted to the CPR by the BC government for railway construction in the interior was sold back to the province in 1912. A further 1.2 million acres (486,000 ha) of land was turned over at no cost to the Eastern Irrigation District—the organization of farmers in southeast Alberta—along with all of the infrastructure associated with the CPR-built irrigation works in that area.

The last 887,000 acres (359,000 ha) of land granted to the CPR was sold in 1964 to Marathon Realty Company, a subsidiary of the CPR, most of which consisted of lots within the boundaries of Canadian cities and towns. By 1997, virtually all of this acreage had been sold for commercial development.[24] Over a period of more than one hundred years, Canada's pioneer transcontinental railway had played a leading role—unprecedented anywhere in the world—in attracting people to the New World and settling the country's Golden Northwest.

ACKNOWLEDGEMENTS

CONSIDERING CANADIAN Pacific's critical role in Canada's creation as a coast-to-coast entity and its numerous involvements in the promotion and development of the country throughout the first century of its existence, it's perhaps not surprising that historians have not attempted to chronicle the full measure of these contributions to the national makeup.

Much has been written about the political foundations and economic consequences of building Canada's first transcontinental railway, as well as the enormous physical challenges imposed by the country's expansive and often inhospitable geography in accomplishing that remarkable engineering feat. But that chapter in the company's history, momentous as it was, proved to be only a prelude to the myriad activities with which the CPR would insinuate itself into the nation's journey toward mature statehood.

A number of those corporate endeavours have been touched upon in a variety of published works dealing with immigration, transportation, settlement, irrigation, resource development, tourism, and a host of other topics. In researching *New World Dreams*, I have benefitted greatly from the efforts of more than one hundred of these narratives—listed in the bibliography—and for that I am grateful to the diligence of their authors in chronicling many of the individual stories and vital contributions of the men and women who turned an ambitious national dream into a growing and thriving reality.

In the same vein, I have been able to take advantage of several of the many substantial and comprehensive archival collections available in Canada for public consultation and have been the recipient of much valuable assistance from their knowledgeable and accommodating staff members, notably those at Library and Archives Canada, the Glenbow Western Research Centre of the University of Calgary, and the Canadian Pacific Archives, now located at the Exporail/Canadian Railroad Historical Association Archives and Documentation Centre. Largely as a result of the depth of these collections, I was also able to mine pertinent historical facts and quotations from more than eighty newspapers and periodicals, national and international.

As for the photographs and other illustrations used to supplement the text, my greatest resource was the extensive Library and Cultural Resources Digital Collections at the University of Calgary (in part, formerly the photographic collection at the Glenbow Museum and Archives). Other comprehensive collections at Library and Archives Canada, the National Film Archives, and Ingenium/Canada Science and Technology Museum (formerly the National

Museum of Science and Technology) yielded a wealth of salient images, as did the provincial archives of Manitoba, Saskatchewan, and Alberta and the universities of Calgary and Alberta. Notman Photographic Archives at the McCord Stewart Museum in Montreal has had a long historical association with the CPR and proved to be a more unexpected but useful repository for visual documentation relative to my study; and the Thunder Bay Historical Museum Society and the Cobourg [Ontario] Museum Foundation provided rare views from their collections as well.

Most of the images credited to the author's collection were obtained from the Canadian Pacific Archives throughout the fourteen years that I worked there, during which time the department's staff provided thousands of historical photographs at no charge to researchers, movie-makers, magazine and book authors, historical societies and associations, and others as an exercise in public relations, which gained increased exposure with the CPR's travelling clientele and much good will from the man on the street. Many of these images should still be available from Exporail, where the CPR's former holdings are now housed.

The late Omer Lavallee, the CPR's former corporate historian and a recognized authority on Canadian transportation matters, also gave me several copies for my own use from his personal photo collection, while he was engaged in writing the celebrated history of CPR's construction years entitled *Van Horne's Road*. And I have added to my own files over the years with images given to me by friends and others that I have purchased from private dealers and members of the public and through online websites.

On a more personal note, I would like to thank Paul Clegg, Jim Lanigan, and Don Thomas—all friends and colleagues from the National Dream Legacy Society—along with my lovely wife, Erika Watters, for proofreading the manuscript for *New World Dreams* and offering useful suggestions. In addition, I'm grateful to Jim for allowing me to copy several images from his own collection of brochures and documents relating to Canadian immigration and colonization, and to my fellow researcher, CPR pensioner and co-volunteer at the Glenbow, Doug Phillips, who generously shared hard-to-find images of Canadian Pacific Railway rolling stock from his personal collection, as well as his encyclopedic knowledge of railway passenger equipment. Lastly, I'm indebted to graphic artist Dave Kromand of Breathe Communications for executing professional digitized maps and other images from my own rough sketches, and to Rick Robinson for scans.

Thank you one and all.

NOTES

Chapter 1: This Land Is Your Land

1. Statutes of Canada, 44 Victoria, chapter 1 (1881).
2. The president of the CPR, George Stephen, and his cousin and fellow syndicate member, Donald Smith, would put up much of their personal fortunes to get the railway through rough financial times. In the 1870s, Sandford Fleming, a government surveyor and engineer, estimated the price of constructing the national transcontinental to be about $100 million. By the time the last spike was driven in 1886, the overall cost would be even greater.
3. Statutes of Canada, 44 Victoria, chapter 1 (1881).
4. Shelagh D. Grant, *Polar Imperative* (Vancouver: Douglas & McIntyre, 2010), 144.
5. Wikipedia, "Rupert's Land." en.wikipedia.org/wiki/Rupert%27s_Land.
6. Andrew McIntosh and Shirlee Anne Smith, "Rupert's Land," *The Canadian Encyclopedia*. thecanadianencyclopedia.ca/en/article/ruperts-land.
7. Bob Beal and Rod Macleod, *Prairie Fire: The 1885 North-West Rebellion* (Toronto: McClelland & Stewart, 1984), 49.
8. Ibid.
9. Statutes of Canada, 44 Victoria, chapter 1 (1881).
10. Douglas Barnett, "The Deville Era: Survey of the Western Interior of Canada," *Alberta History* 48, no. 2 (Spring 2000): 19.
11. Statutes of Canada, 44 Victoria, chapter 1 (1881).
12. *London Truth*, September 1, 1881.
13. W.L. Morton, "Gladman, George," *Dictionary of Canadian Biography*, 9. biographi.ca/en/bio/gladman_george_9E.html.
14. Pierre Berton, *The National Dream* (Toronto: McClelland & Stewart, 1970), 32.
15. Ibid., 35.
16. Ibid., 18.
17. Statutes of Canada, 33 Victoria, chapter 3 (1870).
18. Omer Lavallee, *Van Horne's Road* (Montreal: Railfare Enterprises, 1974), 60.
19. John Macoun, *The Autobiography of John Macoun, M.A., Canadian Explorer and Naturalist 1831-1920* (Ottawa: Ottawa Field-Naturalists Club, 1922), 185.
20. Thomas Shaughnessy to Sir Oliver Mowat, April 4, 1897, CPCA, Records Group 2, Shaughnessy letterbook 51, p. 785.
21. William Archibald MacIntosh, *Prairie Settlement: The Geographical Setting* (Toronto: MacMillan, 1934), 40.
22. Macoun, *Autobiography*, 182.
23. Ibid., 184-85.
24. John H. Archer, *Saskatchewan: A History* (Saskatoon: Western Producer Prairie Books, 1980), 69.
25. W. Kaye Lamb, *History of the Canadian Pacific Railway* (New York: Macmillan, 1977), 180.
26. Comments by Van Horne to the directors of the Canadian Pacific Railway were reported in the *Montreal Herald*, Sept. 27, 1884.
27. Lamb, *History of the CPR*, 112.
28. Ibid., 81.
29. In November 1924, Pearce wrote a lengthy memorandum for posterity in which he gave a brief synopsis of the history of the railway's main line as well as its Crow's Nest Pass Railway, CPCA.

30. James Daschuk, *Clearing the Plains: Disease, Politics of Starvation and the Loss of Aboriginal Life* (Regina: University of Regina Press, 2013), 108.

31. Statutes of Canada, 44 Victoria, chapter 1 (1881).

32. Bob Joseph, *21 Things You May Not Know About the Indian Act* (Saanichton: Indigenous Relations Press, 2018), 15.

33. Wabi Benais Mistatim Equay (Cynthia Bird), "The Numbered Treaties," *Canada's History*, drawing on Alexander Morris, *The Treaties of Canada with the Indians of Manitoba and the North-West Territories* (1880. canadashistory.ca/explore/settlement-immigration/the-numbered-treaties).

34. Treaty 7 Elders and Tribal Council with Walter Hildebrandt, Dorothy First Rider, and Sarah Carter, *The True Spirit and Original Intent of Treaty 7* (Montreal: McGill-Queen's University Press, 1996), 80.

35. Rodger D. Touchie, *Bear Child: The Life and Times of Jerry Potts* (Victoria: Heritage House, 2005), 224.

36. Treaty 7 Elders and Tribal Council, *True Spirit*, 74.

37. Father C. Scollen to Lieutenant Colonel A.G. Irvine, April 13, 1879, no. 14924, Indian Affairs Archives, Ottawa; quoted in Hugh A. Dempsey, *Crowfoot: Chief of the Blackfeet* (1972), 105, with a note that both men had been present at the treaty signing.

38. Lynda Gray, *First Nations 101: Tons of Stuff You Need to Know About First Nations People* (Vancouver: Adaawx Publishing, 2011), 166.

39. Hugh A. Dempsey, *The Great Blackfoot Treaties* (Victoria: Heritage House, 2015), 56.

40. Ibid., 59.

41. Ibid., 115-16.

42. Lamb, *History of CPR*, 87-88.

43. Charles Aeneas Shaw, *Tales of a Pioneer Surveyor* (Toronto: Longmans, 1970), 105.

44. The story is told by Pierre Berton, in his usual colourful manner, in the second volume of his history of the building of the Canadian Pacific Railway, *The Last Spike* (Toronto: McClelland & Stewart, 1971), 234.

45. Daschuk, *Clearing the Plains*, from Maureen Lux, *Medicine That Walks: Disease, Medicine and Canadian Plains Native People 1880-1930* (Toronto: University of Toronto Press, 2001), 141.

46. Hugh A. Dempsey, *The CPR West: The Iron Road and the Making of a Nation* (Vancouver: Douglas & McIntyre, 1984), 60.

47. Beal and Macleod, *Prairie Fire*, 76-77.

48. Egan to Van Horne, April 27, 1883, CPCA, Records Group 1, Van Horne correspondence.

49. D.J. Hall, *From Treaties to Reserves: The Federal Government and Native Peoples in Territorial Alberta, 1870-1905* (Montreal: McGill-Queen's University Press, 2015), 132-33.

50. Pierre Berton, *The Last Spike* (Toronto: McClelland & Stewart, 1971), 235.

51. Ibid., 236-37.

52. Dempsey, *The Great Blackfoot Treaties*, 148.

53. Treaty 7 Elders and Tribal Council, *True Spirit*, 166.

54. Letter from Dewdney to John A. Macdonald, June 28, 1883, Macdonald Papers, LAC.

55. Hall, *From Treaties to Reserves*, 192.

56. Donald B. Smith, *Seen but Not Seen: Influential Canadians and the First Nations from the 1840s to Today* (Toronto: University of Toronto Press, 2021), 82.

57. Gray, *First Nations 101*, 57.

58. Daschuk, *Clearing the Plains*, 104.

59. Ibid., 107.

60. Ibid., 124.

61. James B. Waldram et al., *Aboriginal Health in Canada* (Toronto: University of Toronto Press, 1995), 62.

62. Daschuk, *Clearing the Plains,* 164.

63. Berton, *Last Spike*, 404.

64. Dempsey, *The Great Blackfoot Treaties*, 182.

65. Berton, *Last Spike*, 232.

66. Le Roy Barnett, "How Buffalo Bones Became Big Business," *Canadian Geographical Journal* 88-89 (July/August 1974): 20-25.

67. Ibid.

68. Don C. McGowan, *Grassland Settlers* (Victoria: Cactus Publications, 1980), 23.

69. Barnett, "Buffalo Bones."

Chapter 2: Homesteaders, Speculators, and Urban Planners

1. *Calgary Herald*, August 3, 1929, the story "Progress of West Since Early Days Is Ably Reviewed" includes the reminiscences of land agent F.W. Russell.

2. *Manitoba Free Press*, October 24, 1881.

3. From a flyer advertising government lands, Image NA-1472-7, Glenbow Western Research Centre, University of Calgary.

4. Reverse side of flyer advertising government lands, Image NA-1472-8, Glenbow Western Research Centre, University of Calgary.

5. *Manitoba Free Press*, May 5, 1881.

6. Cited in Kaye Lamb, *History of the Canadian Pacific Railway* (New York: Macmillan, 1977), 216; emphasis in original.

7. Barry Broadfoot, *The Pioneer Years 1895–1914: Memories of Settlers Who Opened the West* (Toronto: Doubleday, 1976), 28.

8. Fort Garry was a North West Company post named Fort Gibraltar until that fur-trading company merged with the Hudson's Bay Company in 1821.

9. The trading centres set up by fur-trading companies were known as factories. They were called factories not because anything was manufactured there but because the officials of the companies were called factors.

10. Irene M. Spry, *The Palliser Expedition: The Dramatic Story of Western Canadian Exploration 1857–1860* (Calgary: Fifth House, 1963), 38.

11. John Thomas Culliton, *Assisted Emigration and Land Settlement* (Montreal: McGill University Press, 1928), 23.

12. The 1871 Census was the first regularly scheduled collection of national statistics. However, enumerators only collected detailed information for Ontario, Quebec, Nova Scotia, and New Brunswick. Population figures for Manitoba, BC, and the Northwest Territories were still rough estimates.

13. Secretary, Department of Agriculture to William Hespeler, April 18, 1881, LAC, Records Group 17, Letterbook volume 2318, file 489, quoted in David Monteyne, *For the Temporary Accommodation of Settlers* (Montreal: McGill-Queen's University Press, 2021), 93.

14. *Manitoba Free Press*, March 10.

15. Berton, *Last Spike*, 52.

16. George Henry Ham, *Reminiscences of a Raconteur* (Toronto: The Musson Book Co., 1921), 57.

17. *Winnipeg Sun*, March 3, 1882, quoting from the *Ottawa Free Press*.

18. *Winnipeg Times*, June 14, 1882.

19. *Toronto Globe*, March 21, 1882.

20. Monteyne, *Temporary Accommodation*, 100.

21. Arthur S. Morton, *History of Prairie Settlement* (Toronto: MacMillan, 1933), 23.

22. Berton, *Last Spike*, 52.

23. David Laurence Jones, *Tales of the CPR* (Calgary: Fifth House, 2002), 43.

24. Ibid., 44.

25. Eileen M. McFadden, "Instant City: The Birth of Brandon," *Beaver,* Summer 1982, 18.

26. "Brandon Was Created by the CPR," *Brandon Today*, November 22, 1989.

27. Ibid.

28. McFadden, "Instant City," 21.

29. *Manitoba Free Press*, January 2, 1882.

30. Lavallee, *Van Horne's Road*, 70.

31. Berton, *Last Spike*, 103.

32. McFadden, "Instant City," 20.

33. Hartwell Bowsfield, "Early Days in Brandon," *Manitoba Pageant* 3, no. 1 (January 1957): 14.

34. *Manitoba Free Press*, December 24, 1881, quoting a story from the *London Morning Advertiser*.

35. Berton, *Last Spike*, 79.

36. Report of Commissioners in Rejoint Townships, Department of the Interior, Ottawa, December 1900, Glenbow Western Research Centre, University of Calgary.

37. Charles S. Lee, ed., *The Canada North-West Land Company (Limited): Land to Energy, 1882–1982* (Calgary: Canada Northwest Energy, 1982), 8.

38. Ibid., 12.

39. Donna McDonald, *Lord Strathcona: A Biography of Donald Alexander Smith* (Toronto: Dundurn Press, 2002), 308.

40. Ibid., 308.

41. Alexander Reford, "Smith, Donald Alexander, 1st Baron Strathcona and Mount Royal," *Dictionary of Canadian Biography*, 14. biographi.ca/en/bio/smith_donald_alexander_14E.html.

42. Alexander Reford, "Richard Bladworth, Angus," *Dictionary of Canadian Biography*, 15. biographi.ca/en/bio/angus_richard_bladworth_15E.html.

43. John A. Turley-Ewart, "Osler, Sir Edmund Boyd," *Dictionary of Canadian Biography*, 15. biographi.ca/en/bio/osler_edmund_boyd_15E.html.

44. Zenon Gawron, "Scarth, Willian Bain," *Dictionary of Canadian Biography*, 13. biographi.ca/en/bio/scarth_william_bain_13E.html.

45. Report of Commissioners in Rejoint Townships, Department of the Interior, Ottawa, December 1900, Glenbow Western Research Centre, University of Calgary.

46. Lavallee, *Van Horne's Road,* 77.

47. *Saskatchewan Herald* (Battleford), September 30, 1882.

48. J. William Brennan, *Regina: An Illustrated History* (Toronto: James Lorimer, 1989), 12.

49. Ibid., 14.

50. Monteyne, *Temporary Accommodation*, 106.

51. Brennan, *Regina*, 18.

52. P. Turner Bone, *When the Steel Went Through* (Toronto: MacMillan, 1947), 46.

53. Aileen Garland, "Gardens Along the Right of Way." *Manitoba Pageant* 22, no. 2 (Winter 1977): 6.

54. Ibid., 6-7.

55. Ronald Rees, *New and Naked Land: Making the Prairies Home* (Saskatoon: Western Producer Prairie Books, 1988), 118.

56. Douglas E. Barnett, "The Deville Era: Survey of the Western Interior of Canada," *Alberta History* 48, no. 2 (Spring 2000): 21.

57. Max Foran, "Choosing the Calgary Townsite: The C.P.R. and Other Interested Parties," *Fort Calgary Quarterly* 6, no. 4 (1986): 12.

58. Ibid., 13.

59. John Egan to William Van Horne, August 1, 1883, CPCA, Records Group 1, Van Horne correspondence, file 2056.

60. Lee, *Canada North-West Land Company*, 14.

61. John McTavish to William Scarth, (forwarded by CPR secretary Charles Drinkwater), CPCA, Records Group 1, Van Horne correspondence, file 9724.

62. Ibid.

63. Ibid.

64. William Pearce, "Reservation of Land at Calgary," *Alberta History* 27, no. 2 (Spring 1879): 26.

65. Lee, *Canada North-West Land Company*, 38.

66. James B. Hedges, *Building the Canadian West: The Land and Colonization Policies of the Canadian Pacific Railway* (New York: MacMillan, 1939), 37-38.

67. Ibid., 39.

68. Ibid., 40-41.

Chapter 3: A Hard Sell

1. Simon M. Evans, "The Origin of Ranching in Western Canada: American Diffusion or Victorian Transplant?" *Great Plains Quarterly* (Spring 1983): 82. The order-in-council was an amendment of the 1872 Dominion Land Act.

2. Jimmy M. Skaggs, *Prime Cut: Livestock Raising and Meatpacking in the United States, 1607-1983* (Texas: A&M Press, 1986), xx.

3. David H. Breen, "Ranching History," *The Canadian Encyclopedia*, 2009. thecanadianencyclopedia.ca/en/article/ranching-history.

4. Evans, *Origin of Ranching*, 80.

5. Ibid., 83.

6. Ibid., 84.

7. Barry Potyondi, *In Palliser's Triangle: Living in the Grasslands, 1850-1930* (Saskatoon: Purich Publishing, 1995), 50.

8. Craig Brown, ed., *The illustrated History of Canada* (Toronto: Lester & Orpen Dennys, 1987), 358.

9. Byfield, Ted, ed., *Alberta in the 20th Century*, vol. 1, *The Great West Before 1900* (Edmonton: United Western Communications, 1991), 215.

10. Ibid., 217.

11. Ian MacLachlan, "The Historical Development of Cattle Production in Canada" (1996, 2006), unpublished manuscript, University of Lethbridge Research Repository. opus.uleth.ca/handle/10133/303.

12. Canadian Pacific Railway advertising booklet, "The Canadian North-West: Dairy Farming, Ranching, Mining" (1890), 39.

13. Ibid., 43.

14. Ibid., 40.

15. Canadian Pacific Railway pamphlet, "An Account of the Working and Results of the Canadian Pacific Railway Co's Experimental Farms" (Winnipeg, 1884).

16. Ibid.

17. George Stephen, Canadian Pacific Railway Official Memorandum, Montreal, December 12, 1882.

18. Experimental Farms Service, Canadian Department of Agriculture, "Fifty Years of Progress on Dominion Experimental Farms 1886-1936" (Ottawa: King's Printer, 1939), 20.

19. Canadian Pacific Railway pamphlet, "An Account."

20. Ibid.

21. *Canadian Society of Technical Agrologists (C.S.T.A.) Review*, no. 16, (March 1938).

22. Experimental Farms Service, "Fifty Years," 19.

23. Archer, *Saskatchewan*, 121.

24. Quoted in the report of Lieutenant Colonel Thomas Barwis (who visited the Northwest and the vicinity of Calgary, in particular, in the summer of 1884) with "valuable information for the intended settler."

25. Speech of A.W. Ross, M.P. for Lisgar, Ontario, to the House of Commons, June 19, 1885, on the subject of the Pacific Railway and its relations to the Canadian West.

26. [Toronto] *Globe*, June 13, 1884.

27. Potyondi, *In Palliser's Triangle*, 56.

28. Hedges, *Building the Canadian West*, 71.

29. Archer, *Saskatchewan*, 71.

30. Michael Dawe, "They Didn't All Homestead," *Alberta History* 51, no. 4 (Autumn 2003): 14+. Gale Academic OneFile (accessed April 7, 2023). https://o-link-gale-com.aupac.lib.athabascau.ca/apps/doc/A109578875/AONE?u=atha49011&sid=bookmark-AONE&xid=a107b7a3.

31. Philip Creighton, "Moore, John Thomas," *Dictionary of Canadian Biography*, 14. biographi.ca/en/bio.php?id_nbr=7608.

32. Dawe, "They Didn't All Homestead."

33. Hedges, *Building the Canadian West*, 71.

34. Norman Fergus Black, *A History of Saskatchewan and the Old West* (Regina: North West Historical Co., 1913), published online by ElectricCanadian. electriccanadian.com/history/Saskatchewan/sask/chapter43.htm.

35. Archer *Saskatchewan*, 71.

36. John Eagle, *The Canadian Pacific and the Development of Western Canada* (Kingston: McGill-Queen's Press, 1989), 176-77.

37. From notes compiled by Jim Shields, assistant archivist, Canadian Pacific Corporate Archives, and Doug Phillips.

38. E.L. Meeres, *The Homesteads That Nurtured a City: The History of Red Deer, 1880-1905* (Red Deer: Red Deer and District Museum Society, 1977), 54.

39. Hedges, *Building the Canadian West*, 108.

40. *Gananoque Reporter*, May 1886.

41. Van Horne to McTavish, December 17, 1884, CPCA, Records Group 1, Van Horne correspondence.

42. D. Carskaden (*The Times*, Chicago) to Egan, January 6, 1885, Canadian Pacific Corporate Archives, Records Group 1, Van Horne correspondence.

43. Hedges, *Building the Canadian West*, 113.

44. Armstrong to Shaughnessy, September 14, 1885, CPCA, Records Group 2, Thomas Shaughnessy correspondence.

45. Van Horne to Daly, December 10, 1894, CPCA, Records Group 1, Van Horne correspondence.

46. Report of a CPR travelling passenger agent to colonization agent L.O. Armstrong for the week ending Saturday, November 17, 1894, Canadian Pacific Corporate Archives, Records Group 1, Van Horne correspondence.

Chapter 4: The Call of the New World

1. Hedges, *Building the Canadian West*, 94-95.

2. Hugh Fraser, *A Trip to the Dominion of Canada* (Halifax: n.p., 1883), 29.

3. David Cruise and Alison Griffiths, *Lords of the Line: The Men Who Built the CPR* (New York: Viking, 1988), 99.

4. Stephen to Macdonald, February 26, 1882, Macdonald Papers, LAC.

5. Manitoba Historical Society, "Alexander Begg (1839-1897)." mhs.ca/docs/people/begg_a.shtml.

6. Hedges, *Building the Canadian West*, 95.

7. Ibid., 98.

8. *Manitoba Free Press*, February 4, 1886.

9. Stephen to Macdonald, December 13, 1881, Macdonald Papers, LAC.

10. Quoted in an address by George Hodge, manager of the CPR personnel department, to the Officers' Luncheon Club, Montreal, entitled "Sir William C. Van Horne, K.C.M.G.: The Story of His Contribution to Canadian Pacific History," February 19, 1936.

11. Dave McIntosh, "Go West Young Woman," *Beaver*, December 1992-January 1993, 38-39.

12. Rees, *New and Naked*, 16.
13. Ibid., 17.
14. Hedges, *Building the Canadian West*, 98.
15. *Canadian Gazette*, June 18, 1903.
16. Begg's report on the work of the CPR's emigration department in London, England, during the winter and spring 1883-84, CPCA *Canadian Gazette*, June 18, 1903.
17. *Canadian Gazette*, June 18, 1903.
18. Begg to Van Horne, May 15, 1886, CPCA, Records Group 1, Van Horne correspondence, file 13080.
19. Baker to Van Horne, September 12, 1885, CPCA, Records Group 1, Van Horne correspondence, file 10453.
20. *Canadian Gazette*, June 18, 1903.
21. Archer Baker, Report on British and Continental Emigration to Canada, 1885 to 1894, CPCA.
22. *Canadian Gazette*, June 18, 1903.
23. Ibid.
24. Baker to Van Horne, 1894, CPCA, Records Group 1, Van Horne correspondence.
25. *Manitoba Free Press*, January 30, 1891.
26. Van Horne to J.H. Redman, September 4, 1884, CPCA, Records Group 1, Van Horne letterbook 7, pp. 410-15.
27. Hedges, *Building the Canadian West*, 104.
28. Van Horne to R.V. Martinsen, November 21, 1884, CPCA, Records Group 1, Van Horne letterbook 8, pp. 689-92.
29. Van Horne to J.H. Redman, November 27, 1884, CPCA, Records Group 1, Van Horne letterbook 8, pp. 841-47.
30. Thomas E. Appleton, *Ravenscrag: The Allan Royal Mail Line* (Toronto: McClelland and Stewart, 1974), 123.
31. Mark Zuehlke, *Scoundrels, Dreamers & Second Sons* (Vancouver: Whitecap Books, 1994), 20.
32. Quoted in "Read this Pamphlet on Manitoba, The North-West Territory and the Provinces of Ontario and Quebec," published by the Allan Line in 1883.
33. From a late-nineteenth-century Beaver Line advertising card.
34. Ralph Allen, "The Land of Eternal Change," *Macleans Magazine,* June 25, 1955, 16.
35. John W. Niddrie, *Niddrie of the North-West: Memoirs of a Pioneer Canadian Missionary* (Edmonton: University of Alberta Press, 2000), 15-16.
36. Lavallee, *Van Horne's Road*, 22.
37. Daniel Oliver, "James J. Hill: Transforming the American Northwest," FEE Foundation for Economic Education, 2001. fee.org/articles/james-j-hill-transforming-the-american-northwest/.
38. Lavallee, *Van Horne's Road*, 23.
39. Douglas R. Phillips, "Historical Significance of Canadian Pacific Colonist Sleeping Car 2658," prepared for Heritage Park Historical Village, February 2008.
40. *Railway World*, July 1867.
41. *Manitoba Free Press*, Wednesday, August 27, 1884.
42. Douglas Sladen, *On the Cars and Off: Being the Journal of a Pilgrimage Along the Queen's Highway to the East, from Halifax in Nova Scotia to Victoria in Vancouver's Island* (Ward, Lock & Bowden, 1895), 228.
43. *Saskatchewan History* 6, no. 1 (Winter 1953): 3.
44. Van Horne to Egan, December 10, 1885, CPCP, Records Group 1, Van Horne letterbook 14, pp. 548-50.
45. *Daily State Democrat* (Lincoln, Nebraska), August 20, 1887.
46. *Winnipeg Daily Times*, March 11, 1881.
47. *Manitoba Free Press*, May 14, 1881.
48. The location in the Lake Nipissing District known as Callander in the 1880s is now called Bonfield. Another Town of Callander is just west of there.
49. Lamb, *History of the CPR*, 94-97.
50. Ibid., 97.
51. Ibid., 101.
52. Text on a Canadian Pacific Steamship Line poster, printed by the American Bank Note Company, of New York, for the 1884 inauguration of service.
53. *Owen Sound Advertiser*, April 24, 1884.
54. Van Horne to John Lowe, March 14, 1884, CPCA, Records Group 1, Van Horne letterbook 5, pp. 98-99.
55. Van Horne to Whyte, March 27, 1884, CPCA, Records Group 1, Van Horne letterbook 5, p. 261. William Whyte was at that time general superintendent of the Ontario & Quebec Railway, headquartered in Toronto.
56. Van Horne to Whyte, April 28, 1884, CPCA, Records Group 1, Van Horne letterbook 12, pp. 641-43.
57. David Laurence Jones, *Famous Name Trains: Travelling in Style with the CPR* (Calgary: Fifth House, 2006), 110.
58. Ibid., 111.
59. Ibid., 112.

Chapter 5: True Believers Head West

1. Michelle Cabana, background to R.L. Richardson, *British Association Report of Their Visit to the Canadian North-West* (Winnipeg: McIntyre Bros, 1884), online at Bell Barn Society, bellbarn.ca/british-association-visit-to-the-bell-farm-1884.

2. R.L. Richardson, *British Association Report of Their Visit to the Canadian North-West* (Winnipeg: McIntyre Bros, 1884), online at Bell Barn Society, bellbarn.ca/british-association-visit-to-the-bell-farm-1884.

3. Berton, *Last Spike*, 287.

4. Archer, *Saskatchewan*, 72.

5. Marquis of Lorne, K.T., *Canadian Life and Scenery with Hints to Intended Emigrants and Settlers* (London: The Religious Tract Society, 1886), 164-65.

6. John Hawkes, *The Story of Saskatchewan and its People* (Chicago: S.J. Clarke Publishing, 1924), xx.

7. W.A. Waiser, "Bell, William Robert," in *Dictionary of Canadian Biography* Vol. 14 (University of Toronto/Universite Laval, 2003) accessed October 25, 2020. biographi.ca/en/bio/bell_william_robert_14E.html.

8. *Moose Jaw News and Qu'Appelle Record*, October 10, 1884.

9. LAC, Department of the Interior, Dominion Lands Branch (Lister-Kaye Papers), volume 93, file no. 80274.

10. Don C. McGowan, *Grassland Settlers: The Swift Current Region during the Era of the Ranching Frontier* (Victoria: Cactus Publications, 1980), 58-59.

11. Ibid., 61.

12. Ibid., 61-62.

13. Archives Society of Alberta, "76 Ranch." albertaonrecord.ca/76-ranch.

14. Hedges, *Building the Canadian West*, 123.

15. Alexander McPherson to Mr. Fyffe, July 2, 1883, from "Letters of Emigrants from the Property of Lady Gordon-Cathcart in the Long Island," Appendix A-xxxii of *Napier Commission in the Outer Hebrides*. napier-outerhebrides.blogspot.ca/2010/08/appendix-xxxii.html.

16. Wapella History Book Committee, *Mingling Memories: A History of Wapella and Districts* (Altona, MB.: Friesen Printers, 1979), 207.

17. Lee, *Canada North-West Land Company*, 17.

18. Salina MacDonald, from "Letters of Emigrants from the Property of Lady Gordon-Cathcart in the Long Island," Appendix A-xxxii of *Napier Commission in the Outer Hebrides*. napier-outerhebrides.blogspot.ca/2010/08/appendix-xxxii.html.

19. Bert McKay, "The Crofters from the Western Isles," *The Western Producer* (Thursday, December 5, 1974).

20. Black, *History of Saskatchewan*.

21. *The Encyclopedia of Saskatchewan*. esask.uregina.ca.

22. Jane McCracken, "Cannington Manor," 2006, *The Canadian Encyclopedia*, thecanadianencyclopedia.ca/en/article/cannington-manor.

23. Berton, *Last Spike*, 222.

24. Archer, *Saskatchewan*, 123-24.

25. Statutes of Canada, 44 Victoria, chapter 1 (1881), Clause 15.

26. Lamb, *History of the CPR*, 157.

27. Ibid., 158.

28. Crystal City Chamber of Commerce, "A Brief History of Crystal City." web.archive.org/web/20170307220705/www.crystalcitymb.ca/profile/history.html.

29. Chester Martin, "Dominion Lands Policy," in *Canadian Frontiers of Settlement*, ed. W.A. Mackintosh (Toronto: MacMillan, 1938), 77-80.

30. *Manitoba Free Press*, December 20, 1883.

31. Alex Campbell, "The Manitoba and North Western Railway," *Manitoba Co-operator*, October 11, 2017. manitobacooperator.ca/country-crossroads/the-manitoba-and-north-western-railway.

32. Andrew A. Marchbin, "Early Emigration from Hungary to Canada," *Slavonic Review* 13, no. 37 (July 1943): 129-30.

33. Hedges, Building the Canadian West, 119.

34. Ibid., 119-20.

35. Wikiwand, "Langeburg, Saskatchewan." wikiwand.com/en/Langenburg,_Saskatchewan.

36. Hedges, *Building the Canadian West,* 122.

37. Meeres, *Homesteads,* 53.

38. Ibid., 74.

39. Ibid., 71.

40. *Calgary Herald*, July 22, 1890.

41. House of Commons Debates, May 5, 1890, 4419-21.

42. R. Douglas Francis, "Establishment of the Parry Sound Colony," *Alberta History* 29, no. 1 (Winter 1981): 23-24.

43. Michael J. Dawe, *Red Deer: The Memorable City* (Red Deer: City of Red Deer, 2013), 82.

44. Meeres, *Homesteads*, 149.

45. F. Marie Imandt, "Among Canadian Settlers," *Alberta History* (Winter 2019): 16.

46. Ibid., 17.

47. *Calgary Herald*, April 24, 1894.

48. *Manitoba Free Press*, December 21, 1889.

49. Ibid.

50. Douglas N.W. Smith, "Passenger Service on CP's Maine Line to the Maritimes," *Passenger Train Journal* (June 1989): 17.

51. Stephen to Macdonald, September 11, 1889, from Joseph Pope, *Correspondence of Sir John Macdonald: Selections from the Correspondence of the Right Honourable Sir John Alexander Macdonald, G.C.B.: First Prime Minister of the Dominion of Canada* (Toronto: Doubleday, Page & Company, 1921), 455.

52. Macdonald to Stephen, September 13, 1889, from Pope, *Correspondence of Sir John Macdonald*, 455-56.

53. Van Horne to Macdonald, February 4, 1891, CPCA, Records Group 1, Van Horne correspondence.

54. Van Horne to the Honourable J.B. Plumb, April 4, 1884, CPCA, Records Group 1, Van Horne letterbook 5, pp. 418-23.

55. William McGirr to Edgar Dewdney, April 11, 1892, Glenbow Western Research Centre/University of Calgary, Canadian Pacific Settlement and development fonds, file M-320, p. 2251.

56. *Calgary Herald*, October 24, 1893.

57. CPR pamphlet, "Manitoba and the North-West territories: Advice to Settlers," 1890.

58. *Calgary Herald*, October 20, 1893.

59. Broadfoot, *Pioneer Years*, 28.

60. Van Horne to Kipling, April 12, 1908, Van Horne fonds, Archives and Documentation Centre of the Canadian Railway Historical Association, Exporail: The Canadian Railway Museum.

61. *Daily State Democrat* (Lincoln, Nebraska), August 20, 1887.

62. Broadfoot, *Pioneer Years*, 116.

63. Berton, *Last Spike*, 223.

64. *Globe*, April 2, 1885.

65. Beal and Macleod, *Prairie Fire*, 32.

66. Lewis G. Thomas, ed., *The Prairie West to 1905: A Canadian Sourcebook* (Oxford: Oxford University Press, 1975), 337.

67. Broadfoot, *Pioneer years*, 240.

68. Anonymous, *The British Colonist in North America: A Guide for Intended Emigrants* (London: Swan Sonnenschein, 1890), 2.

69. *Lethbridge News*, quoted in Ted Byfield, ed., *Alberta in the 20th Century: The Great West Before 1900* (Edmonton: United Western Communications, 1991), 235.

70. Frimann B. Anderson, *Immigration and Settlement on Vacant Lands in Manitoba and North-West* (Winnipeg: n.p., 1887), 10.

71. Ernest Way Elkington, *Canada: The Land of Hope* (London: A and C Black, 1910), 90.

72. Byfield, *Alberta*, 246.

73. *Saskatchewan Herald*, November 17, 1888.

74. *Medicine Hat News*, July 6 and July 13, 1899.

75. Hamilton to Van Horne, October 25, 1894, CPCA, Records Group 1, Van Horne correspondence, file 78150.

76. Broadfoot, *Pioneer Years*, 240.

77. Lavallee, *Van Horne's Road*, 122.

78. Charles W. Anderson, *Grain: The Entrepreneurs* (Winnipeg: Watson & Dwyer, 1991), 2-3.

79. Ibid., 3.

80. Van Horne to Norquay, February 4, 1884, CPCA, Records Group 1, Van Horne letterbook 4, pp. 677-78.

81. Van Horne to Free Press, December 24, 1883, CPCA, Records Group 1, Van Horne letterbook 4, pp. 10-26.

82. Ibid., 10-26.

83. Anderson, *Entrepreneurs*, 135.

84. D.B. Hanna, *Trains of Recollection* (Toronto: MacMillan, 1924), 76.

85. Anderson, *Entrepreneurs*, 134.

86. G.R. Stevens, *Ogilvie in Canada: Pioneer Millers 1801-1951* (privately published, 1951), 28-30.

87. Begg to Van Horne, January 8, 1885, CPCA, Records Group 1, Van Horne correspondence, file 8216.

88. Anderson, *Entrepreneurs*, 7.

Chapter 6: The Twentieth Century Belongs to Canada

1. *Montreal Gazette*, February 24, 1891.

2. Ibid.

3. Van Horne to Laurier, 1896. Quoted in Walter Vaughn, *The Life and Work of Sir William Van Horne* (New York: The Century Co., 1920), 270.

4. Hedges, *Building the Canadian West*, 116.

5. David J. Hall, "Sir Clifford Sifton," *The Canadian Encyclopedia*, 2008. thecanadianencyclopedia.ca/en/article/sir-clifford-sifton; David J. Hall, "Sifton, Sir Clifford," *Dictionary of Canadian Biography*, 15. biographi.ca/en/bio/sifton_clifford_15E.html.

6. John Murray Gibbon, *Steel of Empire* (Toronto: McClelland & Stewart, 1935), 347.

7. 60-61 Victoria, Chapter 5, 29 June 1897 (Crow's Nest Pass Agreement).

8. Pierre Berton, *The Promised Land* (Toronto: McClelland & Stewart, 1984), 14.

9. Howard Palmer, *The Settlement of the West* (Calgary: University of Calgary/Comprint Publishing, 1977), 77.

10. Wendy Owen, "The Last Best West: The 'Wheat King' and the New Farmers," *Beaver*, June-July 1991, 33.

11. Ibid., 31-33.

12. Ralph Allen, "The Land of Eternal Change," *Maclean's Magazine*, June 25, 1955, 12.

13. MacEwan, *Eye Opener Bob*, 33.

14. Gladys M. Rowell, "Memories of an English Settler," *Alberta History* 29, no. 2 (Spring 1981): 14.

15. Sir Clifford Sifton, K.C.M.G., "The Immigrants Canada Wants," *Maclean's Magazine,* April 1, 1922, 16.

16. Ibid., 16.

17. Berton, *Promised Land*, 5.

18. Hedges, *Building the Canadian West*, 132.

19. John W. Dafoe, *Clifford Sifton in Relation to His Times* (Toronto: Macmillan, 1931), 320.

20. Ibid., 320.

21. Jaroslav Petryshyn, "Canadian Immigration and the North Atlantic Trading Company 1889-1906: A Controversy Revisited," *Journal of Canadian Studies* 32, no. 3 (1997): 55-76.

22. Berton, *Promised Land*, 227-28.

23. Petryshyn, "Canadian Immigration," 55-76.

24. Berton, *Promised Land*, 229.

25. Sifton, *Immigrants*, 16.

26. P.J. Lazartowich, "Ukrainian Pioneers in Western Canada," *Alberta Historical Review* 5, no. 4 (Autumn 1957): 17.

27. Sandi Krawchenko Altner, "Stalwart Peasants in Sheepskin Coats." sandialtner.com/2011/04/02/stalwart-peasants-in-sheepskin-coats-2/.

28. Ibid.

29. Ibid.

30. *Alberta Tribune*, July 30, 1898.

31. *Manitoba Free Press*, May 24, 1899.

32. Berton, *Promised Land*, 76.

33. Ibid., 80.

34. Ibid., 81.

35. Lynne Bowen, "Barr: An All-English Agrarian Settlement in the Prairies," *The Canadian Encyclopedia*, 2013. thecanadianencyclopedia.ca/en/article/barr-colonists-muddle-through-feature.

36. Berton, *Promised Land*, 102.

37. Wikipedia, "Isaac Barr." en.wikipedia.org/wiki/Isaac_Barr.

38. Eric J. Holmgren, "Westward, the Land Beckons!: The Story of the Barr Colony and the Founding of Lloydminister," unpublished manuscript, 57. Glenbow Western Research Centre/University of Calgary, Canadian Pacific Railway Settlement and Development fonds, file M8857.

39. Berton, *Promised Land*, 116-17.

40. Ibid., 118-19.

41. Alice Rendell, "Letters from a Barr Colonist," *Alberta Historical Review* 11, no. 1 (Winter 1963): 13.

42. Ibid., 14.

43. Helen Evans Reid, "The Clerical Con Man Who Helped to Settle the West," *Maclean's Magazine*, December 14, 1963.

44. Ibid.

45. Rendell, "Letters," 15.

46. Ibid.

47. Reid, "Clerical Con Man."

48. *Manitoba Free Press*, April 8, 1903.

49. *Saskatoon Phoenix*, April 24, 1903.

50. *Winnipeg Tribune*, April 7, 1903.

51. *Globe*, April 13, 1903.

52. *Ottawa Citizen*, April 14, 1903.

53. *News*, April 14, 1903.

54. Holmgren, "Westward," 68A.

55. Reid, "Clerical Con Man."

56. Holmgren, "Westward," 66.

57. Berton, *Promised Land*, 122.

58. Holmgren, "Westward," 68.

59. Reid, "Clerical Con Man."

60. Ibid.

61. Berton, *Promised Land*, 135.

62. Laura A. Detre, "Immigration Advertising and the Canadian Government's Policy for Prairie Development, 1896–1918" (PhD diss., University of Maine, 2004), 191.

63. James S. Woodsworth, *Strangers within Our Gates* (Toronto: University of Toronto Press, 1972), 9.

64. George M. Gould to Van Horne, October 4, 1897, CPCA, Records Group 1, Van Horne correspondence, file 83186.

65. James H. Gray, *Boomtime: Peopling the Canadian Prairies* (Saskatoon: Western Producer Prairie Books, 1979), 34.

66. Hedges, *Building the Canadian West*, 133.

67. Berton, *Promise Land*, 171.

68. Harold Martin Troper, *Only Farmers Need Apply* (Toronto: Griffin House, 1972), 49.

69. Ibid., 52–53.

70. Hedges, *Building the Canadian West*, 134.

71. Berton, *Promised Land*, 172–73.

72. Hedges, *Building the Canadian West*, 140–41.

73. Donna McDonald, *Lord Strathcona: A Biography of Donald Alexander Smith* (Toronto: Dundurn Press, 2002), 450.

74. Ibid., 451.

75. Jean Bruce, "The Last Best West: Advertising for Immigrants to Western Canada," "Advertising in Britain, 1900–1916," Canadian Museum of History. historymuseum.ca/cmc/exhibitions/hist/advertis/ads3-02e.html.

76. Anthony Wilson-Smith, "Canada's Century: Sir Wilfrid Laurier's Bold Prediction," *The Canadian Encyclopedia*, 2016. thecanadianencyclopedia.ca/en/article/canadas-century-sir-wilfrid-lauriers-bold-prediction.

77. Gibbon, *Steel of Empire*, 361.

78. Archer, *Saskatchewan*, 123.

79. T.D. Regehr, *The Canadian Northern Railway: Pioneer Road of the Northern Prairies, 1895–1918* (Toronto: Macmillan, 1976), 22–26.

80. Ibid., 51.

81. Ibid., 74–75.

82. Ibid., 78–79.

83. Ibid., 228–29.

84. Gibbon, *Steel of Empire*, 361.

85. House of Commons Debates (July 30, 1903), 7559–60.

86. Ibid., (August 28, 1903), 10023, 10029.

87. Gibbon, *Steel of Empire*, 362.

Chapter 7: Growing the Business

1. Gibbon, *Steel of Empire*, 157.

2. *Manitoba Free Press*, November 2, 1901.

3. Hedges, *Building the Canadian West*, 161.

4. Ibid., 163.

5. F.T. Griffon to E.B. Osler, vice-president, Canada Northwest Land Company, February 21, 1902, quoted in Hedges, *Building the Canadian West*, 142.

6. *Manitoba Free Press*, May 14, 1902.

7. Hedges, *Building the Canadian West*, 146–47.

8. Ibid., 153–54.

9. Stephen to Macdonald, August 13, 1883, LAC, Macdonald Papers, vol. 267.

10. Andy Albert den Otter, *Civilizing the West: The Galts and the Development of Western Canada* (Edmonton: University of Alberta Press, 1982), 148–49.

11. Ibid., 107–8.

12. Ibid., 200–1.

13. Ibid., 153.

14. Ibid., 201.

15. *Lethbridge News*, June 8, 1892.

16. Stan Klassen and John Gilpin, "Alberta Irrigation in the Old and New Millennium," *Canadian Water Resources Journal* 24, no. 1 (1999).

17. David Breen, "Pearce, William," *Dictionary of Canadian Biography*, 15. biographi.ca/en/bio/pearce_william_15E.html.

18. C.A. Magrath, *The Galts, Father and Son: Pioneers in the Development of Southern Alberta* (Lethbridge: Lethbridge Herald, 1936), 15.

19. John Gilpin, *Quenching the Prairie Thirst* (Altona, MB: Friesen's Corporation, 2000), 20.

20. Pearce to Van Horne, Pearce Papers, University of Alberta Archives, quoted by John Gilpin in *Quenching the Prairie Thirst*, 20).

21. George G. Anderson, Report on the St. Mary's Irrigation Canal, Alberta, N.W.T., 1897, CPCA, Records Group 2, Shaughnessy correspondence, file 45236.

22. Andy Albert den Otter, *Irrigation in Southern Alberta 1882–1901* (Lethbridge: Whoop-up Country Chapter, Historical Society of Alberta, 1975), 15.

23. Shaughnessy to Galt, January 5, 1898, CPCA, Records Group 2, Shaughnessy letterbooks.

24. Den Otter, *Civilizing the West*, 226.

25. *Calgary Herald*, July 13, 1894.

26. McDonald, *Lord Strathcona*, 478.

27. Ibid., 400.

28. Canadian Pacific Railway Company, *The Canadian Pacific Railway Company's Irrigation Project: A Handbook of Information Regarding this Undertaking* (Victoria: Colonist Presses, 1906).

29. Van Horne to Macdonald, October 28, 1890, Macdonald Papers, C-1690, pp. 13189-96.

30. C.P.R. Report, 1902; Shaughnessy to the shareholders, October 1, 1902.

31. Claude Gardiner, *Letters from an English Rancher* (Calgary: Glenbow-Alberta Institute, 1988), 60.

32. Shaughnessy to E.B. Osler, February 23,1903, CPCA, Records Group 2, Shaughnessy letterbooks.

33. Lamb, *History of the CPR*, 245.

34. *Montreal Gazette*, February 18, 1903.

35. *Montreal Gazette*, February 24, 1903.

36. Gibbon, *Steel of Empire*, 359.

37. *Financier and Bullionist*, February 26, 1903.

38. Baker to Shaughnessy, February 25, 1903, CPCA, Records Group 2, Shaughnessy correspondence, file 7039.

39. George Musk, *Canadian Pacific: The Story of the Famous Shipping Line* (London: David & Charles, 1981), 23.

40. *Lloyd's List*, April 7, 1903.

41. Broadfoot, *Pioneer Years*, 5.

42. Berton, *Promised Land*, 49.

43. Musk, *Canadian Pacific*, 24.

44. Ibid., 23.

45. Heather Robertson, "Salt of the Earth," *Weekend Magazine* (*The Albertan* supplement) 24, no. 43 (October 26, 1974): 7.

46. Musk, *Canadian Pacific*, 27.

47. *Montreal Gazette*, May 14, 1906.

48. Colonel George H. Ham, "There Were Giants in Those Days," *Maclean's Magazine*, March 15, 1921, 52-53.

49. Ruth Steeves, *No Englishmen Need Apply* (Mill Bay, BC: The Cowichan Press, 2008), 21.

50. Lamb, *History of the CPR*, 248.

51. *Saint John Daily Telegraph*, October 8, 1909.

52. Lamb, *History of the CPR*, 248.

53. C.P.R. Report, 1913; Shaughnessy to shareholders, October 1, 1913.

54. Woodsworth, *Strangers*, 9.

55. *Canadian Pacific Staff Bulletin*, November 1, 1937, 5.

56. *Calgary Herald*, April 18, 1904.

57. "Narrative of a Journey from Liverpool to Calgary," *Alberta History* 32, no. 3 (Summer 1984): 13.

58. Arthur E. Copping, *The Golden Land: The True Story of British Settlers in Canada* (London: Hodder and Stroughton, 1911), 19.

59. *Winnipeg Free Press*, June 28, 1904.

60. Letter from Jeannie, the great aunt of Christine Pickess of Brentwood, Essex in England. Jeannie sailed to Canada from Glasgow on May 22, 1909. A copy of the letter was forwarded to Canadian Pacific Railway Archives in June 1999.

Chapter 8: The Boom Years

1. Thomas Shaughnessy, statement from the "Office of the President," May 1, 1901, CPCA, Records Group 2, Shaughnessy letterbook, 74.

2. *Railway and Shipping World*, January 1904.

3. Nanton to E.B. Osler, April 13, 1901, cited in John Eagle, *The Canadian Pacific Railway and the Development of Western Canada* (Montreal: McGill-Queen's University Press, 1989), 74.

4. *Canadian Railway and Marine World*, May 1914, 216.

5. Shaughnessy to L. Zuckermandel, February 11,1902, CPCA, Records Group 2, Shaughnessy letterbook, 76.

6. "Colonel J.S. Dennis An Empire Builder Dies at West Coast," *Canadian Pacific Staff Bulletin*, January 1, 1939.

7. Meeres, *Homesteads*, 31.

8. A. Mitchner, "The Bow River Scheme," in *The CPR West: The Iron Road and the Making of a Nation*, ed. Hugh Depsey (Vancouver: Douglas & McIntyre, 1984), 264.

9. George Freeman (compiler), *Flow Beyond the Weir: The Jubilee Edition 1944-1994*, 22-24.

10. Peter L. Neufeld, "Colonel J.S. Dennis: Catalyst of Prairie Development," *Western Producer*, April 12, 1973.

11. Hedges, *Building the Canadian West*, 176.

12. Ibid., 178.

13. Ibid., 178.

14. A. Griffin, "The D.N.R. and Its Part in the Development of the West," *Canadian Pacific Staff Bulletin* (n.d.): 4.

15. Grant MacEwan, "The Birth of Twin Provinces," *Beaver*, Summer 1980, 14.

16. Ibid., 15-17.

17. David J. Hall, "Oliver, Frank," *Dictionary of Canadian Biography.* biographi.ca/en/bio/oliver_frank_16E.html.

18. Troper, *Only Farmers*, 22.

19. "Immigration Act, 1906," Canadian Museum of Immigration at Pier 21. https://pier21.ca/research/immigration-history/immigration-act-1906.

20. Hall, "Oliver, Frank."

21. Valerie Knowles, *Strangers at Our Gates: Canadian Immigration and Immigration Policy, 1540-2015* (Toronto: Dundurn, 2016), 109-10.

22. Department of Interior, Western Canada, 10.

23. Gray, *Boomtime*, 42-46.

24. Majorie Wilkins Campbell, *The Silent Song of Mary Eleanor* (Saskatoon: Western Producer Prairie Books, 1983), 4-5.

25. Ibid., 5.

26. Steeves, *No Englishmen*, 7-15.

27. Ibid., 29.

28. Ibid., 29-30.

29. Robert W. Sloan, "The Canadian West: Americanization or Canadianization?" *Alberta Historical Review* 16, no. 1 (Winter 1968): 3.

30. Sir Clifford Sifton, "The Immigrants Canada Wants," *Maclean's Magazine*, April 1, 1922, 16.

31. "Immigration Prospects" (editorial), *Edmonton Bulletin*, January 21, 1905.

32. "High Grade Immigration" (editorial), *Lethbridge Herald*, November 15, 1905.

33. *Winnipeg Tribune*, July 6, 1907.

34. "The Heart of the Famous Saskatchewan Wheat Belt," booklet, Saskatoon and Western Land Company, 1906.

35. Andy Albert den Otter, "Adapting the Environment: Ranching, Irrigation, and Dry-land Farming in Southern Alberta, 1880-1914," *Great Plains Quarterly* 6, no. 3 (Summer 1986): 171-89.

36. "Manitoba, Alberta, Assiniboia, Saskatchewan: The Four Great Fertile Provinces of Western Canada Described and Illustrated," pamphlet, Canadian Pacific Railway, 1892.

37. Marc Choko and David Jones, *Posters of the Canadian Pacific* (Toronto: Firefly Books, 2004), 24.

38. Beckles Willson, *From Quebec to Piccadilly and Other Places: Some Anglo-Canadian Memories* (London: Jonathan Cape, 1929), 94.

39. Grand Trunk Railway pamphlet quoted in Ralph Allen, "The Land of Eternal Change," *Maclean's Magazine*, June 25, 1955, 14.

40. *Morning Post* [London], March 26, 1908; *Ottawa Journal*, March 28, 1908.

41. Ibid., April 23, 1908; April 25, 1908.

42. Gladys M. Rowell, "Memories of an English Settler," *Alberta History* 29, no. 2 (Spring 1981): 13.

43. Allen, "The Land of Eternal Change," 15.

44. Broadfoot, *Pioneer Years*, 31.

45. Lindalee Tracey, *A Scattering of Seeds: The Creation of Canada* (Toronto: McArthur & Company, 1999), 127.

46. "Immigrants Flooded into Saskatchewan Sixty Years Ago," *Saskatoon Star-Phoenix*, June 8, 1965.

47. Ibid.

48. Copping, *Golden Land*, 234.

49. *Calgary Tribune*, May 1, 1899.

50. Many CPR pamphlets in the late 1890s and early 1900s included this paragraph under the heading "Advice to Settlers"; other headings included such as "Homestead Regulations," "Choosing a Location," "Settlers' Effects" (Freight Regulations), "Available Lands," "Climate," etc.

51. "Words from the Women of Western Canada," CPR booklet, 1903, 3.

52. Ibid., 14.

53. Ibid., 25.

54. Sarah Carter, *Imperial Plots: Women, Land and the Spadework of British Colonialism on the Canadian Prairies* (Winnipeg: University of Manitoba Press, 2016), 143.

55. Ibid., 144.

56. Canadian Pacific Railway land sales database, Glenbow Western Research Centre/University of Calgary, glenbow.ucalgary.ca/archives-cpr-land-sales/.

57. biographi.ca/en/bio/oliver_frank_16E.html.

58. Carter, *Imperial Plots*, 53.

59. CPR European manager Archer Baker's letter to Charles Urban on May 6, 1902, cited in Greg Eamon, "Farmers, Phantoms and Princes: The Canadian Pacific Railway and Filmmaking from 1899-1919," *Cinemas (Journal of Film Studies)* 6, no. 1 (1995): 11-32, includes the more modest proposal. However, notes in the CPCA collection from CPR publicity man Norman Rankin indicate that Shaughnessy gave considerably more assistance, as does the list in *Urban Film Subjects* (London: Charles Urban Trading Company, 1903), which mentions the "special engine" assigned to the film crew. Eamon also erroneously identifies a "T. Bell" as being a CPR photographer.

60. Jones, *Tales of the CPR*, 186.

61. Sam Kula, "Western Settlement and Steam Movies," *Archivist* 12, no. 4 (1985): 6-8.

62. Jones, *Tales of the CPR*, 186-88.

63. *The Bioscope*, January 20, 1910, 12-17.

64. Jones, *Tales of the CPR*, 186.

65. Peter Morris, *Embattled Shadows: A History of Canadian Cinema, 1895-1939* (Montreal: McGill-Queen's University Press, 1978), 43.

66. Ibid., 223.

67. "Immigration Act, 1910," Canadian Museum of Immigration at Pier 21. pier21.ca/research/immigration-history/immigration-act-1910.

68. William Scott, "Immigration and Population," in *Canada and Its Provinces*, ed. Adam Shortt and Arthur Doughty. (Toronto: Publishers' Association of Canada, 1913), 7: 573.

69. Knowles, *Strangers*, 111.

70. *Globe*, September 24, 1896.

71. Hugh J.M. Johnston, *Jewels of the Qila: The Remarkable Story of an Indo-Canadian Family* (Vancouver: UBC Press, 2011), 20.

72. Troper, *Only Farmers*, 131.

73. Colin A. Thomson, "Dark Spots in Alberta," *Alberta History* 25, no. 4 (Autumn 1977): 31.

74. Troper, *Only Farmers*, 135.

75. Gwen Hook, The *Keystone Legacy: Recollections of a Black Settler* (Edmonton: Brightest Pebble Publishing, 1997), 33.

76. Troper, *Only Farmers*, 137.

77. Ibid., 145.

78. Thomson, "Dark Spots in Alberta," 35.

Chapter 9: The Last Best West

1. *Edmonton Bulletin*, November 25, 1905.

2. *The Railway and Shipping World*, April 1903, 139.

3. Douglas R. Phillips, "CP Colonists Cars and the Restoration of #1202," *Canadian Rail*, January-February 2009.

4. Ibid.

5. *Calgary Herald*, April 7, 1906.

6. Muriel Holden, "The Normans Come to Calgary," *Alberta History* 28, no. 3 (Summer 1980): 26.

7. Hedges, *Building the Canadian West*, 200.

8. *Canadian Gazette*, April 28 and June 16, 1910; May 25 and July 13, 1911.

9. Ibid., 207-10.

10. Herman Ganzevoort, *A Bittersweet Land: The Dutch Experience in Canada, 1890-1980* (Toronto: McClelland & Stewart, 1988), 14.

11. Ibid., 15.

12. Ibid., 46.

13. *Daily Mail* [London], January 10, 1910.

14. Ibid.

15. *Evening Standard*, March 23, 1910.

16. Gibbon, *Steel of Empire*, 371.

17. "Moving Pictures and Settlers," *Gleichen Call*, April 28, 1910, 7.

18. *Canadian Gazette*, May 5, 1910.

19. Ibid.

20. John Mather to Van Horne, March 6, 1885, CPCA, Records Group 1, Van Horne correspondence, file 8739.

21. Hamilton to Van Horne, October 25, 1894, CPCA Records Group 1, Van Horne correspondence, file 78150.

22. *Strathmore Standard*, October 9, 1909.

23. Dennis to Shaughnessy, August 15, 1910, CPCA, Records Group 2, Shaughnessy correspondence, file 93754.

24. Copping, *Golden Land*, 98.

25. *Calgary Herald*, July 13, 1911.

26. "More Ready-Made Farms," *Strathmore Standard*, September 3, 1910.

27. *Verdant Valleys—In and Around Lougheed* (Lougheed: Lougheed Women's Institute, 1972).

28. Elsa Lam, "A Fertile Wilderness: The Canadian Pacific Railway's Ready-Made farms, 1909-1914," *Journal of the Society for the Study of Architecture in Canada* 35, no. 1 (2010): 9. Settler quote and

anecdotes were originally printed in Frank Snowsell and Edwin Snowsell, "Starting Over on a Ready-made Farm, 1911-1916," *Western People*, no. 14, 1982.

29. Dennis to Shaughnessy, August 15, 1910, CPCA, Records Group 2, Shaughnessy correspondence.

30. Hedges, *Building the Canadian West,* 241.

31. Ibid., 242-43.

32. Ibid., 243.

33. Lam, "Fertile Wilderness," 9.

34. *Gleichen Call*, May 4, 1911. The ship was reported in the *Globe* to be the *Empress of Britain*, but it was actually the sister ship, *Empress of Ireland*. The full story of Miss May is told in great detail in Carter, *Imperial Plots*, 222-35.

35. Carter, *Imperial Plots*, 227-29.

36. Ibid., 230.

37. *Canadian Gazette*, December 22, 1910.

38. Hedges, *Building the Canadian West,* 225-26.

39. *Medicine Hat News*, January 5, 1911.

40. "Making Girl Farmers," *Gleichen Call*, April 21, 1910.

41. H.G. Ahern, "In Search of a Homestead," *Alberta Historical Review* 13, no. 2 (Spring 1965): 16.

42. "CPR-Irrigation Block, Bow River Valley, Southern Alberta, Canada," pamphlet, Canadian Pacific Railway, 1909.

43. "Some Recollections of the Site of Old Strathmore," an interview with Frank Bates in *Strathmore: The Village That Moved* (Strathmore: Strathmore Alberta History Book Committee, 1986).

44. T.M. Schulte, "See You at the Depot: A Nostalgic Look at Strathmore's Railway Station," in *Strathmore: The Village That Moved* (Strathmore Alberta History Book Committee, 1986).

45. "Agricultural Demonstration in the Bow Valley of Alberta," *Grain Growers Guide* 2, no. 36 (April 6, 1978).

46. *Canadian Gazette*, December 15, 1910.

47. Ibid.

48. Ibid.

49. L. James Dempsey, "The CPR Demonstration and Supply Farm, 1908-1944," *Alberta History* (Autumn 2011): 21.

50. George Freeman, "Canadian Pacific Railway Demonstration and Supply Farm," in*Strathmore: The Village That Moved* (Strathmore Alberta History Book Committee, 1986).

51. *Albertan*, September 27, 1911.

52. Hedges, *Building the Canadian West,* 261-64.

53. "The Movement to Canada," *Gleichen Call*, April 21, 1910, 4.

54. *The Railway and Shipping World*, no. 94 (December 1905): 571.

55. *The Albertan*, January 17, 1906.

56. Archer, *Saskatchewan*, 157.

57. *Olds Gazette*, December 6, 1912.

58. *Canadian Pacific Staff Bulletin*, no. 41, July 30, 1912, 4.

59. The original list of potential "illustration mixed farms" was published in *CP Staff Bulletin*, no. 41, July 30, 1912; an update in the August 1, 1914, edition of the *Bulletin* said that thirteen farms had been established; but a detailed report shows that only twelve were actually developed (Glenbow Western Research Centre/University of Calgary, Canadian Pacific Railway Settlement and Development fonds, file M2269-16).

60. Andre Sigel and James Hull, "Made in Canada!: The Canadian Manufacturers' Association's Promotion of Canadian-Made Goods, 1911-1921," *Journal of the Canadian Historical Association* 25, no. 1 (2014).

61. *The Standard* [Stavely, AB], June 13, 1912.

62. *Manitoba Free Press*, May 22, 1912.

63. den Otter, *Civilizing the West*, 307.

64. Gilpin, *Quenching*, 67-68.

65. Mary Wilma Hargreaves, *Dry Farming in the Northern Great Plains, 1900-1925* (Cambridge: Harvard University Press, 1957).

66. This was an anecdote told by Harry Cresswell, chief commissioner of CPR's Department of Immigration and Colonization, at a luncheon meeting of the Canada Colonization Association at Winnipeg, February 21, 1949.

67. Hedges, *Building the Canadian West,* 259.

68. *Popular Mechanics*, February 1913, 161; *Country Life*, February 26, 1913, 11.

69. *Strathmore Standard*, April 10, 1910.

70. Naismith to J. Murray, president of British "Ready-Made" Farmers Association, Lougheed, Alberta, March 15, 1913; and Naismith to Dennis, January 20, 1914, Glenbow Western Research Centre/University of Calgary, Canadian Pacific Railway Settlement and Development fonds, files M2269-18 and M2269-38.

71. Elsa Lam, "Fertile Wilderness," 12.

72. O'Farrell to Shaughnessy, June 26, 1913, CPCA, Records Group 2, Shaughnessy correspondence, file 101558.

73. Rutherford to Dennis (copy to Shaughnessy), July 25, 1913, CPCA, records Group 2, Shaughnessy correspondence, file 101558.

74. Most of the more well-known ready-made farm colonies are listed in studies such as Lam, "A Fertile Wilderness:," and Shona Gourlay, "Just Add People: CPR's Ready Made Farms," *Alberta History* 67, no. 4 (Autumn 2019): 2-7. The more obscure colonies within the irrigation block were identified in a year-end statement from the CPR's Department of Natural Resources, now at Glenbow Western Research Centre/University of Calgary, Canadian Pacific Railway Settlement and Development fonds, file M2269-58.

75. The ready-made farm in British Columbia is referenced in Glenbow Western Research Centre/University of Calgary, Canadian Pacific Railway Settlement and Development fonds, file M2269-13.

76. Gilpin, *Quenching*, 69.

77. Ibid., 69.

78. Renie Gross and Lea Nicoll Kramer, *Tapping the Bow* (Brooks: Eastern Irrigation District, 1985), 7.

79. *Bassano News*, May 26, 1911.

80. An anonymous family member produced a booklet about the trip of Johan and Judithe Wulff from Denmark to Canada in 1912–13. It was published in 1985 under the title *Johan and Judithe*.

81. Ibid., 28-29.

82. Ibid., 29-30.

83. Gross, *Tapping*, 37-38.

84. David Finch, *The Brooks Aqueduct: A Technological and Engineering History, 1912-79*, Environment Canada, Canada Parks Services Report Series 360 (1988), 64.

85. David Finch, *Much Brain and Sinew: The Brooks Aqueduct Story* (Brooks: Eastern Irrigation District, 1993), 40.

86. Simon Evans, "The Passing of a Frontier: Ranching in the Canadian West, 1882-1912" (PhD diss., University of Calgary, 1976), 58; quoted by A. Mitchner, "The Bow River Scheme," in Hugh Dempsey, ed., *The CPR West: The Iron Road and the Making of a Nation* (Vancouver: Douglas & McIntyre, 1984), 261.

87. Letter from M.L. Kropinak, secretary-treasurer for Village of Hussar, Alberta, to Eric J. Holmgren, Geographic Board of Alberta, January 21, 1972. Holgren was the author of *Place-Names in Alberta* (1972).

88. From a translation of "What We Found in Canada," in the Russian-language newspaper *Pacific Ocean*, published in San Francisco, September 2, 1914.

89. Ibid.

Chapter 10: A World in Disarray

1. James Davenport Whelpley, *The Problem of the Immigrant* (London: Chapman & Hill, 1905), 28.

2. Ibid., 37-39.

3. Gibbon, *Steel of Empire*, 371.

4. Musk, *Canadian Pacific*, 32.

5. *Financial Times*, April 23, 1913.

6. *Chicago Examiner*, October 19, 1913.

7. Gibbon, *Steel of Empire*, 372.

8. Omer Lavallee, "Our Austrian Adventure," *Spanner* [CPR employee publication], May 1957, 13.

9. Musk, *Canadian Pacific*, 235.

10. Ibid., 29.

11. "Memorandum of the personnel, organization and activities of the Department of Natural Resources of the Canadian Pacific Railway Company," Montreal, March 14, 1916, Glenbow Western Research Centre/University of Calgary, Canadian Pacific Railway Settlement and Development fonds, file M2269-430.

12. J.S. Dennis memorandum, presented the CPR Department of Natural Resources Advisory Committee, June 3, 1916, Glenbow Western Research Centre/University of Calgary, Canadian Pacific Railway.

13. *Canadian Pacific Staff Bulletin* 77A, June 1, 1915, 15.

14. Joseph A. Boudreau, "Western Canada's 'Enemy Aliens' in World War One," *Alberta Historical Review* 12, no. 1 (Winter 1964): 1.

15. Ibid., 2.

16. Shaughnessy to Martin Burrell, August 26, 1914, Borden Papers 674 (2), Library and Archives Canada.

17. Boudreau, "Western Canada," 3.

18. Ibid., 2.

19. William Pearce, William Pearce Manuscript, 32, unpublished manuscript reformatted by J.A. Jaffary of the Alberta Provincial Library in 1925, edited by William's grandson Doug Pearce in June 2013, in the Pearce [William] Papers, University of Alberta Archives, William Pearce Fonds, Accession #74-69-459.

20. J.S. Dennis memorandum, April 1, 1915, Glenbow Western Research Centre/University of Calgary, Canadian Pacific Railway Settlement and Development fonds, file M2269-459.

21. Ibid.

22. Beatty to Dennis, June 28, 1916, Glenbow Western Research Centre/University of Calgary, Canadian Pacific Railway Settlement and Development fonds, file M2269-459.

23. J.S. Dennis, Immigration and Colonization brief, Calgary, December 29, 1915, Glenbow Western Research Centre/University of Calgary, Canadian Pacific Railway Settlement and Development fonds, file M2269-459.

24. *Agricultural and Industrial Progress in Canada* [CPR Department of Colonization and Development at Montreal] 1, no. 1 (October 1919): 6.

25. *Montreal Gazette*, December 2, 1918.

26. *Montreal Gazette*, June 5, 1919.

27. *Agricultural and Industrial Progress in Canada* 1, no. 1 (October 1919): 6.

28. *Lethbridge Herald*, December 1, 1916.

29. *Agricultural and Industrial Progress in Canada* 1, no. 1 (October 1919): 6.

30. "Memorandum of proposed routine of C.P.R. Bureau of Canadian Information at New York, Chicago, and London," Glenbow Western Research Centre/University of Calgary, Canadian Pacific Railway Settlement and Development fonds, file M2269-472.

31. An Act to Incorporate Canadian National Railway Company and Respecting Canadian National Railways, 1919, S.C. 1919, c. 13. Archive.org, archive.org/details/actsofparl1919v01cana/page/36/mode/2up.

32. *Alberta Farmer*, May 20, 1920.

33. *Agricultural and Industrial Progress in Canada* 2, no. 7 (July 1920): 1.

34. Kelley, Ninette and Michael Trebilcock, *The Making of the Mosaic: A History of Canadian Immigration Policy* (Toronto: University of Toronto Press, 2010), 186–87.

35. *Agricultural and Industrial Progress in Canada* 2, no. 7 (July 1920): 122.

36. Ibid., 124.

37. *Montreal Herald*, September 27, 1920.

38. *Canada West Magazine*, n.d. (post 1917).

39. Jones, *Tales of the CPR*, 189.

40. Dennis to Chairman of Advisory Committee, Saskatchewan, May 12, 1921, Department of Immigration and Development, Glenbow Western Research Centre/University of Calgary, Canadian Pacific Railway Settlement and Development fonds, file M2269-472.

41. *Strathmore Standard*, August 3, 1921.

42. *Montreal Gazette*, March 21, 1922.

43. Potyondi, *In Palliser's Triangle*, 98.

44. *The U.F.A.: Official Organ of the United Farmers of Alberta* 2, no. 7 (April 16, 1923).

45. Naismith to Nanton, October 26, 1923, Glenbow Western Research Centre/University of Calgary, Canadian Pacific Railway Settlement and Development fonds, file M2269-511.

46. Naismith to Nanton, October 31, 1923, Glenbow Western Research Centre/University of Calgary, Canadian Pacific Railway Settlement and Development fonds, file M2269-511.

47. *Albertan*, October 31, 1923.

48. *Calgary Herald*, January 12, 1924.

49. *Albertan*, February 28, 1924.

50. *Popular Mechanics*, March 1924, 189.

51. *Montreal Gazette*, May 16, 1923.

52. Jones, *Tales of the CPR*, 141–42.

53. *Canadian Pacific Staff Bulletin* 196 (May 1, 1925): 25.

54. Musk, *Canadian Pacific*, 168.

55. Peter Pigott, *Sailing the Seven Seas: A History of the Canadian Pacific Line* (Toronto: Dundurn Press, 2010), 103.

56. P.A. O'Farrell (Shaughnessy's secretary) to Col. Dennis, from Grosse Isle, November 22, 1922; I.M.R. Sinclair (passenger) to A.D. MacTier, CPR vice-president, November 28, 1922.

57. Frank H. Epp, *Mennonites in Canada, 1920–1940: A People's Struggle for Survival* (Toronto: MacMillan, 1982), 139–79.

58. Ibid.

59. Hedges, *Building the Canadian West*, 369.

60. Ibid., 369.

61. Musk, *Canadian Pacific*, 24–25.

62. Epp, *Mennonites*, 139–79.

63. Musk, *Canadian Pacific*, 15; Hedges, *Building the Canadian West*, 374.

64. Jim Wilkie, *Metagama: A Journey from Lewis to the New World* (Toronto: Doubleday, 1987), 63.

65. Hebridean Connections, "Emigration on the SS *Metagama*." hebrideanconnections.com/historical-events/27104.

66. Wilkie, *Metagama*, 66.

67. Ibid., 80.

68. *Calgary Herald*, April 11 and 12, 1924.

Chapter 11: Spanning the World

1. Immigration statistics 1867–1987 from Canada Employment and Immigration Commission.

2. Kelley, *Making of the Mosaic*, 199.

3. Reg Whitaker, *Canadian Immigration Policy Since Confederation* (Ottawa: Department of Political Science, York University, 1991), 12.

4. Ibid., 13.

5. Ernie Bies, "My Parent's Journey to Becoming Canadians," June 12, 2019, OntarioHistory.org. ontariohistory.org/bies-parents.pdf.

6. *Calgary Herald*, August 10, 1925.

7. Bies, "My Parent's Journey."

8. Hedges, *Building the Canadian West*, 379.

9. Field supervisor, "General Report on the Clan Donald Colony, Vermilion, Alberta," November 1, 1926.

10. A number of relevant letters and newspaper translations on the topic of Russian immigration from Harbin, Japan, and Soviet Russia can be found at Glenbow Western Research Centre/University of Calgary, Canadian Pacific Railway Settlement and Development fonds, files M2269-676, 679, 712.

11. Flood, Whicher & Elves to CPR Department of Natural Resources, September 19, 1925, Glenbow Western Research Centre/University of Calgary, Canadian Pacific Railway Settlement and Development fonds, file M2269 79.

12. Grant Grams, "Der Volksverein Deutsch-Canadischer Katholiken: The Rise And Fall of a German-Catholic Cultural And Immigration Society, 1909-52," *The Catholic Historical Review* 99, no. 3 (July 2013): 480-98. jstor.org/stable/23565368.

13. Dennis to Forke, November 1, 1926.

14. Kelley, *Making of the Mosaic*, 214.

15. "To Canada Two Pounds," pamphlet, Canadian Pacific Railway, 1926, 3.

16. Phyllis Harrison, ed., *The Home Children* (Winnipeg: Watson & Dwyer, 1979), 259.

17. "To Canada Two Pounds," 1.7.

18. *Agricultural and Industrial Progress* 9, no. 9 (1927).

19. *Agricultural and Industrial Progress* 10, no. 9 (1928).

20. Central Womens' Colonization Board to applicant for domestic help, n.d., (1927), Glenbow Western Research Centre/University of Calgary, Canadian Pacific Railway Settlement and Development fonds, file M2269-1007.

21. Colley to Van Scoy, March 7, 1928, Glenbow Western Research Centre/University of Calgary, Canadian Pacific Railway Settlement and Development fonds, file M2269-732.

22. Ibid.

23. Colley to Van Scoy, April 30, 1928, Glenbow Western Research Centre/University of Calgary, Canadian Pacific Railway Settlement and Development fonds, file M2269-732.

24. Barbara Roberts, *Whence They Came: Deportation from Canada, 1900-1935* (Ottawa: University of Ottawa Press, 1988), 117-23.

25. Ibid., 120.

26. Draft agreement of Canadian Pacific Company and Hudson's Bay Company Land Settlement, August 24, 1928, Glenbow Western Research Centre/University of Calgary, Canadian Pacific Railway Settlement and Development fonds, file M2269-837.

27. Hedges, *Building the Canadian West*, 380.

28. Colonel J.S. Dennis, Memorandum for private circulation to officials of the Department of Immigration and Colonization, July 8, 1932, CPCA.

29. *Montreal Star*, August 8, 1928.

30. Glenbow Western Research Centre/University of Calgary, Canadian Pacific Railway Settlement and Development fonds, file M2269-754.

31. W.H. Vanwyck to Colley, August 31, 1928, Glenbow Western Research Centre/University of Calgary, Canadian Pacific Railway Settlement and Development fonds, file M2269-754.

32. Colley to Van Scoy, September 14, 1928, Glenbow Western Research Centre/University of Calgary, Canadian Pacific Railway Settlement and Development fonds, file M2269-754.

33. *Winnipeg Free Press*, December 27, 1928.

34. Ibid.

35. *Winnipeg Free Press*, December 28, 1928.

36. *Montreal Gazette*, December 29, 1928.

37. *Winnipeg Free Press*, December 31, 1928.

38. *Montreal Star*, January 11, 1929.

39. "Family Settlement in the West," pamphlet, Canada Colonization Association, 1929.

40. Canadian Pacific Railway/Secretary of State for Dominion Affairs Land Settlement Scheme, Glenbow Western Research Centre/University of Calgary, Canadian Pacific Railway Settlement and Development fonds, file M2269-752.

41. *Agricultural and Industrial Progress* 6, no. 2 (February 1924): 23.

42. *Edmonton Journal*, May 18, 1929.

43. *Medicine Hat News*, May 8, 1929.

44. Ibid.

45. Imperial Order Daughters of the Empire, "Wecome to British Settlers Service," October 2, 1929, Glenbow Western Research Centre/University of Calgary, Canadian Pacific Railway Settlement and Development fonds, file M2269-818.

46. *Calgary Herald*, January 5, 1929.

47. Ibid.

48. *Wilts & Gloucestershire Standard*, August 11, 1928.

49. *Agricultural and Industrial Progress* 10, no. 10 (1928).

Chapter 12: Dark, Dreary, and Deadly Days

1. *Montreal Gazette*, January 10, 1930.

2. *Montreal Gazette*, February 20, 1930.

3. Musk, *Canadian Pacific*, 41.

4. Ibid., 35.

5. Pigott, *Sailing*, 111.

6. Immigration Table 1867–1987, Canada Employment and Immigration Commission.

7. *Regina Leader-Post*, April 12, 1930.

8. Professor W.J. Elliot, "C.P.R. Demonstration Farm: A Centre of Agricultural Information for Settlers," in *Strathmore, the Village that Moved* (Strathmore Alberta History Book Committee, 1986), 24.

9. Ibid., 23.

10. Bosworth to Sam Porter, manager of DNR, July 13, 1932, Glenbow Western Research Centre/University of Calgary, Canadian Pacific Railway Settlement and Development fonds, file M2269-525.

11. *Canadian Pacific Staff Bulletin*, August 1, 1935.

12. *Liverpool Post and Mercury*, June 14, 1930.

13. *Peterborough Examiner*, August 16, 1930.

14. Hedges, *Building the Canadian West*, 378.

15. "The Prairie Provinces and the Proposed Agricultural Credits," an address by E.W. Beatty (CPR president) to the Winnipeg Board of Trade, February 16, 1931.

16. East Irrigation Districrt, "History of the EID," 2015. https://www.eid.ca/about.html. (The brochure consulted is no longer available at eid.ca/documents/publications/Brochure_Irrigation_District.pdf.)

17. *Los Angeles Daily News*, December 19, 1933.

18. Memorandum from Chief Commissioner J.N.K. Macalister, January 25, 1934, Glenbow Western Research Centre/University of Calgary, Canadian Pacific Railway Settlement and Development fonds, file M2269-476.

19. Memorandum for the Chairman and President from J.N.K. Macalister, May 7, 1936, Glenbow Western Research Centre/University of Calgary, Canadian Pacific Railway Settlement and Development fonds, file M2269-476.

20. Irving Abella and Harold Troper, *None is Too Many* (Toronto: Lester & Orpen Dennys, 1983), 5.

21. Ibid., 75.

22. Ibid., 285.

23. Pigott, *Sailing*, 129.

24. A. Mitchner, "The Bow River Scheme," in *The CPR West: The Iron Road and the Making of a Nation*, ed. Hugh Dempsey (Vancouver: Douglas & McIntyre, 1984), 268.

25. Pamphlet: "Agricultural Settlement Opportunities in the Prairie Provinces of Canada," Department of Immigration and Colonization, CPR, 1940.

26. *Agricultural and Industrial Progress in Canada* 24, no. 7 (July 1942).

27. *Montreal Star*, September 22, 1943.

28. *Vancouver Sun*, December 15, 1943.

29. *Agricultural and Industrial Progress in Canada* 25, no. 3 (March 1943).

30. Ibid.

31. *Winnipeg Tribune*, June 19, 1943.

Chapter 13: To Canada by Sea and by Air

1. *Spanner* [CPR employee publication], October 1947, 8.
2. *Canadian Pacific Staff Bulletin*, April–May 1947, 24.
3. Ibid., September 1947, 6.
4. Kelley, *Making of the Mosaic*, 321.
5. John Murray Gibbon, *New Colour for the Canadian Mosaic: The Displaced Persons* (Toronto: McClelland & Stewart, 1951), 7.
6. Musk, *Canadian Pacific*, 192.
7. Gibbon, *New Colour*, 7.
8. Musk, *Canadian Pacific*, 192.
9. Ibid., 193.
10. *Spanner*, April–May 1952, 11.
11. *Spanner*, April 1950, 14.
12. Alma Jorgensen, "From Denmark to Magrath," *Alberta History*, Spring 1999, 21–22.
13. Henry Cresswell, chief commissioner of the CPR's Department of Immigration and Colonization, and president, Canada Colonization Association, speech at a staff meeting of the latter organization held at Calgary, February 23, 1951, CPCA.
14. Ibid.
15. Letter from Holmgren to Professor Harald Troper at the Ontario Institute for Studies and Education, December 1, 1981 (copy in author's collection).
16. Cresswell address, February 23, 1951.
17. Holmgren to Troper, December 1, 1981.
18. *Spanner*, March 1957, 9.
19. CPR press releases, Montreal, April 2, April 7, May 19, May 26, 1960 (author's collection).
20. Liverpool Ships. liverpoolships.org.
21. CPR press release, Montreal, April 25 (author's collection).
22. Canadian Pacific pamphlet, Canadian Farmers Abroad 1960, CPCA.
23. CPR public relations memorandum, 1962, CPCA.
24. "Land Grants: Getting Railways Built," Communications & Public Affairs, Canadian Pacific Railway, April 2006, CPCA.

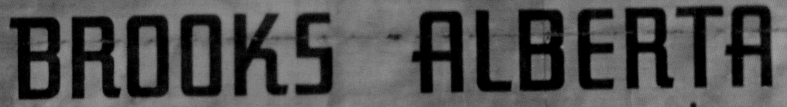

BROOKS – ALBERTA
HEADQUARTERS OF CANADA'S
LARGEST IRRIGATION SYSTEM
EASTERN IRRIGATION DISTRICT
FARMER OWNED & OPERATED

BIBLIOGRAPHY

Archival Sources

Canadian Pacific Corporate Archives (CPCA) brochure and pamphlet collection (now housed at Exporail, the Canadian Railway Museum in Delson, Quebec, as part of the Canadian Pacific Railway Company fonds of the Canadian Railway Historical Association (CRHA) Archives and Documentation Centre)

Canadian Pacific Railway, Land Settlement and Development fonds, Glenbow Western Research Centre/University of Calgary

Canadian Pacific Steamships Limited fonds, Ingenium/Canada Science and Technology Museum, Library and Archives

Borden [Robert] Papers, Library and Archives Canada

House of Commons Debates, Library and Archives Canada

Lister-Kaye [John] Papers, Library and Archives Canada, Department of the Interior, Lands Branch

Macdonald [John A.] Papers, Library and Archives Canada

Pearce [William] Papers, University of Alberta Archives. Includes the William Pearce Manuscript, reformatted by J.A. Jaffary of the Alberta Provincial Library in 1925, edited by William's grandson Doug Pearce in June 2013, Accession #74-69-459

Shaughnessy [Thomas] Papers, Records Group 2, CPCA (now housed at Exporail/CRHA Archives and Documentation Centre)

Statutes of Canada, 44 Victoria, chapter 1 (1881), Library and Archives Canada

Statutes of Canada, 33 Victoria, chapter 3 (1870), Library and Archives Canada

Van Horne [William] Papers, Records Group 1, CPCA (now housed at Exporail/CRHA Archives and Documentation Centre)

Newspapers

Alberta Tribune (Calgary)
Albertan
Bassano News
Calgary Herald
Chicago Examiner
Daily Mail (London)
Daily State Democrat (Lincoln, Nebraska)
Dundee Courier
Edmonton Bulletin
Edmonton Journal
Evening Standard (London)
Financier and Bullionist (London)
Gananoque [Ontario] *Reporter*
Gleichen Call
Globe (Toronto)
Journal of Canadian Studies
Lethbridge Herald
Liverpool Post and Mercury
London Morning Advertiser
London Times
London Truth
Los Angeles Daily News
Manitoba Free Press [Winnipeg Free Press, after 1931]
Medicine Hat News
Montreal Gazette
Montreal Herald
Moose Jaw News
Morning Post (London)
News (Toronto)
Ottawa Citizen
Ottawa Free Press
Ottawa Journal
Owen Sound Advertiser
New York Times
Peterborough Examiner
Qu'Appelle Record
Regina Leader-Post
Saint John Daily Telegraph
Saskatchewan Herald (Battleford)
Saskatoon Phoenix [later Star-Phoenix]
Standard (Stavely, Alberta)
Strathmore Standard
Times (Chicago)
Toronto Star
Vancouver Sun
Western Producer
Wilts & Gloucester Standard
Winnipeg Sun
Winnipeg Times
Winnipeg Tribune

Periodicals

Agricultural and Industrial Progress in Canada

Alberta Farmer

Alberta History

Alberta Historical Review

Beaver

Bioscope

Canadian Gazette

Canadian Pacific Staff Bulletin

Canadian Rail

Canadian Railway and Marine World

Canadian Water Resources Journal

Canada West

Country Life

CP Rail News

Fort Calgary Quarterly

Grain Growers Guide

Great Plains Quarterly

Journal of Canadian Studies

Journal of the Canadian Historical Association

Journal of the Society for the Study of Architecture in Canada

Lloyd's List

Maclean's Magazine

Manitoba Pageant

Passenger Train Journal

Popular Mechanics

Railway and Shipping World

Railway World

Saskatchewan History

Slavonic Review

Spanner

The U.F.A.: Official Organ of the United Farmers of Alberta

Weekend Magazine

Western People

Western Producer

Books

Abella, Irving, and Harold Troper. *None is too Many*. Toronto: Lester & Orpen Dennys, 1983.

Anderson, Charles W. *Grain: The Entrepreneurs*. Winnipeg: Watson & Dwyer, 1991.

Anderson, Frimann B. *Immigration and Settlement on Vacant Lands in Manitoba and North-West*. Winnipeg: n.p., 1887.

Anonymous. *The British Colonist in North America: A Guide for Intended Emigrants*. London: Swan Sonnenschein, 1890.

Appleton, Thomas E. *Ravenscrag: The Allan Royal Mail Line*. Toronto: McClelland and Stewart, 1974.

Archer, John H. *Saskatchewan: A History*. Saskatoon: Western Producer Prairie Books, 1980.

Beal, Bob & Rod Macleod. *Prairie Fire: The 1885 North-West Rebellion*. Toronto: McClelland & Stewart, 1984.

Berton, Pierre. *The Last Spike*. Toronto: McClelland & Stewart, 1971.

———. *The National Dream*. Toronto: McClelland & Stewart, 1970.

———. *The Promised Land*. Toronto: McClelland & Stewart, 1984.

Bone, P. Turner. *When the Steel Went Through*. Toronto: MacMillan, 1947.

Brennan, J. William. *Regina: An Illustrated History*. Toronto: James Lorimer, 1989.

Broadfoot, Barry. *The Pioneer Years 1895-1914: Memories of Settlers Who Opened the West*. Toronto: Doubleday, 1976.

Brown, Craig, ed. *The Illustrated History of Canada*. Toronto: Lester & Orpen Dennys, 1987.

Byfield, Ted, ed. *Alberta in the 20th Century: A Journalistic History of the Province in 11 Volumes*. Edmonton: United Western Communications, 1991.

Campbell, Marjorie Wilkins. *The Silent Song of Mary Eleanor*. Saskatoon: Western Producer Prairie Books, 1983.

Carter, Sarah. *Imperial Plots: Women, Land and the Spadework of British Colonialism on the Canadian Prairies*. Winnipeg: University of Manitoba Press, 2016.

Choko, Marc, and David L. Jones. *Posters of the Canadian Pacific*. Toronto: Firefly Books, 2004.

Copping, Arthur E. *The Golden Land: The True Story of British Settlers in Canada*. London: Hodder and Stroughton, 1911.

Cruise, David, and Alison Griffiths. *Lords of the Line: The Men Who Built the CPR*. New York: Viking, 1988.

Culliton, John Thomas. *Assisted Emigration and Land Settlement*. Montreal: McGill University Press, 1928.

Dafoe, John W. *Clifford Sifton in Relation to His Times*. Toronto: Macmillan, 1931.

Daschuk, James. *Clearing the Plains: Disease, Politics of Starvation and the Loss of Aboriginal Life*. Regina: University of Regina Press, 2013.

Dawe, Michael J. *Red Deer: The Memorable City*. Red Deer: City of Red Deer, 2013.

den Otter, Andy Albert. *Civilizing the West: The Galts and the Development of Western Canada*. Edmonton: University of Alberta Press, 1982.

———. *Irrigation in Southern Alberta 1882-1901*. Occasional Paper No. 5. Lethbridge: Whoop-up Country Chapter, Historical Society of Alberta, 1975.

Dempsey, Hugh A. *Crowfoot: Chief of the Blackfeet*. Edmonton: Hurtig, 1972.

———. *The Great Blackfoot Treaties*. Victoria: Heritage House, 2015.

Dempsey, Hugh A., ed. *The CPR West: The Iron Road and the Making of a Nation*. Vancouver: Douglas & McIntyre, 1984.

Eagle, John. *The Canadian Pacific and the Development of Western Canada*. Kingston: McGill-Queen's Press, 1989.

Elkington, Ernest Way. *Canada: The Land of Hope*. London: A and C Black, 1910.

Epp, Frank H. *Mennonites in Canada 1920-1940: A People's Struggle for Survival*. Toronto: MacMillan, 1982.

Finch, David. *Much Brain and Sinew: The Brooks Aqueduct Story*. Brooks: Eastern Irrigation District, 1993.

Fraser, Hugh. *A Trip to the Dominion of Canada*. Halifax: n.p., 1883.

Freeman George (compiler). *Flow Beyond the Weir: The Jubilee Edition 1944-1994*. Red Deer: Advisor Graphics, 1994.

Ganzevoort, Herman. *A Bittersweet Land: The Dutch Experience in Canada, 1890-1980*. Toronto: McClelland & Stewart, 1988.

Gardiner, Claude. *Letters from an English Settler*. Calgary: Glenbow-Alberta Institute, 1988.

Gibbon, John Murray. *New Colour for the Canadian Mosaic: The Displaced Persons*. Toronto: McClelland & Stewart, 1951.

———. *Steel of Empire*. Toronto: McClelland & Stewart, 1935.

Gilpin, John. *Quenching the Prairie Thirst*. Altona, MB: Friesen's Corporation, 2000.

Grant, Shelagh D. *Polar Imperative*. Vancouver: Douglas & McIntyre, 2010.

Gray, James H. *Boomtime: Peopling the Canadian Prairies*. Saskatoon: Western Producer Prairie Books, 1979.

Gray, Lynda. *First Nations 101: Tons of Stuff You Need to Know about First Nations People*. Vancouver: Adaawx Publishing, 2011.

Gross, Renie, and Lea Nicoll Kramer. *Tapping the Bow*. Brooks: Eastern Irrigation District, 1985.

Hall, D.J. *From Treaties to Reserves: The Federal Government and Native Peoples in Territorial Alberta, 1870-1905*. Montreal: McGill-Queen's University Press, 2015.

Ham, George Henry. *Reminiscences of a Raconteur*. Toronto: The Musson Book Co., 1921.

Hanna, David Blyth. *Trains of Recollection*. Toronto: MacMillan, 1924.

Hargreaves, Mary Wilma. *Dry Farming in the Northern Great Plains, 1900-1925*. Cambridge: Harvard University Press, 1957.

Harrison, Phyllis, ed. *The Home Children*. Winnipeg: Watson & Dwyer, 1979.

Hawkes, John. *The Story of Saskatchewan and Its People*. Chicago: S.J. Clarke Publishing, 1924.

Hedges, James B. *Building the Canadian West: The Land and Colonization Policies of the Canadian Pacific Railway*. New York: MacMillan, 1939.

Hook, Gwen. *The Keystone Legacy: Recollections of a Black Settler*. Edmonton: Brightest Pebble Publishing, 1997.

Johnston, Hugh J.M. *Jewels of the Qila: The Remarkable Story of an Indo-Canadian Family*. Vancouver: UBC Press, 2011.

Jones, David Laurence. *Famous Name Trains: Travelling in Style with the CPR*. Calgary: Fifth House, 2006.

———. *Tales of the CPR*. Calgary: Fifth House, 2002.

Joseph, Bob. *21 Things You May Not Know About the Indian Act: Helping Canadians Make Reconciliation with Indigenous Peoples a Reality*. Saanichton: Indigenous Relations Press, 2018.

Kelley, Ninette, and Michael Trebilcock. *The Making of the Mosaic: A History of Canadian Immigration Policy, 2nd ed*. Toronto: University of Toronto Press, 2010.

Knowles, Valerie. *Strangers at our Gates: Canadian Immigration and Immigration Policy, 1540-2015*. Toronto: Dundurn, 2016.

Lamb, W. Kaye. *History of the Canadian Pacific Railway*. New York: Macmillan, 1977.

Lavallee, Omer. *Van Horne's Road*. Montreal: Railfare Enterprises, 1974.

Lee, Charles S., ed. *The Canada North-West Land Company (Limited): Land to Energy, 1882-1982*. Calgary: Canada Northwest Energy, 1982.

Lougheed Women's Institute. *Verdant Valleys—In and Around Lougheed*. Lougheed: Lougheed Women's Institute, 1972.

Lux, Maureen. *Medicine That Walks: Disease, Medicine and Canadian Plains Native People 1880-1930*. Toronto: University of Toronto Press, 2001.

MacEwan, Grant. *Eye Opener Bob*. Edmonton: Institute of Applied Art, 1957.

MacIntosh, William Archibald. *Prairie Settlement: The Geographical Setting*. Toronto: MacMillan, 1934.

Macoun, John. *The Autobiography of John Macoun, M.A., Canadian Explorer and Naturalist 1831-1920*. Ottawa: Ottawa Field-Naturalists Club, 1922.

Magrath, C.A. *The Galts, Father and Son: Pioneers in the Development of Southern Alberta*. Lethbridge: Lethbridge Herald, 1936.

Marquis of Lorne, K.T. *Canadian Life and Scenery with Hints to Intended Emigrants and Settlers*. London: The Religious Tract Society, 1886.

Martin, Chester. "Dominion Lands Policy." In *Canadian Frontiers of Settlement*, ed. W.A. Mackintosh. Toronto: MacMillan, 1938.

McDonald, Donna. *Lord Strathcona: A Biography of Donald Alexander Smith*. Revised ed. Toronto: Dundurn Press, 2002.

McGowan, Don. C. *Grassland Settlers: The Swift Current Region during the Era of the Ranching Frontier*. Victoria: Cactus Publications, 1980.

Meeres, E.L. *The Homesteads That Nurtured a City: The History of Red Deer, 1880-1905*. Red Deer, AB: Red Deer and District Museum Society, 1977.

Monteyne, David. *For the Temporary Accommodation of Settlers: Architecture and Immigrant Reception in Canada, 1870-1930*. Montreal & Kingston: McGill-Queen's University Press, 2021.

Morris, Alexander. *The Treaties of Canada with the Indians of Manitoba and the North-West Territories*. Toronto: Willing & Williamson, 1880.

Morris, Peter. *Embattled Shadows: A History of Canadian Cinema, 1895-1939*. Montreal: McGill-Queen's University Press, 1978.

Morton, Arthur S. *History of Prairie Settlement*, Toronto: MacMillan, 1933.

Musk, George. *Canadian Pacific: The Story of the Famous Shipping Line*. London: David & Charles, 1981.

Niddrie, John W. *Niddrie of the North-West: Memoirs of a Pioneer Canadian Missionary*. Edmonton: University of Alberta Press, 2000.

Palmer, Howard. *The Settlement of the West*. Calgary: University of Calgary/Comprint Publishing, 1977.

Pigott, Peter. *Sailing Seven Seas: A History of the Canadian Pacific Line*. Toronto: Dundurn Press, 2010.

Pope, Sir Joseph. *Correspondence of Sir John Macdonald: Selections from the Correspondence of the Right Honourable Sir John Alexander Macdonald, G.C.B.: First Prime Minister of the Dominion of Canada*. Toronto: Doubleday, Page & Company, 1921.

Potyondi, Barry. *In Palliser's Triangle: Living in the Grasslands, 1850-1930*. Saskatoon: Purich Publishing, 1995.

Rees, Ronald. *New and Naked Land: Making the Prairies Home*. Saskatoon: Western Producer Prairie Books, 1988.

Regehr, T.D. *The Canadian Northern Railway: Pioneer Road of the Northern Prairies, 1895-1918*. Toronto: Macmillan, 1976.

Roberts, Barbara. *Whence They Came: Deportation from Canada, 1900-1935*. Ottawa: University of Ottawa Press, 1988.

Scott, William. "Immigration and Population." In *Canada and its Provinces*. Vol. 7. Ed. Adam Shortt and Arthur Doughty. Toronto: Publishers' Association of Canada, 1913.

Shaw, Charles Aeneas. *Tales of a Pioneer Surveyor*. Toronto: Longmans, 1970.

Skaggs, Jimmy M. *Prime Cut: Livestock Raising and Meatpacking in the United States, 1607-1983*. Texas: A&M Press, 1986.

Sladen, Douglas. *On the Cars and Off: Being the Journal of a Pilgrimage along the Queen's Highway to the East, from Halifax in Nova Scotia to Victoria in Vancouver's Island*. London: Ward, Lock & Bowden, 1895.

Smith, Donald B. *Seen but Not Seen: Influential Canadians and the First Nations from the 1840s to Today*. Toronto: University of Toronto Press, 2021.

Spry, Irene M. *The Palliser Expedition: The Dramatic Story of Western Canadian Exploration 1857-1860*. Calgary: Fifth House, 1963.

Steeves, Ruth. *No Englishmen Need Apply*. Mill Bay, BC: The Cowichan Press, 2008.

Stevens, G.R. *Ogilvie in Canada: Pioneer Millers 1801-1951*, privately published, 1951.

Strathmore Alberta History Book Committee. *Strathmore: The Village That Moved*. Strathmore: Strathmore Alberta History Book Committee, 1986.

Thomas, Lewis G., ed. *The Prairie West to 1905: A Canadian Sourcebook*. Oxford: Oxford University Press, 1975.

Touchie, Rodger D. *Bear Child: The Life and Times of Jerry Potts*. Victoria: Heritage House, 2005.

Tracey, Lindalee. *A Scattering of Seeds: The Creation of Canada*. Toronto: McArthur & Company, 1999.

Treaty 7 Elders and Tribal Council with Walter Hildebrandt, Dorothy First Rider, and Sarah Carter. *The True Spirit and Original Intent of Treaty 7*. Montreal: McGill-Queen's University Press, 1996.

Troper, Harold Martin. *Only Farmers Need Apply*. Toronto: Griffin House, 1972.

Vaughn, Walter. *The Life and Work of Sir William Van Horne*. New York: The Century Co., 1920.

Waldrum, James B., D. Ann Herring, and T. Kue Young. *Aboriginal Health in Canada: Historical, Cultural an Epidemiological Perspectives*. Toronto: University of Toronto Press, 1995.

Wapella History Book Committee. *Mingling Memories: A History of Wapella and Districts*. Altona, Man.: Friesen Printers, 1979.

Whelpley, James Davenport. *The Problem of the Immigrant*. London: Chapman & Hill, 1905.

Whitaker, Reg. *Canadian Immigration Policy Since Confederation*. Ottawa: Department of Political Science, York University, 1991.

Wilkie, Jim. Metagama: *A Journey from Lewis to the New World*. Toronto: Doubleday, 1987.

Willson, Beckles. *From Quebec to Piccadilly and Other Places: Some Anglo-Canadian Memories*. London: Jonathan Cape, 1929.

Woodsworth, James S. *Strangers within our Gates*. Toronto: University of Toronto Press, 1972 (reprint).

Zuehlke, Mark. *Scoundrels, Dreamers and Second Sons*. Vancouver: Whitecap Books, 1994.

INDEX

Bulgaria, 401
Bulgarian immigrants, 327
Burdett-Coutts, Angela, 131
Burns, Pat, 349

Cairnhill Colony, 283, 303
Calder, James Alexander, 321, 327
Calgary
  administrative centre, 208, *218*, 241, 243, 300
  corruption in, 301
  CPR routes, 137, 142–43, 245, 275
  vs. Edmonton as capital, 245
  entertainment in, *368–69*
  founding and settlement of, 51–54, 57–60, 68, 174–75, 243, 254, *278*, 283, 353, 365
  irrigation projects, 242
  products of, 56, 63, 78, 129, 293
  radicalism in, 365
  women workers of, 257, 358
Calgary & Edmonton Railway, 142, *143–45*, *147*, 148, 199, 210, 372
Calgary Colonization Company, 243
Calgary sleeping cars, 274
Canada
  British character of, 83
  CPR's role in establishing, 5
  Northwest Territories acquisition, 5–7
Canada Central Railway, 113
Canada North-West Land Company, *46*, 47, 49, 51, 54, 57, 58, 59–60, 113, 130, 131, 207, 307
Canada West magazine, *277*
Canadian Agricultural, Coal and Colonization Co., 128–30
Canadian American Land Company, 208
Canadian Christian Council for Resettlement of Refugees, 393, 394, 395

Canadian Colonization Association, 326–27, 330, 336, 347, 371, 372, 373, 374, 383, 391, 393, 399
Canadian Co-operative Colonization Co., 133
Canadian Gazette, 84, 89, 91, 148, 293
Canadian Government Railways, 205, 325
Canadian Land and Ranch Company, 130
Canadian National Land Settlement Assocn., *328*
Canadian National Railways, 325, 327, 328, 329, 330, 345, 347, 350, 352, 365, 371, 373, 379, 381, 385, 389, 391, 393, 395
Canadian Northern Railway, 142, 171, 192, 199–205, 271, 275, 295, 296, 297, 300, 319, 320, 324–25
Canadian North-West Irrigation Company, 216–17
Canadian Pacific Airlines, 396, 397, *403*
Canadian Pacific Irrigation Colonization Co., 243, 244, 273–74, 275, 278, 282, 285, 287, 300
Canadian Pacific Railway Co.
  beginnings, 31
  "Better Farming" trains, 296, 297, 329
  construction and maintenance crews, 15, 20, 40, 44, 137, 138, 140, 242, 262
  Dept. of Colonization and Development, 321–22, 327, 329, *370*, 377, *378*, 389, 391, 396, 397
  Dept. of Immigration and Agricultural Development, 399, *400*, 401
  Dept. of Immigration and Colonization, 321, 377, *378*, 391, 396

Dept. of Natural Resources, 299, 300, 301, 309, 318, 320, 321–22, 330, 375, 377, 379
  dispute with Austria, 313–15
  Exhibits Branch, 275, *277*
  experimental farms, 70–73, 127, 135–36, 255, 291, 296, 308, 339
  fares, 94, 108, 122, 137, 145, 153, 275, 365
  government support for, 5, 7–8, 133–34, 137–38, 150, 169, 171, 271
  irrigation projects, 304–11
  land grants to, 8–9, 57, 59, 61, 135, 150, 156, 170–71, 203, 207, 210, 217, 401–3
  land sales of, 31–35, 44–48, 55, 58–59, 61, 74, 76, 124, 127–28, 135, *141*, 155–56, 161, 207, 208–9, 210, 242–43, 260, 269, 278–79, 281, 285, 286, 287, 295, 309, 311, 322, 325, 330, 375, 387, 403
  London offices of, *90*, 91–93, 401
  "Made-in-Canada" trains, 299
  "monopoly clause," 133–34, 135, 137–38, 171
  movies by, 260–62
  Numbered Treaties and, 15, 20
  opposition to, 10, 171
  Pacific route, 11–15, 37
  propaganda and immigrant recruitment, 7, 32, 55, 56, 68, 70, 76–93, 96, 123, 149, 152–53, 157, 193–96, 218–19, 260–62, 275–79, 295, 300, 301, 318–19, 324, 327–29, 331–32, 342–43, 350–52, 357–64, 375, 379, 381–83, 391–92, 396–97
  Publicity Branch, 275, 277
  ready-made farms, 251, 277, 280–87, 295, 298–99, 301–3, 318, 323–24, 349, 363, 372

station gardens, 55–56, 71–72, 175, 293
  stations, 40–43, 44, 48, 50, 51, 54, 57–58, 59, 67, *103*, 106, *114*, 158, 163, 183, 188, *193*, 233, 235, 237, *246–48*, 277, 291
  town planning influenced by, 8–9, 40, 43, 47, 49–54, 57–59
  See also Canada North-West Land Company
Canadian Pacific Steamships
  origins, 219–24, 332
  Allan Line and, 94, 96, 97–98, 140, 219, 223, 225–27, 230, 316, 323
  Beaver Line and, 94–98, 220–21, 223, 224, 314
  Canadian Pacific Ocean Services, 317–18, 322, 329
  fares, 220, *355*, *360*, *362*, 372
  third-class passage, 353–57
  war requisitioning of, 317, 379, 387
Canadian-American Land Company, 242–43
Cannington Manor, 131–33
Carberry, 51
Card, Charles Ora, 212
Cardiff, *181*
Cardston, 212, 217, 296
Carey, Frank, 224
Carsland sleeping cars, *274*
Cassils, 309, 318
Castle Mountain, 320
Cathcart, Emily, 130–31
cattle cars, 67–68, 254
Central Women's Colonization Board, 358
Chancellor, 323
Cheadle, 291–92, 303
Chestermere Lake, 242

Chicago, 27, 65, 67, 115–16, 151, 153, 272, 288, 324, 381, 383
children, 37, 44, 51, 78, 100, 159, 180, 193, 224, 226, 232–33, 255–56, 296, 316–17, 320, 334, 340, 353, 355, 356, 357–63, 367, 371, 372, *378*, 386, 394, *395*, 397, 401
Children's Overseas Reception Board, 386
Chinese immigrants, 263–65, 305, 306
Chinook Belt & Peace River Railway Company, 142–44
Clan Donald Colony, 349
Claresholm, 289, 358
Clark, G.H., 296
coal, 12, 40, 78, 135, 211–13, 215, 375
Coal Banks, 211, 212
Coaldale, 299, 303, 323, *338*, 339
Cochrane, *208*, 296, 299, *382*
Cochrane, Mathew H., 63
Cochrane Ranch, 63, *64*
Code, Elias, 145
Colley, James, 358, 361, 365, 374–75, 388
Colman, Dalton, 391–92
colonist cars, 107–13, 129, 130, 153, 186–88, 231, 235–36, 237, 272, 273, 281–82, 350, 365
Colonization Finance Corporation, 383
commissary cars, 183, 281
communists, 365
Conservative Party, 169
Cornwall Canal, 118
Cotton, Almon James, 173–74
Countess of Dufferin, *105*, 106
Coutts, 212
CPR Contract Holders' Association, 330
Craigellachie, 48, 121, 142
Crandall, C.R., 381–83

Grand Trunk Railway, 55, 84, 85–86, 94, 96, 107–8, 111, 114–15, 116, 149–50, 152–53, 203–5, 219, 227, 239, 253, 261, 325

Grand Valley, 43, 44

Great Lakes, 10, 103–6, 111, 114, 116–21

Great Northern Railroad, 14, 203

Great West Canadian Festival, 368, 369

Great Western Line, 96

Great Western Railway, 111–12

Greenway, Thomas, 135–36, 138, 171

Gretna, 112, 135, 136, 165, 180

Griffon, Frederick T., 208

Grosse Isle, 227–31, 336

"guest children," 316–17

Gull Lake, 71, 128, 130

Halifax, 94, 96–97, 102, 149–51, 183, 205, 231, 232, 332, 353, 355, 379, 392

Ham, George Henry, 38

Hamburg, 176–77, 181, 228, 313, 332, 346, 352

Hamburg America line, 92, 180, 314, 316, 318, 332–33, 357

Hamilton, Lauchlan Alexander, 58, 159–60, 208, 282, 283

Hansen, Peter, 208

Harrington, Roger, 180

Haultain, Frederick, 244

Hawreliak, Mr., 350

Hays, Charles Melville, 203, 205

Head, Jeremiah, 213

head tax, 263, 265

Hebrides, 130, 338, 339–43

Hebrides, 340

Hector, James, 9, 10

Hedges, James, 76

Herzer, Traugott Otto Francis, 336, 383

High River, 242

Hill, James Jerome, 12, 14, 43, 48–49, 106, 107

Hind, Henry Youle, 10–11

Hohenlohe Colony, 140

Holden, Muriel, 273

Holmgren, Marius, 396–97

Holt, Herbert, 142, 199

Home Stock Farm, 135–36

Homestead Act, 320–21

Homestead Act (US), 34

Horan, Vic, 396–97

horses, 26, 37, 65, 68, 70, 125, 129, 131–33, 147, 161, 215, 222, 223, 293, 306, 330, 351, 378, 379–80

housing, 34, 44, 51, 54, 174–75, 181, 183, 189–91, 208, 233, 235, 273, 282, 283–86, 320, 358, 361, 365, 373, 378
See also speculators

Huascaran, 394

Huba, Jan, 384

Hudson Bay, 5, 137, 314

Hudson Bay Railway, 203, 325

Hudson's Bay Company, 5, 7, 8, 15, 31, 35, 48, 51, 57, 58, 107, 138, 212, 218, 240, 363–64

Hughes, Sam, 200

Hundred Cottage Scheme, 372

Hungarian immigrants, 139–40, 181, 339, 347–49, 352, 358, 371, 374–75, 385, 396, 397–98

Hun's Valley, 139

Hussar, 308, 330

Hysop, David, 55–56, 288–89

Icelanders, 26, 140, 149, 255

I.G. Baker Co., 57, 58

Imandt, Franziska Marie, 148

immigrants
    Atlantic crossings, 185–86, 222–28, 333–37, 340–42, 355–57, 394–96, 398

deportations, 263, 303, 313, 326, 347, 361
experiences of, 98–102, 154–57, 158–61, 235–36, 247–48, 254–55, 257, 273, 284, 305–6, 349, 365–66
Immigration Acts, 245, 262–63
internment camps, 319–20
policies and prejudices, 25, 34, 37, 92, 111, 140, 157–58, 173–74, 175–80, 181, 185, 189, 192, 245–48, 255, 262–69, 300–301, 303, 313–15, 319–20, 322, 327, 330–31, 345–47, 352–53, 367–71, 386–89, 393
propaganda and recruitment, 7, 25, 32–33, 46, 55, 56, 68, 70, 76–93, 96, 123, 130, 149, 152–53, 157, 174, 175–79, 193–99, 218–19, 251–54, 260–62, 275–79, 295, 300, 301, 313–14, 318–19, 324, 327–29, 331–32, 342–43, 350–52, 357–64, 375, 379, 381–83, 391–92, 396–97

Immigration Act (1906), 245
Immigration Act (1910), 262–63
immigration halls, 37, 38, 102, 118, 174–75, 179, 180, 183, 233, 235, 247, 282, 333, 365, 366

Imperial Order Daughters of the Empire, 374

Imperial Order of the Daughters of the Empire, 269

Indian Act, 25

Indian Head, 20, 48, 73, 124, 125, 127, 131, 133, 154, 167

Indigenous Peoples
    agricultural training of, 73
    buffalo and, 27–29
    impact of railroads, 26
    Métis people, 26, 27, 35, 37, 50, 54, 57, 127, 134

Numbered Treaties, 7, 15–26, 57, 173
    resistance of, 19–20, 24, 26, 35–36, 75, 127, 155, 241
    Saskatchewan population, 50
    segregation of, 54

Innisfail, 145, 194

Intercolonial Railway, 96–97, 111, 149–51, 205, 325

International Mercantile Marine, 222

internment camps, 319–20

Irish immigrants, 10, 55, 100–102, 157, 185, 222, 227–31, 247, 255, 281, 349, 366–67, 402

Irricana, 282–83, 284, 303, 308

irrigation, 14, 211–19, 240–44, 272–79, 281, 285, 287, 289, 293–95, 299, 304–11

Italian immigrants, 173, 245, 329, 334, 401

Jacobson, Sebina, 259

Japan, 271, 293, 313, 329, 350, 379

Japanese immigrants, 267, 305, 389

Jaschke, Manfred Terry, 396

Jaschke, Mrs. Alfred, 395–96

Jewish immigrants, 149, 158, 173, 181, 185, 263, 362, 373, 385–87

Josephsburg, 149

J.P. Morgan, 222

Kainai People, 19, 21

Kaiserin Auguste Victoria, 332

Kansas City, 274–75

Kaposvar, 139–40

Kappelle, Lily, 382

Kenaston, Frederick Eugene, 209

Kenora, 56, 166, 240, 257

Kerr, Robert, 260

Kipling, Rudyard, 251–54

Kittson, Norman, 107

Klaehn, Otto, 351

Ku Klux Klan, 369

Lacombe, 349

Lacombe, Albert, 23

Lacombe & Northwestern Railway, 349

Laidlaw, George, 114

Lake Champlain, 221, 224, 314, 318

Lake Dauphin Reserve, 61

Lake Erie, 221, 222, 314

Lake Huron, 183

Lake Manitoba, 91, 185–86, 221, 222, 236, 317, 318

Lake Manitoba Railway and Canal Company, 171, 199–203

Lake Michigan, 221, 222

Lake Newell, 305

Lake of the Woods Milling Co., 166

Lake Shebandowan, 103

Lake Superior, 183

Lamb, W. Kaye, 14, 227

Land Explorers Excursions, 137

Langenburg, 140

Last Spike, 48, 121, 156

Latta, Robert Gilmore "Jock," 334–36

Laurier, Wilfred, 169, 170, 171, 173, 196, 197, 204, 205, 244, 245, 251, 299, 377

Lawlor's Island, 231

Leoville, 278

Lesley, James, 28

Lethbridge, 12, 211–13, 214–17, 296, 299, 300, 303, 320, 323, 339, 396

Lethbridge, William, 211

Lethbridge Experimental Farm, 339

Lethbridge Land Company, 212, 216

Lewis, 339–40

Libau, 149, 336

Lilge, Andreas, 149

Lister-Kaye, John, 126, 127–30

Lister-Kaye, Natica, 127

Lithuanian immigrants, 395

Liverpool, 94, 98, 100, 152, 185, 186, 222, 224, 227, 231, 281, 316, 322, 323, 332, 334, 353–55, 379

Livingston, Sam, 68

"Palace" sleeping cars, 115
Palliser, John, *9, 10–11, 35*
Palliser's Triangle, 9, 11, 12, 14, 61, 63, 70, 73, 74, 210, 272–73
Parisian, 123
Parry Sound Colony, 145
Partridge Island, 231
Paterson, Isabel, *382*
Peace River, 372–73
Pearce, Thomas, 145
Pearce, William, 14, 59, 213–15, 217, 241, 320–21
Pearson, Stanley and family, *334*
Peterson, Charles Walter, 274, 285, 287
pets, 155, *156*
Piapot, 20
Pickersgill, Jack, 397
Pierce, Edward Mitchell, 131, 133
Piikani People, 19
Pilipiwski, Ivan, 180
Pocklington, William, 25
Polasczuk, Gregorz, *378*
Polish immigrants, 102, 140, 158, 179, 181, 245, 250, 329, 347, 358, 362, 367, 371, 385, 394, 395–96
Pope, John Henry, 35
Port Arthur, 10, 103, 111, *117,* 118, 121, 131, 133, 161, *162, 163, 164,* 203, 257, 271
Portage la Prairie, 37, 39, 43, 138, 163, 199, 248–50, 278
Portland, ME, 115, 149–50, 205, 221
Potts, Jerry, 16, *18*
Poundmaker, 27
Powder River Ranch Company, 128
Preston, William Thomas Rochester, 176, 177
Prince Albert, 54, 142, 183, 199, 240
Prince Edward Island Railway, 325

Qu'Appelle, 28, 47, 51, 59, 131, 140, 183, 247
Qu'Appelle, Long Lake & Saskatchewan Railroad and Steamboat Company, 142, 183, 199, 209, 210
Qu'Appelle Valley Farming Company, 123–27
Quebec, 5, 10, 96, 98, 102, 150, 244, 314
Quebec, Montreal, Ottawa & Occidental Railway, 114–15
Quebec City, *179,* 180, 205, 221, 224–25, 231–33, *316,* 329, 332, 355, *361*
Queensberry, Lord, 127
Quirk, John, 211
Quorn Ranch, 63

Railway Agreement, 345, 347, 352–53
ranching, 63–70, 128–30, 195, 211, 212, 214, 242, 254–55, 269, 290, 304, 349, 372, 380, 384
See also farms, farming life
ready-made farms, 251, 277, 280–87, 295, 298–99, 301–3, 318, 323–24, 349, 363, 372
Red Deer, 74–75, 76, 142, 145–48, 342, 343, 349
Red River, 5, *11,* 35, 37, 51, 103, *104*–6, 112, 135, 138, 161, 214
Red Star Line, 227, 234
Regehr, Theodore D., 200
Regina, 47, *49,* 50–51, 59, 142, 192, *253, 278, 361*
Rendell, Alice, 186
"return men," 92
Revelstoke, 56
Riel Resistance, 127, 241
Robert Reford Company, 94–96
Robson, Marjory, *382*
Romania, 401
Romanian immigrants, 149, 158
Rosemary, 303, 309

Rosenthal, 149
Rosenthal, Joe, 260
Ross, Arthur Wellington, 73
Ross, James, 142, 199
Rosser, Thomas Lafayette, 40–41, 43
Rosthern, 142, 183, 336, *338*
Rowell, Gladys M., 254
Royal Agricultural Shows, 89
Rupert's Land, 5, 7, 8
Rush Lake, 71, 128
Russia, 7, 37, 148–49, 271, 313, 336, *338,* 350, 351
Russian immigrants, 36–37, 134, 140, 145, 148–49, 157, 158, *177,* 183–85, 236, 300, 309, 313, 329, 336–39, 349–51, 362, 367, 371
Ruthenia, 314
Ruthenian immigrants, 139, 140, 158, 314, 319

Saint John, 150–51, 183, 186, 231, 233, 281, 286, 322, 340, 342, 355, 379, 394, 395
Saltcoats, 131
Salvation Army, 282, 329
Sardinian, 100
Sarmatian, 100–102
Saskatchewan
buffalo bones trade in, 28
First Nations of, *16,* 19–21
founding of, 244, 271
internment camps, 320
propaganda and immigrant recruitment, 86
routes to, 14–15, 142, 204–5
settlement of, 11, 50, 74–76, 140, 184, 254–55, 269, 278, 300, 319, 336–39, 371–72, 387
training farms in, 289, 299
Saskatchewan Land & Homestead Co., 74–76, 145
Saskatchewan Valley & Manitoba Land Co., 203, 209–10

Saskatoon, 28, *187,* 188–89, *189*–92, 254, 271, 275, 278, 300, 336, 339
Sayre, A.J., 243, 244
Scandinavian, 98, 99
Scarth, William, 47, 48, 49, 55, 58, 130
schools, 8, 19, 37, 173, 244, 247, 255, 387
Scottish Immigrant Aid Society, 342, 347, 349
Scottish immigrants, 35, 84, 130–31, 157, 173, 175, 185, 232, 285, *338,* 339–43, 374, 388
Scottish Ontario and Manitoba Land Company, 49
Scoy, Van, 361, 365, 366
Seba, *378*
Second Northern Reserve, 61
"section" system, 8–9, 19, 31, 34, 36, 40, 47, 51, 57–58, 61, 74, 140, 142, 154, 155, 156–57, 183, 189, 192, 203, 207–8, 210, 212, 218, 240, 289, 295, 320
Sedgewick, 283, 286–87, 299, 301, 384
seed, 34, 55–56, 72–73, 279, 282, 295–96
Selkirk, 11, 35–36, 183, 255
Selkirk, 104–5, 106
Selkirk, Lord, 35
Sellers, Matthew, 163–65
Selwyn, Alfred, 123
Shaughnessy, Thomas, 12, 78, 217, 219–21, 227, 239, 243, 252–54, 255, 260, 262, 280, 281, 287, 288–89, 300, 315, 317–18, 323, 339
Shawbridge Boys' Farm, 359
sheep, 65, 69, 70, 129, 130, 133, 140, 155, 296, 318, 379, 380, *381*
Shidzuska Maru, 349

"Short Line," 150–51, 199, 233
Sicilia, 180
Sifton, Clifford, *170,* 171–74, 175, 176–80, 183, 185, 189, 193, 195, 196, 214–15, 217, 244–45, 247, 248, 261
Sifton, John, 171
Sikh immigrants, 266–67
Siksika People, 19, 21–23, 57
silk, 76
Sintaluta, 199
Skinner, Thomas, 47, 84
Slidge, 163
Slovak immigrants, 139, 181
Smart, James, 176, 177, 179, 189
Smith, C.E., *159*
Smith, Donald (Lord Strathcona), 31, 48, 106–7, 176, 197
Smith, John Obed, 183
Smith, Luke, 102
Smzt, Lucan, 102
Sokol, Piotr, *371*
Solberg, Johanna, 259
"Soo Line", 153, 193, 255, 275, 290
Sorensen, Mark, 386–87
Souris, 135, 366
South Eastern Railway, 115
Southampton, 332, 334, 336, 355, 373
speculators, 12, 38, 39, 43–44, 45–46, 50, 57–58, 68, 170, 208–10, 243, 245
See also housing
Springfield, 56
St. Julien, 323
St. Lawrence, 94, 96, 97, 98, 115, 224, 227, 230, 356
St. Mary's River Railway Company, 217
St. Paul, 106, 111, 112, 123, 151, 210, 273, 275, 318, 329
St. Paul & Pacific Railroad, 14, 48, 106–7
St. Paul, Minneapolis & Manitoba Railway, 12, 43, 107, 112–13, 135

St. Walburg, 373

Stair, 71, 128

Standard, *367*

station gardens, 55–56, 71–72, 175, 293

stations, 40–43, 44, *48*, 50, 51, 54, 55–56, 57–58, 59, 67, *103*, 106, *114*, 158, 163, 183, 188, *193*, 233, 235, *237*, 246–48, 277, 291

Stavely, *148*, 299

Stephen, George, 34, 45, 48–49, 51, 84, 85, 91, 107, 113, 114, 115, 137, 140, 150, 166, 211, 281

Stewart, A.W., *156*

Stewart, William, 224

Stickney, Alpheus Beede, 43, 58

stock cars, *66, 67*

Stornoway, 340–42

Strathcona, Lord (Donald Smith), 31, 48, 106–7, 176, 197

Strathmore, 278, 282, 290–95, 301–3, 318, 358, 379–80

Sudeten Germans, 373, *386*

suffragettes, 259, 260

Sundance, *385*

Sutherland, Duke of, 285, *287*

Swamp Cree, 18

Swan River, 61

Swedish immigrants, 84, 140, 145, 149, 321, 358, 385

Sweetgrass (Cree chief), 7

Swift Current, 21, 28, 54, 71, 127–28, 130, 158, 255, 278

Swiss immigrants, 385, 392, *395*

tariffs, 171, 251, 299, 301

Temperance Colonization Society, 76

Territorial Grain Growers' Association, 199

Thingvalla, 140

Thomas Cook & Sons, 386

Thornton, Henry, 330–31, 371

Thunder Bay. *See* Port Arthur

Tilley, 71, 309, 318, 323, 380, *382*

Tims, F. Fraser, 28

Tirpitz, 357

Toe Laer, R.R.H., 89, 92

Toews, David, 336

Toronto, 111, 113–14, 115, *152*, 161, 169, 180, 205, *250*, 352, 399

Toronto, Grey & Bruce Railway, 114, 115, 116, 239

Torrance, John, 221–22

Touchie, Rodger, 16

Touchwood and Qu'Appelle Colonization Company, 76

tourism, 116, 121, 127, 186, 219, 262, 274–75, 313–14, 327, 353, 356–57, 363, 379, 397, 398, 400, 403

Trans-Canada Air Lines, 397

Treaties, Numbered, 16–19, 21–25, 57, 173

Trego, W.D., 330

Trieste, 314

Tunisian, 332

Tsuut'ina People, 19, 21

Tupper, 373, *386*

Turkish immigrants, 327

Tyler, Henry, 85–86

Tyrolia, 314

Uist, 130, *338*, 342

Ukrainian immigrants, 158, 179–81, *215*, 245, 319, 329, 350, 367, 394

Union Pacific Railroad, 80, 195

United States

  effects of Civil War, 63

  immigrants from, 76, 78–80, 89, 96, 136, 145, 149, 151–54, 173, 175, 193–96, 203, 204, 210, 242–43, 248–50, 262, 269, 273, 275–77, 295, 310, 316

  immigrants to, 84, 152, 157, 248

  rivalry with Canada, 12, 14, 152, 157, 159, 169

subsidies to railroads, 7–8, 9, 107

Van Aaken, Father, 278

Van Horne Colony, 323

Van Horne, William

  background, 31–32, 56, 169

  Atlantic steamship service and, 221

  Blackfoot people and, 21–23

  Clifford Sifton and, 171–72

  colonist cars and, 111

  dealings with competitors, 85–86, 96–97, 138, 219, 221, 252, 272

  exhibition car and, 78–80

  free trade views of, 169

  grain elevators encouraged by, 162–63

  on the Hudson's Bay Company, 218

  immigration and, 151–52, 154, 181, 195, 247, 263

  James Freer and, 261

  land speculation opposed by, 43, 44, 58

  Pacific route and, 14

  railway fares and, 148

  ready-made farms and, 282

  Regina townsite and, 51

  Rocky Mountains Park and, 241

  station designs by, *48*

  steamship service and, 117–18

  wheat milling interests, 165–66

Vancouver, 56, *98*, 153, 192, 252, 267, 397

Vanderhoof, Herbert, 275

Vaughan, Josephus Wyatt, 43

Vegreville, 145, *181*

Vermilion, 347, 358, 363

Victorian, 223, 224, 225

Virden, 47, 51, 163, 299

Virginian, 223, 224, 225

Vulcan, *298*, 299, 351

Wallis, J.M., 44

Walrond Ranch, 63, 65

Walton, Archibald S., 281

Wapella, 130–31, 149

War Beryl, 322

War Peridot, 322

Wardner, 303

Wascana Creek, 50, 51

water tanks, 40

Wayne, 330

weather, 10, 44, 73, 85, 109, 121, 127, 128, 138, 151, 213, 251–55, 260

Welsh immigrants, 84, *101*, 140, 157, 281, 300

Western Canada Colonization Association, 326

Western Canadian Immigration Association, 210

Western Irrigation District, 387

Wetaskiwin, 145, 146–47, 349

wheat

  crop yields, 73, 86, 127, 161, 165, 173, 250, 288, 295

  grain elevators for, 162–67

  harvest workers, 180, 250, *291*, 364–67

  Marquis, 255

  Red Fife, 72, 161–62, 163, 165, 170, 255

  transportation routes, 14–15, 151

Wheeler, Seeger, 255

White, William J., *193*, 194

White Star Line, 227, 235

Whitehead, Charles, 43–44

Whitehead, Joseph, 43, 106

Whitewood, 109, 133, 140, 149

Whyte, William, 55–56, 91, 117, 118, 138, 239, 243, 287–88, 295

Winder Ranch, 63

Windsor Station, 115, 233, 236

Winnipeg

  domestic workers, 257

  founding and settlement of, 31–32, 37, 54, 113, 154, 180, *182*, 183, 188, *193*, 195, 236–37, *246*, 247, 248, 257, 278

  harvest workers transiting, 180, *250*, 364, 367

  internment camps, 320

  real-estate boom, 37–38, 44, 207

  routes to and from, 14, *39, 43*, *103*, 106, 111, *112*, *118*, 121, 133, 134–35, 138, 163, 203, 205

  weather, 44

Wintering Hills, 330

Winton, Francis Walter de, 131

Wittrick, Louisa May, 286

Wolseley, 51, 56

women, 78, 86, 100, 108, 111, *184*, 188, *193*, 235, 255–60, 286, 288–89, *307*, 340, 358, *360*, *361*, 374

World War I, 299, 311, 315–23, 325, 326

World War II, 379, 386, 387–91

World's Fair, 153–54, 318, *383*

Wulff, Johan, 305–6

Wylie, D.J. "Joe," 128

Wynyrd, 299, 303

Yellowhead Pass, 11, 12

York Farmers' Colonization Co., 75–76

Yorkton, 109, 138, 183, *184*

Yugoslavia, 401

Yugoslavian immigrants, 358, 370, 371

Zboray, Theodore, 140

ABOUT THE AUTHOR

DAVID LAURENCE JONES is the former manager of internal communications at Canadian Pacific Railway. A history graduate from Concordia University, he worked for fourteen years in the railway's corporate archives, researching and collecting stories and anecdotes about the CPR's rich heritage. He is the author of *Railway Nation: Tales of Canadian Pacific—The World's Greatest Travel System*, as well as *The Railway Beat*, *Tales of the CPR*, *See This World Before the Next*, and *Famous Name Trains*.

PHOTO BY RICK ROBINSON